☆
☆ ☆

Americans No More

Americans No More

Georgie Anne Geyer

The Atlantic Monthly Press
New York

Published simultaneously in Canada
Printed in the United States of America

FIRST EDITION

Library of Congress Cataloging-in-Publication Data

Geyer, Georgie Anne, 1935–
    Americans no more / Georgie Anne Geyer. — 1st ed.
        p.   cm.
    Includes bibliographical references and index.
    ISBN 0-87113-650-3
    1. Immigrants—United States.   2. Illegal aliens—United States.
  3. Americanization.   4. Citizenship—United States.   I. Title.
  JV6455.G49   1996
  323.6′0973—dc20   96-15308

Design by Laura Hammond Hough

The Atlantic Monthly Press
841 Broadway
New York, NY 10003

10 9 8 7 6 5 4 3 2

To Newton Minow,
the late Morris Leibman,
and Mary McDermott Coder,
three incomparable friends and
fellow citizens who believed in this book

☆
☆ ☆

Acknowledgments

My thanks go first to my splendid editor, Allison Draper, who was willing to take a chance on a "different" book and to offer solace and excellent advice at every turn. Also to my publisher, Morgan Entrekin, and to our fine copy editor, Patty O'Connell, who in so many ways helped to clarify a complicated manuscript. Behind all of this was my agent, Richard Curtis, whose determination, good taste, and support I deeply appreciate.

The book could never have been written without the support of the Annenberg Washington Program, whose fellowship enabled me to spare the necessary time from my usual substantial workload. I am deeply and affectionately indebted to so many at Annenberg: Amb. Walter H. Annenberg, who set out to do good many years ago and has surely done it; Newton Minow, the amazing Chicago attorney who is unquestionably one of America's wise men; Yvonne Zecca, who ran the Annenberg office with such efficiency and flair; Theresa Rosato and Libby Dehning, the two splendid interns from my alma mater, Northwestern University, who did such fine work—conducting complicated interviews and backing me up generally—that they put me light years ahead of where I would have been without them.

My wonderful part-time assistant, Rita Tiwari, was an invaluable aide in every way. I thank her, as well as my excellent occasional typist, Linda Matthews, and the young woman who really made it all possible, Melissa Hampton, the computer whiz who somehow managed to teach me the computer without my collapsing of frustration while I was writing the book.

Harry Swegle, John Fonte, and Scipio Garling critically read parts of the work in progress and were influential in my final thinking; I thank them. Two wise professor friends, Richard Walker and Mike Hummel, guided me on a fascinating trip along the American-Mexican border, where I was pleasantly overwhelmed by the uncomplicated patriotism of America's Hispanic-American community. Ed and Janet Harte of Corpus Christi influenced me on this book early on, as did so many.

I must add thanks to Universal Press Syndicate, to our incomparable president John McMeel, and to our wonderful vice-president Kathleen Andrews, not to mention my treasured editors Elizabeth Andersen and Alan McDermott. The dozens and dozens of columns I have written for them on the subject of citizenship over the years—and their encouragement and love—are the bedrock of this book. As are the hundreds of letters that I received (and tried always to answer) from my readers, who showed me firsthand how deeply so many Americans feel, naturally and spontaneously, about the death of citizenship.

I would like to thank all the people around the world—from Bosnia to India to Mexico—who gave me their thoughts and their time, who opened their memories and often their hearts to me. I want to thank, too, the new citizenship thinkers in America, the immigration and Border Patrol officers, and the various groups on all sides who care very much about what they believe about America today. I have tried to reflect fairly the convictions of those with whom I deeply, but respectfully, disagree, although my own convictions are hardly hidden, and my conclusions are, of course, wholly my own.

☆
☆ ☆

Contents

☆
☆ ☆

Preface

I want to stress that this is a journalist's book. I know the special prejudice aimed at journalists who have the rashness to make any pretense to the scholarly or, on the other hand, reserved for scholars who dare to write clear or felicitous prose. But this book does not pretend to reflect the world of the theoretician or philosopher. These words are the honed and considered thoughts of a highly trained and experienced observer who has for thirty-two years watched the unfolding of astonishingly similar events in incredibly diverse countries on the international stage, and who sees the frightening implications of these events for her own country. Above all, I am a true universalist, appreciating every culture, speaking five languages, exploring the countries of the world with the passion of the lover *because* I know who I am and where I am from. I am always, first of all, a citizen of the United States; without that grounding in my own nation, I would not have had the emotional or analytic tools to know or understand others.

I was born on the South Side of Chicago in 1935 into an American family that gave me both a solid moral grounding, in the most traditional sense of that term, and the street savvy that has been one of my greatest boons as a journalist. *Americans No More*, therefore, is grimly realistic but also optimistic—the observations of a professional journalist and very lucky American, blessed to have come from a family and community characterized by love, moral concern, and artistic creativity, and concerned with the reconstruction of my own country at a time when everywhere we look nations are suffering internal conflict.

My love affair with the world began when I first traveled abroad to study. This grew into a passion for traveling all over the world, interviewing whomever I chose, and courteously but insistently busting into anyone's business with the magic moniker of "foreign correspondent." Today I am a syndicated columnist and overjoyed to belong to Universal Press Syndicate, a place where every kind of newspaper talent comes together in a commercial enterprise that should give lessons to the world on how to be simultaneously moral and successful.

My interest in citizenship evolved naturally as I traveled, observing, studying, and writing about the same questions in many diverse countries. I saw the century develop from the iron rod of Communism's dictate to a disintegration of nation-states that seemed finally to know no borders. Everywhere, I saw people wrestling with the same crucial problem that seems to me the key to everything: *Who belongs, and why?* It seems obvious but bears repeating that all cultures are not alike or equally amenable to development at any given time. Throughout history, various countries or empires have at different times found within themselves the confluence of cultural elements to throw them to the top. My largely German relatives, for instance, were dancing naked around the fires of northern Europe when Rome was already a decadent and aging empire. And anyone who has traveled across the Iraqi deserts and come breathlessly upon the gorgeous ruins of the old Parthian empire capital of Hatra would understand the unevenness of cultural development throughout time. Anyone who has seen a sunrise off Bombay and had the famous—but still amazing—epiphany that, at one time, the sun never set on the British Empire, would realize it.

I am aware that more utopian Americans will sometimes conflate an understanding of differences in cultural achievement—or even, in a sloppy way, patriotism—with racism, nativism, or xenophobia. But in my experience the world cannot be known or examined through falsity or wishful thinking, and the glossing-over of difference is not the same thing as cultural respect. Moreover, the fact that I love Latin America enough to have lived there for five years and risked my life repeatedly to tell its story has never in any way challenged or undermined my love for my own country.

In order to shed some journalistic light on the subject of citizenship, I have of course drawn on history, literature, geopolitics, military thinking, and the psychology of peoples. I believe that journalists are uniquely positioned to cross borders of the land and frontiers of the mind, constantly, repetitively, in every area of the world, so that we are able to see both the precursors to changes and the aftermaths of those changes. Moreover, as a journalist, I am interested in exploring what we *can* know, not in theorizing or speculating about what we don't or cannot know.

I am convinced that we must free ourselves of the emotional and severely limited ideological terms that so often attend any discussion of citizenship, immigration, or nationhood—unhelpful delineations, at least in today's contradictory world, such as "liberal" or "conservative," "immigrant" or "alien," "patriot" or "nativist." We desperately need a new terminology to fit the mind-set that the times demand. If we are to arrest the current decline, we must first discard its vocabulary of old and prejudicial terms so that we can think lucidly and anew.

This is a controversial book, although it deals with questions whose answers were so generally assumed and accepted by the American people for more than two centuries—and by the forefathers of democracy for at least four centuries before that—that many Americans might wonder why they and this volume should be controversial at all. It is a measure of how far we have traveled from a strong sense of our national identity that the old questions that gave form to America—*What makes an American citizen? Who belongs to the American polity, and why?*—should now need to be posed again.

I am not an unhopeful person. Indeed, I am a very hopeful one. For, knowing history, I know that there were deliberate steps that led us to where we are today. If we want to change the results of these acts, we can and will do so.

Washington, D.C.
April 17, 1996

☆
☆ ☆

Americans No More

1

The New Balkabarians

I man a checkpoint; therefore, I am.
political scientist Fouad Ajami, commenting
on the spirit of Lebanon's militarism

When the United States government put forward a new "citizen-ship" test for recent immigrants in 1986, at the very time that the rite of citizenship was most threatened, the test was designed to symbolize restructured immigration laws, in particular the Immigration Reform and Control Act of 1986. Duly, the Immigration and Naturalization Service (INS) issued the test, which was composed of a neat list of one hundred questions, all supposedly concerning American history and government. And of all those questions, which would supposedly test the eager would-be citizen's commitment to the nation through his or her knowledge of its history, ethos, and principles, question 86 best illuminated what was happening to American citizenship.

It asked: *"Name one benefit of being a citizen of the United States."*

One might pause here to reflect upon the profundity of the historical "social compact" or "contract" between the citizen and the state and how it grew and was nurtured organically through all the long and turbulent stages of modern European civilization, at each and every step making the individual human being more free *because* that lone individual had made a solemn commitment to a nation. One might stop to leaf through the books of Hector Saint John de Crèvecoeur, the immensely popular French-American author of the Revolutionary War, whose works were inspired by love of his adopted country and who wrote the famous words, "He is an American . . . who is a new man, who acts upon new principles."

Or one might pause to consider the philosophical nature of man choosing democratic community above either extreme individualism or totalitarian collectivism. One might find on one's lips the eloquent words of Jean-Jacques Rousseau, the great eighteenth-century French philosopher of freedom, concluding even two centuries ago that only a free contract between citizen and government allows the individual "to bind himself to all while retaining his free will."

But such musings would no longer be relevant. For there were only three acceptable answers to question 86: "to obtain federal government jobs, to travel with a U.S. passport, and to petition for close relatives to come to the United States to live." These were not just random answers to the question, they were the *only* answers to the question; and, although in later years there would be several other acceptable answers added, they were minor and did nothing to change the "spirit" of the test.

Moreover, the rest of the test proceeds in the same style. From the rich heritage of American heroes who might inspire immigrants with such an American sense of universalism that human beings of any background could accept them as their own, only seven are mentioned: George Washington, Abraham Lincoln, Thomas Jefferson, Patrick Henry, Francis Scott Key, Martin Luther King Jr., and a generic American Indian.

Indeed, as Philip Marcus of the J. William Fulbright Foreign Scholarships Board points out in an article about the test in *Chronicles*, the critical intellectual journal:

> Facts about three wars must be known; that our first was against England, that Lincoln presided over the Civil War to "free many slaves" and that in World War II our allies included the Soviets. We have two holidays, the Fourth and Thanksgiving; Inauguration and federal election days are the other notable events on the calendar.
>
> The Constitution receives a decidedly democratic reading. One question requires its identification as the "supreme law of the land," while two other questions detail the process and extent of its amendment. There is nothing about the ideas of the Constitution beyond stating that the "most important" right is to vote (nothing is said about taxes).

Another question, number 84, also characterizes the ambiguity of thinking about American citizenship. It asks: "Whose rights are guaranteed by the Constitution and the Bill of Rights?" The answer? "Everyone's (citizens and noncitizens living in the United States)." This statement marks still another recently created "citizenship doctrine," because the Constitution in its entirety clearly distinguishes between citizen and person, reserving to citizens certain political rights, whose possession and nurture separates the *citizen* from the *person*. Indeed, this change in the idea of constitutional protection is the perfect antithesis of traditional ideas of American citizenship.

But this test is only a small part of what some thinkers are calling the "commoditization of citizenship" in America. (*Commodity:* convenience, useful, profit, advantageous, expediency.)

When President George Bush signed still another immigration bill, the Immigration Act of 1990, he called it "the most comprehensive reform of our immigration laws in sixty-six years." Advocates praised its "streamlining" of the process of citizenship. And perhaps it was that. Nevertheless, after this bill, the historical and beautiful courthouse ceremonies—in which new citizens were sworn to fealty to their new nation, reciting the Oath of Allegiance before a judge of that nation in a solemn courtroom scene—became "optional." At every turn, the entire process of citizenship was being made more remote, the old one-on-one relationship of citizen to state, diminished: There was talk of getting citizenship by mail, there were plans for taking the citizenship English test by phone; by 1995, voting by mail was "in." There were some possibilities of being sworn in under even less formal circumstances.

As immigration lawyer Mark Mancini put it wryly at the time, "You might as well be at the Department of Motor Vehicles."

One of the few newspapers even to take note of these dramatic changes in the rituals of citizenship, The *Washington Times* editorialized:

> The ritual is—or was—important because, like birthdays, weddings and funerals, it commemorated a major transition in human life. By means of the naturalization ceremony, men, women and children from countries and cultures all over

the world, who shared nothing in common before, suddenly
found themselves linked by a single thread. They had become
Americans. . . .

It might have occurred to the lawmakers who drafted and
passed the law that citizenship means something more than the
abstract legal rights and obligations it confers. Citizenship involves a profound psychological and moral commitment, which
is why admission to it is registered by an oath. That oath abjures
loyalty to "any foreign prince, potentate, state or sovereignty"
and binds the citizen with an obligation to support and defend
the Constitution and laws of the United States against all enemies, foreign and domestic, including by bearing arms for the
country. If you fraudulently obtain American citizenship, it will
be stripped away from you. If you violate its obligations, you can
go to jail. Citizenship in any country means a lifelong commitment at least as sacred as marriage, and in a country where citizens govern themselves, it involves the responsibility to assume
the burdens as well as the privileges of ordered freedom.

But the possible ways to become an American citizen (without
fuss or bother!) did not end there. Under that same 1990 law, there
is another provision by which, at one minute past midnight on
Columbus Day, would-be immigrants and their lawyers can dump
tens of thousands of applications into waiting bins in American
post offices. The first forty thousand applications thus received
will qualify automatically for the green card that signifies legal permanent residency in the United States. We were one step away
from citizenship-as-lotto!

Many of the new citizens or petitioners for citizenship came
from countries whose cruel histories had doomed perfectly worthy
and capable human beings to lives ruled by whim, or the accidents
of fate. Now, America, instead of offering the old transformational
experience into the new values that *it* historically embodied, was
only confirming and perpetuating the vagaries of chance these
people wanted to escape.

There were many other changes in the process of citizenship.
For citizenship applicants over fifty years of age who had lived in
the country for over twenty years, the requirement of English as
the spoken language was eliminated. Another bill would further

exempt those over fifty from knowing anything about the civics of the country. A certain number of visas were reserved for foreign millionaires, as though citizenship were for sale—and, in fact, it was.

But what was overwhelmingly important beyond any single example of ludicrousness was the fact that, on interwoven levels, sometimes in accidental but more often in deliberate ways, citizenship in America was being demeaned and destroyed—not at all by the immigrants themselves, nor by would-be citizens, whose fault it is not, but by America herself.

☆

This, then, is a book about the silent but real death of American citizenship. If allowed to persist, this phenomenon will surely destroy America as we have known it. This slow but steady destruction is occurring, incredibly enough, even at that moment in history when America has won the "war" for the ideological context of the world, and at a time when democracy and capitalism are celebrated as *the* means for humankind's development and for the massive freeing of the human spirit. Thus, one might expect for this journalistic journey to begin and continue in America itself. But its parameters are immeasurably broader than that.

The major question to absorb and confront us at the turn of this century—*Who belongs?*—is a quandary that America shares with the world. This issue also invokes the largely unrecognized saga of how other nations are affecting America's most profound union, its citizenship, while dealing with equally troubling and directly related questions of their own.

The story does not really start in New York, or Omaha, or Sacramento, although it surely ends there; the story begins in Berlin.

In June of 1991, I traveled first to a schizophrenic Berlin before moving on to a gradually reviving Poland, a rapidly disintegrating Yugoslavia, a long-suffering Israel, a stunned Kuwait trying to regain its senses after the Gulf War, and finally the once-hopeful "secular and democratic" state of India that was by then on the verge of violent breakup into component pieces.

It could have been one of myriad "normal" trips to places that I had by then been involved in for nearly thirty years, but it was not.

I had been quite aware of the world's stubborn and astonishing fissiparous tendency for many years. As early as 1985, I had written a groundbreaking lead piece for the *Encyclopaedia Britannica Yearbook* in which I traced the way that modern nation-states, countries, and internationally recognized legal entities that we had always thought stable and unchanging were now collapsing before our very eyes. But I had never seen this frightening syndrome acted out in such a disturbing manner as I did that spring/summer—and, most important of all, acted out with such profound implications for the future of our own American democracy.

It was late June when I arrived in the old German city, and Berlin was beautifully green and still luxuriating in the stunning aura of hope that had effused the country after the breakup of the rigid, brutal East German Communist state. After all, the "impossible" had happened only two years earlier, in 1989. The "wall" that had so brutally and bitterly imprisoned the Communist East from the democratic West since 1962 had finally fallen—that demise soon would symbolize the inner collapse of the Communist mentality. Now the East Germans would surely face a time of "democracy and free enterprise" for everybody, and a cornucopia of now-realizable hope "obviously" lay ahead!

Only that was not exactly what was happening.

Not unexpectedly, American Secretary of State James Baker III chose that moment to give a prophetic speech. In a press conference at the Aspen Institute in Berlin, this sophisticated diplomat began in a sentimental tone; "When I visited you in 1989, the Wall had just become a Gateway. . . . And now, in 1991, I have the honor of meeting in the capital of a united Germany . . ."

The secretary spoke eloquently of the experience of both Americans and Germans in Berlin: Together they had preserved the great city's freedom for forty-four years! Indeed, said Baker, the "trans-Atlantic relationship stands for certain Enlightenment ideals of universal applicability. These values are based upon the concept of individual political rights and economic liberty rooted in European ideas of the seventeenth and eighteenth centuries, and first planted in the new American nation."

Now, once again, in this post-Communist age, the two countries were grappling valiantly with those "shared values" now moving beyond European and American shores; those formerly purely "Western" values were permeating long-closed parts of the rest of the world. "The communities of value section of the speech," American diplomats explained in background briefings to reporters, "tries to explain the origins of Western values and their basis, making the key point that the values started in Western Europe and that the United States was the first democratic experiment." Not only did those values transcend national borders now, but "this speech . . . talks about extending the trans-Atlantic community to Central and Eastern Europe, and to the Soviet Union. Hence the phrase 'incomplete pieces of our architecture.'"

The briefings continued: "So it goes beyond linking the United States to Western Europe under new conditions. [It includes] language about objectives such as a Europe whole and free and a Euro-Atlantic community that extends east from Vancouver to Vladivostock. . . ."

Secretary Baker spoke clearly about the changes in the nation-state—and thus changes also in the demands and joys of citizenship in the nation-state itself. Perhaps the most striking phenomenon across all of Europe today, he said, was the combined and simultaneous devolution and evolution of the nation-state, because "while the nation-state remains by far the most significant political unit, its political role is being increasingly supplemented by both supranational and subnational units. In other words, some of the nation-state's functions are being delegated 'upward' and others 'downward.'"

But while in Western Europe citizens were transferring more and more functions from the national to the larger, supranational level, it was quite a different story in the suddenly free (and already increasingly unsure) Eastern Bloc. There, "with the collapse of Communism, ethnicity has reemerged as a powerful political force, threatening to erect new divisions between countries, and, even more acutely, within multinational states. . . ." But, not so in the United States, according to Baker!

"The United States is a nation of ideas, not of blood, birth, or creed, " he went on, and it was therefore not a country threatened by divided and warring ethnics, but rather a nation of self-affirming citizens freely consorting with one another and empowering their government to act for their benefit. Up against that American idea and ideal, there now stood countries like Yugoslavia, where the West found it incumbent upon itself to "overcome the reemergence of the old nationalisms and ethnic divisions. . . ." Along the way, he spoke of course of Marxism, that experiment in universalism supposed to transcend national borders, but in the end unsuccessful.

Listening to these words there, and reading the transcripts and background notes to Baker's wise speech in Berlin, I realized that I was hearing something very special indeed. Somehow the words spoke profoundly to me, but I was not to understand exactly why—and why it had so much to say to us Americans—until later.

As I moved along, I soon began to have the distinct feeling that I was not on a normal trip at all but that I was walking through the national psychiatric wards of the world. Nowhere did I have that feeling more so than in Belgrade, the gray, dour capital of the long-admired "independent socialist state" of Yugoslavia. To me what had been Yugoslavia now looked like an animated picture puzzle, where all the pieces suddenly began jumping out by themselves and, indeed, that was what had happened.

I went on that spring to Yugoslavia, arriving in Belgrade on the day in late June that the post–cold war's "first ethnic war" began. Indeed, when I arrived in the Belgrade airport that night from Berlin, a kind of furtive, quiet terror hung in the air. No one spoke. Slovenia had just declared independence, the militarized Serbs would begin attacking the other Yugoslav republics, and "Yugoslavia," the great experiment, would fall into ruin. But those ruins did not come accidentally; they were organized and orchestrated, plotted and planned. . . .

Earlier, in the fall of 1989, I had deliberately traveled to Yugoslavia for some days of investigation because I was certain it was to become "the" symbol and model for breakdown in the East Bloc and perhaps in the world. As a matter of fact, the beginnings were already evident.

Budimir Kosutic, professor of political systems at the faculty of law of the University of Belgrade, gave me one of the first hints, as he so early on demolished the idea that all of these ethnic hatreds were about to spring to the surface *spontaneously*. "I believe that the differences in our country are not consequences so much of differences in nations, but more the consequences of bad politics," he began. The economic paralysis led to ethnic problems?

"Absolutely! And I should point out that the divisions in the country are much less the divisions within the political leadership. *Each of the political leaders presents himself as the defender of the interests of his nation.*" So they have to create differences in order to hold onto political power? "Your conclusion is absolutely right," he averred.

One after the other, I found that the professors, political thinkers, and journalists that I was interviewing were all saying much the same thing: The crisis that was coming was not spontaneous or unavoidable at all but was one deliberately and cynically created by aggressive men whose long-burning ambitions had been suddenly freed from the restraints of the Communist system.

"The fights are not between nationalities, you see," Dr. Vladimir Stambuk, secretary general of the Communist League of Serbia, told me on another day, "but between political leaderships. When you are going downhill, you try to grab from others as much as you can. The Serbian leadership is split, so the idea of 'Greater Serbia' is put forward as an attempt to stop the changes."

Some saw this dangerous moment in larger historical terms. "You see, in the nineteenth century, only Serbia and Montenegro had their own states," said Deputy Foreign Minister Milivoje Maksic. "Now, some of us are living through this statehood as others did in the nineteenth century. So we have a problem, where Europe is undergoing integration and yet we have groups, as in the nineteenth century, which want everything for themselves." He paused, then added, "This is simply a phase we will have to live through."

The strange, whispering, deliberate man plotting and orchestrating the breakup of Yugoslavia since 1987 was Slobodan Milosevic; here we have an archetypal figure to study for some understanding of all of the breakups in the Eastern Bloc. The round-faced, small-eyed, fanatical Milosevic, the consummate bureaucratic Communist Stalinist, was elected, thus having the benediction of those in the West who naïvely believed that democracy would solve problems around the globe. But anyone who even cursorily studied Milosevic would soon have noted that he was a classic figure of dictatorship. Small, fat, and physically homely, he was as banal as evil can be, and from the time he arose in the Communist Party bureaucracy, he marketed in fear, terrifying his people with tales of Serbian destruction at the bloody hands of a world that hated him. He worked in secret, like the leader of a revolutionary cult, often in underground offices, destroying with the worst calumnies the men who had helped him to the top. "Little Slobo" had a sad life, he did; both parents, also Communists, committed suicide—it was that kind of family. The intellectuals helped him, in 1987 issuing a famous white paper extolling Serbia's great role in the world. And then the man the American ambassador called "the slickest con-man in the Balkans" took over. As a matter of fact, the moment he took power legally and "democratically," he began plotting for the demise of Yugoslavia and for the rise of a "Greater Serbia" that would eclipse all the other five Yugoslavia republics and take over in whatever way necessary all historically (or mythologically) Serbian land within them. The real purpose was quite simple: It was a blatant and cynical means of staying in power.

As early as that prophetic fall of 1989, the American ambassador to Belgrade, Warren Zimmermann, posed this rhetorical question: "What does Milosevic want?" Then he answered in a talk with me: "He wants to destroy Yugoslavia and pick up the pieces in a 'Greater Serbia.' That is the only theory that explains all the facts. For the last few years, most of his actions were against the unity of Yugoslavia. He gave aid to the autonomous Serbs in Croatia. He tried twice to destroy the Yugoslav presidency. He formed and unified groups of Serbs in Bosnia for autonomy. Even when the Croats and Slovenes were willing to work out a loosely federated Yugoslavia, Milosevic said that would 'not be Yugoslavia,' and so Serbia should look out for the Serbs. . . ." He could have added that Milosevic already was brilliantly and terrifyingly propagandizing the Serbs. With an almost total control of television even then, he orchestrated fear of outside influence through hour upon hour of mournful Orthodox Church music, films of Serb graveyards and churches and battlefields (where they had always, not incidentally, lost their battles). The xenophobic message was clear: The Serbs were a uniquely persecuted people throughout history and must finally become the great nation the world had always stopped them from being.

But, back to 1991: The very day that I arrived in Belgrade those last days of June, (just after Jim Baker had rushed to be there and warn the Yugoslavs against breaking up, ironically enough), the war started and the diabolical breakdown of prosperous and independent Yugoslavia into a modern hell began. And as I looked out across the lovely but moldering old city of Belgrade, I found it ominously quiet. (Strangers to war expect cities to be excited and violent at moments such as this; instead, they are frighteningly silent.) On the streets, people everywhere looked deeply depressed, and officials seemed almost in a state of emotional breakdown. Everyone feared—and some beamed evil smiles about—the fact that "Yugoslavia was about to be no more."

The first two northern "republics" of Yugoslavia, Slovenia and Croatia, had proclaimed their independence on June 25, thus indirectly starting the war that Milosevic had so long been crafting with his Machiavellian moves. For at least three years, arms had been smuggled into all the republics—but the Serbs had mountains of arms behind them, not to speak of their fanaticized Serb militias made up of usually drunken, often criminal, lumpen "mountain Serbs."

That Friday afternoon, in the federal palace, the impressive, silver-haired, sober-minded prime minister, Ante Markevic, best defined this extraordinarily dangerous moment in modern history. At times nearly in tears, this courageous man spoke with a group of journalists in a voice close to despair. "Unfortunately, in our community today, these complex ethnic, national, and religious conflicts will soon lead to an identical response from others," he said. "That response will lead inevitably to a 'Lebanonization' of our country."

That evening, sitting in the Belgrade Inter-Continental looking across the Danube River at the somber city huddled on the opposite banks, bathed in an eerie silence as though for a moment something had stopped in history, I counted up the number of the disconsolate, restless, and determined ethnic groups who could and would now take heart at the possibility of separation. Ethnic Albanian and Muslim Kosovo in the South had long wanted to separate and secede; a Sandzak Autonomy group of Muslims in Bosnia, Croatians and Hungarians in the area of Vojvodina, and even the Italians of the Istrian Peninsula were preparing to secede if things got too bad. At that time, I counted at least thirty movements that would restructure internal and perhaps even external borders in what would be little less than a geopolitical nightmare.

I kept thinking: "Is it humanly possible that we're heading for a new Dark Ages?"

By the time I returned again to Yugoslavia in October of 1992, the war was raging at full speed. The new Dark Ages had indeed come down upon the world with the vengeance of an Old Testament God, and Belgrade had become a kind of Old Testament city, the capital of one of the most deadly paranoid delusions in history. It was the fortress from which the mass hysteria and self-pitying blood lust of so many of its young men would flow; many in the world had come to equate the word *Serb* with "mass genocidal murderer."

The cynical Milosevic had fed "Serbs" with the fanatic ideas that Serbs were the master race who deserved a "Greater Serbia" and that the Roman Catholic Croats, and particularly the Bosnian Muslims, must now be eliminated. But what the world did not recognize was the fact that the rampage of the Serb militias and irregulars to kill every "other" had not occurred *spontaneously*, it had been nurtured and orchestrated. Now Milosevic and his group of Communists-turned-nationalists totally controlled all television except for two courageous local shows, Studio B and Polytyka-TV, and the results were Orwellian, brutally challenging all the hopeful talk about information and global villages. In Kosovo, the threatened Albanian area in the South that the Serbs ruled as a police state, I one day sat before Serbian TV (the only TV the Kosovars could get) watching the surreal picture of Serb soldiers being "thanked" by Bosnian Muslims for "liberating" them. I was seeing, in the last decade of the twentieth century, the total mesmerization of a people.

It was a strange war, a different war, but it was by far not the inexplicable quagmire that the West portrayed it to be. It was not a war of "courageous" World War II Serb guerrillas fighting the invading Nazis, it was a war of deliberately fanaticized "mountain Serbs" or "wild Serbs" destroying the beautiful Renaissance and Venetian cities of Bosnia, Croatia, and Dalmatia with masses of artillery, all left behind by the well-endowed Yugoslav army when it collapsed in 1991. The fighters were largely criminal thugs, psychopaths, and would-be World War II "Chetniks," whose "specialties" were slitting throats and cutting off limbs while the victims were still alive and setting up "rape camps" for women they would then murder. Indeed, their units were so thrown together that troops often were wearing paper emblems on their sleeves denoting their rank.

In sad, gray Belgrade that October, Milos Vasic, the courageous antiwar Serbian editor of *Vreme* (*Time*) magazine and a leading war analyst, offered *the* key to the gunmen's and the war's character. "This war is definitely anthropological," he told me, sitting in *Vreme*'s grim and busy offices. "We always divided our population more by altitude than by language or ethnic group. First, there is the mountain-cattlemen approach. Then there is the farmers' approach. The cattlemen perceive the world in terms of space for their herds; the farmers, in terms of time for their crops. That is why the 'wild mountain men' with no sense of humor are the driving force of this war. And that is why Sarajevo and Mostar were so savagely destroyed. These cities are a different civilization to guys frustrated by not being able to settle in them."

Vasic might have added that churches and cultural monuments were the constant and cynical targets of savage Serb fighters for the same reason. Four hundred Croatian churches, many of them exquisite historic monuments, had been destroyed in the first eighteen months of war; the Serb gunmen had consistently used UNESCO flags, supposedly protecting historic monuments, as markers to destroy those monuments. Over and over in the smitten cities, the gunmen would hit a church with artillery and journalists at the scene could hear the "yea, yea" in the background.

The West early on determined to do nothing against the Serbs—it was too difficult because these were "World War II Serb guerrilla-fighters" and airpower "could not deter them." So this first real example of classic disintegration through rational exploitation of irrational nationalism in modern ages continued. The carnage went on and on. The West was failing the first test of the post–cold war world.

Nor was this deliberate and calibrated regression-to-the-past limited to Yugoslavia. Throughout the region, analysts such as those from Radio Free Europe were seeing "the potential for new authoritarianisms built on racial and religious suspicion and hatred." Like Serbia's Milosevic, politicians from Russia to Romania to Hungary, to Slovakia and Moldova, for example, were seeking to advance themselves as defenders of "threatened" peoples. The

syndrome was growing everywhere, as the great secular ideologies and institutions of the twentieth century collapsed and vacuums of both spirit and power beckoned such men like modern
Loreleis.

☆

As it happened, I moved on that summer of 1991 to India. Surely,
I thought, I would leave these experiences and symbols of breakdown and terror and human division behind. . . .

India had been such a hopeful new nation in the 1950s and '60s.
Not really a country, it was rather a throbbing universe of peoples,
religions, and races; and it was to be *the* example of "secular democracy" riding high on the waves of hope in that postcolonial
world after World War II. When the aristocratic Indian leader
Jawaharlal Nehru, with his elegant and aloof mien, marched into
the Bandung conference in Indonesia in 1955, he and the others of
that first postcolonial leadership in the Third World of Africa, Asia,
and the Middle East were widely assumed to be ushering in a brilliant new phase in the world. He and his "brothers" in the other
nations were, after all, the "real national and nationalist elites"
finally come to power, and they were filled with the heady and
innocent idea that development would come to them and their
new countries magically. Colonialism was finally gone, and the
white man with all his self-styled and self-conscious "burdens"
had finally gone home; nirvana was on the horizon!

How all that hope was squandered and wasted by decent
but arrogant leaders and how it ended in the political rise of basically criminal forces presented me with still another tragic
story, made even more dramatic for coming so directly on the
heels of Yugoslavia.

That hot summer, whipped by the monsoon winds, I found
that India too was in the process of breakup and breakdown—into
tribal and ethnic groups—and that India's process too was filled
with a ferocity carrying people back to earlier, more primitive
times. India was like a dervish whirling ever faster, with its peripheries spinning off into other nights as the dervish nation sped
out of control. On that universe's peripheries, Sikhs in the Punjab,
Kashmiri separatists in "beautiful" Kashmir, Assamese in the Indian state of Kashmir, and Tamils in neighboring Sri Lanka all

were deeply involved in civil wars or in the tragic dismemberment and retribalization of India.

"An increasingly violent political culture," one commentator wrote. "A country of madmen full of madness and intensity destroying all that Indians hold dear," another declared, while still others wondered whether the wrath of the ancient war-god Shiva had suddenly been loosed on the unprepared country.

One could study any of the areas—and any of the "liberation" movements or, more accurately said in this situation, "secessionist" or "terrorist" movements in any of these areas—and the analysis would be revealing. But since it was the first movement to threaten the continuation and coherence of the Indian state, I will offer as my example the Sikh movement in the rich, advanced, agricultural Punjab of the North.

"You ask me how this all could have happened," the famous and polished Sikh journalist Khushwant Singh remarked, shaking his head sadly. "It is amazing how an educated people like the Sikhs could have fallen under the spell of a demented hatemonger. . . ."

Four years earlier when I had interviewed the legendary Singh, he had greeted me in a tasteful Nehru suit in one of those picturesque Delhi villas surrounded by sensuously rippling trees. He was the very picture of the confidence of the Indian elites. This time, the scene was depressingly different. He greeted me from within a first-floor apartment set back from the street. Indian troops were encamped, complete with live-in tents, in the park just outside his door; Khushwant Singh, like so many others, had been put on the vicious Sikh radicals' "hit list."

This distinguished man, who knew he could be wiped out at any minute by his own people, tried to explain to me what had really happened in the Punjab. It was made diabolically and tragically bewildering by the fact that the Punjab was no poor or desolate area of India, but rather the richest sector, the historic "breadbasket," and the area of the most educated and probably most able people in all of India. Indeed, the "green revolution," pioneered in the Punjab, offered the world hope that agriculture could be immeasurably if not indefinitely expanded, and it brought increasing mechanization of agriculture to the Punjab.

What did the sons of the agricultural owners do? They went to the city and became unemployed and half-educated intellectuals—and soon became the angry, undigestible backbone of the violent anti-India Sikh movement. They believed that an independent and separate state would solve their poverty, but the real problem was their alienation.

"If you want to go to the roots of 'the thing,' it started with younger men giving up the beards, becoming secularized," Singh began. "Many became Sikhs worshiping as Hindus. There was the danger of the community disappearing. Now, there are only two ways of dealing with such situations: by appealing to the inner strength of the community or appealing to the fear of outside."

He spoke then of the infamous "demented hatemonger," Jarnail Singh Bhidranwale, who started out as a kind of Robin Hood and, much like Slobodan Milosevic, ended up employing every tool of mind control and ethnic hatred and throwing into turmoil what had been the most accomplished and promising province of India. "He referred to 'born-again' Sikhs," Singh went on. "He appealed to them not to drink, not to take opium, and not to clip their beards, but to say their prayers and to be good Sikhs. Bhidranwale started with appealing to the inner strengths and ended with appealing to the fear of outside. The analogy with the Ayatollah Khomeini and Iran is quite pertinent; it is just what Khomeini did."

Indeed, as with Khomeini and Milosevic, the Sikh radicals began to seek a return to the "pure" past, in this case an all-Sikh state of Khalistan. *Khalsa* means "pure," and when a people begin returning to "purity," whether the Khomeini boys with keys to heaven around their necks pouring across minefields into Iraq or the massacring Serb legions in Bosnia, one can justify any barbarity in purity's name. I knew then that this could all well end with the dismemberment of India.

Concerned analysts rightly blamed such alienation, which spread from the Punjab to Kashmir to Assam and Bihar, on the breakdown of secular democracy and of the traditional party politics that had arisen out of British colonialism and had served India so well in those early years. Indeed, it marked a series of events noticeably similar to those in Yugoslavia.

Equally dangerous, the British-inspired secular law that had held such a universe of peoples together was breaking down at the behest of peoples returning to their own past history and to their own isolated hothouse of religious groups. As the leading Indian military strategist Shri K. Subramanian explained to me in 1991, "The majority in India is ready for common civil law for everyone. But the minorities want their personal law. Polygamy was abolished here, but the Muslims want it. The Muslims are still led by an obscurantist leadership."

This new specificization of the law, this breaking-down of one secular law for everyone to the benefit of the specific demands of every group, was another of the characteristics common to the process of breakdown that I saw spanning many and quite different nations. While I was there, Dinesh Singh wrote in the *Times* of India that the next step for India was a "criminalization of Society." And S. K. Ghost, director of the independent Law Research Institute of Calcutta, carried the idea further by writing that "our politicians have surrendered their powers to gangsters."

Still another part of the Indian experience eerily parallels and shadows its American social counterpart—affirmative action as a means of breaking down its vicious and humiliating class and caste system.

An ominous example of the forces that were at play: In 1994, 120 demonstrators, 30 of them children, died in Nagpur, in the western state of Maharashtra, when 40,000 protestors from the Gowari caste clashed with police. They had gathered together there for an odd but very New Age demand: that their caste should be added to a growing list of "economically and socially-backward communities," which would entitle them to preferential access to government jobs and college spaces. The day after the protest, the state government gave in and acceded to their demands.

What was going on here? Basically, the intention of the government was good, even noble by historic standards. India was one of the most class- and caste-ridden states in the world, a situation that stemmed from early Aryan invasions of India from the North, in which dark-skinned Indians were pushed south. The hierarchy thus established rivaled the courts of Egypt or Persia. Brahmins (priests) at the top gave way to Kshatriyas (warrior-landowners), followed by Vaisyas (merchants) and Shudras (craftsmen). At the bottom were the "untouchables," with each level divided into thousands of complexly related and confused local communities. These latter "backward castes" are particularly numerous in the South, where they form up to 75 percent of the Hindu population; on the national level, they are about 52 percent.

The coming of Christian missionaries during the British colonial period was the first challenge to the ugly caste system; but it was not until the first years of independence in the early 1950s, when Dr. B. R. Ambedkar arose on the scene, that real efforts were made by government to reform this regressive and violent social thinking. Ambedkar was an untouchable who, amazingly, rose to be a minister in the first independence government, and he was able to secure a constitutional commitment that 22.5 percent of government jobs and college places would be reserved for untouchables. Thus, the noble beginning.

What started out as so reasonable, so right and just, soon became a government social leviathan. In 1990, the government awarded special treatment to another 27 percent of the Hindu population, the so-called "other backward classes." Even while the Indian Supreme Court moved to cap the total setting-aside of jobs and academic privilege for the lowest of the low at 50 percent, the percentages kept rising because of the cynical maneuvers of ambitious politicians to gain more votes. In 1993, the state of Tamil Nadu had set its quota for the outcaste classes at 69 percent, while neighboring Karnataka set its for 73 percent.

Those dramatic changes have, ironically, brought little to the really poverty-stricken, although they have benefited the "caste politicians." What they have done is to *increase* caste awareness and class differences in India; indeed, resentment between and among the castes and classes has dramatically increased. Quarrels over economic benefits have dramatically increased, while the economy has not grown nearly enough to deflect the effects of these affirmative action programs. Again, India's experience is dramatically similar to that of the United States, a truth self-evident to anyone who studies these intricate new-style problems of justice and privilege in today's world.

These were the steps: first, the weakening of the traditional political and other secular institutions (inclusive of all groups) in the country; next, the beginnings of a break *away* from the center on the part of groups that find or are propagandized into seeking alternative forms of cohesiveness, such as religion or ethnic heritage; then, disintegration of the center, caused by lack of confidence within and violent attacks on those fissiparous peripheries; and, finally, as traditional forms and answers fail, a partial or total criminalization of politics and of social and economic life!

That was the pattern that India showed me, and it was terrifying. It belied all of our blithe suppositions that the story of the world in our times was one of cohering rather than of collapsing, one of ever evolving toward higher human and institutional forms of life.

Indeed, by the time I was in India that hot, ominous summer of 1991, one entire state had already *become* a criminal enterprise. The eastern Indian state of Bihar, just northwest of Bangladesh, was, in the 1950s, the third richest state in India; in 1991, it was not only one of the poorest but also a state whose politics were almost totally controlled by caste-based gangster armies employing atrocious violence against their enemies. To note only one example: Of an overbloated "government" of seventy-four ministers, fourteen of them were publicly known as hardened criminals.

In my long life as a journalist, I had been able to foresee many developments, but I had never dreamed that, at this point in the development of nations, the greatest danger would be that states would be turned over to their worst and most deviant elements. Equally as bad, the Indian middle class—the class we depend upon for sanity and rational behavior everywhere in the world—had become itself a violent and extremist class. It was the middle class that gave its support to the radical Hindu party, the Bharatiya Janata Party; soon the BJP was violently battling the Muslims, riots were sweeping Indian cities, and India was on the verge of total civil war, with each caste, each ethnic and/or religious group, demanding its own privileges, rights, and laws.

Those events had their zenith, though surely not their end, in an Armageddonesque explosion of hatred that shook India to its ethnic roots. In December of 1992, Hindu fundamentalists marched on an ancient mosque in eastern India built by the first Mogul emperor Babur. In three days of savage rampages, they ravaged and destroyed the historic holy place.

But we must pause for a moment to note that, just as in Yugoslavia, in India these strange and frightening events did not come out of nowhere; they were neither spontaneous or inevitable.

The bitter attack on the mosque was carried through not by poor, illiterate villagers in kurtas and dhotis, but by clerks, boys from urban lower-middle-class families, the educated unemployed.

They are, say two writers, I believe correctly, young men—similar to those in Algeria, Egypt, almost all of Africa—"frustrated by the lack of good jobs and opportunities . . . victims of modernization, seeking to victimize others . . . whose expectations have run well ahead of available opportunities. . . ." The remarkable article in the March 1993 *New Republic*, "Modern Hate," by Susanne Hoeber Rudolph and Lloyd I. Rudolph, meticulously traces the reasons for the rise of this "ethnic hatred" in India, and comes, despite the obvious cultural differences, very close to the conclusions that I had reached about Yugoslavia: The events in India were also carefully orchestrated by groups interested in the radicalization of Hindu nationalism and through the use of TV series and shows that radicalized the public's understanding of Hinduism.

The writers, who are professors of political science at the University of Chicago, comment, "'Ancient hatreds' are thus made as much as they are inherited. To call them ancient is to pretend they are primordial forces, outside of history and human agency, when often they are merely synthetic antiques. Intellectuals, writers, artists and politicians 'make' hatreds. Films and videos, texts and textbooks, certify stories about the past, the collective memories that shape perceptions and attitudes."

President Clinton and others "too easily invoke 'ancient hatreds' to explain what are really contemporary conflicts," the authors sum up. "The question, in other words, is not why old conflicts are flaring up anew, but rather why traditionally harmonious mosaics have been shattered."

One of the most brilliant thinkers on development and its myriad attendant stresses, Mahbulbool Haq, the Pakistani economist, explains the changes in India and the subcontinent in larger terms. "We see two trends that look contradictory but are not," he told me one day, sitting in his U.N. office in New York. "On the one hand, you see globalization. On the other, you see this search for ethnic roots, this search to belong. . . . The nation-state in the middle is being whittled away. That is what we see in Pakistan and India, an assault on the nation-state.

"People find themselves so threatened by globalization—even in Pakistan, cooks and drivers talk about CNN bringing the Gulf War into their living rooms—that they revert to ethnic searchings.

At the same time, these new 'liberation movements' are more and more indigenous. Their origins are not from outside. . . ." His words reminded me of the other wise man who, discussing the stresses of modernity, said that "to use the telephone, you do not need to understand the philosophy behind it."

As this trip, this odyssey, drew to a finish, with more and more of these dread cases of national disintegration facing me across the globe, I realized where it had all started.

☆

Before "Lebanon" in 1975, despite warning signs here and there, we all assumed that nation-states would basically hold steady; that the form of the future was certain to be one of more and more peoples coalescing into new states of their own; and that breakdown and anarchy were signs of an ancient past. After "Lebanonization," we could assume nothing.

Lebanon, before it began to disintegrate into warring clans in the mid-1970s, had been a small paradise of a country. With its glorious green mountains and legendary cedar groves, with rich Christian, Muslim, and Druze villages descending to the azure blue of the Mediterranean, Lebanon had worked out a special social compact among its sectarian members.

By the 1980s it had become hell in a small place, as its hatreds imploded. Christians killed Muslims without quarter. Muslims killed Christians with a ferocity not seen since the Crusades. Druze and Palestinians entered the dark fray, until at any one time there were as many as fifty-three "irregular" armies fighting in Lebanon. Indeed, the "Lebanon syndrome," as I originally termed it, became the very metaphor for irregular warfare and purposeless killing in our times.

American Secretary of State George Shultz said in those days that Beirut should be "quarantined," and many nodded sage heads in urgent agreement. "A city once orderly and familiar had contracted a social and political malady, a pathology beyond redemption and cure," the brilliant Lebanese intellectual Fouad Ajami wrote.

The men and women of Beirut had turned it into a world short
of all the certainties and restraints. Just beyond the familiar world,

on the other side of the banalities and pretensions of this
Levantine city, men created a new hell. Ruin came to Beirut. But
the ruins had claimants and lords. . . .

Men began as ideologues and ended up as bandits. The
claimants came forth with guns and pamphlets, but the pamphlets were soon discarded and the game was reduced to its es-
sentials: Banditry and extortion. "I man a checkpoint; therefore,
I am." The checkpoints were sources of power—and revenue. The
warlords of the ruins—all of them, the Palestinians, the Maro-
nites, the Shiites, all the rest—marked out turfs, put the turfs
beyond the rule of law. The bandit became master and king. The
bandits claimed the ports of the country, opened new ones, imposed "taxes," ran protection rackets, flaunted the wages of banditry. The "lieutenants" of the Iranian-sponsored "Party of God"
went around the city in BMWs, those of a rival Shiite militia in
Volvos. . . .

What had happened in paradise? The tragedy was played out
in four predictable acts.

First, the country had been held together by a 1943 pact ham-
mered out between the country's traditionally warring sects and
clans, which gave each side a part of the power. For thirty or so
years, the social compact worked quite well. Second, the balance
began to unravel—at first, only underneath the surface—when the
Muslim birthrate in the late sixties began to surpass that of the
Christian population. Third, the change in the balance of internal
power was known by everyone, but no one dared say anything
about it publicly for fear of upset or upheaval. Fourth, the explosion finally came in 1970 and 1971 when the Palestinians thrown
out of Jordan in the war with King Hussein poured like political
quicksilver into Lebanon, thus destroying whatever was left of the
crucially important population balance. At that point, the country
was doomed.

I had been covering Lebanon as a foreign correspondent since
1969; but once the war started, I could hardly bear to see it in ruins.
When I did return to Beirut in the spring of 1977, I wanted to know
what the war really had been like inside. "What is striking here,"
explained a member of a French architectural team, standing in the

midst of this perverse devastation, "is that it is as if there were a willful and deliberate effort to destroy."

Umayam Yaktim, one of a group then studying the Lebanon syndrome for the American University of Beirut, told me, "Both sides wanted to kill innocent people. All the hospitals were hit— from all sides. I could go into Freud—that people were born with innate aggressive impulses—but I think it's more than that."

Actually what the world was seeing was a totally new kind of war. Once the various sides saw that no group could win, at any cost, each side began to bomb its own people, hit its own neighborhoods with artillery, and bomb theaters in which its own people were innocently watching movies. American General Andrew Goodpaster told me this was "irrational warfare." But, as with Serbian militias, there was also a kind of cynical new "rationality" about it.

Whatever title one wanted to give it, it was not really war, it was the *breakdown of war*. And it catapulted the foreign correspondent—as well as all the other "in-between people," such as diplomats, businessmen, missionaries, Red Cross workers—into a new kind of danger that we thought was impossible in our "modern" times.

In these dark new wars, there were no borders. There were no recognized civilians; indeed, the "civilians" became the deliberate targets. And there were no respected neutrals. Red Cross trucks and hospitals were intentionally hit, instead of being protected. Children fought and were killed, without bothersome second thoughts about "noncombatants."

What we were seeing in this postcolonial period was the breakdown of the Great Powers' ability to keep even the minimal peace they had kept before. With this breakdown had come an almost total dismissal of such niceties as the "rules of war" and the "rules of noncombatancy" that had been built up over the centuries. To die in Spain's civil war was to be a hero to the generations; to die in Beirut was to die without benefit of clergy or embassy, and on page 35 of the newspaper.

One fine political scientist, Benjamin R. Barber, director of the Walt Whitman Center for the Culture and Politics of Democracy at Rutgers University, began in the early nineties to see that, contrary to all we had expected in the world, "just beyond the horizon of current events lie two possible political futures—both bleak, neither democratic. The first is a retribalization of large swaths of humankind by war and bloodshed: a threatened 'Lebanonization' of national states in which culture is pitted against culture, people against people, tribe against tribe—a 'Jihad' in the name of a hundred narrowly conceived faiths against every kind of interdependence, every kind of artificial social cooperation and civic mutuality. . . ." And this "jihad," or holy war, against the West— and what the Islamicists see as a sick and odious Western secular culture—delivers a set of virtues that takes the place of the old, traditional citizenship values. Barber lists these as "a vibrant local identity, a sense of community, solidarity among kinsmen, neighbors and countrymen. . . ." (In short, all the elements that people in these situations believe are missing from their lives.) "But it also guarantees parochialism and is grounded in exclusion," Barber contends. "Solidarity is secured through war against outsiders."

Even a wildly incomplete list of the peoples wanting and demanding autonomy, secession, or any one of a series of choices on "liberation" would include the Kurds, Basques, Puerto Ricans, Ossetians, East Timoreans, Québecois, Catholics of Northern Ireland, Abkhazians, Kurile Islanders, Zulus, Catalonians, Tamils, and Palestinians—peoples who are, in Barber's apt words, "seeking smaller worlds within borders that will seal them off from modernity." As Barber puts it, "These are cultures, not countries; parts, not wholes; sects, not religions; rebellious factions and dissenting minorities at war not just with globalism but with the traditional nation-states." They are "people without countries, inhabiting nations not their own, seeking smaller worlds within borders that will seal them off from modernity. . . ."

By the end of 1992, *Jane's Defense Weekly* of London had identified no fewer than seventy-three flash points around the globe that threatened regional or international stability, as well as twenty-six wars or insurrections. "We continue to live in the most dangerous decade of the century and possibly ever," publisher Pale Beaver summed up. And every year the numbers of wars— no longer interstate but now intrastate—grew.

I realized that I was seeing far more than the breakdown of Communism in the world; I was seeing virtually every major *multinational* and *multiethnic* country on the verge of disintegration. (The countries of one people and one heritage were infinitely more secure and seemed almost totally exempt from this syndrome.) But these movements toward revolutionary change were not pitted against a tyranny, as they had been in the past, and were not even particularly *for* an ideology. Far from the old protests against political oppression, these ironically were protests arising out of the new inner upheavals within man and against the emptiness of a world that had changed dramatically in too short a time and left its inhabitants existing precariously, without context or meaning. That, of course, made them much more bedeviling and dangerous.

But by far the overwhelming truth at work here was the fact that, in each of these cases of political and human disintegration, the crisis was basically the same: It was a crisis of belief in commonality, of the death of commitment to the whole, and above all of the weakening of the citizenship bond.

☆

But there were also countertrends, and they too were spreading everywhere. Some looked as though they would tie nation-states and societies together, often with new cultural and especially economic principles that creatively crossed national boundaries: sometimes they did, sometimes they did not, and sometimes they were creating a world so new that we could not yet really judge it.

The summer and fall of 1995, as I traveled around the world, I seemed to find myself in one "seminar" after another on the kickiest new subject in the world—"globalization." Everywhere I went, whether we were talking about political, economic, or social issues, it was "globalization" that was the most urgent and compelling new theme of discussion. Indeed, from all the attention given the concept, one would have thought the future of the world depended upon it, and in many ways perhaps it does.

The idea—the hope and the threat—of globalization caused otherwise sober men and women to predict that soon the "nations" of the world would become simply "counties" of the new world economic order. Many believed that soon the formerly powerful and aggressive states of the world would find themselves in effect only supine launching pads for complex international companies and webs of production that would have no known nationalism but were tied together solely by perhaps some Internet of finance. Boundaries would crumble, as at the touch of a magic wand, and the financial elites of all countries would bond together in a kind of amorphous international citizenship.

Dr. Chai-Anan Samudavanija, the respected Thai thinker, predicted that the nation-state would soon be "bypassed" by these new and pregnant businesses-of-the-world, and that a kind of "globalized communitarianism" would soon emerge, particularly across Asia, replacing the old boundaries forced upon these peoples by nineteenth-century colonial powers. "No modern economy can any longer be limited to its country's borders," he says. Meanwhile, writer Richard Rorty, in his famous essay "Post-Modernist Bourgeois Liberalism," characterizes the next civil society of the liberal bourgeois type as "a bazaar surrounded by lots and lots of exclusive private clubs."

Such thinking only caused the perspicacious Christopher Lasch to retort dryly, "But a well-ordered bazaar presupposes nothing, after all, in the way of common beliefs or shared values. It presupposes nothing more than acceptance of a few procedural rules." Then he went on to identify what is missing from such a world: "urban amenities, conviviality, conversation, politics—almost everything, in short, that makes life worth living." And when the bazaar preempts all the public space, and sociability has to "retreat" into private clubs, people are "in danger of losing the capacity to amuse and even to govern themselves."

But what *is* globalization? And, particularly, what is the complex and sinuous but very real connection it has to the future of American citizenship?

When I spent a week in South Korea that July, the Koreans were telling a light little joke about globalization that in some ways captured the youthful headiness among these, the world's new economic cognoscenti:

A dutiful mother cat was trying hard to catch a mouse to feed her hungry babies. Finally she cornered the poor creature in his hole and tried to trick him by barking like a dog. At first, the clever mouse thought to himself, "No, that is only the cat barking. . . ."

But eventually he was taken in by the ruse and came out of his hole, only to be snatched swiftly away by the mother cat. As her children applauded, the mother told them proudly, "And that is globalization!"

Well, learning the languages and psychology of other people is indeed part of globalization; but beyond that, globalization first announces an entire new economic network for the world and, second, directly affects the most consequential issue that the world faces as the millennium looms: *Who belongs, and to what?*

When I talked with Kim Kihwan, the experienced chairman of the big Korea Trade Promotion Corporation in Seoul, he explained that globalization simply meant the opening of the world economies to an interdependence that began in the 1970s and '80s, never before known in human history. "Globalization means the world market becomes one," he said. "Every industry must have production facilities all over the world. Even in your own market, as well as abroad, your own firms compete with foreign firms—and competition is no longer between small and medium-sized industries but between large internationalist companies. Soon it will be harder to identify products in terms of nationality—say, as a Japanese, Korean, or American car—because their parts will be made all over the world."

We were sitting in his ultramodern offices in booming downtown Seoul, and it occurred to me, as it had many times on the trip, to recall that the impoverished and destroyed Korea of the 1950s was now the world's twelfth-largest economy and also that it was now building on its earlier government-induced economic success to become one of the maven nations of globalization. Then he began musing about what globalization of the world's economies would mean to the very personality of the Koreans. "It means we also need a new kind of Korean," he went on, "one who is less nationalistic, who realizes his life is dependent upon what foreigners do, as much as what his own country does." He paused, then added, "Koreans must be eager to consider the entire globe as their playground."

The next day, I went to see the country's handsome and gentlemanly prime minister, Lee Hong Koo, and we continued the globalization conversation. "In many ways," he began, "we consider the present moment one of crucial transition. We are carrying the banner of globalization—even our cabinet is called the 'globalization cabinet.' The changes we are witnessing are really epochal, but they represent much more than the end of the cold war. The 'information revolution' is like the industrial revolution of two centuries ago. If you are not at the starting line, you will be in the background for years to come."

South Korea was determined to be at that "starting line," and it had more and more determined competitors on that line across a suddenly awakening world: From Singapore and Malaysia to Chile and Argentina to the United Arab Emirates and the Sultanate of Oman, economies were opening to others, vying directly with one another for the first time in history. Everywhere, companies and industries were being reorganized, denationalized, and deracinated. An American company could have a Latin American CEO in one place, a Japanese in another, an Egyptian in another. Mexico nearly disintegrated because of the sudden flight of all the promiscuous "hot money" flying around the world looking for a profitable nesting place; yet, in a counterbalancing trend, many governments of those old and supposedly self-satisfied nation-states were finding that the imperatives of the new syndrome were forcing them to balance their budgets and maintain fiscal sobriety—or they would not be candidates for the attention of that "hot money."

It was surely a strange world to any traditional commercial thinker. The organizational structure of the old corporate world was vertical; this one was horizontal. Little Singapore, with only 3 million people, was exporting $25 billion in services and commodities to the world market, while huge Brazil, with 150 million, exported half that much. "Statist corporations" were globally owned, and investments could flow from any country and into any country. There were caveats: Where capital was liquid, the state had no control; but where it was an asset, the state had definite controls and, of course, could still erect barriers wherever it wanted. Above all, capital didn't have a flag anymore, as it did, to name just one example, with the aggressive East India Company in the nineteenth century.

Diplomacy was also being transformed. That summer in Korea, I was invited to the July Fourth party at the luxurious Korean-style American embassy residence, which is one of the most beautiful in the world. But when I entered, I stood there, stunned. The beautiful red, white, and blue tables were filled to overflowing with rich and tasty food, but everywhere you looked, there were signs to designate the benefactors: McDonald's, Wendy's, Burger King.

When I mentioned to the American ambassador the next day that I found it a little strange that American diplomacy—and, thus, America—with its complex mix of politics, culture, power, and psychology, had been reduced to this shameless huckstering of the omnivorous international marketplace, he grumbled in sympathy. "We have simply become peddlers," he said.

Like the Koreans, the more forward-looking of the new leaders were willing to take the risks of transforming their national character and mind-set in the service of an economic globalization in which "the market" seemed to have subsumed even the very culture and psychology of whole peoples in its cool and unemotional (but surely not passionless) grip. So it was natural that many of the conversations of that time moved on to questions of borders, immigration, the movements of peoples, culture, and—perhaps above all—citizenship.

One beautiful sunny day that October, for instance, I was sitting in Muscat, the lovely capital of the Sultanate of Oman at the bottom of the Arabian peninsula, in the exquisite offices of the development ministry talking with the minister of state for development affairs, Mohamed Al Yousef. He expressed both the hopes and the fears of so many of the best people in the developing world today.

"With globalization, governments are losing control of a lot of their economic and political tools," he began. "Most cannot control their exchange rates because of currency trading. Work can be done anywhere—through satellites, through computers. . . . So the borders of the nation-states are being taken over by globalization. The only way to meet the challenge is not to fight the globalization train but to be prepared, to have trained people, and to join the technological revolution. There is no sense in just sitting and thinking you can maintain traditions and build a fortress around you; only with strategic thinking can you win!"

Then the minister began to muse less buoyantly about the future of the nation-state, and thus about the future of citizenship itself. "Despite everything, the nation-state is needed for maintaining the social fabric of the state," he went on, "but who will provide roads, water?" A thoughtful pause. "Although, I think that the nation-state will even lose control of education."

He paused again, his hesitation to make pat statements showing the ambiguity of much of the thinking about globalization, and then continued in a more positive mode. "There are a lot of articles on 'global citizenship,' but at the same time we are becoming very tribal societies—look at the wars in Bosnia, in Kashmir, in Karachi. . . . Citizenship will continue because no matter what globalization there is, we still have human beings, and people want always to be in ever-larger families."

Another pause, and then he took off on yet another road. "Actually, maybe the trend will go the other way, become more nationalistic," he suggested, "as the fight for survival becomes more intense and we struggle for resources."

I soon came to realize that what I was seeing in the entire globalization phenomenon and debate was a dramatic manifestation of the decitizening of America, and for two reasons: (1) American corporations and indeed the entire American economy were being disconnected economically, politically, and morally from "America" as we had known it when what was good-for-General-Motors was good-for-America, and not necessarily the world; and (2) the new American elites—the people that Robert Reich calls "symbolic analysts" because they manipulate the symbols of the modern world—were also becoming disconnected from any real sense of deep patriotism for America, and they were replacing it with loyalties to their far-flung brother and sister elites-in-globalization. And so, in place of the great old families of America—with their "old money," traditional patriotic civic conscience, and ethic of investing in all levels of citizenship and community—we have new elites who live separately, act internationally and think free-enterprisingly.

First, the corporations. "Like American products . . . the 'American' corporation is being disconnected from America . . . ," Reich writes in the seminal *Work of Nations*. Corporations are fast becoming "parts of global webs in which much of the value of what they sell comes from other places around the world—including, importantly, high-value problem-solving and identifying." At the same time, "national savings increasingly flow to whomever can do things best, or cheapest, wherever located around the world." American capitalism is now "organized relentlessly around profits, not patriotism." He quotes a top executive of Colgate-Palmolive as saying, "There is no mindset that puts this country first."

These globalized companies often pride themselves on being "good citizens" of other countries as well as America, but that is highly questionable. Citizenship is a complex weave of factors, not reducible to almsgiving around the world, as agreeable to the receiver as that may be—or seem to be at the moment.

Next, the people. Reich's term "symbolic analyst" has become the standard expression for the Americans who serve this globalized community and fly from their most often restricted neighborhoods to foreign countries, where they mix with the same sorts of people as they are, but in other languages and with exotic food and clothing, and never quite know where "home" is, except that it is wherever they are at whatever moment.

To simplify, they are people who work not so much with old-style product as with abstract concepts and symbols and who "produce" symbolic information. This work can include anything from journalism to the stock market to the culture of Hollywood across the world.

"Many of them have ceased to think of themselves as Americans in any important sense, implicated in America's destiny for better or worse," the brilliant social critic Christopher Lasch writes, continuing that "multiculturalism suits them to perfection, conjuring up the agreeable image of a global bazaar in which exotic cuisines, exotic styles of dress, exotic music, exotic tribal customs can be savored indiscriminately, with no questions asked and no commitments required. The new elites are at home only in transit, en route to a high-level conference, to the grand opening of a new franchise, to an international film festival, or to an undiscovered resort. Theirs is essentially a tourist's view of the world—not a perspective likely to encourage a passionate devotion to democracy."

Lasch, finding these trends profoundly alarming for the future of the republic, goes on to say that

> the cosmopolitan man or woman with a sense of global citizenship is thus able to maintain appropriate perspective on the

world's problems and possibilities. . . . But will the cosmopolitan with a global perspective choose to act fairly and compassionately? Will our current and future symbolic analysts—lacking any special sense of responsibility toward a particular nation and its citizens—share the wealth with the less fortunate of the world and devote their resources and energies to improving the changes that others may contribute to the world's wealth?

Here we find the darker side of cosmopolitanism. For without strong attachments and loyalties extending beyond family and friends, symbolic analysts may never develop the habits and attitudes of social responsibility. They will be world citizens, but without accepting or even acknowledging any of the obligations that citizenship in a polity normally implies. . . . Without a real political community in which to learn, refine, and practice the ideals of justice and fairness, they may find these ideals to be meaningless abstractions.

Indeed, some commentators think these "citizens" have already "seceded" from America, while others just find them uninterested in America except as a "base from which to skim the world."

In short, the globalization phenomenon, which will surely rule the economic life and thinking of the world for many decades to come, does more than change all the rules, it also changes the very character of the people who are effectively becoming citizens of the world economy: It rewards the single-minded ambition of the aggressive upward-striving and threatens to leave the more amenable average citizen behind.

These globalized Americans—and, remember, they are Americans with a remarkably wide scope of interests, who in other eras would have been citizen-leaders—simply do not belong to a really American "political community" any longer. They belong to a very arcane world. At home, they (and of course other types of Americans as well) often live in "gated communities," where two scholarly analysts have found they are "using barricades and gates with increasing frequency to isolate themselves" and where both disinterest in nation and fear of crime and the other is "fueling the drive for separation, distinction, exclusion and protection."

In *Fortress Communities: The Walling and Gating of American Suburbs*, the scholars Edward J. Blakely and Mary Gail Snyder note:

The resulting loss of connection between citizens in privatized and traditional communities loosens social contact and weakens the bonds of mutual responsibility that are a normal part of community living. As a result, there is less and less talk of citizenship. The new lexicon of civic responsibility is that of the taxpayers who take no active role in governance but merely exchange money for services. . . .

With segregated, disconnected living spaces and social interactions, the result is atomized citizenship, in place and in style. Democracy is in part based on the mutuality of citizenship, the structure of communities which tie individuals together across their dissimilarities. . . . We question whether American society can prosper without inclusive community undergirding the practice of citizenship. Can the nation have any wholeness when communities are fragmented and pitted against one another socially, politically, or economically?

The trend toward privatized government and communities is part of the more general trend of fragmentation, and the resulting loss of connection and social contact is weakening the bonds of mutual responsibility and the social contract. We no longer speak of citizens, but rather of taxpayers. . . . Can this nation fulfill its social contract in the absence of social contact?

It used to be, of course, that citizenship made insiders of strangers, but now, the authors sum up, by "creating outsiders of fellow citizens . . . we must question whether democracy founded on a citizenship and community base remains possible." We must question whether current trends and practices are making strangers of citizens.

Not surprisingly, the hoary practices of peculiarly American citizenship are withering away under the onslaught of changes. In his seminal works about America in the 1830s, Alexis de Tocqueville saw above all that America was a nation of joiners, that they "are forever forming associations." That truth defined the richness of American community life, whether citizenship was defined by the sewing bee or the cooperative barn-raising, by helping a neighbor in trouble, by organizations pushing for criminal justice, for just about everything and anything. Most local and personal problems were taken care of by the people themselves—not through the revolutions of Europe but through the practice of citizenship. Thus, human beings evolved to ever-higher forms.

All that changed. By the 1990s, one of the most perceptive of American social critics, Professor Robert D. Putnam of Harvard University, noted that from the 1960s onward participation in voluntary associations in the United States went down between 25 and 50 percent. "Americans today are significantly less engaged with their communities than was true a generation ago," he wrote. Above all, he blamed television. The average American was spending fully 40 percent of his free time watching television, which discourages "social trust and group membership." Part of the problem was that television gives such a negative picture of society that "heavy watchers of TV are unusually skeptical about the benevolence of other people, overestimating crime rates, for example. . . . Heavy TV watching may well increase pessimism about human nature."

This state of affairs seems even more alarming when we realize that globalization has also redefined the economic life of many countries and it is redefining the world of work so profoundly that, today more than ever, it is not natural resources or even the wealth of companies that is important but the "human resources" that are applied. And, of course, unlike the old capital of the corporation, those human resources are fungible. If people leave, they take knowledge with them. This means that the individual human being has greatly enhanced power. But for citizenship, this means a further distancing of any person from his fellow citizens.

Finally, we cannot fail to mention the other international phenomenon that is changing and diluting the nation-state, and upon which national citizenship of course depends. This is the development not only of international organizations such as the U.N., which by the 1990s was fast becoming the world's major diplomat, but of the increasingly influential nongovernmental organizations, NGOs. These NGOs can be anything from church organizations to humanitarian groups to agricultural development organizations; they have money and they have people, and they are increasingly involved in new forms of "global governance," crossing borders on the humanitarian and developmental level in the same way as globalized corporations on an economic level. As the Commission on Global Governance states in its "Our Global Neighbourhood" report:

Global governance, once viewed primarily as concerned with intergovernmental relationships, now involves not only governments and intergovernmental institutions but also non-governmental organizations (NGOs), citizens' movements, transnational corporations, academia, and the mass media. The emergence of a global civil society, with many movements reinforcing a sense of human solidarity, reflects a large increase in the capacity and will of people to take control of their lives.

☆

There are a few social problems that accompany all of these developments: (1) The new American elites are disconnected from America; (2) other Americans from the working class and many parts of the middle class who still patriotically believe in country, flag, and patriotism are left behind and alienated; and (3) divisions of class that America has not known are likely to appear and become problematic. What will happen to them, the old "common people," the members of the working class that indeed I came from, when, without the safety of reasonable patriotic protections, they have to face all the new challenges—from the remoteness and "threat" of globalization to the abstract alchemies of many new information networks?

The American working classes will not be speaking English with counterpart Indonesians and drinking Scotch with Singaporeans at conferences in Alexandria, Bucharest, and Bellagio. No, they risk being left in the backwaters of all these grand new theories and phenomena; they fear them, and they are right. Their self-respect has been taken away from them: the factories and businesses that they sustained and that sustained them are the same ones that globalization has replaced. Worse, the very symbols of their nation have been weakened, if not derided and destroyed, by ethnic controversies, by multiculturalism, and by snide dismissals by new activists in odd union with symbolic analysts to destroy what is left of the civic culture that alone sustains citizenship, particularly among the "less privileged."

And so the workable old social equality of America is direly threatened by the conjunction of all of these trends and tendencies. There is no place to hide from change anymore, and there are fewer and fewer places even for the different classes to meet, work on common problems or projects, or even get to know one another.

As the thoughtful *New Republic* editor Mickey Kaus writes: "The most serious threat to democracy in our time comes not so much from the maldistribution of wealth as from the decay or abandonment of public institutions in which citizens meet as equals."

When we are talking about globalization, then, we are really talking about the emasculation of the nation-state, the emasculation of American citizenship, and the gradual breakdown of America by class.

We are seeing the formation of a world where the most intelligent and upwardly mobile people are apolitical, sitting in front of their machines "communicating" passively with people they will never see or truly talk to or share anything real and palpable with, while many of the lesser-educated are left behind, alone, to uphold national citizenship. But will people die for Internet?

Robert Reich fears that

> America may simply explode into a microcosm of the entire world. It will contain some of the world's richest people and some of the world's poorest, speaking innumerable languages, owing many allegiances, celebrating many different ideals. These individuals will be efficiently connected to the rest of the globe—both economically and culturally—but not necessarily to one another.
>
> Our collective identity will fade. There will be no national purpose, and no pretense of one. . . . In contrast to most inhabitants of the planet, who still live in nations that impose on them substantial responsibilities for the well-being of their compatriots, the well-being of the people who live within the borders of the United States will inhabit a kind of free, universal zone, obligating them only to refrain from causing one another bodily injury and stealing one another's property. There will be no sense of national community. . . .

And this would be ineffably sad, for it would mean an end to the "American experiment," to "creating a diverse society bound together not only by its love of individual liberty but also by its sense of justice. It robs America of a moral authority transcending and preceding the cold war with Soviet communism—an authority derived from its unique confluence of tolerance and fairness."

It would be amazing, going against everything we know about human nature and waves of social change, if some of the humiliated and resentful human beings threatened by these developments did not respond in some irrational and violent way. In fact, it was bound to happen, and so of course it did.

☆

One afternoon in the early spring of 1995, I was walking across the lobby of National Airport in Washington on my way to Chicago when a porter that I had gotten to know over the years ran up to me. He looked stricken, and I soon found out why. "They've blown up the federal building in Oklahoma," he said. And soon the whole nation was stricken by the sickening news.

My first thought, as that awful day progressed and the gruesome pictures of that skeletal Alfred P. Murrah Federal Building were seared into our national consciousness, was that this horrible act had to be the work of Islamic extremists. It was exactly the kind of car bomb the terrorists used in Beirut, and Oklahoma and its part of the Deep Midwest had been home to members of many extremist groups from the Middle East as well as their major conferences. But the "Islamic fundamentalist threat" was not the answer this time.

Instead, with the bomb that tore asunder that huge public building, finally killing 169 men, women, and children and injuring more than 500, there came revelations of deep secrets about American society that few had even suspected and that even the press had only barely discovered. Day after day, new wellsprings of violence were suddenly opened to the light of day; and day after day the nation grew more shocked, horrified, and bewildered by what was revealed.

It seems that there was a substantial group of Americans who had existed in an arcane and largely hidden world of incipient rebellion against the U.S. government and its authority. Many called them the Far Right, but that was really not accurate, for they were not the traditional Right at all. Theirs was a paranoid world more akin to the Serbian militias of the mountains of Bosnia, defined by similar tales of nearly ripe conspiracies and nourished by fears of destruction of a mythical former life—in the case of the Serbs, their former medieval glory as a state; for the Americans, their memory of the frontier.

Members told Armageddon stories of American troops hovering over their lands in black helicopters, coming to get them after changing the interstate road signs so that only they could read them. (The reason it sounds more like Beirut than Billings is that *it is*.) Theirs was a cabal with its own code words—government bureaucrats were called "public masters" instead of public servants, and "Chunged," after TV anchorwoman Connie Chung, meant "to be treated shabbily by the media"—and their movement was well into devising aggressive tactics against that hated government.

Paranoid militiamen, right here in America? Disillusioned "citizens" who felt they had nowhere to turn? Disaffected and alienated young men, whose violence was erupting outside of traditional societal controls in gunfire and conspiracy? To the great shock of the rest of America, it was true.

Very quickly, the FBI arrested not any Islamic radicals but an American, the unsmiling and tight-lipped Timothy McVeigh. His frighteningly expressionless face was on every front page as he refused to give authorities anything more than his name and date of birth—for was he not a "political prisoner," just like all those similar men from Latin America to the Middle East to Asia? The *Washington Post* detailed his biographical evolution in its long and comprehensive profile of him weeks later:

> He lived the divorce revolution, age 10 when his parents split in 1978. . . .
>
> He was an underachiever in high school, uninterested in college.
>
> He hit the job market in the mid-1980s as it ran out of room for young men with blue-collar skills. Aware of affirmative action for women and minorities, he began to feel shortchanged as a white male.
>
> He worked dead-end jobs, voiced fears of going nowhere, tried a well-trod escape route—the Army—but bailed out as the military downsized with the fall of Communism. Like millions in his generation, he ended up back home as an adult, a man sleeping in a boy's room, headed exactly where he'd feared: nowhere. . . .

The story moved on to the dénouement of the saga, in many ways predictable, at least in hindsight. Soon he had an obsession with guns, he was beginning to arm himself to "fight alone in an apocalyptic war," and he was making and exploding bombs in a "survivalist bunker." And finally, "Americans were shocked to learn that the prime suspects in the Oklahoma City bombing were not foreign terrorists but men from the nation's heartland. The plot was not hatched in Beirut or Baghdad but possibly in the backwoods of northeast Michigan by a paramilitary cell. . . ."

Now that the public had been alerted by the horrors of the bombing, the profile of this "cell" began to fill out with flesh and blood. What investigators discovered was no less than a vast subculture, hiding in the shadowy corners of America and readying itself to defeat its "tyrannical government and its co-conspirators," who could be everything and everybody from the liberal media to feminists to gays, immigrants, Jews, and even the Freemasons. The image of these men was not what would be expected: They were most often dressed not in jungle fatigues but physically and psychologically in the garb of the respectable working-class Right, which made the whole phenomena only more confusing to analysts. Its groups had often innocuous and misleading names: the Historic Preservation Association, the Institute of Historical Review, the Council of Conservative Citizens. But in fact these supposedly "respectable" groups went from being fanatically anti–civil rights to denying the Holocaust to accusing the government of a conspiracy to create a black-ruled "Republic of South Africa" in the South. (Interestingly, even the names they so pretentiously chose paralleled the guerrilla and militia groups across the world that they in so many ways resembled: Were they perhaps rhetorical brothers to the Popular Front for the Liberation of Palestine?)

Many of the members of the American militias walked around with copies of the Constitution in their pockets; they bubbled out of the same ferment that, *Time* magazine notes, "produced such widely divergent events as the Oklahoma City bombing and Ross Perot's recent proposal to launch a new political party." The case of Nevada cattleman and Nye County Commissioner Dick Carver is exemplary: On July 4, 1994 (it was no accident, of course, the choice of the day), Carver decided he had had enough of the federal government. So he took his old D-7 Caterpillar bulldozer and threatened to run down a U.S. Forest Service agent who had challenged his opening a road across a national forest without federal permission. Carver compared his act of "civil disobedience" to a "frontier Boston Tea Party," justified because of the "tyranny" of the government. That day, no one got hurt, but that day was only the beginning.

As the case against Timothy McVeigh and several of his cohorts began taking form, the newspapers finally got into high gear with this story: There were by then at least twenty-five thousand members of militias in the country—and perhaps up to two hundred thousand—and they lived, organized, and moved in at least eighteen states. Great numbers of militia members were, not surprisingly, from western or midwestern states where recent economic disasters of struggling farm and factory towns had added to the sense of disenfranchisement and humiliation that underlay all of their activities.

In their "constitutional rebellion," these groups and militias— and farmers and ranchers who can range from conservative angries to paranoid crazies—had developed their own arsenal of tactics to confront the government and its power. One of the major approaches was "jury nullification," a concept of antagonism between the jury (the people) and the judge (the state) unfamiliar to most Americans. The idea, expounded in depth at militia meetings by its rural gurus and "philosophers," was that the government could exercise no power over its citizens if jurors would not enforce the government's laws. Even a few jurors could neutralize tax and gun laws, for instance, if they refused to convict a defendant in very specifically chosen cases and despite ample evidence of a violation. Jury nullification was a direct threat to the government's power in the courtroom, and militias looked upon it as a "citizen's" challenge to government.

A typical case study of a rustic guru of the movement: The *Washington Times* found one of the jury nullification leaders in Isabella, Missouri, deep in the Ozarks, in September 1995—George Gordon, who teaches "his peculiar mix of biblical and statutory law, promising to show his students how to represent themselves in court and disconnect themselves from the everyday snares and

entanglements of government authority." The reporter characterizes Gordon's revealing message thus: "Learn to live life without
cash, lawyers, a Social Security number. . . . *Live without citizenship,*
a credit card, a mortgage, a driver's license, a marriage license or
an obligation to send your children to public schools. And, most
important, without taxes. Learn the laws of man in order to adroitly
sidestep them. . . ." (Italics mine.)

Live without citizenship? But, of course. The militiamen and
women were turning their backs upon everything that tied them
to the hated American government and authorities, including citizenship. Since their version of citizenship was so sacred to them,
they had to deny it to those authorities.

There had, of course, been American paranoics with weapons
since the days of the Whiskey Rebellion two hundred years ago,
right up to the neo-Nazis and skinheads of the early 1980s; but two
different elements came into play with these new groups. First,
they were using the most advanced technologies of the modern
world. They posted their meetings on the Internet and used the
new technology to spread the types of theories that in earlier days
of conspiracy were whispered in dark bars and around the street
corners of mill towns.

The *Wall Street Journal* noted that "this newfound public relations and technological savvy allows once-isolated individuals,
who may previously have preached only to a few friends and
neighbors, to reach a wide audience—including other, formerly
isolated people." It quoted a leader of one of the front organizations, the "Southern League": "The Internet and desktop publishing help groups like ours circumvent the mainstream media and
get the truth out." The end result, summed up the *Journal,* "is an
alternative gush of information and opinion upon which thousands now feed, yet which remains virtually unseen and unheard
by the rest of the nation."

Second, their fears were not only of the federal government,
forestry and fishing officers, and people they can see; their paranoia stretched to the hated "one-world government" they saw at
the nation's very doorstep. They see such sinister global forces that
many of them believe a "U.N. Army" is veritably on its way to take
over America. (The rather obvious fact that, even as this paranoia

was at its very height, those U.N. armies were the laughingstock of the entire world did not seem to sink into their consciousness, despite the fascination with information technology.)

As the uncovering of the militia movement and all of its different groups continued dramatically after the Oklahoma City bombing, it became clear to the country that these groups were particularly inspired by what they saw as two recent cases of federal "murder"—the "Standoff at Ruby Ridge" in August of 1992 and the "Siege of Waco" in the spring and summer of 1993—which gave them "sacred causes" and proof that the federal authorities were out to get anyone who did not think their way.

But what was even more distressing to many was that some of the movement's dissension was reflected in America's *non-militia* center.

An April 1995 Gallup poll found that no fewer than 39 percent of Americans thought that the federal government "poses an immediate threat to the rights and freedoms of ordinary Americans" and that 49 percent of the public thought that the CIA was involved in the assassination of John F. Kennedy. A rabid and paranoid spirit was obviously infecting usually rational parts of the country, not just the militia.

☆

Two social psychologists from Northern Texas University, Don Beck and Christopher Cowan, have done some of the best analysis of what was happening with these movements in America. "This is an extremely dangerous time," they write in a memo to me.

> The "evil empire" no longer provides a common enemy. The end of the Cold War also thawed the ice sheet that covered deep value system divides. Hot ethnic survival cores are now bubbling and boiling everywhere—in the Balkans, Africa, and even here.
>
> Cultural diversity taken to the extreme is polarizing society. The loss of high niche jobs is a threat. Affirmative action, especially as imposed by the federal government, has alienated many white males. The crime rate is high. The political process creates and freezes left wing vs. right wing stereotypes. Radio talk shows have reached an inflammatory stage. Open media teaches everybody, everything—even how to make bombs—and quickly

spreads rumors. We are going through the final decade of the 20th Century and we are facing the Second Millennium, and this will be a crazy time, full of prophets, apocalyptic forecasts and bizarre visions.

These are the conditions of existence in the milieu that create the mood, atmosphere and driving forces that are shifting core attitudes and shaping a major restructuring of our society.

Focusing directly on the "Oklahoma version of domestic terrorism," the two professors write that

> the atmosphere is inflamed by the alarming increase in the number of Americans who are anti-federal government, paranoid about the threats and loss of control, and are hunkering down in cults, brigades, militias, patriotic cells and isolated enclaves. Unhappily, the alphabets (FBI, AFT, even FEMA) are replacing the EVIL EMPIRE in the minds of those who desperately need the huns to be at the gates. You see identical systems in Arkansas in the Aryan Nation, Ku Klux Klan, White Posse, White Supremists. . . . The same profiles are in the Jihad, the Hammas, extreme Zionist groups, Black Panthers, Maoist Red Brigades. All of these systems come out of identical brains and the same seam in the terrorism strata. They are psychological twins.

In one of the books that is "sacred" to many in the militias, *Warrior Dreams: Violence and Manhood in Post-Vietnam America*, author James William Gibson explores similar themes. He traces how "the independent warrior" stepped in to fill the dangerous void of manhood created by the American failure in Vietnam and comments that the "disruptions of cultural identity" that began in the 1960s with civil rights and ethnic pride movements led to this new creation, the "paramilitary warrior."

What is different in this scenario from earlier "wars" is that the old Western hero, when he moved to the frontier, left behind a stable world—these men do not. In fact, they feel that they are leaving behind no society at all, that they must reconstruct it on new frontiers they alone will rule; so they are symbolically carrying their citizenship with them. Ironically, these men think, seriously no doubt, that it is *they* who are the perfect citizens.

☆

I began to wonder: What were the common elements within such civil breakdown in different societies? Did the United States share them with other countries of the world?

As a matter of fact, there were and are remarkably similar factors that tend to cross and crisscross every country and every group. I am not talking theoretically but rather in terms of what I have witnessed in parts of the world that we believed were extremely stable. I do not deal in theory but in indicators of change that have proven almost as predictable as scientific equations.

In many cases, such as Yugoslavia and in former parts of the Soviet Union—Tajikistan and Azerbaijan, Georgia and Abkhazia—the first major factor in societal weakening is the death of an all-encompassing ideology whose "truths" provide the answer to every question of man. Core beliefs are no longer valued and no longer held; and so the historic facts and principles behind them are ignored, forgotten, buried. It was always difficult for Americans to understand the dominating, pulsating, fanatical power of Marxism and how, despite its crimes and distortions, it nevertheless gave meaning to the lives of tens of millions in the succor of its ideological empire that then stretched from Moscow to Saigon, and from Luanda to Kabul to Havana. Marxism was indeed a religion—the modern age's answer *to* religion and, in one philosopher's words, "a Christian heresy." It gave life form, and it claimed to leave behind in an outdated history all the old differences and hatreds that divided men so murderously according to tribe, clan, and creed.

When Communism collapsed and the full truth of its shabbiness and criminality emerged in the sudden light of day, those tens of millions of persons were suddenly "free"—but that freedom signified to most of them only that they were now floating alone in a meaningless world. They also now knew of their conscious or subconscious complicity in atrocities during those years of obedience to the state. So what they did, massively, was very simple: They returned to the only other thing they knew, which was to renew the old hatreds against their neighbors. But in no place did this occur spontaneously. Those hatreds could be orchestrated, nurtured, and re-created (as in Yugoslavia, Georgia, and Russia itself) or muted, mediated, and controlled (as in Bulgaria, Macedonia, and Kirgizstan).

Language is the next mighty sword in these silent wars of breakdown. Language was the prime mover in the breakdown of Sri Lanka, the beautiful and once-felicitous island of Ceylon, where Tamils and Sinhalese had lived together in an enviable harmony until, in the 1950s, the Sinhalese insisted upon imposing their language on the island. Now, tens of thousands of dead later, the once-paradisal island remains in ruins. Language is equally the problem in Belgium, Canada, and many parts of Africa and the Arab world.

In *many* cases, breakdown comes when agreed-upon measures to keep different groups living peaceably together suddenly no longer hold. This was the primary and quintessential lesson of Lebanon, just as it was part of the problem in Oklahoma City; but, particularly overseas, this phenomenon is almost always linked to changes in demography. When one population grows inordinately large, whether slowly or suddenly, another population comes to feel threatened and is fearful. Unless there are extraordinarily wise politicians and leaders (and there do not seem to be many around these days), violence begins, spreads, and probably finally overwhelms all attempts to dampen it down.

Further, when a new population enters the society and polity, particularly if it is perceived by the mainstream (in Lebanon, the Christians and the Muslims) as hostile and illegitimate (the Palestinians), there comes a moment of reaching critical mass in population and thus of power through numbers, when liberal and tolerant ideas of "living together" just naturally fall by the wayside. At that moment, when the new group suddenly realizes it is large enough and strong enough to take power, it virtually always acts in some way that evinces violence, usually from the threatened and outnumbered group.

Still another important area in societal disintegration is that of the law. The impulses toward breakdown become extremely important and dangerous when new groups, which are identified or identify themselves as "different" (peculiar to themselves and cutting themselves off from the mainstream), insist upon their own laws. This is what has been happening in India, where minority groups put great new stresses upon a society and weakened the polity at its point of greatest vulnerability, the law. Those stresses affect a society socially, culturally, and economically as well as in terms of security. When a multinational society has to accommodate so many different demands, which can include court procedures and public papers in many languages, in addition to actual changes in the laws to suit various cultural tastes, a country is inevitably bound not only to divide into conflictive camps but also to decline economically; there is simply no way that a country can, with such expensive and disruptive demands, keep up with the much more easily functioning one-culture, one-language, and one-heritage countries.

When I was a young reporter in Chicago in the early sixties, the man who most profoundly understood these changes in the world—and who analyzed them best psychologically—was the late Dr. Heinz Kohut. Professor at the University of Chicago, this brilliant psychoanalyst became a treasured mentor and friend and often patiently tried to help me to understand what was really going on underneath the surface of all of these disturbing and kaleidoscopic events across a changing world. Too many countries, repressed and backward, were pitting themselves against a country such as the United States, which both inspired change and thwarted it.

"Then came the shah in Iran, Ataturk in Turkey, Nasser in Egypt," he told me one day. "In order to make their people more capable of self-respect, the message is 'Modernize!' But if the changes made are made abruptly, within one or two generations, that threatens the continuity of the ethnic self. It is much like the individual self. We were once children, then adolescents, then mature adults. When a person feels discontinuous, that is a terribly painful feeling. You do not hang together. People will do almost anything to avoid that.

"What happens when it is not within the capacity of people to change is that they want to overthrow those who forced them to move. Change is experienced as an agent of someone else. Discontinuity arouses tremendous anxiety. So when someone comes like Khomeini or Yassir Arafat, with something of a 'new world,' there is a sense of tremendous healing. They do anything for it, so long as the sense of continuity is reestablished.

"The riches that oil wells give does not give them self-esteem—that can only come from being master of one's own fate. Then there is a degree of sadism that is mobilized: Give them (the foreign agents of change) a dose of that medicine that they inflict on others.

They feel shamed by us, so they need to shame us. And they know that they can have tremendous power over us because they are at that stage of development where their goals are compatible with dying. Ours are not. We can't say we'll do the same to you. We are at a totally different stage of selfhood in dealing with them. It is important to give them a sense of respect so they don't need to shame us."

Then Kohut summed up what the West, by simply existing and being the agent suggesting change, did to the less developed countries: "We took a picture of their poverty."

Finally, in every case of breakdown, one discovers that the dominant society and leadership group waited too long to confront the divisive elements. It gives in and gives in—all the while destroying its historical self-knowledge, which endows a people with confidence—instead of standing on principle from the very beginning. It also gives in, thinking itself liberal and tolerant, to new and different interpretations of national commitment— of *citizenship*— that are at heart antithetical to the traditional beliefs and needs of the society. And by the time the elite intellectual and political group realizes the danger, it really *is* too late. The ties that have held the society together have been ineluctably rent; worse, rent by its own hand.

But if Americans and others no longer understood what and why citizenship was, sadder voices across the world certainly did. In one spring 1993 *Washington Post* dispatch from war-torn and brutalized and starving Somalia, for instance, another child of breakdown and savagery, one Kalif Shira Hossein, a government employee whose wife had just been killed, is quoted: "The only thing I'm worried about now are the people left in Somalia, who are being starved and killed by those who don't know the meaning of a nation." And that same week, on Mount Trebevic in Bosnia, while Milosevic's forces were massacring the poor, unarmed intellectuals of Bosnia, the Bosnian Muslim leaders kept nevertheless repeating pitifully that they sought only a "citizens' state" with "equal rights for all."

☆

We Americans inherited and will inhabit the only country that early arrived at a coherent national expression of what a univer-

salist nation should be: which is, one embracing all kinds of
human beings and cultures but unmistakably within one ideology based upon political democracy and economic freedom. To
quote just one of many cogent thinkers on the roots of this American unity, columnist and intellectual Charles Krauthammer has
said that it was "built on a tightly federalist politic and a powerful melting pot culture. Most important, from the very beginning
of the republic, Americans voluntarily chose to deal with the
problem of historic differentness (ethnicity, race, even gender) by
embracing a radical individualism and rejecting the notion of
group rights."

For their part, Americans most often took their historic good
luck as natural (after all, it *seemed* natural to them). They assumed
it to be automatic. To our forefathers, the American way of life was
not only a pragmatic agreement among human beings but also one
that every man and woman on the globe could have, if they only
put their minds to it and did what was necessary to achieve it.

From the very beginning of the republic, Americans knew in
their hearts and minds that America was something different and
blessed, and they came too to realize that their country was the
very example to the world of the modernized nation-state; as such,
it was marked by God and history for all the other struggling, less
lucky "old" countries to follow.

Thus, from the very beginning, America seemed to be exactly
the opposite of those threatening "case studies" such as Yugoslavia, India, or Lebanon. America "worked" because it arose out of
the Protestant-ethic societies of Northern Europe, whose secret for
success lay in the fact that its individuals, respecting the rights of
their fellow citizens, had developed a unique compact for a healthy
society that was based upon citizenship. These rare societies—
where men seldom killed one another over power—would accept
the decision of the majority in political and even social affairs, following certain civilized norms. This equilibrium would be realized
in the name of justice and evolution toward a human society that
could finally enjoy the benefits of the amity and harmony the
prophets had predicted. It was in this sense, certainly to the Founding Fathers, that "America" was the secular fulfillment of religious
prophecy.

But Americans could strive to put into practice these dreams only because the majority of the people were committed citizens who believed in the same principles—or at least accepted them as a basis for their acts—and exercised the same impulses. The magic of this compact was that it allowed, encouraged, and forced the passions and talents of the society to turn away from those old clan, tribal, and ethnic conflicts that had seemed eternal during earlier stages of man's development, and focus instead on science, architecture, literature, physics, geography, geology, animal husbandry, agriculture, philosophy. . . .

Americans were to live governed by an inner morality, with inner controls exercised by responsible and self-motivated human beings. The destructiveness of the past, where all the energies of the group went into fighting for group position and privilege, was to be left behind—and, in general, was.

There was, of course, violence within this new American society, sometimes terrible violence, and deceit and corruption. The Founding Fathers most definitely did not believe in the perfectibility of man; but they did believe that, given the right principles, institutions, and intentions, man could and would evolve to ever-higher forms.

While there were threats from outside, despite the protection of the two great oceans, still very few Americans ever dreamed that any threat could seriously challenge it from within. But the fact is that "America the Unbreachable" *is* being assaulted today, on one level or another, by every one of the same problems afflicting those "remote" dissolving countries of the world.

In a mostly nonviolent version of Yugoslavia, America is deeply involved in a vast conflict of individual versus group rights, with group rights at the moment gaining. Like Sri Lanka, Belgium, and Québec, language has become a major problem: American English is being challenged by groups demanding that teaching in the schools be carried out in virtually every language of the world. As in India, more and more ethnic and religious groups in America are demanding the imposition of their own laws and the legalizing of old customs (female circumcision, to name only one example) that the great mass of Americans rightly find alien and abhorrent.

In little potential Lebanons across America, group leaders are creating a rigidly adversarial atmosphere that is overwhelming the civic life of the country. Instead of working for the old "common good," the political/civic picture of America today is that of group constantly fighting group and activist/leader fighting advocate/leader for power and privilege, which leads only to disruption and division. As in parallel developments from Australia to the North of Europe, multiculturalism has become ascendant in America's schools, universities, and scholarly associations, direly challenging the radical individualism that alone assured true individual rights under the Constitution and the law. Prominent social scientist Francis Fukuyama has summarized what is happening in America by saying that "multicultural proponents argue either that the United States never had a single culture beyond its universalistic political and legal system, or else that the dominant European culture of generations past was oppressive and should not be a model to which all Americans must conform."

At the same time, often without realizing what is happening, the nation has passively allowed its preparation and its testing for citizenship to become little more than a joke and a fraud. All can become "citizens" with little study and often without even reasonable English proficiency, without knowing much about the history (and thus, the meaning) of the society they are joining, and without having to make most of the traditional commitments to it. So, of course, they remain what they were when they approached America: strangers.

Meanwhile, buoyed by new neutralist dreams of borderless worlds, utopians in American universities and in international organizations weave fantastic *Thousand and One Nights* tales of "new forms of citizenship." More often than not, these new forms deliberately bypass the old nation-state, while they envision human beings traveling on the Internet and identifying with a global economy. These new people are supposed to live in "virtual realities" in (one can only suppose) a brave new world of uprooted "virtual citizens." But the "non-virtual reality" is really Oklahoma City.

☆

Given these admitted upheavals within America, one can only ask: Where do we start?

There is a place to start—the one area of breakdown in America that provides the key to unlocking the riddle of all the others. This key opens the door to both warnings and answers. And yet this area is little addressed or even debated in America today.

It is citizenship.

More and more as I have spoken around the country these last years, whenever I mention citizenship, someone always asks, usually with a kind of puzzlement: "But why is it important?" I have asked myself repeatedly: Is it possible that many of us Americans no longer even know what it is?

The dictionary definition of *citizenship* is actually much too simple; it says only that it is "the status of being a citizen, a membership in a community, the quality of an individual's adjustment, responsibility or contribution to his community." In fact, national citizenship developed first in England in the fifteenth century and found its apogee in the American republic and then, less rationally, in the French Revolution. It can be compared loosely to marriage, except that in citizenship the individual promises his fealty to his nation and broader principles, not to one person or one family. For its part, the nation promises to protect and secure him, and to give him all the manifest benefits of living in and communicating with a civilized polity.

It has been called many things—the bond, commitment, contract, compact—thus reflecting its intrinsic complexity. Essentially, citizenship organizes society by defining who belongs and who does not, and by honoring the voluntary decisions of individual human beings. Yet, citizenship is not totally exclusionary: In most countries of the world, foreigners or "aliens" (that strange and discomfiting word, indicating as it does a world of antagonists) can, by applying appropriately, studying the history of that nation, and forsaking previous citizenship bonds, join and even be welcomed into the new community.

But citizenship is more than just a banding-together for protection against enemies. Citizenship, particularly as it has evolved throughout the Western world, is the unique and ennobling story of the postfeudal, modern relationship of the individual human being to the state, of the state to the individual, and of the human being to his fellow man. It is a dignified commitment of respect, responsibility, even friendship and love. In contrast to the irrational acts in today's Yugoslavia, citizenship offers a rational and voluntary covenant and a social contract, made in free will and in the integrity of the individual's conscience.

Citizenship is the cornerstone of all of the other commitments—marriage, baptism, school, university—that people make. It is the only commitment that everyone living in a nation *can* make. It guarantees virtually every right and duty that come together to keep a nation healthy and sane.

Man's development to the stage of citizenship represented the moment when the nobodys of history became somebodies, and when human beings were suddenly equal in the eyes of the state and the law, for the first time regardless of ownership of land, station of birth, or even level of intelligence. As the great philosopher Hannah Arendt has written, "It is citizenship that confers equality, not equality that creates a right to citizenship." Or as Christopher Lasch wrote just before his death, "Citizenship appeared to have given even the humbler members of society access to the knowledge and cultivation elsewhere reserved for the privileged classes."

What we do know—palpably, practically—is that, without citizenship, groupings of people who find themselves occupying the same territory on earth have little protection of the law inside their own communities and at the same time no security from the worst aggressions of outsiders. Essentially, this was what James Baker was talking about in the "communities of value" part of his speech in 1991 in Berlin, when he spoke so eloquently about the "trans-Atlantic community" and all that it had in common—and about extending those values and principles post–cold war to the rest of the world.

But, even while we Americans are today busy giving lessons in "civic culture" to the rest of the world (Hungary, Russia, the Czech Republic, Latin America, South Korea, China . . .), citizenship is ironically threatened in America itself. This development is even more dangerous for us than it would be in other nations because America is an artificial country, which needs a social compact far more than countries such as France or Italy or England, where blood ties and shared historical memories can be counted upon to bind the countrymen together in times of crisis. America is a nation based upon an idea, the "outrageous" concept that men can live together rationally and respectfully, united only by the commitments they make voluntarily to one another. And, even more outrageous, they would thus prosper!

But today it is not going too far to say that there is a real possibility that the idea and practice of citizenship in America may for all intents and purposes die in our lifetimes unless we act to reverse certain trends that are detailed on these pages.

2

Citizenship-as-Carnival

Anyone who wants to emigrate has a right to be in this city.
Documented or undocumented, you have a right to be in this city.
Moises Perez, Dominican activist in New York City, on *60 Minutes* (1993)

I am not an American. There is nothing about me that is American.
I don't want to be an American, and I have just as much right
to be here as any of you. . . .
young immigrant testifying at the National Endowment for Humanities
"National Conversation on American Pluralism and Identity" (1994)

Takoma Park just outside of Washington, D.C., looks deceptively apple-pie and middle-class Americana. It is classic suburbia/ exurbia, with old Victorian and Colonial homes and leafy streets, in the hills of Maryland. Most of the people are young profession- als who work in the nation's capital but choose to raise their fami- lies in the more amenable atmosphere of the suburbs. It looks "typical," but it is not.

In 1985, while the bitter civil war in El Salvador was still at its height, Takoma Park declared itself a "City of Refuge" for immi- grants fleeing persecution, war, and atrocities; some two thousand Salvadorans and Guatemalans flocked there. It also declared itself a "nuclear-free zone." Once, the town of sixteen thousand attempted to secede from Prince Georges County because the county was so stodgy and regressive in spirit. Both friends and enemies liked to refer to it as the "People's Republic of Takoma Park" because it had become an American laboratory and a social, political, and demo- graphic greenhouse for all the "progressive" issues of the 1960s, '70s, and '80s.

This was natural because so many Takoma Park residents were sixties-generation radicals who had migrated there in their thirties from the Berkeleys, Wisconsins, and Chicagos of those years of tumultuous change. Soon they put their mark of distinction on the small and otherwise unremarkable little community that ironically had once been the headquarters for the Seventh-Day Adventist Church: in those days, everything was closed on Saturdays, making Takoma Park not exactly the interesting place it is today!

But it was in November of 1991 that Takoma Park tore itself apart by doing something that few could readily have imagined: Takoma Park voted to give non–U.S. citizens the right to vote in city elections. Though the measure was approved by only a 51–49 percent margin (1,199–1,107), and though this vote meant only that noncitizens could vote in *local* elections, the ballot came as a bombshell whose fallout included broader changes to come. For analysts and individuals who had been watching the increasingly dangerous changes in the reality and rituals of citizenship on so many levels, Takoma Park was to become *the* example of what would happen elsewhere.

On the "anti" side of the issue, a former state delegate, Thomas J. Mooney, wrote critically in the *Prince Georges Journal* at the time that

never have I heard of anything so ridiculous, so devoid of merit and so blatantly anti-American as the recent proposal to allow aliens (legal or illegal) the opportunity to vote in city elections. . . . If I went to Mexico or El Salvador, I would not expect to be involved in their electoral process. I am an American citizen and my allegiances are to the USA. . . . Voting is much more than supporting one candidate over another. It is a positive affirmation of our system of government. It is an act of involvement, a right of passage for defining American citizenship. It is a vital piece of our common culture that is under intensely strident attack by "the Hate-America-First" crowd. By allowing aliens to vote, we demean that act which legitimizes our government and is one of the essential unifiers of our society.

We don't need to create another special interest group with an agenda that may be radically different from that of permanent

residents. After all, politics is about power and influence. Outsiders with transient or peripheral stakes in the community and
primary allegiance to other countries should not be awarded the
opportunity to push their platform.

Many black American residents also came in with angry responses, presaging clearly the black/Hispanic division in American life that was soon to spread in many parts of the country. "As
one who was born here in the U.S. and had to pay the poll tax as
a citizen in order to vote and fought to get rid of that tax, it just
seems to me there ought to be some residency requirement," the
late respected newspaper publisher Calvin Rolark, an African-
American, remarked at the time.

But the decision did not end there. Only four months after the
Takoma Park vote, two D.C. City Council members took an interesting and initially unannounced trip to El Salvador. Frank Smith
and Harry Thomas flew to San Salvador on March 23, 1992, without notifying either the American embassy or the Salvadoran embassy in Washington; they traveled around for a week, largely to
formerly Marxist rebel–held territory.

Members of the curious sixteen-member delegation, which
included some of the pro-immigration Hispanic activists who had
supported the Takoma Park vote, made it clear when they returned
home a week later where their sympathies lay. They spoke of observing naked children running around town squares and of an
undetonated bomb on church steps labeled with the words: "MADE
IN THE U.S.A."

"We were on an emotional roller coaster the whole time we
were there," Yvonne Martinez Vega was quoted when she returned
home. As the executive director of Ayuda, a pro-immigration legal
services agency in D.C.'s Adams Morgan neighborhood, where
largely Salvadoran riots had erupted in the spring of 1991, she had
a special interest in Salvadoran immigration and the "rights" of
Salvadorans in the United States.

The trip might have seemed to be only an aftermath of the controversial thirteen-year American involvement in the bitter Salvadoran conflict. However, the delegation in fact went there with a
larger agenda: It was going to propose in the City Council of the

District of Columbia that noncitizens be permitted to vote in D.C. city elections!

But when Councilmen Smith and Thomas came home, they seemed hesitant about their original intention. El Salvador was, after all, finally at peace, making it far more difficult to put forth the traditional argument that the Salvadorans in Washington were there as "political refugees." Moreover, despite awful times in American aid to Salvador, times when it seemed American policy was supporting a repressive military instead of progress, the undeniable fact by 1992 was that American policy in Central America had indeed finally forced a reform of the military in El Salvador and thus had opened the way to a peace treaty.

So Smith and Thomas were suddenly saying that perhaps they should let the *voters* decide in a referendum whether resident aliens should vote in local elections. (Cynics, of course, felt that the two black councilmen had seen the writing on the wall: Giving too many votes to aliens would surely disadvantage their own black constituents.) The outcome of the trip was an indefinite postponement in bringing up the idea of the noncitizen vote to either the council or current voters in the city. The trip and its intent nevertheless showed the extent to which the idea was growing.

Actually noncitizens—and there are some twenty million of them—were already voting all over the country. Long before Takoma Park, several small communities in Maryland had already given the vote in local elections to any resident, legal or illegal. As early as the late 1960s, a radical move occurred in New York City, where, with the decentralization of the New York City schools, all parents, legal or illegal residents, were given the right to vote in the thirty-two community school board elections.

In New York City, noncitizens were voting not only in elections for school boards but, interestingly, on policy boards that were in charge of distributing antipoverty funds to community groups. (This was a fact of substantial importance. It was one of the first harbingers of the divorce of government benefits from citizenship. It also began tying noncitizens immediately into the system of Big Government largess.) With 1.2 million immigrants in New York, noncitizen voting advocates had created a new category of voter—an undocumented immigrant with children in public schools could register to vote as a "parent voter"; and government grants had created a new kind of "politician"—the dispenser of welfare monies.

Meanwhile, in California, Leticia Quezada, the first Latina president of the Los Angeles school board, in 1992 also formally proposed allowing noncitizen parents to vote in school board elections. She called it a "parent empowerment" proposal, but it was widely interpreted by opponents as a barely masked attempt to expand her constituency. When black Americans protested, Latino parents threatened to pull their children out of school in protest. This again showed that, rather than quelling those fabled feelings of "impotence" on the part of the poor, acts that undermine legal and accepted processes actually bring forth violence. Nevertheless, a confident Quezada said that "we are at the infancy stage of a new movement."

And the undeniable fact was that, in the shadowy worlds-within-worlds of immigration fraud, illegal aliens were already voting all over the country.

When *Target 7*, an investigative show in Chicago on WLS-TV, undertook a comprehensive investigation of illegal aliens and the vote in February 1983, the five-part series detailed as never before the presence of massive fraud. *Target 7* found that the Chicago Board of Elections was making voters' cards available to just about anyone, even though it is technically a felony for a noncitizen to vote in Illinois. In fact, all a person had to do was obtain some "identification": a fraudulent Social Security card or even a homely library card would do. Or noncitizens could just go to the Chicago Board of Elections and get their cards directly, no questions asked, even if they didn't speak English!

When confronted with the massive evidence, U.S. Attorney Dan Webb was quoted on the show: "I'm quite disturbed when I see the vast number of illegal aliens that appear to be registered to vote in the city of Chicago. What bothers me the most is that when you have this number of illegal registrations what you're doing is you're laying the groundwork to have fraud on election day."

Some of the conversation in the series:

ROBERTA BASKIN: Carlos is a citizen of Mexico. But he had no trouble registering to vote in Chicago.

CARLOS: I go to the city hall and they give it to me easy. They don't ask for identification.

ROBERTA BASKIN: Jose LaRiosa is a citizen of the Philippines. He voted for the first time in November, after registering at his local library.

And you told them that you were not yet a citizen?

JOSE LARIOSA: Yes, I told them that I am not yet a citizen.

ROBERTA BASKIN: But they said it was okay?

JOSE LARIOSA: Yes.

ROBERTA BASKIN: Shokumbi is a citizen of Nigeria. But he is registered to vote in Chicago.

SHOKUMBI: I told him I was born here, you know. He said that was good enough.

ROBERTA BASKIN: Where did you say you were born?

SHOKUMBI: Kentucky.

ROBERTA BASKIN: And did he say anything about that?

SHOKUMBI: No, he didn't.

ROBERTA BASKIN: Mario Castaneda. One day after the November election, he was arrested by Immigration carrying his proof that he voted in his pocket. He was using his voter's registration card to try and get a U.S. passport.

Andres Garcia. He's voted in at least three elections.

Ramon Ramirez. He has proof of his Dominican Republic citizenship . . . right next to his Chicago voter's card.

Theresa Alvarez de Lopez. She bought a set of documents in the name of a dead woman, Ofelia Moreno. Then she used the voter's card to vote in the gubernatorial election.

Julio is a Mexican citizen but he casts his ballot right here in Chicago.

JULIO: I had the illusion that being Latino, if we did vote, maybe we could get better service. . . .

The new logic behind noncitizen voting found its most eloquent spokesman in an assistant professor of law at Washington's American University, Jaime Raskin. For Raskin, a curly-haired, gregarious, committed young thinker of the sixties, the first arguments are consummately "practical" ones. "They may be aliens from a national or international perspective," he said at the time of the Takoma Park vote, "but locally they are taxpayers, neighbors, and parents of kids in schools." He fell back on a trusted old Americanism: "No taxation without representation, remember?" He and his group like to make the argument that people without access to normal channels of political participation will find "other ways and perhaps violent ones, to make their voices heard."

But after those homey and "Watch out!" arguments, Raskin reveals a far more complicated and convoluted side to his arguments. "One man at the subway told me that 'they shouldn't vote because they're not citizens—period,'" he told the *Los Angeles Times*. I urged him to look up the meaning of 'citizen' in the dictionary. The primary definition is 'an inhabitant of a city or a town.' The second and logically distinct definition is 'a member of a state.' Thus one can be a citizen of Takoma Park but not of the United States. It may be counter-intuitive, post-modern even, but it makes democratic sense."

Yet, Raskin at the same time makes this very vote seem like some onerous burden, a most interesting turnaround. Instead of the vote being a privilege and a joy, to be exercised by free men, the vote is a reward for all the hardships to be put up with in American life. "City residents born in other lands have all the obligations of Takoma Park citizenship but lack the right to vote," Raskin argued. "They pay property taxes and sales taxes. They spend untold hours sorting their garbage into esoteric recycling categories. They call the police and fire departments. Their children go to city schools and play in city parks. . . ."

He then moved on systematically from the "voting-as-therapy" and "voting-as-everyman's-right" to the related "America-the-guilty" explanation. "The argument for expanding suffrage at the local level is particularly compelling now," he said, "because many noncitizens in the United States have fled violence in El Salvador and Guatemala, nations whose military-controlled governments have won substantial American aid for many years now. Surely if the federal government can promote democracy for Salvadorans living in El Salvador *by sharing weapons with their rulers,* local governments can promote democracy for Salvadorans living in American cities *by sharing the right to vote.*" (Italics mine.)

In an interview for this book, Raskin played out this "new logic" even further, revealing still more where his group of thinkers really are headed. "It makes a certain amount of sense to say

that Canadians should not be able to vote in American presidential elections, because the interests of Canada and the United States
may often conflict. But it makes no sense to exclude a Canadian
neighbor from voting in Takoma Park City Council elections because he has exactly the same interest as citizens in city affairs. It
is very compelling logic, which I think will begin to spread across
the country."

Then he put forward the argument, important in all of this
thinking, that basically only "economic man" mattered. "Think of
it this way," he went on. "In a privately owned corporation, aliens
who own stock get to vote their shares. Cities are municipal corporations. If you own land in a municipal corporation, you get to
vote your shares."

Raskin then explained that he was really speaking of an international syndrome. "As the world becomes more of one economic
market, pressures will accelerate to become more of one political
market. If we are going to have a free trade zone, and we are going
to have mobility in capital, shouldn't we have mobility of voting
rights in local elections?"

Finally, he stressed the "patriotism versus nationalism" difference, calling to mind the great George Orwell, who wrote about
the tragic inanities of Communism and secular faiths. "Nationalism is based on fear and a hatred of the other," he went on, "but
patriotism is based on love and respect and admiration for your
neighbors, the institutions of your society. It is the very patriotic
thing to do. It reflects a love of your own democratic institutions
that is so strong that you want to bring other people into it. . . .

"It is said that immigrants' rights are the civil rights of the
1990s. By that logic, noncitizen voting is the suffrage movement
of the decade."

Idealists find it hard to quarrel with such arguments. Yet others
see the situation far differently—and far more darkly. "How can
this be a self-governing society," Roger Conner, the original director of the Federation for American Immigration Reform (FAIR),
asks, "when somebody who shares none of our history can walk
in one day and have exactly the same impact on the choice of the
people that govern us as the people who have been here for generations? What then does self-government mean? It is no longer
'We, the people of the United States of America,' it is 'We the

people *in* the United States,' or 'We, the people *who happen to be in the United States on any one day!'*"

But noncitizen voting, though historically curious, is by far not the end of the challenges to an informed and committed citizenry. In 1993, shortly after Bill Clinton became president of the United States, Democrats in Congress pushed through the notoriously named "motor-voter" bill, which would permit aspiring voters to register when they apply for a driver's license, establish a uniform national system of registering by mail, and require that voter registration forms be offered at offices that provide public assistance, unemployment compensation, and other social services. In short, voter registration would be equated with a government handout instead of civic privilege and personal responsibility.

☆

After the Takoma Park vote, critics of giving the vote to noncitizens asked, "What is next?" And soon they saw what was next. In the D.C. City Council, two city councilmen put forward a bill abolishing the Pledge of Allegiance to the United States at the beginning of every council meeting. They wanted to substitute a "moment of silence" for the pledge, which they said was like a "loyalty oath" that smacked of McCarthyism. The motion was not passed, at least at that time. Yet the country soon would see "ethnic pledges of allegiance" arise to take over from American ones: Hispanic students would be pledging allegiance to Mexico on "Cinco de Mayo" day and some African-Americans to Africa.

Meanwhile, in July of 1993, the *New York Times* ran a front-page story that shocked many readers. Its headline was "IMMIGRANTS FORGOING CITIZENSHIP WHILE PURSUING AMERICAN DREAM." It showed that, unlike fifty years ago when the majority of immigrants routinely sought to naturalize, today "only slightly more than a third of legal permanent residents now apply to become citizens. . . . Most immigrants now exist in a state of legal limbo, many nourished by the dream, often an illusion, that they will someday return home."

The *Times* reported that these people in legal and social limbo now number up to ten million nationally and "form a growing population of tax-paying residents without the right to vote or to serve on juries, police forces or in many federal jobs. At a time when ethnic and racial tensions are fracturing the harmony of many cities, the immigrants' status—seen by some as an unfair disenfranchisement and by others as a failure to integrate—has become a cause of concern."

And once again, as in question 86 of the U.S. citizenship test, the *Times* ran a box in which it listed the "Benefits of Citizenship": "citizens can vote, citizens travel freely, and citizens can sponsor more relatives."

The children of immigrants were not assimilating, either. The *New York Times* in June 1993 reported, "Today's immigrants . . . are most likely to settle in inner-city neighborhoods, where assimilation often means joining a world that is antagonistic to the American mainstream."

But it was not only the immigrants to America who were realizing—implicitly and also explicitly—that America no longer prized itself, and so they no longer considered belonging to it the "prize" it had always been to the peoples of the world. This was the realization of Americans themselves.

Money magazine headlined in July 1994, "ESCAPE FROM AMERICA." It ticked off the astonishing new indicators: "Driven by rising crime rates and limited job opportunities, as many as 250,000 Americans are leaving the country for good every year. And millions more are seriously considering it. According to an exclusive 'Money' poll, 1) Nearly one out of five Americans are thinking about moving abroad, 2) Fully 26 percent of those with incomes of $50,000 or more have contemplated it, and 3) One in four college-educated adults have thought about emigrating."

The 250,000-a-year number is up from approximately 160,000 a decade ago, according to Census Bureau estimates. As many as half of those emigrating are now native-born Americans, while 80 percent of those who left for good between 1900 and 1980 were former immigrants returning home.

And there is evidence that more skills are draining from the country than are added to it through immigration. The magazine somberly summed up that "the growing flight of America's top achievers is . . . ominous, recalling historic 'brain drains' experienced by countries around the globe—from Germany in the 1930s to the Philippines in the 1960s to, most notably, the departure of well-heeled British from tax-burdened England, also in the 1960s."

The magazine quoted Ikubolajeh Logan, expert on population shifts at the University of Georgia in Athens: "There are insidious implications when you lose your best and brightest citizens. Economic and social progress are slowed and the country's expectations about itself are reduced."

☆

In the past, there was no question as to what made a United States citizen. In those "old days" of citizenship, certain clear and unbendable rules governed the rights and duties of American citizenship.

The new citizen had to either be born in America or take the Oath of Allegiance to the United States of America, almost always in an awe-inspiring judicial ceremony presided over by a sober, black-robed judge. As in marriage, the petitioner to citizenship had to forsake all other loyalties in order to undertake this new bond. If a person was a citizen of America, he could never be a citizen of another country; the bendable forms of "dual citizenship" that other countries allowed or encouraged were to have no place in life in America. History and language tests were rigorous and, in general, enforced by immigration officers who were most often exacting teachers. The petitioner for citizenship had to reside in the United States for five years, be of good moral character, have an "attachment to the Constitution," give a formal declaration of intention, and provide witnesses as to character and intent. The FBI did regular checks on the moral character, and of course any criminal record, of potential citizens. A criminal record would shut out the person forever from citizenship in the United States.

New citizens were helped to move into their new country by tens of thousands of "mediating institutions" that made up the very body and bloodstream of America: political parties, ward organizations, settlement houses, community organizations, church and synagogue groups, and educational establishments. All of them served both citizens and would-be citizens as stepping-stones to new relationships.

Across the board, citizenship was considered not only a very serious thing, but so meritorious that the petitioner had to agree that he or she would never serve in a foreign army or in any political or military position in a foreign country. That would open the dangerous possibility of dual loyalties, and those would lead only to anarchy and chaos. (The Founding Fathers knew this well: was not that the curse of the Europe they had left behind?) It is important to realize that these sorts of common-sensical stipulations not only kept the United States organized according to duties and responsibilities, but also served to keep the world organized and as rational as it could be, at least at this stage of evolution.

For its part, the nation-state committed itself to protecting and defending its citizens, both at home and in foreign countries. Indeed, in earlier years, there was so little hesitation on this matter that an American president would reach out far beyond American shores to take care of "his people." No story better typifies that era, which one immediately contrasts to the disaster of the American hostages in Teheran in 1979 and '80, than does this one:

It seems that just before the Republican national convention in 1904 an American citizen, Ion Perdicaris of New Jersey, and his son-in-law had been kidnaped from his elegant villa outside Tangier in Morocco.The kidnaper was the rapscallion warlord Raisuli who was trying to use the Americans against the sultan of Morocco.

When the sultan refused to give in to the warlord, President Theodore Roosevelt simply ordered a U.S. Navy squadron already close to the Mediterranean to move directly to Tangier. The squadron was backed up by tough and very realistic talk about landing the American marines to seize the Tangier customshouse, thus forcing the reluctant sultan to negotiate with the devilish Raisuli. The sultan soon acquiesced, but not before an amazing moment at the Republican convention when delegates leapt to their feet, shouting secular deprecations against "that old body-snatcher!" And one delegate shouted, "Out in Kansas we believe in keeping the peace but in fighting against wrong."

President Roosevelt then masterfully used the crisis to gain political points in the campaign—and his words of warning at the time went down in history as the very exemplar of American determination to protect its own citizens regardless of any threat. The famous cable that went out to the U.S. consul general at Tangier said, "WE WANT PERDICARIS ALIVE OR RAISULI DEAD."

Perdicaris and his son-in-law were freed. It was the spirit of the era in America.

But by the 1990s, the transformation of the old concepts of U.S. citizenship—what the citizen gave and got, what the country gave and got—was in many areas complete.

Dual citizenship? America has now made it possible, thus diluting a person's commitment and making citizenship akin to bigamy. The old "five-year" rule? The new citizen does not have to live in America at all. Moral character? No one ever asks about that, not in America's permissive new epoch, and the FBI has been excluded from the old checks because they discovered so few breaks in the law when they were involved. (The critics never dreamed that such a statistic might simply be a *result* of the FBI checks, which kept aliens with criminal records from coming forward to seek citizenship.)

That old "attachment to the Constitution"? The very idea is laughable. It is hard to figure out how aliens can be expected to have such an attachment when virtually no serious schooling in the history or civics of their new nation is required of them. In fact, today, given the abysmal lack of "citizenship socialization" in America, by the time they are naturalized, new citizens probably do not even know what the Constitution is, much less have any "attachment" to it! (On the other hand, they need not feel left out or mistreated, for American students are not being citizenship-educated, either.)

Lose your citizenship by serving in a foreign army or government? By now hundreds, perhaps thousands, of young American men and women have served in the Israeli army. That change in the citizenship law allowing for such service, which came after the formation of the new state of Israel in 1948 and which was pushed by the highly organized American Jewish community, marked the first breaking point to the old rule. Then, in the aftermath of the fall of Communism, Baltic-Americans, Yugoslav-Americans and many others actually served as leaders of the new countries, with not the slightest complaint from America. To name only two, American citizen Milan Panic served as prime minister of Serbia during most of 1992, while Estonian-American U.S. Army Colonel Aleksandr Einseln became an Estonian general, training native soldiers in the new Estonian state; in 1995, the defense minister there remarked tellingly that the American had given Estonia "all his strength, love and skills."

Despite the best of intentions, the undeniable fact was that such acts had built into them the contradictions and threats of dual loyalties and the confusion in responsibility that America had, throughout its entire history, always tried assiduously to avoid.

As for the historic citizenship tests, they had become dumbed down so severely that the would-be citizen scarcely had to study at all. Perhaps saddest was the fact that this country was asking almost nothing of the would-be citizen, thus not only severely denigrating the very meaning of citizenship but also denying him or her the truly "equal" chance to be challenged—and thus to grow in the same manner in which earlier citizens had been challenged to grow, by an America that believed in them and believed they too could become more than they had been.

Instead, the new "multicultural" America not only allows but encourages them to be imprisoned in their old ethnic categories. As Christopher Lasch notes, this America, in the hands of "an insidious double standard, masked as tolerance, denies the minorities the fruit of the victory that they had struggled so long to achieve: access to the world's culture."

The advertisements for the tests make the petitioner for citizenship appear an incapable child, who needed to be coddled and patronized, a mascot of the elites. Over and over the ads stress that the tests are "EASY . . . EASIER THAN EVER . . . YOU WILL NOT BE ASKED QUESTIONS ABOUT HISTORY OR GOVERNMENT AT YOUR IMMIGRATION AND NATURALIZATION SERVICE INTERVIEW. . . . AND I.N.S. WILL NOT HAVE A RECORD OF YOUR SCORE IF YOU DO NOT PASS. . . ."

It gets worse. In the last twenty years, the testing of potential citizens has in many cases been deliberately taken away from the INS—and given to various religious and ethnic interest groups. These groups prepare people for testing and often *make the judgments* as to who passes and who fails. "No failures are reported," one of the designers of the new tests told me, "so you can come back again and again."

Was it really good to make the test so much easier?

"I think it was a good thing to do," he answered thoughtfully. "What the government wants to do is making sure people are taking an 'interest' in the country."

Leave the "interest" in the country aside for the moment. It is abundantly clear that these activist groups, whether Roman Catholic, Hispanic, or other immigrant rights groups, have their own limited, self-interested agendas—and that those agendas are seldom directly consonant with the broader political, social, and economic interests of the nation. All of them actively *want* more citizens, particularly new citizens dependent upon them and upon their goodwill and thus ready made to be part of a larger constituency for them (not to speak of more federal and foundation grants and better jobs for the activist/leaders). Often, representatives of these special-interest groups are there right after a new citizen's swearing-in, ready on the spot to register him or her for the political party of choice—most often, the organization's choice.

Rather obviously, the greatness or glory of a nation and its historic achievements have little place in such a system. Indeed, they are easily drowned in this belching quicksand of transcendent personal ambition, easy money, and unrepresentative power.

I have personally walked into the cheerful offices of some of these groups and been handed the citizenship questions, along with the answers. In fact, the INS also hands them out together. Cheerfully. And why not? It's a cheerful business—for them.

It gets *still* worse. In the newest trend, not only have these special-interest groups taken over the "substance" of the citizenship of the nation, but much of the process is now being "privatized." One has to wonder: Even in a country of more and more putative "rights," what possible right do private companies have to decide the substance and spirit and process of citizenship in the nation?

But wait. Did I mention "advertisements" to encourage aliens to take an "interest" in country and in citizenship, as though America were hawking something in a really hard sell? I'm afraid I did. Instead of treating American citizenship as a rare and desirable privilege, the INS has now developed a truly "remarkable" public relations outreach. The program is designed to bring folks in; it's a wonder they have not yet hired callers or stage managers with hooks to pull the innocents into the citizenship carnival! All of this seems even more curious when one realizes that so much of the world's population *wants* to come to America.

It is not, then, only the spirit of citizenship that has been so severely altered but, most important, the mechanics of it—and, indeed, the changes in the mechanics have not surprisingly led directly to the changes in the spirit. None of these events have occurred accidentally, none have been spontaneous. And, as the 1990s progress and the mechanics of citizenship become ever more contorted, more observers are beginning to compare what is happening in America with what is clearly happening in other countries threatened by similarly fissiparous tendencies.

Writing in 1995 on the question of whether black university students should have the right to exclude whites from leadership positions in the black student union, columnist John Leo said that "the separatist instinct—even black yearbooks, and black parents associations at integrated schools—should be fought. Those who believe this is one nation, and not a larger version of 'the former Yugoslavia,' ought to start undermining segregation wherever it appears."

Noting that there are now 323 different languages spoken in the United States, Wisconsin Republican Congressman Toby Roth looked at the razor-thin vote of Québec not to secede from Canada in the fall of 1995 and called it a "red warning light" for Americans. Then he asked: "Could America fragment like Canada almost did?"

There are no clear answers—as yet.

☆

In the spring of 1989, two patrolmen of the U.S. Border Patrol and I drove south from thriving, glistening San Diego, where the gringos live like rich gringos do, and soon we found ourselves in a wasteland of landscape, filled with the silence of lonesome cactus and abandoned junk cars. Looking in any direction, you could see some spectral vehicle—a car or a small truck—on some desolate horizon, despite the fact that there were only eight hundred of the Border Patrol trying to enforce the law on this strange and contradictory border. Occasionally, we heard the whir and buzz of a Border Patrol helicopter overhead.

But that momentary omnipresent feeling of emptiness was grossly misleading. Fifty-four million people pass through this Tijuana–San Isidro passing every year, the patrolmen told me soberly, and in any one year roughly three million of them are illegals. As dusk came, small darkened figures, like shadows coming out of the unknown corners of the Third World, poised eagerly and insistently on the Mexican side, where the Tijuana slums push boldly up against the border, held back only by a drainage ditch, roughly fifty feet across, and by a weak and aged wire fence.

As it grew darker, the figures began to run across, then dart back, and finally take a real rush at the fence; by full darkness, they were hanging on to the fence like spiders to a web, vastly outnumbering the gringos and daring the Border Patrol to catch them as they prepared to make their end run for the "promised land." They were certainly not invisible, but their effects on America—and particularly on California—were invisible until recently, when the United States began to realize for the first time the effects of their undocumented presence.

By the onset of total darkness, these illegal aliens would be plummeting over the fence and running to hide in the backstreets of San Isidro. Then it was on to San Diego and Los Angeles, to Portland, Chicago, and Detroit. The Border Patrol arrested an average of 1,225 every twenty-four hours and duly sent them "home." They merely turned around the next day and came back.

It is a tragic picture, an Orwellian picture; and it is in many ways the metaphor for the mass movements of displaced peoples in the world today, moving from country to country, driven more and more by overpopulation, sometimes by tyranny, and always by the sheer economic attraction of other worlds they yearn to enter. . . .

It is this picture, arresting and frightening, that leads us to the ditch.

One must first realize that 90 percent of the border is wild mountainous terrain, far too dangerous and threatening for humans to cross. The immigrants have come across almost entirely in two spots: the Tijuana and El Paso crossings. Near the Tijuana crossing, there was one small area, a shallow kind of ditch with an old and disintegrating fence, that offered one of those keys to how to control the border. For it was this shallow ditch that people-smugglers and drug dealers, in their souped-up cars and with their despicable talents, streamed through.

And so the Border Patrol, along with those who would "rationalize" the border, came up with a relevant idea that they thought would work: They suggested digging a deep ditch in that small area, hurting no one but perhaps stopping the parade of criminals and dope dealers who had made this passing their own private little highway to the glories of "El Norte."

"There has been so much emotionalism and misinformation about this ditch that it is really almost unbelievable," Dale Cozan, the chief of the Border Patrol in San Diego, told me then, as we sat in his simple office out in that desolate stretch of land. "It was a very narrow and restricted area that we were trying to control, but it was one that had great numbers of vehicles driving across it at will. You see, there is only this four-and-a-half-mile area where people can literally drive back and forth. The cars don't stop, they are lawless. Basically, we were only talking about constructing a simple drainage ditch, not drowning people. The smugglers know very well we are not going to take any action that would endanger lives. Why, they hold up babies as shields."

But this ditch, which was to become a metaphor for a supposed American "impotence" in border control, created an uproar. The San Diego City Council, activists in San Diego, and Mexican "human rights" groups along the other side of the border all made it sound as if the Americans were erecting concentration camps there.

One day, I sat with Peter Nunez, the former U.S. Attorney for San Diego, and he, better than anyone, described the situation. "There are really no obstacles to Third World migration to the United States," Nunez, a handsome Hispanic-American lawyer, began. "It used to be that the mountains and deserts were obstacles. Today, if you can get to Mexico, you can get to Detroit. But if you say these things, you will be immediately branded a racist by the minority community. Take 'the ditch.' The City Council expressed outrage about building a ditch because it 'sent the wrong signal to Mexico.' We had a hearing—basically it was to condemn the ditch. Now the idea is basically tabled.

"At one meeting, I put the American immigration bill on the desk. I said, 'This is the law of the United States. It says it is illegal to enter the United States illegally. You must support that. Violations of the law are all over the place. We have a terrible drug problem. Leave the methodology to the people in the field, who know what works best; and if Mexico is offended by that, I'd say, 'Too bad!' It is not your position to determine how the Border Patrol does its job.'"

Nunez, who had been U.S. Attorney for six crucial years during the eighties, then discussed the never-never land in which activist groups, minority "spokesmen," and ethnic lobbies—and "nice" Americans who above all did not at any cost want to appear intolerant—operate, assuming every immigrant, legal or illegal, is an asset to the community and assuming everyone has some amorphous "right" to come to America (even though they can't explain what that "right" quite is). "The San Diego police are even under orders of the City Council and the mayor not to arrest an illegal alien," he went on. "A police officer, knowing that a crime has been committed, can't do anything about it. San Diego police say they are not allowed to draw conclusions that someone is here illegally; yet, ninety-nine of one hundred illegals will freely admit it."

Here he paused for emphasis, looked out over the supermodern downtown of San Diego that so well masked the shantytowns just beyond it. "Even if the person admits this to you," he continued, "you can't say he is here illegally. The city is just paranoid about this.

"It's okay to build a ditch as long as it doesn't work," he summed up. "It's okay to build a fence that's shredded because it doesn't work. Now they are saying it's okay to have a token force so long as it doesn't do the job." He paused, wondering at the absurdities of this strange out-of-control border world, then added, "You either have people standing shoulder-to-shoulder from the Pacific to the Gulf of Mexico, or you deal with the two hundred miles that is the biggest problem."

But the ditch was not the end of the story at all. By 1991, south of San Diego near the border, a five-mile stretch of Interstate 5 was offering an even more unique immigration problem. The problem began with many undocumented aliens crossing I-5 near what is known as the San Clemente checkpoint in North County. Indeed, between 1987 and 1991, more than one hundred aliens had been killed there, all trying to cross the freeway. The fact that what they were doing was also breaking American law seemed to register with almost no one. Indeed, in July 1991, the news was dominated by furious Hispanic activists screaming at officials of the California Department of Transportation (CalTrans) that "ignoring traffic deaths was tantamount to murder."

Then, instead of dealing with the aliens, who were clearly disobeying and even arrogantly challenging the law by sneaking into the United States, CalTrans actually closed two southbound and two northbound lanes on I-5, from just south of Imperial Beach to the border: *They acted to make it easier and safer for the aliens to break the law!* But like all of these stories, it still does not end even there.

Members of a San Diego task force were then duly appointed to deal with the subject "at its source," and they met with Mexican officials to discuss pedestrian freeway crossings. The task force consisted of a collection of elected officials, law enforcement officers, and transportation experts. Ideas conceived by the task force included removing brush in some areas where undocumented aliens were known to hide before attempting to cross the freeway, and installing black-and-yellow signs along the freeway warning motorists to watch for people running across the road—all to protect the aliens! One real idea put forward, which seemed to have the support of only the Border Patrol, was to erect a barrier on the median of the road; but since that might actually serve to stop the aliens from breaking American law, the task force quickly brushed it aside.

Thus, illegal aliens, committing an illegal act by entering the United States, became the reason for the closing of part of a superhighway on American soil—and all because Hispanic activists said that the traffic deaths of people entering the country illegally were murder!

The not surprising consequence of such incredible actions was that thousands of aliens—by then, their numbers were reaching a record of twenty-two hundred a day—were coming into the country and marching right down the unclosed median lanes after the four outside lanes were closed. Smugglers, along with both female prostitutes and male transvestites, were becoming even more brazen, while one alien "coyote," or smuggler, was so bold that he simply held up his arm and stopped traffic on the two remaining northbound lanes so that his twelve migrant followers (most of whom are terrorized by such smugglers) could pass more readily into the United States. Even the border police, who thought they had seen just about everything, were stunned to find prostitutes performing acts of prostitution right *on* the freeway.

What the United States effectively had done was to encourage often the most vicious lawbreakers, who should instead have been apprehended and punished. But instead of making it *harder* for them to enter the United States, the county bowed to political pressure to make it *easier* for them to enter. In the end, the Border Patrol was forced to bow to "safety concerns" and announced that it would not apprehend undocumented aliens found congregating in the median.

The American government was now actually aiding and abetting the breaking of its own laws!

Yet the fact remained that not only the vast majority of Americans in general but the vast majority of Hispanic-American citizens desperately wanted border control and limits to illegal immigration. Every poll—from those done by Torrance & Associates, a subsidiary of Gallup, to those conducted by the University of Texas in Austin—indicated such wishes. Polls showed that two-thirds of the Hispanic-American citizens in California and San Diego supported increased repair of shredded fencing along the border (another source of dispute), 73 percent approved of employer sanctions against illegals, and 35 percent of all citizens even wanted to militarize the border!

When we look at this syndrome of "pro-immigration leadership," we find a classic case of what we might call "unrepresentative representation." For what we find is a tiny group of activists that has been pushing illegal immigration, immigration "rights," and weaker border controls, and which has been effectively writing the public agenda, even while it really represented nobody!

In San Diego, for instance, the "spokesman" for these causes is a man named Roberto Martinez, who is head of the American Friends Service Committee (Quakers) Coalition for Law and Justice, and who likes to say things such as "We should be building bridges, not ditches." He is always out on the street protesting against any effort to control immigration, and he always has with him ten or twelve adherents—but only ten or twelve! Nevertheless, he has become *the* spokesman for the immigrants due to the philosophy of the press in recent years to "always get the other side."

Peter Nunez says: "These men profess to be speaking for the Hispanic community, but polls always show that Hispanic-Americans want controls. Journalistic ethics requires you find the other point of view. So-and-so says X! So you see these guys quoted over and over, and it looks as though the power and ideas are 50 percent pro and 50 percent con. It's not true, but no one ever looks into who these people are and whether they really represent anyone or not."

And so adversarial journalism covers these groups as if these advocacy groups were equal in numbers and conviction to the majority, when in truth they have no or little actual status as spokesmen.

Meanwhile, Southern California is breaking down under the inundation of so many unabsorbable people and infinite needs.

☆

Meanwhile, on the other coast of the United States, American officials—not having yet seen the enhanced horrors of Oklahoma City—were calling the bombing of New York's World Trade Center in the spring of 1993 "the single most destructive act of terrorism on American soil." Eight people were dead in one lethal afternoon, and the entire country lay in a state of shock. The terrible reality was that a Middle Eastern terrorist named Mohammed Salameh with stunning ease had been able to drive into the underground garage of the largest building on earth, in a rental van crammed with explosives, set them off, and nearly bring crashing to bits a building of eighty stories in the very heart of the richest city in the world!

But it was what Salameh did then that was so telling. Even while New York was in total turmoil, even while desperate and smoke-blinded people were making their way down the back stairs of the enormous building, even while no one knew who did it or why such a horrendous thing could have happened, the sweatshirted, diminutive Salameh (he stood only five foot, six inches tall) actually proceeded calmly to the agency where he had rented the van. Salameh was a practical man, and he wanted to report his van "missing." No wastrel here! He could get his four-hundred-dollar deposit back!

But the story gets worse.

The director—the "mastermind," the inspirer of this terrible deed and thus the real perpetrator of it—was also still at large. That man was an aged Egyptian sheikh, long blinded, a "holy" man whom the Islamic fanatics of the Middle East venerated and whom normal people rightly feared, Sheikh Omar Abdel-Rahman. In Egypt, the sheikh was famous—notorious, really—for his alleged involvement in the 1980 assassination of President Anwar Sadat.

Indeed, he had been on the State Department's star list of those involved in terrorist groups since 1991. Of late, in New Jersey, he had been busily preaching his hatred-filled and politicized-firebrand form of anti-Western (and particularly anti-American) Islam in the El Salam Mosque, where the resourceful little Mr. Salameh worshiped. Preaching violence against any non-Muslims, the sheikh had been able to inspire the World Trade Center bombing for one simple reason: The Immigration and Naturalization Service had let him in!

Easy! No sweat! The hoary man, whose picture had been on the front pages of every newspaper in the Middle East for at least twelve years, had simply gone to the American embassy in Khartoum, the capital of the Sudan—where one hundred million dollars a year in Iranian money passes through to support terrorist organizations in Egypt, Algeria, and elsewhere in the Middle East—and applied for a visa to America.

The entire transaction could be compared to Adolph Hitler or Joseph Stalin going through Geneva in 1939 and applying for a visa. "Adolph Hitler?" the embassy consular officer would say. "Hmm, sounds like a good solid German name to me! Joseph Stalin? Georgian, you say? They have such good wine! Let 'em roll!"

And so, the United States, through its innocence and carelessness about the nature of humankind and of the world, naïvely welcomed the leading terrorist of the Middle East into its very midst. Later, the INS and the State Department would offer elaborate excuses for why and how it had happened: Nobody had "recognized" him in Khartoum, the visa was "a mistake," et cetera. But underlying this crime was the fact that America had so little a sense of danger in the world that a strange man, living openly in America and known throughout the world as a mastermind terrorist, could—without the slightest alarm bell having rung—walk in and do his deadly business. In this age of refugees and "asylum," he could even do it "legally"!

What we are dealing with in the World Trade Center bombing is another case study of the manner in which citizenship is being shredded in America through the sheer carelessness and innate sloppiness of a rich and (so Americans have thought) "isolated" nation-continent. We are dealing with American asylum policy, which today is actually (my term) "politicized immigration." (Some have said that "political asylum has become a back door to illegal immigration," and basically they are right.)

Political asylum was and still should be one of those rare and sacred gifts of the nation-state. It was designed over the centuries for a very specific and deliberately limited number of men and women facing dire political persecution in their countries of origin. It constituted a noble effort by the civilized countries of the world to deal with the flotsam and jetsam of political tyranny, to offer decent people sustenance and sanctuary and allow the persecuted to rebuild their lives and contribute their talents in America. Indeed, during the 1930s and after World War II, great thinkers such as Albert Einstein and talented musicians and artists from the ruins of Europe fled to America as "refugees" and contributed enormously to American culture.

As Senator Alan Simpson of Wyoming, the congressional specialist in these areas, says, "Asylum is a very sacred thing. It's for someone fleeing persecution or having a well-founded fear of persecution. Gimmick it and you cheapen and debase a remarkable thing."

But by the 1980s and '90s, this sacred right of asylum—like virtually everything having to do with immigration and citizenship—had become corrupted, perverted and contorted beyond the worst nightmares of any normal person. And, as with all the changes occurring in these related areas of citizenship, it had happened so fast!

In 1980, the United States had five thousand asylum applicants, a high percentage fleeing Communist countries, from which "refuge" was routinely considered valid. By 1990, a mere ten years later, the United States was being bombarded by such applicants in excess of one hundred thousand a year! Moreover, the caseloads exhibited a bewildering variety of claims of alleged "persecution" and "oppression" that brought into serious question the noble original intention of asylum: Chinese saying they were escaping their country's "one child per family" policy, for instance.

Some of these asylees were doubtless genuine; but too often America's sloppiness was making con-men out of many people in the world who would otherwise not have stooped to such behavior.

It is commonly known and documented that these "asylum-seekers" get on the plane *with* documents (indeed, they could not get on without them), that they often eat them en route or flush them down the toilet (a great opening act for the sacred right of asylum). When they arrive at, say, JFK Airport, the huddled masses become downright aggressive. They demand asylum, are almost always simply let go; they then disappear into the shadows of American society and more than 50 percent never show up for the supposedly required initial hearing before a judge. All in all, they get more due process than American citizens.

Writer and immigration control activist Ira H. Mehlman wrote perhaps the best exposé of the incredible situation at JFK Airport, "The New Jet Set," published in the *National Review* (March 15, 1993):

It's a slow day at New York's John F. Kennedy International Airport. Mondays usually are. "You should be here on a Friday or a Saturday, that's when the action is," says one of the uniformed immigration inspectors who deal with up to 1,300 political-asylum claimants a month.

At the secondary inspection area in the East Wing of JFK's International Arrivals Building, a Liberian national is entering a claim for political asylum. He is traveling on a British passport which he purchased for $300 in Bangkok. The flight that he arrived on several hours earlier originated in Tokyo.

The man, about 30, has his lines well rehearsed: "My uncle was killed in an attempted coup. He was a soldier in [Samuel] Doe's army."

"What would happen if you would go back?" asks a skeptical officer from the Immigration and Naturalization Service.

"I'm afraid of the situation," replies the Liberian.

"What would happen?" insists the officer, a man who has clearly heard it all before.

"My father was killed," the Liberian states emphatically.

"When?"

A long pause. "February. February '92. My mother is in Ghana."

"When did she go?"

"I don't know."

"Did she go to Ghana alone?"

"I cannot say."

The interview drags on. Both men are going through the charade. The Liberian will be out on the street in a matter of hours— he knows it and so does the officer.

The political-asylum claimant left Liberia in 1988, stowing away by ship to Thailand. Two years later he moved on to Malaysia, then back to Bangkok, followed by a stint in Japan. Frustrated by poor earnings over the past four years, he's decided to try the land of opportunity: the United States.

He has a bogus passport, he's been out of Liberia for four years, but he knows the magic words that will get him past the harried officers at JFK. Once he utters "political asylum" his chances of remaining in the United States are 93 percent.

"We're being deluged. It's scandalous," complains the officer filling out the papers on this case. "In a matter of hours he's going to be walking out onto the street joining the ranks of the unemployed. We don't know anything about him. We don't know if he has AIDS. We don't know if he's a murderer." In most cases immigration authorities don't even find out a real name. It's a complaint heard over and over again from any of the 360 immigration officers who work America's most unguarded border— JFK.

Last year 14,688 excludable aliens attempted to enter the United States through JFK, nearly triple the number just two years earlier. Of these, 9,194, or 63 per cent, asked for political asylum. All but 428 of them had either fraudulent documents or no documents at all.

The deck is stacked in favor of the aliens. The detention center at JFK airport has a maximum capacity of 100 beds and only 12 to 15 vacancies for some 1,300 new excludable aliens every month. For someone contemplating illegal immigration, it's difficult to find better odds. "During fiscal 1992, I detained only 1,169 of the 15,000 inadmissibles who came through JFK," says William Slattery, New York district director for the INS.

In total, only about 7 percent of the inadmissible aliens who come in at JFK can be detained. The rest are simply released onto the street and asked to present themselves for a hearing at a future date. "We have no good, solid data" on how many ever show up for their hearings, says Duke Austin, an INS spokesman. "I know it sounds crazy, but it's just not collected." On background, other INS people concede that probably not more than 5 percent of the airport asylum claimants are ever heard from again.

Nor were Sheikh Rahman and his merry mosque men from New Jersey the only criminal cases linked with the new refugee and asylum scams. In 1993, Mir Aimal Kansi, a Pakistani refugee, shot and killed six people as they waited in their cars outside the CIA offices in McLean, Virginia. He then fled, apparently back to Pakistan, probably to the remote and inaccessible Baluchistan region. Cables from the American embassy in Islamabad urgently pleaded with Washington to do something: "ALIEN SMUGGLING HAS PASSED THE CRISIS LEVEL." The diplomats also said that this human smuggling was abetted by the Pakistan government, it was aided by some foreign airlines, and the odds of anyone getting caught were only one in seven or eight.

In 1992, asylum officers received 103,447 applications for asylum; they approved 4,019 and denied 6,904. At year's end, the INS had a backlog of 215,772 cases, and those did not even include those thousands of foreigners who were immediately put into deportation hearings.

Meanwhile, the global population, standing at 5.4 billion in 1992, was growing by nearly 100 million annually. So, in the absence of reasonable controls from the American side, asylum claims were going to grow into more Mad Hatter craziness. And the story was filtering through the world's population that it was exceedingly easy to brazen your way into the United States. Nobody would even ever know your real name.

☆

On the night of May 18, 1993, in Miami, a mere thirteen people—the Metropolitan Dade County Commission—voted to repeal a thirteen-year-old ordinance declaring English the official language of local government.

While American leaders in Washington were talking soberly about the crushing need to simplify government and to cut the deficit that was choking the nation, thirteen people in Dade County in effect decided to spend millions of dollars to translate county documents, court records, and other complex papers into

Spanish, Creole, and French (for the moment, because surely many other languages would ultimately be included).

"This is not a question of language but a question of respect," Miami Beach Mayor Seymour Gelber was quoted, reflecting in his words the idea of *respeto,* an especially powerful Hispanic honor concept from medieval Spain that happens to be in direct philosophical contradiction to classic American concepts of justice and equality. Many in the commission, including Hispanics, laughed when "Anglos" at the meeting complained that their very way of life was in danger of being destroyed.

That meeting marked the first time that pure competitive demographics prompted a decision to effectively break down the dominance of the unifying American language; it was the first time any government, at any level, in the history of America, was able officially to reject English as the official language; and it was the bellwether of a far larger transformational agenda being pushed on various levels across the country.

To discover its genesis one would have to go back to the Cuban Revolution of Fidel Castro in 1959 and in particular to the later Mariel boatlift of 1980. After 1959, at least one million Cubans fled to American shores. Then in 1980, 125,000 Cubans again spontaneously voted with their rafts and small boats to escape to America, which generously gave them solace, sanctuary, and welcome in the bosom of the most successful society in human history, a society that indeed was so in large part because of its use of the English language.

The original Cubans who came constituted almost entirely the educated middle class and upper class, and they soon invigorated Miami and in general settled well into American life. But after the huge and sudden assault of "Marielitos" in 1980 and after a large second immigration from Nicaragua's civil war, after 1979, the critical mass of Dade County swung away from the English-speaking and toward the Spanish-speaking. (Political and cultural power will always and inevitably swing toward the largest group.)

In 1980 the original, English-speaking American residents in Dade County, alarmed at the huge influxes of Spanish-speaking peoples, voted overwhelmingly for a city ordinance establishing English as the official language of local government. At the same time, the state of Florida also moved to amend its constitution, making English the "official state language." For thirteen years, those acts in effect proclaimed that most government business was required to be conducted in English, as in the rest of the country, although at home, in shops and businesses, Spanish and other languages were widely and freely spoken.

But by the time the vote was taken on the critical issue of language that night in the spring of 1993, the entire situation had changed. Osvaldo Soto of the Spanish American League Against Discrimination felt himself called to announce that Miami was simply no longer even an American city. "Here we are and feel that we are the capital of the Americas," he said on TV. "The young countries, the Mexicans, the Argentineans, the Chileans: they realize that Miami is their capital now." And Miami had indeed become the first U.S. bilingual city, with more than half of the population speaking Spanish as a first language, busy Spanish-language television stations, and a major paper, the *Miami Herald*, which published in both languages.

One "Anglo," who disliked the term because it was obviously meant to be pejorative, wrote to me of her feeling. Maxime Bender Segal of Miami is a writer, teaching writing part-time at Miami-Dade Community College and holding seminars on grammar and business writing. "The last time I looked, a 'nation' was defined as a community which had a common culture, definable borders and a common language," she wrote.

> According to that definition, the United States is losing ground on all three points. Our borders are extending further and further south; current immigrants are unwilling to adapt to or adopt the American culture, preferring to retain their own; and equally unwilling to speak the language of the United States.
>
> I am a second-generation American, most of my roots are East European, and I haven't been able to detect any English descendants. Yet, in Miami, I am referred to as an "Anglo" or a "non-Hispanic white." I am neither and I resent terribly being defined by what I am not. And those tags were hung on me and my family and friends by the people who refuse to become Americans.

And Miami, the "capital of the Americas"? In those words, one can find the first and most dramatic example of geographical re-

districting on an international and transcendental scale being accomplished not by war, not by conquest, and not by purchase, but
by the demographic force of immigrants who refuse to accept or
embrace the central tool of their adopted country's unity—language. Here was a country allowing parts of itself to set up parallel societies and hoping they might, in some utopian world, still
exist "together." Here was one of the first peals of warning that
the United States was losing its sovereignty, which requires control of its borders, as well as its nationhood, and which requires a
common language.

But Dade County surely was not the only such example. Indeed, the syndrome of cultural dividing—and thus economically
impoverishing America through language division—was occurring everywhere. . . .

In 1993 Rhode Island became the second state, after Washington, to declare itself a "multilingual" state; the Maryland House
of Delegates, at the request of Maryland's Office of Hispanic Affairs, introduced a resolution that would have officially recognized
Maryland as a "multilingual and multicultural" state; and Senator John Breaux and Representative James Hayes, both from Loui-
siana, where French was the dominant language until it joined the
Union in 1812, introduced bills in both houses of Congress to add
an amendment to the Constitution of the United States granting
"cultural rights" to all Americans. The Maryland resolution did not
pass, but the two Louisianans were expected to bring up similar
bills again; the intent was to seek official recognition of "multiculturalism" and "multilingualism" as accomplished facts and to
thus impose legal blocks to granting any special protection to
America's historic common language and civic culture—a harbinger of much more to come!

If Puerto Rico, which shares a commonwealth relationship with
the United States that has been substantially successful since the
early 1940s, is brought into the equation, the linguistic question will
become even more problematic. Puerto Ricans are for the most part
loyal American citizens but they do not pay taxes, and Puerto Rico
has been traditionally both English- and Spanish-speaking. But if
Puerto Rico becomes a state, a potentiality that is enormously gaining steam toward the end of the century, that statehood would put
the United States mainland in severe danger of becoming an officially bilingual nation, like Canada with Québec, or like Belgium

with French and Flemish, and with all the intractable problems those linguistic divisions have wrought.

Meanwhile, on another crucial level, the bilingual education world was dividing America still further. Pushed by the New Left ideas of the 1960s, the Bilingual Education Act of 1968 was designed to help immigrants be assimilated into American society and eventually learn English by "removing language barriers to learning." The act mandated three years of study under a new initiative called "bilingual education." It was designed to develop "self-esteem," and to help students master subjects for grade promotion and high school graduation. But by the early 1980s, bilingual education had become still another government program existing in a bureaucratic world of its own: an entire cadre of bilingual teachers were now cemented into the system. Worst of all, most children in the program were spending fully eight years in Spanish classes, which, through some mystification of common sense, was supposed to teach them English.

Although a survey of Los Angeles teachers in 1988 showed that 78 percent of them were opposed to bilingual education, the bureaucratic digging-in of the basically unrepresentative bilingual lobby prevailed, and a master plan was imposed upon the Los Angeles schools that required even more teaching in "native" languages. In New Jersey in 1989, the state Board of Education announced that limited-English students could take the test of basic skills required for high school graduation in any of twelve languages. (How someone testing in Creole could then get a job in an English-speaking society or move on to college was, as usual, never explained.) In New York, the state's avant Board of Regents, which had become a beacon for the consummately "politically correct," even went so far as to legislate that students could go through the entire university system only in Spanish. And in New York City, which was going broke and swiftly descending to Third World status, students were being taught in eighty-two languages, including Kpelle, Nyanja, Twi, Gurma, Ewe, and Cham; while in Los Angeles County, in a state that was virtually bankrupt by 1993, only 54.6 percent of those five years and older spoke English at home.

Meanwhile, English remained the universal language of the world, and these children were thus cut out of the universal culture completely.

The bilingual flight reached its apotheosis in the early years of the nineties in the much-discussed and controversial "Curriculum of Inclusion" produced by a special minority task force in New York State last year. The report argued no less than that "African-Americans, Asian-Americans, Puerto Ricans, Latinos and Native Americans have all been the victims of an intellectual and educational oppression that has characterized the culture and institutions of the United States and the European-American world for centuries."

The task force soon spelled out the hatreds, prejudices, and punishing attitudes in such oppression. Its new curriculum, concentrating on contributions by members of minority groups to the culture, would ensure that minority children "have higher self-esteem and self-respect, while *children from European cultures will have a less arrogant perspective of being part of the group that has 'done it all. . . .'"* (Italics mine.)

Writing about the issue in the *New York Times Magazine*, Richard Bernstein, the *Times*'s national cultural correspondent, came to this conclusion: "What's at stake, then, is nothing less than the cultural identity of the country. Those who argue that bilingual education is a 'right' make up a kind of informal coalition with those who are pressing for changes in the way the United States is perceived—no longer as a primarily European entity to which all others have to adapt, but as a diverse collection of ethnic groups, each of which deserves more or less equal status and respect." No longer the "melting pot," now the "salad bowl"!

Little mentioned in the ideological flurry of language changes in the nation was the "plebeian" cost of it all.

In the fall 1992 elections, many localities moved to give voting help to citizens with limited English proficiency. This was accomplished via the 1992 extension of the 1965 Voting Rights Act, applicable to all counties with ten thousand or more residents who were part of any "language minority." Again, Los Angeles County was in the vanguard. Under this law, the county and its cities were required to give voting help in five languages other than English: Spanish, Chinese, Japanese, Vietnamese, and Tagalog. For good measure, on its own the city added materials in Korean. The city spent initially $125,000 to prepare the materials, which was quite a lot when you consider that only 927 people asked for bilingual materials. In Long Beach, the situation turned out to be even more absurd. Long Beach spent roughly $6,200 preparing multilingual voter information pamphlets, and the city received a total of 22 requests for them.

And the more bilingualism failed—by 1994, reports from New York City, its crucible, made that point unmistakably—the more the education engineers pushed it. Moreover, through such deliberate linguistic separation, the bonds of citizenship were being affected in ways that we are only beginning to understand.

☆

The *Chicago Tribune's* Joseph Tybor wrote as early as 1988 about the way in which new immigrants' habits from "home" were being accepted in many American courts instead of American law.

> A "truth serum" of rooster blood and water replaces the time-honored oath a witness gives in a U.S. courtroom? A judge requires a defendant to apologize to his rape victim instead of imposing a prison sentence? Improbable as they seem, these incidents are drawn from reality. They figure in a remarkable discussion among judges, lawyers and futurists about challenges posed to the nation's courts by a new wave of immigration.
>
> As a result, the U.S. system of government and law finds itself at great odds these days with an increasing number of people living here, and there is growing uncertainty over how to deal with this. Accommodation of cultural mores, rather than the law, may be a consideration in defining criminal blame—but if it becomes an excuse for breaking the law, that affects our basic concepts of right and wrong.

Again, the activists, advocates, and voices that really want to break down the American cultural polity were soon heard from. Jim Daton, a political scientist and futurist at the University of Hawaii who had counseled emerging nations and several states on their court systems, was quoted as saying in contemptuous terms about America: "Nothing will be more rare in the future than a white person, and nothing may be less important than the white man's ways. We can continue to try to force people to behave the way the system assumes, or we can change the system—or at least its assumptions. To fail to do one or the other will lead to enormous social strife in the near future."

Lest anyone think that the American system of law and justice, the model to which the entire world aspires, is not threatened, here is one actual case study cited in *Time* magazine:

In Chicago, two Hmong tribesmen from Laos, a father and son, were charged with assault after they beat up a motorist who had honked at them when his auto was cut off on an expressway ramp. In a pretrial motion, arguing their "cultural differences," the men's attorney asked Circuit Judge Michael Jordan to take part in a formal prayer ceremony with the Hmong and to allow each side to tell its story and then drink a glass of water containing rooster blood. (The Hmong believe that a person who drinks the mixture and tells a lie will die within a year.)

Here, as in so many related cases, we see people from countries with different and most often less developed systems of justice and different historical principles, having voluntarily come to America, wanting to impose upon America's advanced and sophisticated justice system habits and ideas long left behind by most advanced countries.

Fortunately, Judge Jordan was having none of it. He sternly explained that any idea of a "prayer ceremony" was totally impossible because the U.S. Constitution separates church and state; he further explained that "the method they described would harken back to 'trial by ordeal' in ancient history—and that our system does not allow." The jury found the son guilty of aggravated assault and the father guilty of battery. The judge sentenced both to learn English and to study U.S. heritage and culture, as well as sentencing them to thirty months probation, two weekends in jail, and six hundred hours of community service.

"I recognize that they came from a different society and a different culture," this unusual judge said. "But they should be assimilating into our culture, and they should realize we live in a society of law and order."

But the odd "culture war" that has been going on as immigrants come to America and as they face America's unwillingness to define the parameters of its acceptance of change supersedes these court cases—which are, though important, passing pages of history. Far more serious has been the imposition of permanent monuments from the cultures of origin. Not only are these monuments often of heroes and gods of foreign nations whose intrinsic worth has nothing whatsoever to do with America, but they are often entities antithetical to American values. In many places, because of spurious "multiculturalism" and "diversity," they often actually *replace* even the most sacred of American religious holiday commemorations. One extraordinary example:

During the fall of 1994, after considerable and heated discussion, a new statue was unveiled in the city of San Jose, California. The debate addressed how to "honor" the Hispanic contribution to San Jose, and a famous artist, Robert Graham, chose as the subject of such a commemoration the ancient Mexican god Quetzalcoatl, who was worshiped in Mexico before the arrival of the Spanish in the sixteenth century. Vice Mayor Blanca Alvarado told the *San Jose Mercury News* that the statue depicting the god as a coined, feathered snake is "a major statement about the city's desire to recognize and highlight its diverse population."

There was one problem: Quetzalcoatl, although one of the more benign Mexican gods for that sanguinary time, was still a demonic god to whom humans were sacrificed (as were all the gods of that era in the Aztec and Toltec religion). A local Protestant minister, the Reverend Dick Bernal, said at the time, "Quetzalcoatl is a dead, forgotten god who deserved to be dead because of all the lives sacrificed to him. There'll be a curse on San Jose if this statue goes up." And an eminent scholar in Latin American studies, Ronald Hilton of Stanford University, went so far as to file a deposition on behalf of six plaintiffs in a lawsuit against the five-hundred-thousand-dollar statue.

But it is interesting to note that the only real way they could sue was to make a legal challenge on the basis of the separation of church and state. There was no way they could contest the creation of and public payment for a statue to a totally foreign cultural figure, no matter how moral or immoral. Hilton pointed out that Quetzalcoatl had religious significance in Mormon theology (where it is believed that he was Jesus Christ appearing to the Indians of ancient America) and among New Age cults. He further charged that those in Stanford's anthropology department, many of whom had championed the statue, were "in the grips of romantic pseudohistory" over an "extremely bloodthirsty" god who inspired sacrificial massacres and the ritual killing of children. "The people who are pushing this whole business . . . are frankly pretty ignorant and they're politically inspired," he summed up. "I'm not a Catholic, but I think it's intended as an anti-Catholic manifestation."

Just before Christmas, only a few weeks after the statue had been unveiled, the city of San Jose ordered the removal of a Nativvity scene that had been part of the park's Christmas display for fifteen years. Although the crèche had been particularly popular with families, it took up less than 1 percent of the display, which included secular Christmas symbols such as reindeer, elves, and a gingerbread house. From a legal viewpoint, there was no requirement whatsoever that the crèche be moved, because the law required only that, along with religious displays, there must be some that are secular—and there were. True, the Jewish publisher of a weekly city newspaper, Dan Pulcrano, had complained, but other Jewish organizations were mystified about the removal of the Nativity scene.

Meanwhile, the ten-foot-tall, cast-iron statue of Quetzalcoatl, a pagan god from a faraway culture, stood proudly all through the Christmas season, in a nation predominantly Christian, while small Christian displays were banned from public sight.

Another example of "cultural rights" bravado: In June of 1993, the popular Sunday-night television show *60 Minutes* did a segment on the huge Dominican community in New York, which had taken over the old neighborhood of Washington Heights and was by then deeply involved in the drug trade. They interviewed a Dominican activist/"leader," Moises Perez, a neighborhood organizer with the Alianza Dominicana, who minced no words.

"Anyone who wants to emigrate has a right to be in this city," the attractive, dark-haired young man said with a confidence that might suggest he had another life, perhaps as an official at Chase Manhattan bank. "Documented or undocumented, you have a right to be in this city. This is the symbol, this is the Statue of Liberty, this is 'Give me your poor.'"

Interestingly, the interviewer never even questioned such implausible, putative "rights." He never brought up such relevant subjects as citizenship or the law.

Indeed, the fact that such words are *not* being questioned is what has, in great part, led to the new reality that the United States has allowed and even encouraged to grow an entire and bizarre congeries of ideas about American citizenship, "rights," and the future direction of the country.

Other leading Hispanic-lobby activist/leaders have reflected Perez's thinking, saying of today's overwhelming Central and Latin American emigration to the United States: "This is different, they did not come to America, America came to them."

☆

Let us look finally at some more of the strange new ideas that are being put forward for what are basically changes in citizenship (although they are not always called that), in addition to sobering challenges to its centrality in the lives of individual human beings and of nations.

Take the concept of "diaspora" citizenship. The *Chronicle of Higher Education* published a groundbreaking article in June 1992, "World Wide Diaspora of Peoples Poses New Challenges for Scholars," which says, "Scholars have begun to consider how 'diaspora' communities reshape nations, noting that 'diaspora' is the word first applied to the experience of Jews, and later to Armenians, who were forcibly exiled from their homelands. Recently, scholars have expanded the definition to include groups who, sometimes by choice, have moved from one part of the world to another even if they don't intend to move back."

The article quotes Arjun Appadurai, professor of anthropology at the University of Pennsylvania, saying, with typical elliptical ambiguity, "More people are in some sense where they do not belong than ever before. But even those who have not moved are in some sense in greater contact with those who have."

Then the article brings up another new concept that is becoming the fashion in certain basically anticitizenship circles. It describes "non-European and non-white immigrant groups [which] are changing the face of the United States and Europe. They won't or can't easily assimilate. They are committed instead to retaining their cultures and, often, close ties to home. . . ." And so we arrive at a kind of "binational citizenship!"

Mr. Appadurai goes on to say that scholars need to study "the landscape of persons who make up the shifting world in which we live: tourists, immigrants, refugees, exiles, guest workers, and other moving groups and persons (who constitute an essential feature of the world and appear to affect the politics of and between nations to a hitherto unprecedented degree)."

"Global ethnoscapes," he calls them. "Transnational identity" is another term used. And in Europe, the fashionable term is "having multiple identities." Whatever one wants to call these changes, they impact dramatically upon historical and metaphysical ideas of citizenship.

International agencies, caught up in utopian ideas of human nature, often even came to support and advance policies and programs that were helping to break down nation-states. The World Bank, for instance, was deeply involved in the new "plurinationalism" that effectively recognized and encouraged all the splintering and squabbling little nationalisms. And University of Texas anthropologist Richard N. Adams wrote that "the emergence of politically contentious plural societies is one of the major historical events of the present era." As the twentieth century draws to a close, the world "has become an assemblage of peoples struggling over rights and power to rule states."

Certainly, the world is changing dramatically, and most of the changes have to do with the disintegration of borders, with lateral economic links that tie peoples of certain economic levels and groups together, and with mass and uncontrolled movements of peoples.

We are no longer a world of black and white, we now have "gray areas," which involve at least two levels of authority, the official and the unofficial. We now have "global tribes"—the Jews, Chinese, Indians, Japanese, British, Lebanese—whose lateral ties across national borders are becoming in many ways more important than the commercial pyramids within the countries themselves. We now have ethnic factions and religious fundamentalists, militias and international criminal organizations, terrorists and every possible type of informal economic organization.

Here at home, we have the citizen-as-taxpayer, citizen-as-consumer, citizen-as-tourist, citizen-as-stranger, citizen-of-a-cause, citizen-of-a-gang, citizen-as-complainer, citizen-as-claimant, and even citizen-as-cog in the great globalized economic machine.

All of these new groups and new developments have led clearly to the delegitimization of the state, political atomization, and breakdown into smaller and more conflicting interest groups or focuses (characteristics listed by the National Strategy Information Center). They certainly do mean that citizenship—and particularly American citizenship—is being used as never before for questionable purposes having little to do with its original intent, by self-interested groups, by cynical or simply arrogant governments, and by desperate, ambitious, or aggressive individuals.

In short, the threats to a serious and responsible citizenship were coming from all directions: mostly from Americans themselves but also from developments that were both deliberate and accidental, in an increasingly crowded world.

When I travel around the United States and mention citizenship in my speeches, Americans no longer seem to know the history behind it—what it meant, how it had developed, or where it was going. "But why is it important?" people who nevertheless call themselves "Americans" ask me over and over, even in middle-American areas where one would think that citizenship still has the glow of privilege. Indeed, it was after many such discussions that I decided to write this book.

☆

In Belgrade in 1989 and 1991, those of us who cared to could see even then what was happening and how the coming carnage easily could have been stopped before it began—but even a powerful outside world seemed paralyzed until it was too late. Should we not now ask: Are we capable, in our own country, of anticipating related problems before they reach critical mass?

Indeed, if it comes to that, when events backed up by our own lethargy have carried us to the point where there is no longer any arriving at a good balance between what we have and what we must have, the American story will be difficult for future historians to believe:

History's single most successful society—and at the very moment, when America's values were transcendent from one end of the globe to the other—had in effect collaborated in its own murder.

3

From Subject to Citizen— and Back Again?

It is right to prefer our own country to all others, because we are children and citizens before we can be travelers and philosophers.
George Santayana, "The Life of Reason"

Americans seem to have lost the broader sense of politics that goes beyond what governments do. They have lost the names for what citizens do.
David Mathews, president, the Kettering Foundation

The apogee of American citizenship, the furthest point of development from the closed circle of misery in which the great masses of humanity had virtually always found themselves, came at the Constitutional Convention of 1787 in Philadelphia. The event inspired most of the world with the staggering new possibility that even the poorest and most wretched man on earth was no longer destined to remain forever in his despair. It opened the door to true equality among men and women—not the equality of wealth or talent but the only real equality possible, the equality of participation in the creation and constant re-creation of the nation. Although, of course, there had been movement for many centuries toward that moment in history, its transformation into reality came at the convention when, symbolically and within the structure of a single nation, subjects gained the right to become citizens.

Historian James H. Kettern writes how a bold new actor marched onto the stage of history during those months: "The Revolution created the status of 'American citizen' and produced an

expression of the general principles that ought to govern membership in a free society. The notion that individuals had the right to
choose their own loyalty was embedded in the concept of contractual allegiance from the beginning; yet the transformation of the
idea from a mythical construct to a human reality was undeniably
the result of the concrete situation created by the Revolution. *When
subjects became citizens,* they gained the right to choose their allegiance." (Italics mine.)

But Abraham Lincoln, in a speech on Independence Day in
1858 before he became president, had already carried the scope and
reach of American citizenship much further. He remarked to the
assemblage that perhaps half of the American people alive in his
day had had no ancestor present at the nation's actual founding:
If they looked back through their "ethnic history" to try to "trace
connection with those days by blood, they find they have none, that
they cannot carry themselves back into that glorious epoch and
make themselves feel that they are a part of us."

Ah, but if those new Americans of the nineteenth century
would only read the Declaration of Independence and find "that
those old men say 'that we hold these truths to be self-evident, that
all men are created equal,' then they feel that the moral sentiment
taught in that day evidences their relation to those men." For those
principles were meant by their founders for all mankind—they
belonged to all men—because the founders had embodied "the
father of all moral principle." And that meant that immigrants
equally as well as the native-born had a relation to the authors of
the Declaration exactly the same *"as though they were blood of the
blood, and flesh of the flesh of the men who wrote it."* (Italics mine.)

Yet, today, most new citizens and immigrants, and most
younger Americans, have no idea about the importance of the
Constitutional Convention, those principles, or the sacred and
political contract symbolized therein. They understand not a bit the
process that made citizens of subjects on a comprehensive scale for
the first time in human history. In the America that has evolved
over the twentieth century, Americans have not been socialized
into the story and promise of their citizenship; they no longer tell
their story, study it, or honor it.

A brief refresher course follows.

☆

The Federal Constitutional Convention was destined to be one of those breathtaking, watershed moments of change in human history. Modern men of destiny—George Washington, James Madison, George Mason, Gouverneur Morris—strode the halls like giants to "consider the exigencies of the Union."

They argued over the form of their new union, and they debated far into the night; for they were deciding far more than the fate even of their own new nation, born of one of the world's great revolutions a mere eleven years earlier. They were effused with an almost mystical awareness that theirs was no "normal" nation, built upon that ancient greed for power, but truly a new nation created on new principles. Some, perhaps too grandly but certainly sincerely, called America the "epitome of all nations," as though all of human experience somehow had been pared down finally to this essence, to this ideal.

Indeed, these "wisest men politically in recorded history," as historian Henry Steele Commager calls them, "couldn't give a speech or write a letter without talking about posterity." George Washington used the word "posterity" nine times in one speech; Thomas Jefferson talked about the "thousandth and thousandth generation" in his first inaugural address; and after signing the Declaration of Independence, John Adams wrote to his beloved wife, Abigail, "I do not know what will be the outcome of this. We may pay a very high price. But it is certain that posterity will profit from our sacrifice."

Never afraid of noble words or concepts, the Founding Fathers spoke constantly of wisdom, magnanimity, and above all "virtue." Theirs was to be a *virtuous* republic, founded and cared for by citizens striving to be as honorable and expansive in their associations as possible. They were not afraid to talk of goodness or to judge human behavior. Neither were they afraid of genuine charity toward their fellow men or of talking about loving one another.

In the very earliest days, as the *Arabella* approached the Massachusetts Bay Colony, Pastor John Winthrop preached to the Puritans aboard the ship, who were escaping religious persecution in England and facing the unknown: "We must strengthen, defend, preserve and comfort each other. We must love one another, we must bear one another's burdens. We must not look only on our things, but also on the things of our brethren. We must rejoice together, mourn together, labor and suffer together."

At the same time, their profound sense of creating something new was always strengthened by their embrace of those few other shining epochs of mankind. Indeed, to verify their bonds with and their gratitude to the ancients, they even called themselves, while in their own company (and perhaps a little self-consciously), by the names of Brutus, Cato, Publius, and so forth.

The world that the Founding Fathers created was one of great harmony compared to what had come before in mankind's development. Indeed, these men, with their practical genius, were moving politics from the realm of eternal conflict to one that was rational, contractual, and consensual. They did so by creating laws that now bound, and limited, not only princes and lords but every single citizen. The perceptive Arkansas editor Paul Greenberg once commented on these men working in concert, noting with some incredulity how "Washington set out to prove that a republic could do more than prevail in war—that it could endure. How did he manage it? How did he carry off this bold experiment as if it were a formal ritual?"

And he answered that "the clearest and most eloquent explanation may lie, not in scholarly analyses or in Washington's own weighty prose, but in the music of his time. Listen to Haydn and hear the contest between theme and counter-theme, the folk melodies that are given free play but not enough to overpower the final triumph of decorum. Listen to Mozart and hear the stately minuet transformed into a lively rondo, then brought back again to balance and moderation. So with Washington's leadership. . . . Washington's now distant music is really a familiar 18th-century medley. Themes and counter-themes. Folk tunes and acquired formalities. Then the final triumph of balance and stability. Washington's policies changed, but never his grand and civil vision of what could be."

Such was the modest grandeur of the men who laid down the principles that were to bind Americans to their new nation, commit them in love and in charity to one another, and inspire the entire world for centuries to come.

But they were also businessmen; they were practical men of commerce and public affairs, men who addressed themselves always with great realism to the business at hand. The words and phrases they used revealed their spiritual and patriotic passions, but also their relationship to the most ethical worlds of commerce: citizenship would be "a volitionary allegiance . . . a privilege and not a right . . . a band of brethren . . . the social contract or compact or covenant . . . a voluntary commitment of free men . . . a community of allegiance."

Scholar and former U.S. ambassador to the United Nations Jeane Kirkpatrick once said, "Democratic government . . . makes the highest demand of any political culture—it demands that citizens participate and also restrain themselves to legal civil activities which ensures respect for commonality." And so, it was believed, "ordinary" men—through the strength of these voluntary commitments and covenants, and with a representative system of government to back up their efforts—would rise not only above their former "stations" in life, but also above themselves.

In those days, the citizenship that these remarkable men created—with its glories and its duties—was always symbolized in art and ceremony. Citizenship was celebrated in great federal buildings, which monumentally expressed not only the greatness and nobility of American life but the evolution of democratic life down through the centuries. In some of them, one could think oneself a Roman citizen, perhaps of the age of Hadrian. In still others, one could imagine oneself in the Greek temples of Jupiter, Juno, or Minerva.

The political symbolism of marches, parades, and festivals celebrated this deceptively "simple" new democratic world and, above all, the unostentatious nobility of its "ordinary" working citizens. Smithsonian Institution historian Wilcomb E. Washburn has written about how, on February 6, 1788, when Massachusetts became the sixth state to ratify the Constitution, a committee of tradesmen resolved to hold a parade. And what a parade it was, as

. . . their trade and craft groupings (seventy-three blacksmiths, fifty shoemakers, fifty-six tailors, twenty-six hatters, eight tallow chandlers, et cetera), marched over a preplanned route carrying implements of their trades, and symbols of their faith in the new government. Among the symbols was a full-rigged ship named the "Federal Constitution" and pulled by thirteen horses, with a captain, officers, and thirteen crewmen. Another float contained a model shipyard on a platform drawn by thirteen horses, with several builders working on small boats. On the printers' float, composers worked.

As the marchers passed through the streets, hundreds of spectators joined the procession, swelling its numbers from the 1,500 who had begun to nearly 4,000 by the time it had returned to the starting point. All was carried out with what was described by a local newspaper as "perfect order and urbanity . . . dignity . . . and solemnity." Although a band of music was present, and there were various shouts and "huzzas," the citizens watched in almost unbroken silence.

Meanwhile, the greatest thinkers of the world could not praise America and its gallant experiment in human nature enough:

Hector Saint John de Crèvecoeur, the brilliant Frenchman who became enamored of the young republic, wrote, "In this great American asylum, the poor of Europe, leaving sore affliction and pinching penury behind, are seeking a new life—and finding it. . . . Everything has tended to regenerate them: new laws, a new mode of living, a new social system; here they are become men; in Europe, they were so many useless plants . . . mowed down by want, hunger and war. . . ."

Herman Melville, the great writer of sagas, proclaimed, "The Past is dead, and has no resurrection. The Past is the textbook of tyrants; the Future, the Bible of the Free."

Alexis de Tocqueville, the French philosopher/writer who seemed to have been born in order to illuminate the habits and proclivities of this new America in the 1830s, writing the classic *Democracy in America* as he joyously roamed the new land, found that "there is only one country on the face of the earth where the citizens enjoy unlimited freedom of association for political purposes. The same country is the only one in the world where the continual exercise of the right of association has been introduced into civil life and where all the advantages which civilization can confer are procured by means of it."

The respected New York Public Library director and Brown University president, Vartan Gregorian, liked to quote German-Jewish philosopher Hannah Arendt, who knew from her own experience in Nazi Germany how little "safety" there was for the human soul under totalitarianism and who sought and found it in America, in saying that "there is no safety in liberty without a sense of citizenship. It is the concept and the essence of citizenship that transforms the societal contract to a moral transaction. It is the essence of citizenship that ties our pluralistic society. It embodies our social, political and moral commitments."

And the Spanish-born philosopher and poet George Santayana, a naturalized American citizen, wrote that "Americans have all been uprooted from their several soils and ancestries and plunged together into one vortex, whirling irresistibly into a space otherwise quite empty. To be an American is of itself almost a moral condition, an education, and a career."

But it was an obscure and melodramatic play, a four-act drama that opened in Washington in 1908, that perhaps best characterized the experience of American citizenship. Israel Zangwill, novelist, dramatist, and founding father of the Zionist movement, was to become a celebrity from the cities of Europe to the shores of America before World War II for his work, *The Melting Pot*. His hero, David, a young composer, speaks the ringing words: "America is God's Crucible, the great Melting-Pot where all the races of Europe are melting and re-forming. . . . Germans and Frenchmen, Irishmen and Englishmen, Jews and Russians—into the Crucible with you all! God is making the American!"

☆

As America was forming itself, it was natural that its greatest internal discussion should revolve around the question of *who belonged* to this new covenant, who was a "citizen" of this new polity. The philosophers saw, if the average American man or woman did not, how America was passing from the old *ascriptive* citizenship to the new *consensual* form. In a ascriptive system, the person's political membership in a nation was determined by objective and largely unchangeable conditions, say, birth under a particular king or monarch. The principle of consent, on the other hand, defined American citizenship: Free and self-determining men gave voluntary consent to join the new polity; no longer unequals, they were now men—and increasingly, women—among peers.

When the new Americans threw off their allegiance to the British crown, they resolved, in the words of the brilliant Yale law professor Peter H. Schuck, to become something very different: "citizens of a new state constituted solely by the aggregation of their individual consents." Or, as James Kettern writes, "For Americans, these principles of liberty led inevitably to the conclusion that all legitimate power over men depended upon their consent to be governed. All citizenship—and not just that which was created by naturalization or revolutionary election—seemed definable in terms of a legal contract between the individual and the community at large."

Indeed, there was such basic agreement among the Founding Fathers on the responsibilities of this "new man" that citizenship was not even written into the Constitution or defined by it. It was an era of vast open spaces and no population pressures at all. It was an age of inner-directed men and women taught to aim for, if not always to achieve, the highest standards of moral and ethical behavior in their public as well as their personal lives. It was assumed that the individual citizen, whether native-born or naturalized, would realize and accept that he or she was a member of the state to which allegiance was pledged, to the state that in turn agreed to serve as each citizen's protector.

Underlying every other principle of this new citizenship was the idea of *radical individualism,* a concept that differentiated archetypal American thought and practice dramatically from those of the "old countries" of Europe and, later, from those of the twentieth century Communist world, as well as from "multicultural" America. Radical individualism meant that every man and woman was to be judged on his or her own merit, and not at all on the merits or demerits of a group, tribe, clan, sect, or race. (The fact that race outlasted all the other divisions in America and was a matter of profound disgrace to the country does not, however, diminish the principle. This principle, after all, was the impetus for the civil rights fight of the 1960s, as a result of which black Americans finally became full American citizens!)

Writer Bruce Fein has commented: "The individual merit ideal is an enormously unifying, harmonizing and stimulating influence. It pushes toward national unity because all persons are judged by the same standard, and none are arbitrarily disadvantaged or excluded in competition to succeed. The merit ideal turns minds and associations away from divisive preoccupations with race, religion, gender, ethnicity or other congenital attributes it deems irrelevant to social standing."

At the same time, however, even as the Constitution was being drafted in 1787, it was decided unequivocally that the president of the United States must be American-born. It was John Jay, later to become the nation's first chief justice, who persuaded George Washington, then president of the convention, to add the clause barring a foreigner from becoming leader of the nation. Their fear, according to historians, was that a foreign-born president could prove less than 100 percent loyal to his adoptive country and might carry America into the eventuality that perhaps these men most hated and feared: foreign rule. (This requirement was temporarily waived, however, because in fact all the men at the convention were British-born. Not until the eighth U.S. presidency was an American-born president elected—Martin Van Buren [1782–1862]).

In those warm days of May in Philadelphia, the entire legal structure of American citizenship took form under the reigning consciences of the Founding Fathers, most of whom had come out of the town halls of the Massachusetts Colony. Not that there were no conflicts! (The deep conflicts among the delegates as to whether one's loyalties were first to one's own state or to the broader nation led them to put off any real definition of citizenship until after the Civil War.) Not that subsequent cruel and inhuman acts against Native Americans, black Americans, and immigrants didn't happen. They did. But the *principles* were laid down that would allow America, step-by-step, to evolve in time beyond such behavior.

Not inconsequentially, from the very beginning that confusion over the precise mechanistic definition of citizenship—so different from its moral and philosophical clarity, in the minds of the convention—provoked crucial questions that we are still asking today: *Who should take part in modern America in this human and civil bond? How open or how restrictive should citizenship be? What rules and regulations — and/or legal penalties — should guard citizenship or attend it? On what basis should citizenship ever be taken away from the renegade citizen?*

☆

Perhaps we would do well to pause here and review what would become the convictions of this new America regarding citizenship, nationality, and aliens, if only so that we can see how profoundly different they were from those of the tribes, clans, sects, sheikhdoms, sultanates, duchies, feudal kingdoms, city-states, religious entities, nation-states and societies of the past. It is odd, but emblematic of our times, that we need to take a deep breath and go back to origins, for ours is an age of confusion as to principles and wellsprings. At least I am the type, with a literal mind, who needs a small dictionary, to have things spelled out.

CITIZENSHIP: the relationship between an individual and the state, defined by the law of the state, with corresponding duties and rights in that state.

Citizenship is derived from the historical relationship between an individual and history. It implies the status of freedom with accompanying responsibilities. The principal grounds for citizenship have traditionally included birth within a certain territory, descent from a citizen-parent, marriage to a citizen, and naturalization. Generally, political rights, such as suffrage and the right to hold public office, are predicated upon citizenship. Usual incidents of citizenship are allegiance and military duty.

The words *city*, *citizen*, and *civility* all spring from the same Sanskrit root, *sivas*, meaning "friendly, hence dear to one," according to Eric Partridge's *Origins*.

COMPACT and COVENANT: A compact was traditionally an agreement between people, while a covenant was a sacred oath before God. In modern times the latter term became "secularized" along with so many other concepts, and today the two words are often used interchangeably.

NATIONALITY: under the law, membership in a nation or sovereign state.

It is to be distinguished from citizenship, a somewhat narrower term that is sometimes used to denote the status of those nationals who have full political privileges. Before an act of the U.S. Congress made them citizens in the full sense of the word, for example, American Indians were sometimes referred to as "noncitizen nationals."

Individual companies (corporations), ships, and aircraft all have nationality for legal purposes. It is in reference to natural persons, however, that the term finds most frequent use. Nationality is in fact commonly regarded as an inalienable right of every human being. Thus, the U.N. Universal Declaration of Human Rights (1948) states that "everyone has the right to a nationality" and that "no one shall be arbitrarily deprived of his nationality. "

Nationality is of cardinal importance to every person because it is mainly through nationality that the individual comes within the scope of international law and has access to the political and economic rights and privileges conferred by modern states upon their nationals.

ALIEN: in national and international law, a foreign-born resident who is not a citizen by virtue of parentage or naturalization and who is still a citizen or subject of another country.

In early times, the tendency was to look upon the alien as an enemy and to treat him as a criminal or outlaw.

TRAITS OF AMERICA: freedom from external controls made possible by the Protestant ideal of moral autonomy and self-restraint; habits of self-reliance and local government; a belief in natural rights, deriving from the classic liberalism of John Locke and the Declaration of Independence; the common-law tradition and due process of law; the principle against self-incrimination; the tradition of the loyal opposition and the right to dissent; freedom of speech and the appeal to reason in public discourse; traditions of honesty and fair dealing; the high degree of trust and social cooperation made possible by those traits; the rich tradition of voluntary associations and institutions.

☆

Now let's look at what preceded the Constitutional Convention in terms of thoughts on government and citizenship among other societies. The American dream did not spring forth fully formed like Aphrodite out of the waves on Cyprus. To the contrary, it built upon each new moral advancement in human history—from the great thinkers of Greece and Rome, onward to the imperial era of Charlemagne, the Renaissance and the Enlightenment, through the Protestant Reformation in England, to the French Revolution.

Even in ancient Greece, *the* forerunner of all of the philosophies that led to the American experience, the proclivity to consider everyone outside one's own group "inferior" was so ingrained that the great philosopher Aristotle saw the "alien," the early "other," as barbarous, a slave "by nature." But soon this began to change, as the early (300 B.C.–A.D. 200) school of patient philosophers, the Stoics, taught the equality of all men. They were followed by the great historian Plutarch, who wrote that "there should be one Life and one order (cosmos), as it were one flock on a common pasture feeding in common under one joint law."

To emphasize the difference between the secular, reasoned government of the Greeks and the monarchical government, closely allied with religious institutions, that preceded it, the respected Yale classics and history professor Donald Kagan writes, "The Greek city-states were republics. There were no kings with the wealth to hire mercenary soldiers, so the citizens did their own fighting. As independent defenders of the common safety and interest, they demanded a role in the most important policy decisions; in this way, for the first time, political life came to be shared by a relatively large portion of the people."

The ancient Greeks—including their most resplendent philosopher, Socrates—saw themselves as citizens of the "rational universe" or, to use a later term, early "cosmopolitans." This cosmopolitanism was never limited to the Peloponnesian peninsula but would instead influence the entire world. In the Greeks' time, it particularly influenced Alexander the Great, through his studies with the Greek philosophers, and it was he who went on to create the first great Western empire, the Hellenic, based upon many of the first universalist principles. Scholar Patrick Glynn points out that Alexander was the first leader to unify what is now known as "the West."

(Centuries later, in the winter of 1992 to be exact, I was traveling in Central Asia and drove over to remote Kirgizstan from the relatively sophisticated Kazakhstan. There, in gray little Bishkek, the respected Kirgiz president, Askar Akaev, and Kirgiz historians regaled me with stories of how the great Alexander had passed through their lands in those long-ago days. Thus, the redheads and blonds in their region, they told me with absolutely straight faces and apparently genuine conviction; they, the Kirgiz, were the "first Europeans"! Akaev also told me, and this was true, that the early Kirgiz tribes were very democratic; they voted for leaders by throwing stones onto respective piles!)

Much of what the Greeks believed in concerned citizenship; they wanted to rationalize and give animated spirit to the hoary question *Who belongs?* For Aristotle and other, later philosophers, citizenship could exist only through conscious and autonomous civil participation, allowing the individual will fulfillment. Indeed, the Aristotelian idea of a citizen in a democracy is that of a kind of "office-holder-in-waiting."

Glynn further comments that the Romans, "having imbibed Greek learning, revived and reinstitutionalized Greek rationalism, gradually transformed themselves from a republic into an empire." In the Roman Empire, whose sway across all of the Mediterranean lasted from 300 B.C. for six hundred years, we thus find the foundations of American citizenship.

Historian Max Lerner noted that Thomas Jefferson once wrote, reflecting the love of the young Americans of his era for the France of the French Revolution, that "every man has two countries—his own and France." Then Jefferson "corrected" these words, remarking that "a young African writer had amended this to read 'his own and America,'" suggesting the extent to which "people far beyond the boundaries of America have had their imagination touched and their emotions engaged by the American experience. Only one other civilization in history—the Roman—can match this impact."

The similarities that Lerner saw between America and the Roman Empire are many: "a world power span, by land and sea . . . a pride in republican institutions . . . a 'Capitalist' economy . . . vast outlays of monies on public works . . . a cult of magnificence in public buildings . . . the use of military reputation as a road to high civilian office . . . a remarkable system of administration and law . . ." But above all, the "prestige and pride of citizenship in the world's greatest power structure!"

How proud the Romans were to say, "I am a Roman citizen!" They thus proclaimed to the world that they had been transformed and belonged to the greatest and most powerful empire the earth had ever seen. No longer did they belong to the more primitive tribes of the past (in this case, usually the Germanic tribes, a fact that should give some idea of the relativity of human evolution); they belonged to this vast and advanced empire of men, leading the world because they knew what it was to fulfill the formal and the spiritual requirements of citizenship.

But Rome also gives us an important example of the vulner-
abilities that can accompany broad-based citizenship. In the beginning, Roman citizenship was awarded only to those who had been
born or adopted into one of the three original tribes of Rome—in
effect, all males above fifteen years of age who were neither slaves
nor aliens were eligible. Never before in the entire history of the
world had a status been so highly prized or so jealously guarded,
for it alone awarded immunity from legal torture and the right of
appeal against the overzealous behavior of any official in the empire. But it also imposed strict duties: For example, if a man wanted
to go into political life, he had to have performed his military
service.

Then, as Rome expanded—with, at least at first, the attendant
duties—its precious citizenship was extended to others. By 331 B.C.,
Rome had granted citizens' rights to the first conquered city,
Tusculum. Soon Roman citizenship became available to entire Italian peoples. Finally, even plebeians and freed slaves were granted
citizenship. The Greeks were astonished at such daring and often
also thought it arrant foolishness. Moreover, the Roman general
law applied to both citizens and foreigners and (in a unique forerunner of America today) tended toward the idea that aliens also
had rights; meanwhile, the essential idea behind Christianity, that
all humankind was united in "the holy church," also began to influence Roman thinking.

By the third century A.D., Roman citizenship had been extended
to all freemen of the empire, and the era of *Pax Romana* saw the first
real example of the linking of political system and citizen. This
system assured a measure of freedom to individuals while protecting the general peace, but only so long as the citizen pledged his
allegiance to the system.

"Step by step," Patrick Glynn goes on, "the Romans replaced
local laws rooted in local cults and customs with Roman law,
which was rational, universal, and said to be derived from the law
of nature, rationally understood."

But by taking in more new people than it could assimiliate and
by allowing so many essentially uncommitted people and peoples
into an ever-weakened Roman citizenship, Rome also weakened
the core of her polity. There were many reasons for the final fall
of Rome when it was sacked by the Vandals in a fourteen-day orgy

of killing and looting in A.D. 455—epidemics, economic crises, political decadence—but historians are in agreement that a general weakening and diluting of Roman citizenship was surely one of the major reasons. The idea of "Rome" had become so incoherent, so amorphous, that Romans had lost their national confidence and spirit. The first duty of Roman citizens had been to fight for Rome against her enemies. Indeed, one reason the Roman emperors kept expanding citizenship was their interest in protecting the state, as many Romans grew hedonistic and unconcerned with protecting not only the glories that were Rome but their own citizenship as well.

In its last two centuries, as Rome began to decay, she took into her army men from the more primitive Germanic tribes of the North, who were not made citizens: it was a perfect recipe for disaster. Roman Empire specialists assure us that the final decline of Rome was the direct result of the collapse of Roman field armies due to the massive recruitment of German "barbarians" into the ranks of the army as battalions and regiments. The once-fearsome and splendid Roman army split, disintegrated, and ultimately doomed Rome.

The Roman idea of empire was revived briefly under the Emperor Charlemagne, when he unified Europe from the Pyrénées to the Elbe between A.D. 800 and 814, but he was ultimately unable to secure his empire. Once again a period of grand ideas—unity, universality, and ecumenism—gave way to an inevitable dark descent into feudalism and civil wars, and finally to a retreat on the part of human beings to the narrowest and most destructive of ethnic identities.

For more than one thousand years after the disintegration of Rome, tumultuous Europe—mired in the Dark Ages, in the savage and endless religious wars and the injustice of feudal times—would look back upon the era of Imperial Rome as the lamented "Golden Age."

☆

The ongoing evolution of this "order" for mankind—which began in the wisdom of the ancient Greeks and found palpable body and form in the Roman Empire—took place during the Protestant Reformation and the Enlightenment, and then during the dramatic

development of capitalism across the North of Europe. The Protestant Reformation, which began in the sixteenth century, cultivated the concept of radical individualism in citizenship—if man
could now speak directly to God, certainly he could speak directly
to power. The Enlightenment, which blossomed in the seventeenth
and eighteenth centuries, contributed its celebration of the glory
of human reason—if man had the power to understand the universe, then surely, through his own intellectual and civic endeavors, he could transform his community and nation (and perhaps
even the universe, too). The capitalism that flourished alongside
Protestantism in the 1500s offered citizens the capacity to own the
means of production and thus to enhance the wealth and prosperity of their societies through further reinvestment—if man could
create wealth for everyone, instead of investing in pyramids and
cathedrals, then certainly it was possible for the average man to
have, share, and exercise power.

In those same effervescent times of religious, political, and economic change, the nation-state emerged as the "most distinctive
and most effective form of social organization in the modern era,"
according to historians. Before the sixteenth century, humankind
had been divided up into small, unequal, and often warring entities: feudal baronies, principalities, duchies, city-states, sheikhdoms, chieftainships. (Interestingly, these largely unproductive
belligerent entities were dramatically similar to the smaller ones
we are seeing today from the street fights of Lebanon to the mass
graveyards of Yugoslavia to the shantytowns of Africa.) Then, co-
agulative forces were awakened in Europe and began to move
aside the old centrifugal forces that had atomized human societies
for so many centuries; monarchs began to fall and, as larger entities became inclusive nation-states, new and workable contracts
and forms of citizenship began taking shape on a massive scale for
the first time.

One must never dismiss the importance of the French Revolution of 1789, when classes exploded and the word *"citoyen"* (citizen) was on the tongue of every good Frenchman, as men and
women waged one of the classic fights of history to move mankind
(or at least French mankind) from subjects to citizens. Poet William
Wordsworth called it "an hour of universal ferment" when "the
soil of common life was . . . too hot to tread upon." But that

revolution turned out so tragically—catapulting a people from zealotry and mass execution to dictatorship to renewed monarchy—that, while it ultimately inspired the young America with its exquisite rhetoric about "liberty, equality, and fraternity," it gave America little in institutional terms, particularly compared to England.

We know that nation-states arose in the world in this order: England, the United States, France, Germany, Italy, and Japan, in each case replacing native classes, clans, and ethnic groups; and that the nation-state's arrival on history's doorstep came directly from the experience of a common language and literature, that it arrived with the invention of printing, was nurtured in the Protestant Reformation and the Enlightenment, and finally reached its zenith in the mass education systems of the nineteenth and twentieth centuries in Europe. By the sixteenth century, these developments were hastened through the spread of literacy, the growth of bureacracy, and in particular the formation of armies manned not by paid mercenaries but by patriotic citizens.

The nation-state, like most developments in history, was an imprecise creature. There were nations that did not correspond to states (Germany and Italy until the 1860s) and states (the Hapsburg Monarchy) that did not correspond to nations. Still, all represented in some manner this major turnaround in history from small, uneconomic, undemocratic microentities to larger, economic, democratic ones.

It was really the Tudor monarchy in England, having developed one of Europe's first centralized bureacracies under the national church of Anglican Protestanism, which developed into the first nation-state as early as the fifteenth century. Indeed, many of the tenets of modern citizenship must be traced directly to England in those centuries in which the English, before any other people, began emerging so dramatically out of feudalism and into the modern state. It was in England that the light at the end of centuries-long road from subject to citizen really became visible.

Indeed, even as early as the thirteenth century, rural life in England was far advanced over the peasant life of continental Europe. England's break with the static, frozen past of inequality and privilege was possible because England alone was organized according to freeholdings of land, under small farmers who already had the right to keep the land or sell it. Peasants, whether in the Pale of Russia or in Saxony in Germany, traditionally had no rights; but the "new men" of that era, the small farmers of England, did—and constantly seized more. Scholar James Q. Wilson notes: "In England . . . individualism in economic and social life existed, rooted in property rights, inheritances and cash markets. Land was a commodity that could be, and was bought and sold. . . . Fathers could bequeath their land to particular offspring . . . men and women began to hire out for cash wages . . . people moved from one place to another, after centuries of being tied to the land and beholden to the prince . . . and many now knew the daring 'town life' as well as the doughty old village life."

Property was the major economic catalyst for the changes toward equality and citizenship because it was a means not only of support or status but above all of freedom. Its ownership gave the free man the ability to participate in politics and in civic life "independent of others' wills." In short, it gave the individual man an independent power base, apart from royalty or the church.

Some philosophers note that the political personality of the free man was founded in property and "perfected in citizenship." It was in that same England that the citizen began to emerge who would take part in such duties as voting, serving on juries, and paying taxes. England experienced the modern-day realization of Aristotle's idea of the citizen in a democracy, as a kind of "office-holder-in-waiting," a system that gave the citizen practice in governing as a potential legitimized ruler.

Meanwhile, the North of Europe, which only a few centuries before had been the home of primitive tribes dancing around the fires and despised by the proud cosmopolitans of Rome and Constantinople, had come to its moment of quickening and awakening. The Protestant Reformation had changed the patterns of Europe's religious world: Now, Christians did not have to look to the heights of the Roman Catholic Church and obey its strict rulings; now, Christians were to speak directly to their God. As the Reformation empowered men to be responsible for themselves, their minds were freed to enter into the voluntary bond of citizenship. Capitalism, or the use of one's own enterprise to create wealth that would in turn create more wealth, produced still more equality through a vastly expanded and diverse middle class; an evolution in citizenship accompanied such progress. Across the North of Europe, commercial leagues called the Hanseatic Leagues spread prosperity from Hamburg in Germany to Vyborg in eastern Finland, as trade burst its old royal bonds, empowering millions.

(Many centuries later, in 1988, I traveled one night by road from Helsinki, the sophisticated capital of Finland, through the darkness to Saint Petersburg, and on the way I drove through old Vyborg. It was a stunning experience because, even though it had "belonged" to Russia—and, of course, the Soviet Union—since Finland lost it in the "Winter War" of 1939, and even though it was clearly run-down, its buildings were still shabbily elegant, particularly compared with almost anything in the Soviet Union. It impressed me dramatically with the reality of that amazing early Hanseatic prosperity.)

Because of capitalism and citizenship, the world of that era proclaimed an entirely different view of human life, no longer static. With cooperation and investment, both production and human energies could be enormously enlarged in a creativity that constantly increased wealth—and civic virtue at the same time.

After the Revolutionary War severed America from that same Britain who had inspired her, the young Americans immediately set to perfecting Britain's tenets and institutions. As Arthur Schlesinger Jr. has written of the British role before the American Revolution, "Having cleared most of North America of their French, Spanish and Dutch rivals, the British were free to set the mold. The language of the new nation, its laws, its institutions, its political ideas, its literature, its customs, its precepts, its prayers, primarily derived from Britain. . . . For better or worse, the white Anglo-Saxon Protestant tradition was for two centuries—and in crucial respects still is—the dominant influence on American culture and society."

☆

In the new decades of the 1800s in America, as the prestigious *Kettering Review* puts it, America saw that "a flowering of voluntary, civic and reform efforts in America expanded citizens' sense of the public world and the meaning of politics." Alexis de Tocqueville was himself pleasantly surprised again and again in his travels across the country, in the 1830s, to discover with what frequency and fierceness—and distinct pleasure—the public substituted its own activity for that of officials or government. It was then that de Tocqueville made his famous observation that "in America 100,000 citizens might declare their intention to refrain from alcohol, while in Europe, they would have sent a petition to the King."

He further captured the European noncitizen's inability to act in the following remarks:

> There are countries in Europe where the inhabitant feels like some sort of farm laborer, indifferent to the fate of the place where he dwells. The greatest changes may take place without his concurrence; he does not even know precisely what has happened. . . . Worse still, the condition of his village, the policing of his roads, and the repair of his church and parsonage do not concern him; he thinks that all of those things have nothing to do with him at all, but belong to a powerful stranger called the government. . . .
>
> Furthermore, this man who has so completely sacrificed his freedom of will does not like obedience more than the next man. He submits, it is true, to the caprice of a clerk, but as soon as the force is withdrawn, he will vaunt his triumph over the law as over a conquered foe. Thus he oscillates the whole time between servility and licence.

Heightened awareness, public virtues, voluntary efforts at improvement of self and surroundings—all seem to flourish with citizenship and wilt in subjugation.

Despite the turbulence of the nineteenth century, the question of what constituted American citizenship was, in truth, not formally a profound issue. The young country had endless energy and wide-open horizons. The frontier readily absorbed all the misfits, aggressions, disappointments (and enough of the hopes, too!). That a person who came to America wanted to do so in order to become that new man, the American, was simply taken for granted. Distances were great, and one did not travel halfway around the world to see what was there; Christopher Columbuses and Americo Vespuccis were rare. Why else would one risk a life, set aside a past to come to a new country, except to stay? And, most important, what else would he pledge allegiance to except this new polity, which was after all a hopeful affair?

By 1848, the Old World was in decay and chaos, with nasty little student rebellions crashing across Europe, with Russian czars assassinated by a group known tellingly in Russian as "the people," and with the sobering breakdown of the societies that had been evolving in Europe for three hundred years. But in America men and women were eschewing such old political conflicts and exercising their energies in economic production, taming the frontier, and expansion of citizenly duties. Yet, even then, there were some upheavals directly related to the most important question of all: *Who is an American?*

In an early act of nativism, to be repeated many times throughout history, in the 1840s and '50s the "Know-Nothing" party, whose full name was the Supreme Order of the Star-Spangled Banner, banded together to urge the exclusion of the foreign-born and Roman Catholics from public office. When asked about their secret rituals, their answer was always an expressionless "I know nothing." Although the party soon died of attrition, it did constitute a warning.

Still, America could evolve; patriotism did gain in strength, particularly during and after the agonies of the Civil War, in which a nation struggled heroically to keep itself together. And no story of that time, perhaps no story of any era in the United States, characterizes America's profound sense of patriotism more than a trim but compelling book, Edward Everett Hale's *Man without a Country*. Published first in the *Atlantic Monthly* in 1863 and based roughly on the experiences of several real lives, the story involves a "fine young officer as there was in the 'legion of the West,' as the Western division of our army was then called," named Philip Nolan. The young officer from the Southwest, which was still not closely tied to the union, had gotten mixed up in some of Aaron Burr's conspiracies in 1805. When he was brought up before a court-martial with a patriotic old judge, Colonel Morgan, and the president of the court asked him at the close "whether he wished to say anything to show that he had always been faithful to the United States, he cried out, in a fit of frenzy, 'Damn the United States! I wish I may never hear of the United States again!'"

Hale then writes, in his little book that soon sold an astounding half a million copies:

> I suppose he did not know how the words shocked old Colonel Morgan, who was holding court. Half the officers who sat in it had served through the Revolution, and their lives, not to say their necks, had been risked for the very idea which he so cavalierly cursed in his madness. . . . Old Morgan, as I said, was terribly shocked. If Nolan had compared George Washington to Benedict Arnold, or had cried, "God save King George!" Morgan would not have felt worse. He called the court into his private room, and returned in fifteen minutes, with a face like a sheet, to say, "Prisoner, hear the sentence of the Court! The Court decides, subject to the approval of the President, that you never hear the name of the United States again."
>
> Nolan laughed, but nobody else laughed. . . .

This imaginary creature, invented to show the horror of not belonging to the compact of one's fellow men, was placed aboard an American naval ship. Everyone was duly instructed never, ever, to speak of America to Philip Nolan again; he was never to know the slightest detail of what happened in his lost "homeland." And from that day of September 23, 1807, until the day he died on May 11, 1863, although Nolan was a good fellow, and the naval officers liked him, he never heard her name again. "For that half-century and more he was a man without a country."

One day aboard the ship, by accident he came upon a book by Sir Walter Scott, *The Lay of the Last Minstrel,* and began innocently to read it aloud.

> *Breathes there the man, with soul so dead,*
> *Who never to himself hath said:*
> *This is my own, my native land.*

The poem ends:

> *For him no minstrel raptures swell;*
> *High though his titles, proud his name,*
> *Boundless his wealth as wish can claim,*

Despite these titles, power, and pelf,
The wretch, concentrated all in self.

And here, "the poor fellow choked, could not go on, but started up, swung the book into the sea, vanished into his stateroom and never came out for two months. . . . He never was the same man again." Some made friends with him and tried to get the federal government to rescind this terrible punishment, but "it was like getting a ghost out of prison. They pretended there was no such man, and never was such a man. . . ."

Finally, Philip Nolan, the "Man without a Country," lay dying aboard the ship that had been his "country." "Surely you will tell me something now?" he pleaded with a man there. "Stop! Stop! Do not speak till I say what I am sure you know, that there is not in this ship, that there is not in America—God bless her!—a more loyal man than I. There cannot be a man who loves the old flag as I do, or prays for it as I do, or hopes for it as I do." Then the other man relented, telling him of each and every new state, describing for him every president that had served the nation during those long years.

And at the end, on a slip of paper, the dying Nolan had written, "Bury me in the sea; it has been my home, and I love it. But will not someone set up a stone for my memory at Fort Adams or at Orleans, that my disgrace may not be more than I ought to bear? Say on it; 'In Memory of PHILIP NOLAN, Lieutenant of the Army of the United States. He loved his country as no other man has loved her; but no man deserved less at her hands.'"

Writer Hale wrings so much stark emotion out of every moment of his forty-seven-page book that the pathos at times almost overwhelms the reader—or seems quite unbelievable, particularly in terms of the lack of emotion for country on the part of American elites today. But nothing was more typical of the unapologetic grandiosity and exorbitant rhetoric of America's patriotic life in those nineteenth-century decades than that story of Philip Nolan.

☆

In 1893, the frontier was duly and officially announced "closed," and that closing marked a turning point for citizenship.

That vast and wondrous free land of the West, which had saved America so much pain through absorbing her misfits and malcontents and converting America's free energies into ranches and industries, where free men and women had sought their own fortunes, beholden to none, was soon to give way to crowded cities and to intense agricultural competition. In fact, soon America's frontiers would be moving *in* upon her—and then would come the real tests of citizenship.

The superintendent of the census announced that the United States of America no longer had a continuous line of free, unsettled land visible on the American horizon. And, although he did not actually say it, if one listens to historic voices, one knows this really meant that Americans would have to begin to live within some of the limits of other, less blessed countries. Frontier historian Frederick Jackson Turner called it the end of the "first period of American history," but it was that and much more.

Although most Americans did not realize it at the time, the closing of the frontier marked the end of America's age of innocence. Before that, America had had the greatest "escape valve" for its people and its passions of any industrializing country. But after the 1890s, America inexorably began moving toward today's different realities until, by the second half of the twentieth century, the United States had allowed itself instead to become the "escape valve" for the rest of the world.

Philosopher and columnist George Will has written perceptively that that seminal event of 1893 characterized the "perennial American tension—between nature and culture, between the idea of a self-created individual acknowledging no social bonds or debts to society and the individual as a citizen, obligated to the society that shapes him." The frontier, then, was to early American citizenship the very symbol of the space—and, thus, freedom—of the New World (if not always the discipline required to succeed there). One reason American democracy, with all its flaws, "worked" so well so fast—and why its infant citizenship was protected from even worse violence than it suffered at regular intervals—was that it offered all Americans, both citizens and aliens, a "way out" of the confines and corruptions of the cities.

Still, the end of the nineteenth century and the beginning of the twentieth marked a period of great civic culture and activity in America. Americans joined YWCAs and women's clubs, Rotaries and YMCAs, and roaring Lions' clubs and utterly boring community groups, Democratic ward organizations and Republican women's societies, settlement houses, and Christian Sunday schools and Jewish day schools; Americans were said to be so "associational" that many wondered whether, without all their endless associations, they would rightly be called citizens or, for that matter, know what to do with themselves? Farmers' wives got together in the cold winter evenings and made quilts that, stitch by stitch, told the story of their lives; folks "raised" neighbors' barns together; even in the cities, block clubs and fan clubs and girls' and boys' and wives' and husbands' clubs proliferated, and were joined in the twentieth century even by dog and cat shows.

This American "civic spirit" would come to influence the world enormously. Other peoples saw it and understood that they, too, could multiply their blessings and benefits by cooperative work and planning. Christian missionaries carried their religion to the far corners of the globe, yes, but less appreciated was the manner in which Rotary Club members, the Lions, and all the American "do-gooders" went across the seas to help their brothers and sisters over there do well, too.

In 1981, I spoke at a Rotary Club meeting in Cebu, the Philippines. In July of 1995, I was in South Korea when the Lions Clubs International were having their seventy-eighth annual convention. There were over thirty thousand Lions from 138 countries. They were from all races and religions, both genders, and they were genially slapping each other on the back; I have to confess that I was deeply moved. The civic work they do seemed to me more admirable and even wondrous (given mankind's other propensities!) when I read the "Lions Code of Ethics," including these promises, which are really the marks of the good citizen:

- To remember that in building up my business, it is not necessary to tear down another's; to be loyal to my clients or customers and true to myself.
- To hold friendship as an end and not a means. To hold that true friendship exists not on account of the service performed by one to another, but that true friendship demands nothing but accepts service in the spirit in which it is given.
- To always bear in mind my obligation as a citizen to my nation, my state and my community, and to give them my unswerv-

ing loyalty in word, act and deed. To aid my fellow men by giving sympathy to those in distress, my aid to the weak, and my substance to the needy . . .

That summer in South Korea also happened to be the summer when corruption exploded across the society, when two former presidents were imprisoned on corruption charges—and when exactly these precepts, applied, were what the prosperous but troubled society needed to right itself.

But back to America. Perhaps social thinker Charles Murray puts it best (next to the incomparable de Tocqueville, of course) in writing that

> America's political system relies on the civility of its citizens—"civility" not in the contemporary sense of mere politeness but according to an older meaning which a dictionary close at hand defines as "deference or allegiance to the social order befitting a citizen." The wording of the definition is particularly apt in the American case. Civility is not obedience but rather "allegiance" and "deference"—words with old and honorable meanings that are now largely lost. The object of these sentiments is not the government but a social order. And these things are required not of a subject but of a citizen. . . .
>
> Much of what could go under the heading of civility is not readily quantified. Mowing the lawn in the summer or keeping the sidewalks shoveled in the winter, maintaining a tolerable level of personal hygiene and grooming, returning a lost wallet, or visiting a sick friend are not entirely dictated by fear of lawsuits or of retaliation from outraged neighbors. They likely have an element of social engagement, of caring about one's neighbors and community, of what we are calling civility.

Charity has always been an important part of the moral makeup of America, being an integral part of the Christian and Jewish religious spirit. But charity has long been given personally, by individuals, by church or synagogue, and based not only upon need but upon need plus repentance. American charity was underlain by the 1834 reform of Britain's poor-law, reform that was carefully constructed so that the efforts of the poor to raise themselves up was what would be rewarded. Indeed, charity in America has been based upon four sound principles. First, aid recipients were supposed to engage in a certain level of appropriate behavior; second, all healthy people were expected to work; third, special care was given to avoiding negative incentives; and, fourth, help—charity—was given directly. Charity via religious groups and churches ensured a one-to-one contact between giver and receiver.

Respected historian Gertrude Himmelfarb traces the rationale for this arrangement back (again) to the ancient Greeks' influence on the origins of our society and to the prominent place of shame in their ethos, long before "the Christians who introduced the idea of guilt and the Victorians who combined the two in their conception of virtue." She outlines the principle of "less-eligibility," which stipulated that the condition of the "able-bodied pauper" . . . be less "eligible" or less desirable than the condition of the independent laborer; that such a pauper receive the help or charity of society in such a way that it was "stigmatized," so that he would be forced by the mores of society to straighten out his life both physically and morally. This "conditional" charity was almost always the only form of charity available to the individual citizen, and as a matter of fact it worked in bringing millions of poor and indigent into the working class and their children into the middle classes.

Citizenship and participation in society then in general depended upon the all-important mediating institutions—schools, churches, community organizations, the military—which did the actual work of citizenship training as well as the important assimilation of aliens. Civics education in the schools was a serious thing. Immigrants poured into the country, but they met a strong "Americanization" movement; if we judge from the majority of reports and experiences, they largely welcomed it because it helped them to "belong" more quickly. As Allan Bloom writes in *The Closing of the American Mind* about the early immigrant experience, "the immigrant had to put behind him the claims of the Old World in favor of a new and easily-acquired education. This did not necessarily mean abandoning old daily habits or religions, but it did mean subordinating them to new principles. There was a tendency, if not a necessity, to homogenize nature itself."

World War I was not enough to destroy citizenship. Incredibly, the Great Depression, even through all its suffering and humiliation, was not enough to do it. Even World War II, with its hideous mass murder and the sacrifices that America and so many other nations made, was not big enough to do so. But one terrible and seemingly endless event in this century's history had an inordinate and as yet largely unrecognized effect on American citizenship: That event was the cold war, stretching from 1917 to somewhere between 1989 and 1992 and involving America in a standoff with the world's other superpower, the USSR.

☆

The conflict—and the weaknesses it uncovered—finally destroyed Soviet Communism. We are well aware of that today; we see pictures of Russian attempts at democracy and capitalism in newspapers and on television. We hear that many of their best youth are infected with Western ideals, however imperfectly.

But most of us little realize the effects on America of that immense and largely nonviolent conflict that somberly dragged on for more than seventy long years. Most important, most Americans little realize how that persistent and unrelenting grappling with the other universalist ideology affected America. They tend to see only the more overt military and political threat of the Soviet Union, not the intensity and effectiveness of its ideological messages and their capacity for transforming even our society, destroying what had been and come before.

This statement is not meant to resurrect McCarthyism or to encourage looking for "Reds" in every corner; the intent is to discuss the perfectly natural and even inevitable influence of one ideology upon another. This can be particularly dangerous during periods of heightened emotions and exaggerated tensions. What actually happened in terms of culture was far much more serious and insidious on *both* sides than the outer military and security confrontations; the two ideological giants never fought an all-out war, but after 1917—and particularly after 1945—they invaded each other culturally, intellectually, and psychologically.

Mother Russia and Communism were constructed around the idea of implacable class warfare, collective responsibility, collective redemption, "one truth," total control from above and no questioning from below. It was simply a continuation of old Russian czarism, in which insignificant individuals lose themselves in a mystic collective bond with an all-powerful leader. That these ideas ran counter to American individualism, man's one-on-one relationship with God, and human freedom—leading to governments made by and for man—hardly needs to be said. What does need to be said is that it was certainly not unnatural at all that ideas and influences flowed back and forth between combatants in a great conflict that had some noble intentions on both sides; such conflicts usually do.

That is the way the world works, the way empires and religions infiltrate and change one another, until in any conflict each side inevitably takes on some of the characteristics of the other, as in any "marriage." That is also the reason for wise people saying in different ways down through history, "Be careful of what you hate too much."

Indeed, that is what occurs with the grappling of ideologies, whether it be Roman Catholicism and Protestantism, Buddhism and Confucianism, or Islam and Hinduism. Waves of influence and ideas flow back and forth; changes begin around the edges, move to the center of the "other's" beliefs; and, finally, the stronger, or the more ruthless, or the more seemingly true faith overwhelms and overcomes.

Just as democratic and free-enterprise ideas infiltrated the Russians (often, with deliberate help from Western "information" agencies), so did Marxism's leftist or collectivist ideas affect American universities, unions, churches, bureacracies, and corporations (with the help of Soviet intelligence and intellectual agencies). It was a time, after all, when America's youth and its intellectuals regularly and romantically visited Cuba, Russia's Third World surrogate in the Americas, and when very carefully selected Soviets were permitted to visit the West. Three whole American generations, often its best students and thinkers and even labor leaders, were formed with a Marxist component to their thoughts and actions, often without their even knowing it. And this thinking would enormously influence the practice and process of American citizenship.

☆

Communism *anywhere*—whether in Moscow, Budapest, Luanda, Hanoi, or Pyongyang—could have an impact on the evolution of American citizenship. The differences in the Communist and

American systems were illuminated most dramatically to me one day in 1991 in (strangely enough) Seoul, South Korea.

That day, two other Western journalists and I went to talk with the notorious "Miss Kim," a prime North Korean agent who had proudly placed a bomb on a plane over the Persian Gulf on November 29, 1987. All 115 passengers and crew simply disappeared from this earth, but Miss Kim Hyon-hui and her fellow male agent were apprehended in Bahrain. Gradually, particularly when she was taken to Seoul and saw that everything she had been told about South Korea was a lie, she began to think back on her "formation" under the charismatic, messianic, and cruel dictatorship of Kim Il Sung and what "belonging" to that sinister régime had meant.

"When I was born," this beautiful young woman, still looking very troubled, began to tell us that day in a safe house in Seoul, "the first phrase I learned was 'Kim Il Sung.' From kindergarten through the People's School and the university, all subjects concentrated on Kim Il Sung. Besides the studies, everything in society—movies, parties, prayer—all were organized around the subject of Kim Il Sung. They didn't teach anything but Kim Il Sung. I had no choice but to believe that he was the 'Great Leader' and the most important person in the world. So I came to believe that my happiness lay in my loyalty to Kim Il Sung, even at the cost of my life." When the brutal North Korean intelligence recruited her, "I was proud of it at the time," she went on, speaking softly, "especially when I was given the mission to bomb the plane. I was so delighted and proud because, even among the agents, it was difficult to get the mission.

"You see," she continued, "when I was recruited as an agent, I left my family. This meant I was not the daughter of my parents anymore, I was the daughter of the Party. If I had accomplished the mission successfully and returned, I would have been a heroine in North Korea." Kim's trip out of the totalitarian mind control of that Communist state, which could not be more different from the American mind-set, was one of extraordinary pain. "When anyone comes to know the world outside," she murmured at the end, "it is very difficult to remain under the dictatorship."

Her interrogation was the hardest thing of her life, because, as with so many who had been shaped by the unrelenting pressures of Communist "formation," the ability to change one's allegiance was never considered an alternative. "I was at the edge of the cliff," she went on, "and I had to realize that the mission to bomb the plane was not for the purpose of reunification of the North and the South but just a killing of my brethren. It was the most conflicted time of my life. After eight days, I confessed." By the time we talked with her, she was trying devoutly to be a Christian: she prayed, she confessed, she tried desperately to find a substitute for the "true faith" she had known.

It was not easy. The Communist form of "citizenship"—whose compulsions, after all, are those of any messianic régime that proclaims to be the "true faith"—leaves its citizen no voluntary will, no respite, no retreat, and no exit.

☆

In approximately the same years that Communism was building in Russia, a movement was building in America that, while certainly not Marxist, had some of the same tendencies in a Western context toward moving power away from the radical individualism of the past and toward an increasingly powerful state, making the individual more and more dependent upon that central power. This "Progressive" movement began as a healthy and respected reform movement, with the building of bureaucratic government to regulate the abuses of giant corporations. The fine journalist and historian Michael Barone has written that "the narrative continues as politicians built a bigger, more active government to meet the challenges of World War I, the Depression, World War II, the Cold War and civil rights."

Franklin D. Roosevelt's New Deal of course built upon the Progressive movement, as government expanded still further to meet first the needs of Americans during the Great Depression and then the centralized production needs of World War II. But "Progressivism" also had a cultural component, which was in many ways an Americanized version—contorted and adapted—of Marxism's idea that society could be transformed by changing the culture: the Sardinian Antonio Gramsci's "march through the culture." According to this theory, those holding views antithetical to the American way of life would destroy democracy, Christianity, and capitalism by infiltrating and rending impotent every tenet of the culture. In fact, if one listened carefully to Progressivism, one could begin to hear in the background, like a modern Greek chorus that keeps appearing mysteriously onstage out of nowhere and then disappearing, warnings of the "multiculturalism" to come later in the century.

The main early proponent of such change was a "progressive" Jewish philosopher named Horace Kallen, influenced by the pragmatism of William James and John Dewey and disgusted by the harsh "Americanization" movement of World War I; in the 1920s and '30s he was writing that the true ideal of American identity was found not in traditional individual-merit citizenship but in "cultural pluralism." Kallen thought that the United States might be a "federal republic" in form but that it should be a "democracy of nationalities" in fact. Kallen wanted a commonwealth of numerous organized communities that would cooperate voluntarily in the "enterprise of self-realization" (early "New Age" thinking) within culturally distinctive but mutually respectful ancestral groups (early "ethnic rights" groups). In his influential *Culture and Democracy in the United States,* Kallen argued the utopians' eternal and impossible dream: that an enlightened citizen, educated by the experience of diversity, would be "essentially a citizen of the world."

The first warning shot had been fired. The cultural conflagration that would ignite America in the sixties—that would threaten what had constituted "America" with the first change in American culture since its inception in 1776—had begun. And by the 1990s, Michael Barone would write that "government keeps getting more intrusive. Big bureacracies managed by a new mandarin class stifle the creativity of small entrepreneurs, while new technologies make old hierarchies unnecessary."

☆

The new welfare laws and regulations beginning largely in the thirties under the New Deal, resulting in the enormous spread of a government-run welfare society in place of the old private and individualized charities, made the recipients (the increasingly putative "citizens") more and more dependent on the government, while they also effectively isolated the recipients from the manners and behavior that could have helped them escape long-term public "assistance."

Surely not many Americans—not even many academics or politicians—were aware of how this new "welfare state" would affect
citizenship. It was not the intent of most of the Rooseveltian thinkers and doers that their government-sponsored largess would come
in time to demean and diminish the importance of citizenship. Their
intent was the opposite: that a "safety net" provided by government
for the poor would solidify and cement together the polity and
populace. It didn't work out that way. In *Citizenship without Consent*,
Peter H. Schuck and Rogers M. Smith trace how, under the New
Deal and into the 1960s and '70s, the federal government became the
creator and guarantor of "valuable legal statuses and entitlements
enforceable by individuals and groups against public resources."
The federal government emerged as "a major source of wealth . . .
a gigantic syphon. . . . It draws in revenue and power, and pours
forth wealth: money, benefits, services, contracts, franchises, and
licenses. Government has always had this function. But while in
early times it was minor, today's distribution of largess is on a vast,
imperial scale. . . . The law has increasingly expanded the scope of
individual and governmental liability. . . . The law also increasingly
speaks of individuals' 'rights,' the language of entitlement, rather
than those of 'interests,' the language of policy and accommodation.
Moreover, the law increasingly emphasizes the values of equality,
group interest, and non-discrimination."

And, "as to welfare state membership, the individual's actual
consent is virtually automatic and to that extent meaningless. The
price for joining, after all, is almost zero, while the advantages
have never been greater and in some cases may overwhelm all
other considerations." Thus the "norm" for American society has
moved from the autonomous, self-determining citizen to the state-
encouraged dependent.

☆

No change in the United States had a greater impact on citizenship
than the transformation of the system of civic education in the
schools: history, civics, geography, American literature, all the
subjects that had hitherto created citizens out of the lonely crowd.
The decade of the 1960s is an easy target for blame, but in fact
strands of this change in civic education appeared quite earlier, in
the 1930s and particularly after World War II.

The late Morris Janowitz, a professor at the University of Chicago and probably the country's preeminent scholar of citizenship, has traced how "the Great Depression weakened the system of civic education. Tensions and strains of economic collapse undermined social and political consensus. Fragmentation in civic education started to develop during the New Deal and became the norm in the years after World War II. . . . The decline in civic education after 1945 was fashioned to a considerable extent by 'intellectuals' and teachers more concerned with immediate political issues than with an educational format for understanding the long-term trends in the American 'experience.'"

Janowitz continues: "In fact, in the period 1945–75, they were able to transform the curriculum. They were almost able to eliminate that part which deals with the positive and enduring heritage of the political system of the United States. . . . Appeals to patriotism were no longer heard, and little attention was paid to their appropriate reformulation for an interdependent world community."

Among the "new directions" to emerge was the "new communalism," which meant that a far greater "emphasis on ethnic and racial nationalism momentarily outweighed concern with national citizenship. . . ."

At the same time, the teaching of social studies, the very bulwark of citizenship training, was changing dangerously. "After World War II," Janowitz writes,

> social studies changed in content and contributed to the delegitimization of social and political institutions. . . . Elements of the teaching faculty encouraged student confrontation in the name of civil and economic rights, echoing the ethnic and racial nationalists' argument that the strategy of acculturation had failed to assist submerged minorities. During the period of the "new communalism," social studies came to be used to support—but without lasting success—a separatist political ideology that was incompatible with civic education in a democratic polity.

In the primary schools, the hoary *McGuffey Readers,* which had emphasized ethics and morality—what it meant to take an oath,

personal and community civility, honesty, and responsibility—
were disdainfully discarded by the new fashionable new elites. In
their place came the self-interested, self-esteem-focused, "victim"
books that today infect America's schools. William Bennett,
America's wise man, further points out that it was in the sixties and
early seventies that "values clarification" programs started turning up in schools all across America. No longer basing teaching on
sound moral values, teachers encouraged children to "clarify" their
own values (which adults had no "right" to criticize). This strange
movement clarified only wants and desires, in Bennett's opinion:
"This form of moral relativism said that everybody had an equal
right to his own values: all were subjective, relative, personal. . . ."

But even as citizenship was becoming co-opted by the ideologues of the Left, it was also becoming commercialized by the
businessmen of the Right. The idea that citizenship was a noble and
even sacred compact began to give way to an idea of citizenship-
as-commodity. Citizenship was a "product," like soap." In short,
to choose to become a citizen or remain an alien was not much different from choosing what to buy for dinner or what shirt to wear
to impress a potential boss.

The war and the Depression were over—Americans were living for "today." Children began to be raised permissively (a direct
harbinger of today's "permissive naturalization"). The draft, which
was such a training in citizenship for so many, particularly new
immigrants, was over. Charity changed: In sharp contrast to the
mores evident at the country's founding and throughout most of
its history, the giver now not only had no moral right to expect
anything, but he or she was not even supposed to ask for reasonable civic behavior in return for largess. The idea of "direct
democracy" was in the air (and, how many fashionable Americans
knew that it had begun with Mussolini?). "Experts" began taking
over from the tradition-linked "common sense" of Americans.
Patriotic celebrations began what would become a sharp decline
in spirit into cheap, plastic "Elvis" observations, with fleeting emotions. It was the beginning of the "rock age" and the start of the
youth culture that would deconstruct everything in the turbulent
1960s and '70s. An implicit and perverse agreement began to rise

within the new youth culture that all cultures were basically alike and that all people, if left alone by the bad older generation, would live together in harmonious diversified felicity!

In the early twentieth century, citizenship in particular and participation in society in general had depended upon the all-important mediating institutions—schools, churches, community organizations, the military—that did the actual work of assimilation. But, as the century progressed, those organizations, almost unique in American society and utterly crucial to the workings of a democratic society, as well as to the existence of an informed citizenship, soon began to disappear in the miasmic confusion of a new society, one that seemed too often to be without limits and without the old forms.

Indeed, from the Great Depression through World War II, then into the cultural age of the hippie and *On the Road* and the Vietnam War, everywhere one looked there seemed to be a kind of deliberate Balkanization going on.

☆

The new media were also changing the country. Newspapers and radio had brought a sense of community, maybe a sense of nationality. But when television invaded the nation's mind in the 1950s and '60s, it would create not only a new and different communications medium, it would create a different type of American. The new communications created a world which was, in the words of the consummate analyst of that era, Neil Postman, "a 'language' that denied interconnectedness, proceeded without context, argued the irrelevance of history, explained nothing and offered fascination in place of complexity and coherence. Theirs was a duet of image and instancy, and together they played the tune of a new kind of public discourse in America. . . . Television, in other words, is transforming our culture into one vast arena for show business."

On every level, appeals were made not to the old "America" but to many Americas. Markets were no longer able to target simply "one" America but had to try to choose young or old, male or female, urban or suburban or exurban. . . . No one could even figure out anymore what media to use to target whom or what, the society was so fractured.

The cultural institutions of American society too began to engage in a disastrous dividing of the society, so much so that the columnist Charles Krauthammer could write, "Our great national achievement—fashioning a common citizenship and identity for a multi-ethnic, multilingual, multi-racial people—is now threatened by a process of relentless, deliberate Balkanization. The great engines of social life—the law, the schools, the arts—are systematically encouraging the division of America into racial, ethnic and gender separations." Had "We, the people!" become "We, the interest groups"?

☆

All of these trends came into their own in the sixties. Surely too many excesses have been blamed on that miserable decade, but it is important in any discussion of citizenship. Indeed, the *Oxford English Dictionary* by 1961 was describing citizenship in modern terms as devoid of duties and responsibilities, merely as "the position or status of being a citizen with its rights and privileges"!

On the surface, America was being torn apart by a horrendously unpopular war in Vietnam, by assassinations of political figures one after the other, and by an antiestablishment youth culture rampage that was to transmogrify American culture. Social disintegration seemed the order of the day and, with it, the loss of that old, unifying sense of national identity that allowed and encouraged man to promote the common good. The Left began emphasizing individual and group rights and entitlement everywhere at the expense of individual and community responsibility; at the same time, the country was being demographically transformed as large Hispanic and Asian minorities suddenly arrived in America, legally and illegally, but virtually all of them without the prospect of any real assimilation training or socialization into American life.

In the early years of our country, the American genius regarding assimilation was clearly to allow and even to encourage immigrants to keep their traditional ethnic and religious habits and to observe them and even enshrine them, if they wished, in their homes, places of worship or communities. But at the same time that this nation afforded them the freedom to hold on to these customs or leave them behind, it also unashamedly demanded, as only fair exchange for the security and opportunity of America, allegiance to the new, central concepts that brought Americans together in one interconnected and intercommitted political people.

That fine balance was totally and woefully upset when the strong, dominating local political party organizations, which had for so long helped immigrants assimilate and adjust, were replaced by amorphous national television-dependent parties with weak local roots and also by civil rights institutions that effectively—and disastrously—offered new ethnic groups powerful incentives to define themselves now not as one of many ethnic groups, remembering or forgetting their past to whatever degree, but as racially oppressed minorities dependent upon politicizing that past—and being well paid for it!

Immigrants began to lack the inclination to assimilate, and it was hardly their fault, since the United States seemed so ambivalent about the benefits and beauties of its citizenship. The activists who entered the scene in the sixties pretended in their New Left ideology to see no difference between the abilities of diverse peoples. They were equally intent, in their "new utopianism" of "radical egalitarianism" on ignoring any separation between the citizen and the immigrant. The entire history of the nation was simply ignored—or, in the popular and revealing parlance, "deconstructed," taken apart block by spiritual block.

Yet, those of us who were actually working in other cultures, actually out there covering other societies and nation-states, knew that these ideas were all absurd. Every society, every language, every historic memory: all are different. "Different" doesn't mean "not equal," although some ideologues might accuse those of us using that word of making that judgment.

A wise young editor I knew recalled how the impetus for the changes of the 1960s did not stem from young people's idea of overthrowing the existing government; in fact, they saw themselves as "loyal" to their country. Rather, there was a "weird parental dynamic operative in the United States in the sixties, which gave rise to a pure-principle rebellion."

Now, manners were suddenly gone, and discipline had all but vanished from a society that more and more lacked or despised authority. American cities, already plagued by drugs, crumbling infrastructures and crime, began crackdowns against public urination.

"We have conducted a thirty-year experiment in desublimation," Fred Siegel, the Cooper Union social historian, said at one point in the devolution of the new America, "Everyone gets to act out. There are no consensuses. It's been a disaster."

The fictional Kent Amos, who was created by the perceptive columnist William Raspberry as his generic "committed family man," has laid out the dilemma that faces Americans. Raspberry's Amos says in one of his columns:

> "Now, adult neighbors often don't know each other, let alone one another's children. Families are dispersed. There are no neighborhoods and communities as before. The church community is scattered, parishioners often driving many miles to service and then back home, and the churches themselves may be dabbling in everything from politics to real estate development. The government has lost its ability to serve the needs of its constituents in a covenant relationship, as opposed to a process relationship."

It was just that covenant, which was close to a sacred bond between man and man in citizenship, that the men of the Constitutional Convention of 1787 had envisioned. But that bond had become Kent Amos's "process relationship," one based on what you can get from someone or something, including the government. Working hard to get something is not necessarily encouraged today.

Myron Magnet, an editor of *Fortune*, has written of the sixties legacy to the underclass: "During the '60s and '70s, the new culture of the Haves, in its quest for personal liberations, withdrew respect from the behavior and attitudes that have traditionally boosted people up the economic ladder—deferral of gratification, sobriety, thrift, dogged industry, and so on through the whole catalogue of antique-sounding bourgeois virtues." Then he quoted social thinker Irving Kristol as saying that "it's hard to rise above poverty if society keeps deriding the human qualities that allow you to escape from it."

One day in the summer of 1995 in Washington, I saw the juxtaposition of two mind pictures that shocked me into a deep understanding of how far we have strayed from our original purpose as a nation. First, I was walking by the great old post office downtown on Massachusetts Avenue, one of those grand public buildings that the early Americans so loved, and I noticed for the first time a lovely message engraved on one corner: "MESSENGER OF SYMPATHY AND LOVE, SERVANT OF THE PARTED FRIEND, CONSOLER OF THE LONELY, BOND OF THE SCATTERED FAMILY, ENLARGER OF THE COMMON LIFE." I was deeply touched.

Five minutes later, driving home down Constitution Avenue, I saw three strapping, healthy, young "homeless" men, wearing only their undershorts, spreading out their wet clothes all over all the bushes around one of the capital's glorious marble fountains. They had just washed their clothes in the fountain.

"Citizenship, strictly speaking, has always been a legal statute, nothing more," Georgetown University philosopher Phil Gold ruminated with me one day. "What perhaps is dead is civic or public virtue, or the qualities needed to make citizenship a living, effective thing. It's so dead that we don't even have words for what we've lost. Bad as that is, the other half of the equation is even worse: Is this a society where civic virtue is even possible any longer?"

☆

By the 1990s, the American people of course knew that something had gone very wrong. Social isolation was intense—one-fourth of American households consisted of a single person, up from 8 percent in 1940. Volunteering was down by one-sixth; trust was down by one-third. Harvard Professor Robert Putnam created a tempest by saying that Americans were so lonely they were (the ultimate!) *bowling alone!*

Superpollster Daniel Yankelovich compared polling in values, between 1950 and 1990, and he found America had moved in those years from production to consumption, from future gratification to immediate gratification, from sacrifice to greed, from public interest to self-interest, from quality to quantity, from a concern with the long-term to a concern with the short-term. Former Colorado Governor Richard Lamm also tallied up the changes in those key years and found America moving from saving to spending, from delayed to instant gratification, from Ozzie and Harriet to latch-key kids, from certainty to ambivalence, from orthodoxy to skepticism, from investing to leveraging, from neighborhood to lifestyle, from export to import, from public virtue to personal well-being. And that was only the beginning.

When Republican scholar William Bennett began compiling the contents of his *Index of Leading Cultural Indicators* in 1994, in order to provide "an empirical assessment of the condition of America question," he found "substantial social regression" and a nation giving way to it. During the thirty-year period from 1960 onward, he traced a 560 percent increase in violent crime, more than a 400 percent increase in illegitimate births, a quadrupling in divorce rates, a tripling of the percentage of children living in single-parent homes, a drop of almost eighty points in the SAT scores. . . .

And, the "whys" were not at all mysterious to some of the best—and least mentally logjammed—American thinkers.

According to social scientist James Q. Wilson, after post–World War II permissiveness and the sixties explosion of me-ness, "the powers exercised by the institutions of social control have been constrained and people, especially young people, have embraced an ethos that values self-expression over self-control." Daniel Yankelovich found further that our society now places less value than before on what we owe others as a matter of moral obligation, on sacrifice as a moral good, on social conformity, respectability and observing the rules, and on correctness and restraint in matters of physical pleasure and sexuality. The higher value is placed on self-expression, individualism, self-realization, and personal choice.

Other analysts have found a decline in professional values among lawyers, bankers, stockbrokers, and doctors and have analyzed this as part of a collapse in commitment to ideals, as well as a diminishing of the belief that it is appropriate to do your job in an ethical fashion. And a study released by the Times Mirror Center in California in 1994 shows Americans responding by saying they're tired of being nice to their fellow residents (interestingly enough, the word "citizen" was not used). They were fed up with the homeless, the welfare cheats, all those "lazy people" who were eternally whining. That was no surprise; the noble old charitable impulses not only had been pushed too far, but also could no longer connect with genuine need in American society.

An examination of these indicators reveals that every one of them involves citizenship and its commitments. Whereas Americans used to see government as an extension of self, they now see government as "the state," almost as isolated from them as the Soviet state had been from the Soviet people. Those findings constitute the outer warning signal of the real inner problem. That problem is the death of the social compact.

But the hopeful factor is that many, many Americans are also really angry, not passively accepting changes they see as detrimental. Nor, as is so often commonly thought, are Americans lacking in passion or in the civic virtue that the Founding Fathers had insisted upon as the very soil to make democracy possible. To the contrary, even as they feel pushed out of almost every area of the political process, they still believe that they have, in their own neighborhoods, a "wellspring of civic responsibility that nobody is tapping into," in the words of the important Kettering Foundation report on citizenship. Many indicators show that large numbers of Americans still want to behave like *citizens*, whereas factors in American life are instead pushing them again to be *subjects*.

Meanwhile, the process of American citizenship has been dumbed down, simplified, and politicized beyond most Americans' knowledge—or belief.

☆
☆ ☆

4

The New Business of Citizenship

If people knew what was really going on, they'd be amazed.
Mike Miller, retired "historian" of the Immigration and
Naturalization Service (1994)

We have to do as much as we can to promote naturalization. . . .
Naturalization helps counteract anti-immigrant attitudes.
Doris Meissner, commissioner of the INS (1994)

Nowhere can we find a better example of how far we have strayed
from our origins as a nation than in our naturalization process in
general and in our citizenship testing in particular. Most important, nowhere can we better see the characteristics of our next generation of citizens.

The mechanics of citizenship—the "nuts and bolts" behind its
spirit and soul, the *process* by which the subject becomes citizen,
the transformative experience by which the stranger becomes one's
fellow—is where the future takes form. But the entire process of
testing has been dumbed down, and the dignity of citizenship, to
use Daniel Patrick Moynihan's famous term, "defined down."

To understand what we have come to, let us look at one of the
places in today's national life where any of the old nobility and
grandeur of citizenship is still found: Monticello, the home of
Thomas Jefferson in southern Virginia.

More than two centuries after his death, July 4, 1994, dawned
with a heavy curtain of mist and light fog hovering over the beautiful green hills that had been Jefferson's New World home. But
soon after 9 A.M., as the searing summer heat of this part of the
American South began to break the hold of the lingering fog, the
dim whiteness that had hung over the mountains began to lift,

exposing to view the new citizens who had come to take the Oath of Allegiance to the United States of America at this quintessentially "American" spot.

The mood of harmony and hope was a perfect one for new citizens, and Jefferson's exquisite home, Monticello, was the perfect spot to be inducted into and joined with the American polity. Even after two hundred years, the house still uniquely reflected that amazing Renaissance man and his approach to life and history. Georgian in architecture, it exhibits both a sedate look of permanence, with its solid red brick, and the look of a soaring eagle, with its elegant white dome and neoclassic pillars.

Jefferson, born in 1743 in Virginia, was known as "musician, draftsman, surveyor, astronomer, natural philosopher, jurist and statesman"; he searched the world not only for ideas and philosophies that would bring mankind together under accepted rules, but for beauty—Monticello's design, for instance, was based upon the ancient temple of Vesta in Rome. Widely celebrated as the "architect" of American democracy throughout the world, Jefferson was the "American Leonardo," the quintessential American of his era, a man who honored science but who also found truth in history and inside man's natural self.

Typically, Jefferson had built his beautiful home on a hilltop in the backwoods of the New World, three thousand miles away from European civilization. Yet, even there at home—in every move he made, every invention he imagined and gave birth to, and every new principle of democratic life that he followed—he always harkened back doggedly to correct forms. He fervently believed that those forms were above all "natural" to man, at least when blessed with institutions that allowed him to express his better soul.

Midmorning, sixty-two men, women, and babies from twenty-four countries—from the United Kingdom to Vietnam, and from India to Germany—slowly began to make their way to the top of Jefferson's mountain. All were neatly dressed and perfectly behaved as they rode in small buses up the side of the mountain, before taking their seats in long rows that stretched across the dewy lawns. A feeling of reverence suffused the day. Soon, the Charlottesville Band began playing patriotic songs while the sun shone brightly, which it did gamely for the rest of the day.

In short, this was the perfect day, for the perfect American naturalization ceremony, in the perfect American place.

Soon the black-robed judges came and stood in a formal line, while the speaker, the elegant American historian David McCullough, his handsome gray head symbolizing the dignity of the day, began to talk about Thomas Jefferson, about America then and now—and about citizenship.

As he spoke, McCullough "remembered" the summer of 1776: It was a terribly hot summer, with a mood of expectation about it, and Jefferson's wife, Martha, was, again, very sick. How Jefferson yearned to be with his wife at Monticello, to be there in the cool mornings with the exquisite views of the Virginia countryside all around him! But his beloved friend John Adams had insisted that he must write the Declaration of Independence, and so, of course, he followed the commands of his "duty" and did exactly that, in Philadelphia.

"To Jefferson alone fell the task of putting it into words," McCullough began. "There he sat in a Windsor chair in a two-room apartment on Market Street. . . ." There he sat, declaring first with his mind and then with his pen that "all men are created equal. . . ." Soon he was changing the practical John Locke's "life, liberty and property" to "life, liberty and the pursuit of happiness." While others rested in the devastating heat of that summer, Jefferson worked without complaint for a citizenry different from any the world had ever known.

His was a passionate temperament, and he expressed his passions in many ways: in music, the passion of his soul; in mathematics, the passion of his mind; and in politics, the passion of his reason. But his was also a respectful temperament: generous and courteous to other men. And at age thirty-three, what responsibilities he had!

Perhaps most important about Jefferson's travails that historic summer was the fact that he was not led astray by the idea of creating something totally "new in history." Those words later, in the twentieth century, would cause quite enough agony and perversion with the Marxists, revolutionaries, and utopians—who were always trying to start again at the "beginning of history." No, as Thomas Jefferson drafted the declaration of principles for the new state, in terms of philosophy he saw himself as writing not to impose even his or the Founding Fathers' principles but to awaken those principles already waiting for liberation within mankind's nature—"not to find new principles but to put these before people as an expression of the American mind," as McCullough put it.

Remember, the historian went on, Jefferson stressed the term "self-evident." He was not dealing in artificial creations or creatures. No, these were *natural principles*, based upon *natural laws*. To him and indeed to all of the Founding Fathers, all men were truly created equal and endowed with certain inalienable rights—that phrase did not need to be underlined or in quotes.

"Sadly, too, many take the principles for granted, not realizing that they were very novel—very daring—ideas for that time," McCullough went on, "yet, never anywhere in the world had there ever been a government instituted on these principles."

In short, "the Declaration of Independence was not a creation of the gods but of . . . very brave men . . . staking their lives on what they believed." They were "men of honor," which meant that their word, once given, would never be broken. It was the badge of their integrity.

The concepts of their document were not limited to one race, religion, creed, or national origin: they emerged from the spirit and soul of man—not, as in authoritarian governments or dictatorships, imposed from above, but rather to be awakened from below. Moreover, the Founding Fathers fully believed that every human being and every human group, once freed from tyranny, could and would spontaneously embrace these precepts.

These kinds of ideas that would span American history were not reserved to the revolutionary phase of American history. Later, in 1915, President Woodrow Wilson would reflect on similar ideas in a speech to newly naturalized citizens who had just sworn allegiance. Of these new citizens, he said, "They had vowed loyalty to no one, only to a great ideal, to a great body of principles, to a great hope of the human race." Then he voiced a warning for Americans today. "Think first of humanity," he advised, "so as not to divide people into nationalistic camps."

And there, at the very heart of the matter, is what both old Americans and the newest of Americans should have in common. Or, as a friend said once, "My grandparents came to America in 1905, but my political ancestors came with the Pilgrims."

Thomas Jefferson lived from 1743 to 1826. His was an exemplary life; and, for the most part, he lived as he believed. In recent years, Jefferson has been retroactively criticized for holding slaves, for his apparent love affair with a beautiful slave on his own plantation, but, far from diminishing his political legacy, such imperfections only underline the deficiencies of the best of us. On the larger scale of history, he and the other Founding Fathers were blessed men, they shared in the truest brotherhood of man with a dignity and goodness seldom witnessed in history. Indeed, theirs was a brotherhood of ideas that did not enslave their fellow man but ultimately freed everyone. And that brotherhood was perhaps never so exquisitely revealed as at the moment when Jefferson lay dying. Unbeknownst to Jefferson, his beloved conspirator in human freedom John Adams also lay dying.

Jefferson had been asked to speak at the fiftieth anniversary of the signing of the Declaration of Independence, but he was too weak and sick to leave Monticello. He did write a last letter, saying that

> it adds sensibly to the sufferings of sickness to be deprived by it of a personal participation in the rejoicings of that day. . . . I should, indeed, with peculiar delight, have met and exchanged there congratulations personally with the small band, the remnant of that host of worthies, who joined with us on that day, in the bold and doubtful election we were to make for our country, between submission or the word; and to have enjoyed with them the consolatory fact that our fellow citizens, after half a century of experience and prosperity, continue to approve the choice we made.

Both Jefferson and John Adams were determined to remain alive for this fiftieth anniversary. Both lived to see it—but only barely. Jefferson died first, early on the Fourth, saying, "Oh God!" And then, "No, nothing more!" Just before John Adams died later that same fateful day, his own noble last words, uncomprehending of the bitter reality, were "Thomas Jefferson still survives."

Once McCullough's inspirational speech was over, an imposing Yankee judge named James H. Michael Jr., who had presided over the giving of the Oath of Allegiance to the United States of

America at Monticello for many years, heartily welcomed the new citizens. He praised what they could and would bring to America from their former cultures. But then he said pointedly, in words that are the exact antithesis of so much of current naturalization process and thinking: "Today you are Americans. You may describe yourself as 'an American of Cambodian descent,' but first, last and always you are now American!"

The transformation had begun—with dignity, respect, and hope.

☆

While one can still find ceremonies like that one at Monticello, they no longer are the norm.

In terms of sheer numbers, administrative ceremonies (administered by the Immigration and Naturalization Service) have taken over from judicial ceremonies (administered by the courts under the Department of Justice). At the same time, the INS has embraced "standardized testing" in place of the old and more probing personal interviews. As we dumb down and drag down, the standardized testers have, in turn, given parts of the testing and even the actual *approval* of the tests to special-interest lobbies and even to commercial enterprises who are paid for the most unusual "pleasure" of creating new Americans.

As to the testing, petitioners are given so many chances to pass an ever more oversimplified test that any reasonably normal person could hardly fail it. A petitioner's command of English is tested far less nowadays than earlier, the spelling of the English language is totally unimportant, and soon language tests will probably be given over the telephone (symbolizing still *more* distance between new citizen and state). Many ceremonies are already given in other languages, such as the 1994 Arizona naturalization ceremony in Spanish, and the tests themselves are given in many languages. Some of the testers even dream of tests given by computer. (It was inevitable!)

Dual citizenship, formerly not officially recognized by the U.S. government and occurring only when a child of U.S. citizens residing or traveling abroad was granted citizenship in the country where the child was born, is now accepted, with all that means in terms of divided loyalties—or, more and more often, none at all.

And so many Americans of different ethnic descents have gone back to their countries of origin to take political or military positions in the post–cold war world that the former law under which an American could lose his citizenship by serving in a foreign government is not even talked about anymore.

The "motor-voter" bill of 1993 now makes it easy even for illegal aliens to vote through registering his or her car; citizenship has become commensurate with the secular "right" of using the highways and byways. (Could one consciously think of an act more degrading to the original Founding Fathers' idea of citizenship?) And in Oregon, in the winter elections of 1996, voting by mail became possible; no longer any need for that "tiresome" old business of "going to the polls" in the company of one's neighbors. (Had someone once actually been so sentimentally "foolish" as to call voting a "ritual"?)

In short, the degree to which citizenship has been made ever easier replicates Moynihan's syndrome of lowering standards so precipitously and persistently that finally the entire system of standards is defined down to meet the ever-lowered reality, even while maintaining the illusion that the same level of competence holds. That syndrome extends from education to matrimony, personal manners, civic behavior, one's relationship to one's fellow man— until the value of everything has been squeezed out of the nation's heart and soul.

Already, most students and teachers in American classrooms never give the Pledge of Allegiance to the American flag anymore. In California, many give oaths to the Hispanic Cinco de Mayo holiday. But in what would surely be the final insult and indignity, some technocratic and utopian and *psychometric* (more on that key word later) "planners" of the INS want to see the new citizens' Oath of Allegiance to the United States actually omitted from the swearing-in ceremony. They want the immigrant to be able to pass his test, get his citizenship immediately in the same nondescript little flagless room, and then go right on over to the Passport Office with his two photos so he can leave the country as fast as possible—one-stop shopping at the Immigration Service!

In perhaps the most incredible and bizarre turn of all, after the cold war, the United States, using every vehicle from the U.S. Information Agency to new Republican and Democratic institutes to businessmen's groups, plunged into ambitious programs of "civic education" in the former Communist Bloc. From Prague to Warsaw, from Bucharest to Kazan, from Riga to even Moscow, America was teaching the former "totalitarian menace" what true civic life was all about. Only in America was it no longer taught—or practiced, for that matter.

How could this have happened?

☆

When one looks back even cursorily at the transformation of the citizenship process over the last three decades, one can rather easily see what led to the current situation.

Actually, it was soon after the American Revolution, in 1790, that the first U.S. law dealing with citizenship and naturalization gave the judiciary the power to naturalize persons as citizens of the United States of America—and the process remained remarkably the same until well into the present century. Would-be citizens moved through a distinct process: They had to apply to the Immigration and Naturalization Service for papers; then they had to take a test, face-to-face with a trained examiner, to show an appropriate knowledge of American civics and a workable knowledge of the English language.

In the early years almost all of the examiners, INS employees, were lawyers. Some were excellent, some not so good; some were generous and friendly, some unwelcoming and pedantic—but there was at least a vision of purpose to them. They represented the American government and they celebrated the voluntary allegiance of individuals to it and its precepts.

As previously mentioned, there were certain requirements written in stone. The petitioner for citizenship had to have five years' residence in the United States, be of good moral character, have an "attachment to the Constitution," and give a formal declaration of intention, as well as providing witnesses to character and intent. Most questions came from the *Federal Citizenship Textbook Series*, quite good history books prepared by the government's U.S. Printing Office. These books, while clear and factual, were unashamedly enthusiastic about America and expressed pride in its traditions. For instance, from the 1963 book:

Democracy is more than just a word in a book. It is a way of life. And like all living things, it must be carefully attended to. A democracy guided and guarded by the people it serves is a healthy democracy. A democracy ruled by a few is in danger of becoming a democracy in name only. When you are a citizen, you will be able, with your vote, to choose the people you want to represent you in government. This is the right of free people in a democracy. It is also a very serious responsibility.

Once a new immigrant had taken the oral test and passed it, he or she was ready for final papers, the naturalization ceremony, and the privilege—it was not then considered a right—of becoming a full American citizen, with all of its responsibilities and duties. In those days, many immigrants, in gaining citizenship, probably had a more emotional experience of and greater identity with the country than the native-born. So much was asked of them that their knowledge matched their intention. In those days, citizenship was most often a true milestone in a person's life.

But changes occurred in that process, nearly all of them institutional and structural—and all initiated in a spirit of goodwill and intended to adapt the INS to the times and the flow of people in various eras:

In 1906, Congress consolidated immigration and naturalization functions under a Bureau of Immigration and Naturalization, thus marking the first time that a central federal agency was made responsible for both. The examiner system began in 1907. It was also in these years that the "progressive" press and the "muck-rakers," seeing the degree to which new citizens were being pushed through the system by the Democratic Party in election years, fought for greater uniformity in the whole process, which at that point was quite chaotic; reform *was* accomplished.

In 1913, the Bureau of Immigration and Naturalization became part of the newly created Labor Department, with immigration and naturalization separated. Later, the two bureaus were consolidated into the INS, which remained within the Labor Department; and in 1940, still another reorganization took place. Because of America's fear of foreign spies, Congress moved the entire bureau to the Justice Department, where it still resides. While the INS had for years held the responsibility of determining eligibility of applicants for naturalization, actual naturalization functions were always under the jurisdiction of the courts until the watershed year of 1990.

To repeat: Each change developed, at least putatively, in tandem with the real or perceived needs of the country—economic needs, the pressures of political/ethnic organizations and relatives (still in foreign countries who wanted to come to America after other members of the family became citizens), the perceived "carrying capacity" of the nation (although that term was not then used), and, of course and probably most important, the security of the United States.

Morality and loyalty were not embarrassing concepts in those days. The Federal Bureau of Investigation was required to do a check on every potential new citizen; each person was reviewed for criminal and/or subversive activities to determine "fitness on moral and loyalty grounds" to join the American community. Petitioners for citizenship then were asked personal morals questions, such as "Have you ever perjured yourself or stolen anything?" (America's diplomat Averell Harriman used to tell friends about his wife, the famous Pamela Harriman, who had very publicly enjoyed and flaunted love affairs with many of the great men of Europe, being asked, when she took her citizenship test, "Have you ever committed adultery?" Then he would laugh like hell! His response may have been inappropriate, but this anecdote indicates the seriousness of the FBI's inquiry into personal morality.)

Since becoming a citizen of the United States was then considered a privilege, neither the INS nor the American government would ever have dreamed of actually going out to *solicit* citizens.

In fact, immigrants poured into America in those years, just as they do today, albeit in a different manner. They entered then largely New York's Ellis Island, thus creating the grand mythology of that "open door."

Three of my own grandparents came to America that way. Carl Gervens, a lovely, uneducated but natively intellectual young man from the Rhineland, came at sixteen to escape German military service; he never went back. Martha Gums Geyer, a hardworking woman of great natural charm and intelligence, came from what is now Poznan in Poland and was then the home of a substantial

German minority; only in her eighties did she even mention that she had come steerage to America. Oscar Geyer came from Tueringerwald in southeastern Germany, in the middle of Luther and Goethe territory. It may sound as if they weren't much, but as a matter of fact most of the immigrants came to America to escape Prussian drafts, to flee Greek or Italian civil wars, or to search for a better life. All of my relatives were surely transformed by America, which was the idea behind it all.

They did well by working hard, marrying, having children, and being good neighbors, which really meant being good citizens then. Carl Gervens worked in factories and, at the end of his life, with much happiness for the Field Museum; he would have been a great professor in another life. Oscar Geyer started Geyer's Dairy at Thirty-first and Lowe in the "Behind the Yards" Stockyard area, later moving it to Seventy-eighth and Carpenter on the Far South Side. "Oma" Geyer ran the dairy, in hip boots and practical clothes, during the workday; Sundays, she loved to dress in lace and silks. Yes, you're right, there was another grandmother, my mother's mother, Emmaretta Gervens; she was a stern Yankee from Upstate New York; we think she came about the time of the Mayflower from Holland.

No one spoke German much—never at home. Occasionally, I would hear Oma Geyer speaking it to her generation of folks. Oddly enough, after I graduated from Northwestern University, when I went to Vienna on a Fulbright scholarship, I soon learned to speak beautiful German; I seemed to have an "ear" for it.

In truth, much of the saga of the immigrants was not pleasant at all. Desperate people were turned back to the vagaries of the Old World because of disease or (as the century moved on and Communism and radicalism became a threat) ideological differences. Roughly a third of the immigrants who came in the first part of the century tried it, didn't like it, or couldn't make it—and turned back. Contrary to some of the myths today, large numbers spent considerable amounts of time on welfare. The difference between now and then is that previously most resisted the state dole, few came for it, and the broader society encouraged Americanization and independence.

Still, the overall story was one of tremendous success. Most important, if only because they had come so far and because the

"Americanization" movement was so strong in socializing them, the large majority never thought of leaving or of being anything other than American.

In those days, too, the Immigration and Naturalization Service was a popular service. People called it the "agency with a heart." It was personalized because of the interviewers; its personnel generally took pride in a job that they could do well because they had the manpower to do it and they had "the story." Outside of bad times, their job was one of the most wonderful jobs in the world, because it was to tell the story of America and to help to make these fellow humans beings, all of us journeying together in shadows and confusion, into actors and protagonists of the story.

And then it all began to change.

On the purely physical level, by the 1990s the INS offices themselves, which should reflect their status as the concomitantly welcoming and dignified mother agency of the naturalization ceremonies, often had an unkempt air about them. Indeed, this important agency, which oversaw and regulated all naturalization, could not even find a way to open its mail and answer its phones. Up until 1995, there were no computers to check legals, illegals, criminals, angels. The commissioner of immigration presided over an huge corporation—more than nineteen thousand employees in sixty-two offices throughout the country and three overseas—but, as the burden of numbers intensified, was never given the funds or resources to handle it.

The great majority of INS employees, agents, and investigators were a good and responsible lot: hardworking and determined. But, not surprisingly, corruption began to emerge in INS ranks— and why not? Overworked and underpaid INS employees controlled one of the greatest pieces of wealth in the world: the green cards that would give immigrants the right to stay in America.

When the *New York Times* did a long series on the INS in the winter of 1995, for instance, they discovered one corruption case , in the northern Virginia offices of the INS, that made at least that office of the agency look like a poor man's Casablanca. It related how "smooth-talking middlemen took care of the details, bribing immigration service employees with gold jewelry, free vacations and cash-filled envelopes, passed hand to hand in the aisles of a nearby department store; Ghanaians, Lebanese and Salvadorans, among others, flocked to what quickly became a multicultural bazaar. Most came from the Washington area, but others drove hundreds of miles and scribbled phony local addresses. . . ." Not surprisingly, the hands that carried all of this largess to the INS employees were the hands that left with the green cards and other documents.

☆

If there is one legend of the INS, it is Richard "Mike" Miller, who, in his thirty-six years in the bureau, informally became the "historian" of the entire service. Tall and lanky, with the sharp intelligence of the avid, self-taught man, Miller worked on the border with Mexico for four years in the late 1950s and early '60s, when it was a quiet border where "we rarely encountered any unlawful status." He saw the INS through the bracero program, which brought in certain numbers of Mexican farmworkers for limited periods of time, and he saw the INS slide to a point where, by 1986, with an investigations force of only fourteen hundred, it could not begin to stem the tides.

By the time I talked to him, he was retired and, while still filled with INS lore, was a critic more saddened than embittered about how things had changed. He first blamed the change from the beautiful and dignified court ceremony to the INS administrative ceremonies, made possible by the Immigration Act of 1990. He mused, "Under the nineteen-ninety act, individuals for the first time had the option of being sworn in in a court ceremony or in an administrative ceremony; the courts took longer, and so very few selected the courts. . . ."

Like so many changes, seemingly inconsequential at the time, this 1990 change was designed to "streamline" citizenship; although the INS tries very hard to make its naturalization ceremonies as dignified as the court ceremonies and the Monticellos always have been, they don't ever reach the same somber, inspirational level.

Indeed, one of the best INS commissioners, Alan Nelson, originally pushed administrative naturalization; but, after he visited a court ceremony in New York, he did an 180-degree turn and ended up lobbying against the new administrative process. (Incidentally, when Nelson's daughter, a native Californian then living in Washington with her parents, wanted to return to California for university training, she had to pay out-of-state tuition, although by then California was allowing illegals' children to go to school free!)

Miller added in his conversation with me that the surrender of testing to interest groups and ethnic lobbies was the next wrong step. They are largely "people with special interests gnawing at the rules," he went on, "not really caring about the integrity of the system. Hispanic groups, for instance, are big on getting the language requirements reduced. They think the INS is too tough. Some want more people exempt from American history and English. Now, one group wants aged and mentally handicapped exempt from knowledge tests. . . .

"During the legalization program after the nineteen eighty-six Reform Act, ETS [the Educational Testing Service] gained the contract to do naturalization-type testing of a majority of applicants for lawful status. The ETS got out of hand because church groups, and others, were administering the tests, and they not only read the questions, but the answers. Like, 'Who is buried in Grant's Tomb?' When we developed the request for proposals for standardized testing for the naturalization program, we tried to develop strict rules in proctoring, but . . ." He shook his head.

Miller did not mention it, but some of the advocacy groups also were lobbying the Texas legislature for birthing centers—on the American side of the U.S.–Texas border—where Mexican mothers-to-be not only can go to have children on U.S. soil, thus "born" Americans, but also can have America pay it! As unreal as it may first seem, the incontrovertible fact on America's southwestern borders is that mothers-to-be do come over, in massive numbers, just before their babies are to be born. They are almost always granted free medical care, under the Fourteenth Amendment their children are Americans, and, yes, those children in later years serve to bring in those families.

Others in the INS, even those who supported the changes, also saw the 1990 decision as *the* watershed, particularly since that also was the moment when standardized testing began; the ETS of Princeton, New Jersey, was brought in to apply that new form of testing to immigration, and then became the dominant force advocating that more and more special-interest groups be brought into the testing process.

☆

To see what happened—and how and why—one needs first to look at the citizenship test, or what is called the "New Citizens' Exam." The changes in this exam can be gleaned from even a cursory look at the materials "advertising" the tests for citizenship. As was mentioned in chapter 2, all use similar wording: "EASIER THAN EVER!"

And in a special instruction sheet on "INS and Citizenship Testing," this one from the Office of the INS commissioner in 1992, the petitioner is again assured of how *really easy* the test is being made for him. "Before outside testing," it reads, "applicants could only be quizzed during an interview with INS officials. Now, they are able to take the English literacy and civics test before their application and interview process."

It continues: "The citizenship test is a written exam in English of multiple choice questions, including two dictated sentences to be written in English. The test should take less than 45 minutes. . . . Minimum passing score will not be less than 60 percent, including satisfactory completion of one of the two dictated sentences. Questions come from the latest edition of the *Federal Citizenship Textbook Series*." Finally, it duly informs, "Retests are variations of the initial test." (In short, you have to really be a dunce to fail more than once!)

When petitioners take their tests at community centers or with community groups that have in recent years been specially cited and named to give the tests, they are informed ad infinitum that the INS will not know at all if they have passed or not. Here, one already sees an overwhelming truth about the entire devolved citizenship saga: Every benefit of the doubt is given to the would-be citizen, while none at all is given to the nation that that person supposedly has the deepest wish to join!

The debut of the standardized test on the naturalization stage marked the moment of change in citizenship, as indeed it had in all of education, defining it down ever further.

These changes really began in 1986, when the INS decided to do away with the old-version textbooks and hired a publishing firm, Miranda Associates, to revise and update the texts. They devised three different levels of texts: (1) English as a second language, (2) first-to-third-grade reading level, and (3) fourth-to-sixth-grade reading level.

"The instructions that went out to the field with delivery of the new textbooks were exactly as they were with the old series," Mike Miller recalled, "that, with the exception of questions about current officeholders, all questions had to come from the new textbooks. We had no problem if anyone wanted to memorize the texts in order to prepare for the test because they would then have a much better knowledge of the country than most natural-born citizens. Our problem was that many of our offices, without the knowledge or consent of headquarters management, began using the 'One Hundred Questions' written test developed for the Reform Act legalization applicants. Whenever we heard of an office doing this, we would immediately instruct them to cease, but I think some kept it up notwithstanding. . . ."

That did away totally with the power of the old examiner. It also meant that would-be citizens could easily find out what the tests were and did not have to do any original thinking or study. One day in the spring of 1995, I walked into the shabby offices of an allied Hispanic-interest group in Edinburg, Texas, and they automatically handed me both the test questions and the answers. I was surprised; but later I was even more surprised when Cordia Strom, officer for Congressman Lamar Smith's subcommittee on immigration, told me, "One day one of the men working in the cafeteria asked us if we would call the INS to get the test for him. I called and asked them, 'Do you give out copies of the test ahead of time?' They told me that, yes, they did—and they sent us both the test and the answers."

A sample of the questions shows how tough it is to become a citizen today: "Who was the first President of the U.S.? What is the supreme law of the land? Where is the nation's capital? Who is your congressman? How many states in the U.S.?" (Unimpressed, the *Washington Times* called it a "pop quiz.") But the technology-crazy exam mavens at the testing company told the INS examiners that each question was so sensitive, so difficult to devise, that each one cost five thousand dollars to draw up!

In fact, the skeptic or cynic might well say that the would-be citizen needed only to observe George Bush's quip that "half of life is just showing up."

But these changes also marked another passage—the passage, almost unbelievable, toward the businessization of citizenship. By the 1990s, a number of good-sized companies had entered into what we might call the "naturalization game." Too often, the resulting permissiveness toward principle or excellence mirrored what was happening in American education and other areas of "deconstructed" American life.

☆

One sunny day in July of 1994, I walked over to see George Elford at the Educational Testing Service's Washington office located in (appropriately) the 1776 Massachusetts Avenue building. The respected ETS was formed in 1947 by three professional education groups—the American Council on Education, the College Board, and the Association for the Advance of Teaching. Originally, it was only a technical agency formed to do testing, work with client groups, and build national testing programs; but, with its application of cold expertise to the warm soul of education and because of the alleged oversimplification of its tests, ETS would become deeply controversial.

A serious and pleasant man of dignified demeanor, Elford was obviously devoted to his work and proud of it. Like most of the people involved in citizenship today, as with the education establishment for many years, they are almost all nice people: that is not the problem.

"We got involved back in the days of legal immigration, in the late 1980s," he began, "when minority groups perceived INS as a big problem. They said that 'you go for the citizenship test and it's highly unpredictable. You can pass or flunk—that depends upon the examiner.'

"'That's something,' we thought, 'a minority group asking us to do a standardized test!'"

(An admittedly unworthy thought from someone from the South Side of Chicago: Might he not better have thought, "That's something, a minority group asking us to dumb down a test so they can get more citizen members?")

"Our president said then that 'we don't want to be part of the border patrol.' So, we formed a board—with members from the U.S. Catholic Conference, the Hispanic groups, others—to direct us. Our position regarding the board was 'We're here to help the immigrant community.' We worked well together. They guided us

in terms of even *approving the content of the test.* We had to negotiate a level with INS that was acceptable and realistic in terms of
what they could do."

(Another brief pause: Should it not be expected that his job primarily is to help America—the America of everyone, citizens,
would-be citizens, and even all those human beings who in the
future will come to be Americans—and not only "the immigrant
community" at any one time?)

Soon, a great part of America's naturalization process lay in the
hands of special religious and ethnic groups. Indeed, the semi-
official "Guide to the New Citizens Project" lists some of them: the
National Association of Latino Elected and Appointed Officials,
the United States Catholic Conference, Hermanadad Mexicana
Nacional, American Council for Nationalities Service, National
Council of State Directors of Adult Education, the Mexican-
American Legal Defense and Educational Fund (MALDEF), the
Association of Farmworker Opportunity Programs, the Asylum
and Refugee Rights Law Project, Washington Lawyers' Committee for Civil Rights Under Law, the National Immigration, Refugee
and Citizenship Forum, the Language Communications Associates
—and many more.

George Elford sees nothing wrong with this and indeed everything right with it. Although even he admits the interest group /
citizen testers brought a lot of pressure on ETS to replace the examiners, whom they insisted were too hard on immigrants, and
to simplify the tests, so more aliens would be accepted as citizens.

"They are very pleasant to work with," Elford says, "very
appreciative of what ETS has done. They trust us to do serious
work, and we do it. Our goal is to break even: we are a nonprofit
organization. When we began the process, we would tell them we
were thinking of doing something, but only if we could be of service. What we didn't want was to raise the stakes on them—and
we didn't. They do guide us on our policies. We sat around and
talked about what they wanted."

Elford went on: "The test makes it easier. People get two tries,
they get two sets of questions; they can bomb on one and still pass.
We operate through community-based organizations; it makes
them comfortable. No failures are reported, so you can come back
again and again. The pass rate is around eighty percent, which is
typical for minimum competency."

Was it really good to make the test so much easier?

"I think it was a good thing to do," he answered thoughtfully. "What the government wants to do is make sure people are taking an interest in the country."

(My last intrusion, I hope: I thought that these good folk *had* an interest in the country—and that was their reason for wanting to become citizens. Is it really the onerous chore of a great country to convince noncitizens to take "an interest in the country"? Is that not curiously masochistic when that country is considered the most desirable for immigration in the entire world?)

And the principles behind the test questions? Elford shook his head. "I use data," he answered. (The first time he sounded vague, I noticed, was when I asked him about this crucially important area of history and theory. On all the technical matters, Elford was very sure and precise.) "It is not fair, for instance, to ask new citizens things that American children at eleventh grade don't know. I went through the textbooks they used, and then used my own personal judgment. I'm not myself fresh on the Gadsden Purchase, for instance—so I wouldn't use that."

(Truly my last parenthetical comment: It is a good thing he did not use the Gadsden Purchase! James Gadsden happened to be the U.S. minister to Mexico in 1853 and the gentleman who "bought" some thirty thousand square miles of northern Mexico from Mexico that year after the Mexican-American War. Another reason that bringing up Gadsden would not have been a great idea is that many of today's young Hispanic immigrants and some Hispanic-Americans still dream of a state of "Aztlan," reclaiming not only that North of Mexico but the American Southwest. But I digress. . . .)

"Citizenship by mail" has been talked about from time to time but never seriously; it certainly has never been implemented. But today ETS is coming close to that: They are considering "English testing by telephone"!

"We're working on it," Elford said crisply. "What we propose to do is to kind of shadow the INS examiner [as he or she tests someone for English], so we can model what they do. The plan is to do the language testing by telephone. There would be a proctor at the local community center. We would have a check-in screen proctor for voice recognition. The person would answer a series of questions on tape. We would hope to start working on it this year. But of course, we also need security technology."

The degree to which ETS has oversimplified and indeed dumbed down the entire process, with of course the approval of the INS and thus the U.S. government, is stressed by just about everyone in the pro-immigration loop; the latest technologies only reinforce this message. Consider, for instance, Softline Information, Inc.'s Ethnic NewsWatch, a comprehensive collection of newspapers and other periodicals published by the ethnic and minority press in America—on CD-Rom. In 1995, Ethnic NewsWatch advised petitioners for citizenship, correctly, that they had two options: to take the exam that tests their knowledge of U.S. history, civics, and the English language either at the time of their personal interview at the INS or before the interview through the ETS New Citizens Project.

"The INS test is administered orally by the interviewing officer," the NewsWatch related. "The applicant will be asked 20 questions on various historical and current topics and will have to provide correct answers to 12 of them in order to pass." (It then provides a list of the 50 most-asked questions.) "The examiner will then read aloud an English sentence that the applicant must print on a sheet of paper."

Ah, but there is a way out. "The ETS format is far more user-friendly," the NewsWatch goes on,

> and allows the applicant to take the exam without the pressure of having to give oral responses to an INS examiner (except for the one-sentence English test). The ETS exam also consists of 20 questions and the English sentence, but the questions are administered in writing and are multiple choice. Passing the ETS exam allows the applicant to attend the INS interview without having to answer any questions about U.S. history/civics. If the exam is failed, the applicant can re-take it as many times as possible, without fear that the number of failing scores will be reported to the INS. . . . The ETS test is given in two parts—20 questions for A and 20 questions for B. Applicants need to pass on only one of the parts to complete their test requirement.
>
> The English sentence is not graded for punctuation or spelling; rather, it must show the applicant has a clear ability to understand the language. For example, the sentence "The American flag is red, white and blue" is a common one asked. If the appli-

cant spells American as "Amerucan" and blue as "blew," he or she will still meet the requirement.

All of this, not surprisingly, horrifies people like Mike Miller, who remembers the agency that had not only a heart but a head as well. "We were committed to the standardized tests, but we tried to keep it all as honest as possible. There were supposed to be alternate tests, for instance, so no one would know the tests." He paused. "What I am seeing now scares me; we see them giving you the answers on TV."

Seriously dumbed-down? "It's uneven," he said, with his characteristic honesty. He went on, saying that "different Hispanic groups in particular are pushing the changes because, they argue, many of these newcomers come from countries where officialdom is vicious. People 'resent' being naturalized by officials. They say they are 'afraid of all governments.'"

I inserted here that none of those pushing naturalization-by-advocacy-group or naturalization-by-community-group ever seem to pause to think that, by giving in to their fear of governments and police in their countries of origin—and by helping them avoid contact with totally different government and police here—what they are in effect doing is implicitly and even explicitly telling them that the situation is the same in America! They have underlined their fears.

Is this really a way to teach what America is to new citizens?

Miller smiled as he shook his head over these changes, then said, "All the advocacy groups are really moneymakers. When we had the mass registration of new citizens in 1986, the aliens had a choice of where to send their applications—and by far the most applications went not to the advocacy groups but to INS!"

Back to George Elford and the new era in immigration:

One of the problems when ETS came to the immigration testing field, he explained, was that there were basically no records at INS, no history, no memory: the examiners always gave oral exams and there was no record at all of questions and answers. So, when ETS was invited into the process, its testers had nothing solid upon which to base the new standardized test.

Still, how they dealt with this problem remains extremely questionable. History? Memory? The next tests were hardly an advertisement for history and memory, but rather a scattershot swoop-in on a few American factoids. By their own admission, the ETS voluntarily and effectively (and even proudly) gave over to the control of special-interest groups much of the substance of the tests, the testing itself, and even decisions upon the percentages needed to pass. And the fact is that these activist groups—whether religious or Hispanic, serious or slipshod, patriotic or commercial, bent on teaching American history or intent upon distorting it— stood clearly to gain from increasing the number of citizens, citizens of whatever their agenda called for, and from simpler tests. That meant passing people and pushing them through, all for the greater glory of the interest group, not to speak of the fees charged.

Most of them are nice people, many of them are devoted people; that is not the problem. The problem would be the same if every single person in these interest groups were a combination of Mother Teresa, Elie Wiesel, and the Dalai Lama. The problem was that the U.S. government had voluntarily handed over the decisions on what the next generation of immigrants would think of America to interest lobbies and commercial enterprises.

It was where the new American "experts" and education technicians of groups such as the ETS met the ideological groups at the grassroots that American citizenship was being redefined. This was also where a strange new pivot was being put into place, not to hold there but to continue its descent in the dumbing-down process.

This citizenship testing is not the only area in which ETS appears to have been party to a dumbing-down of exams. In 1995, for instance, the Scholastic Aptitude Test, designed by ETS, was restructured so that all of its important achievement expectations were much lower. Presto! SAT scores go up. Why would the citizenship test be any different in the years to come?

It may seem that the farming out of the teaching and even sometimes of the tests to community groups has advantages. People do feel more at home in the resulting settings, and when the teachers are good and serious, there can be a greater human rapport with them than with INS examiners. But this interest-group involvement can also be enormously detrimental to the entire process of citizenship.

The *Chicago Tribune* took a comprehensive look at the INS's new "Citizenship USA" project in April of 1996 and recorded that the INS was pushing people through at breakneck speed, eliminating backlogs and so forth. There were several genuinely touching stories about immigrants studying for citizenship, and then it was duly added that the "INS asked community based groups and educators, working through the non-profit Illinois Coalition for Immigrant and Refugee Protection, to improve the testing process. The educators brought the immigrant's perspective to the process, encouraging the INS to eliminate confusing words." Spelling was downgraded still further—it no longer much matters how the petitioner spells English words—and, astonishingly, something else was altered. Because of the advice and pressure of the coalition and other interest groups, the INS agreed to change "our country" to "our U.S." The *Tribune* noted that the INS realized immigrants might think "our country" was Guatemala, El Salvador, or South Korea, instead of the United States. In doing this, the *Tribune* explained, the INS was agreeing that "immigrants from Latin America already are Americans and might be confused by that usage." In other words: Because of pressures from interest groups, the American Immigration and Naturalization Service, constituted as an important institution of the American nation and paid for by American citizens through their taxes, removed the word "American" from the American citizenship test!

I happen to be a Latin American specialist; I have spent a lot of my life there, written books on it, and love the area. Latin Americans do not think of themselves as "Americans" at all; they cling to their nationalism, even to their regionalism, and to their Catholicism. They admire—and resent—"America." They have always recognized "American" to mean citizens of the United States of America, as does the rest of the world. One could not possibly find a clearer case of how "multicultural" thinking has entered the citizenship process—and of how it can directly undermine the idea of America.

☆

It might shed some light on how to deal with problems of citizenship and naturalization in America if we look at another country also dealing with them halfway around the world. Australia went through a similar series of events in the 1980s, really violent in 1984, with the dumbing-down of citizenship at the combined hands of voracious commercial interests and leftist academics. One courageous dissenter, the respected history professor Jeffrey Blainey, dean of the faculty of arts at the University of Melbourne, has said, "We, more than probably any country in the world, throw away our citizenship. . . .

"Anybody can become a citizen with ridiculous ease. Applicants for citizenship have to live here or claim to live here for only two years, and one of those years can be spent overseas. They need to know no more than a few words of English. If they are over the age of fifty, they need to know no English. They can also maintain their allegiance to a foreign power while becoming an Australian citizen. . . ."

Labour MP Peter Staples summed up the opposing utopian views of many of his colleagues: "If migrants want early citizenship, what right do we have to deny it?"

To which Blainey answered dryly, "A nation has every right to deny a citizenship to those who know nothing about the nation they have entered. As for the question of English, one senator insisted that making English prerequisite in a migrant would be inbuilt discrimination. She did not seem to realize that Parliament holds all its sessions in English. . . . Democracy calls for debate, and a common language is essential if that debate is to be effective. . . . Without that inbuilt discrimination, without a common language or, say, two common languages, we are reduced to the level of monkeys." He paused. Then he added wryly, "Even monkeys probably have a common language."

When Blainey voiced those sentiments in the great 1984 debate, there were demonstrations on campuses where he was to speak. He was constantly attacked in the media (a "supremicist view on immigration and citizenship," one critic ascribed to him), and this distinguished historian was described by the "politically correct" as being "in the vanguard of Australian racism." But he did not give in. "The decline in democracy has aroused virtually no comment," he cried out. "It is not a terminal illness, but one that should be diagnosed. Every system of government is sinkable and liable to be replaced. I point to a few icebergs, large and small, now visible in Australia.

"A sense of citizenship is vital to democracy. The citizens are the final judges in the political process. But, unfortunately in Australia, citizenship is largely the responsibility of the Department of Immigration, and that department is largely the lobby for recent migrants and their relatives who hope to arrive soon. Australia . . . has turned citizenship into a bargain sale."

By the 1990s, Australia changed, began to control immigration and reimpose citizenship requirements. But the debate was so similar to the one ongoing in America as to convince some of us that men really are not islands.

☆

Returning to American history, let us ask: How did it come about that America itself stopped giving the citizenship preparations and testing, and that so many groups were empowered to do it? Here's how it goes, according to the INS itself:

Those wanting to give the test were described fuzzily in a memo (July 2, 1992) from Gene McNary, then commissioner of the INS, in this way: "Any qualified organization may apply to the Service [the INS] for acceptance as an approved testing entity. The agreement between INS and testing groups is non-financial, although the groups can and do charge the immigrants for services given—the Service simply agrees to accept test results from the approved testing entity as evidence of a naturalization applicant's ability to read and write English and U.S. government and history knowledge. . . . Tests are scored by the testing entity, which is also responsible for monitoring the tests, verifying identity of those taking the test, and providing test security and integrity. . . . Quarterly statistic reports and updated test schedules are required by the INS from testing entities. . . ."

Skip Tollifson, the pleasant and informative senior examinations officer of the INS, further explained: "It was June 28, 1991, when the INS came out with its 'Notice of Program.' That started the standardized test as an alternative means of citizenship testing. ETS was the major driving force behind it, and that was because of IRCA."

IRCA, the Immigration Reform and Control Act of 1986, created two brand-new features of U.S. immigration law: rapid legalization of aliens who had been in America for various reasons and sanctions on employers who knowingly hire illegals. What is curious about this moment in time in immigration is that IRCA—and

the consequent change to the standardized, dumbed-down test—
arose directly out of the fact that there were by then so many immigrants, some legal but mostly illegal, working or living in
America without status that the government finally realized something had to be done.

The Reform Act provided for a gigantic amnesty, with more
than three million undocumented aliens able to become legal residents. "It was indeed ironic," Mike Miller recalled. "Because of
IRCA, many aliens, such as students and other long-term temporary aliens, who had made every effort to maintain lawful status
over the years, were now doing everything, including lying and
buying phony documents, in efforts to prove they had been in
unlawful status for the requisite period—so they could gain lawful permanent resident status under IRCA."

"Congress said, 'We'll rescue all these people and make them
lawful residents,'" Skip Tollifson went on, "'but we want them to
meet the demands of citizenship.' ETS was the only one permanent participant in the process. With sixteen thousand to twenty
thousand applicants waiting, that number whetted ETS's appetite
for getting involved more in citizenship. In fact, ETS was behind
the 'Notice of Program.'" He laughed. "It had all the marks of a
brother-in-law deal. INS wrote the loose requirements; ETS wrote
the rest—it was the venerable institution that everybody could
trust."

The next step was for the INS to begin giving licenses—
Tollifson calls the process "an asset in the form of a license"—to
various testing organizations with "proven track records, so that
they could, first, themselves test, and then, second, farm out the
testing even further, to smaller groups. According to the INS list-
ings of 1996, they came into the new INS fold in this order: ETS,
with 389 affiliates nationwide; the Comprehensive Adult Student
Assessment Systems (CASAS), with 100 affiliates, primarily located in California; the Naturalization Assistance Services, Inc.
(NAS), with approximately 170 affiliates nationwide; the Marich
Associates, with 45 affiliates; Southeast College, with 12 affiliates,
primarily in Texas and the Northeast; and American College Testing (ACT), with 112 proposed affiliates nationwide. These licensees, in turn, give licenses to the smaller community and interest
groups, who become licensees of ETS to give preparation help to

immigrants, as well as civic lessons and, occasionally, the ETS tests.

INS is even today not exactly sure what percentages of the petitioners for citizenship use these groups, compared to going directly to the far more demanding INS, but the agency has roughly estimated in materials provided to Congress that it is close to 20 percent of all naturalization applicants who are using the private testing services. The percentages of immigrants passing the test ranges from 85 percent with ETS to 94 percent for NAS to 76 percent for Marich. Different groups charge different fees, most of them not exorbitant.

But back to Tollifson: "The program is set up so that these [ETS] tests on history and English are given full credit," he went on, "so that, when you walk in to your final INS interview, the examiners can't say 'No.' The program has the force of law, and the INS does its best to promote it."

Part of the reason INS is so enthusiastic about it, it turns out, is that they think the immigrants feel better about it. "The whole program is based on psychometrics," Tollifson went on. "The head of ETS told me one day, 'Let me give you the benefit of our research: We compare what happens in an interview in INS or in ETS, and we find immediately that, with INS, people have a high amount of stress. But with ETS, if you fail, they are actually forbidden from reporting failures and, for no additional money, you can go back and take the test a second time."

He paused, his enthusiasm building. "We really believe in standardized testing," Tollifson continued. "From an INS standpoint, this is an Al Gore 'reinventing government' program. We pay nothing for them. When I do an INS interview, I draw from the 'One Hundred Questions.' [Yes, the test of question 86 fame!] I only have fifteen minutes. The time the test takes is monstrous. Fifteen minutes goes by. . . . You can't imagine."

But wait! What is psychometrics and how did it get into citizenship testing? Well, psychometrics is officially the "technique of mental measurements . . . the use of quantitative devices for assessing psychological trends."

What does this mean in real life and language? It means applying modern technological methods to the amorphous realms of civics, emotions, and commitment. It means essentially the abandoning of quality in thinking about testing, and a general abandoning of context; it means measuring intelligence, or knowledge, through exactly such instruments as these tests. It is what ETS and these "technical" and "expert-driven" groups do.

INS officers such as Tollifson are enthusiastic about this new world, and one can understand that, if only because it is finally giving them some hope of catching up on the frightful backlog that a thoughtless America left them. They feel they are catching up—and, to be fair, they are—but at enormous cost to both the new citizens themselves and America. "We recently had a sixty-day period of testing scheduled in Orange County, California," Tollifson went on, as we spoke in the winter of 1996. "We had twenty-four officers doing twenty-seven interviews each a day. We did 19,407 interviews, and 12,665 were granted citizenship." He laughed. "When people ask me what I do," he commented, "I say I work the day shift . . . and the night shift. . . ."

Like many of the new-style INS people, he essentially feels sort of sorry for the immigrants, doesn't want to tax them too much; he brought up the issue of fear, which Mike Miller had also discussed. "Immigration often instills fear in them because of their experience in other countries—Gadhafy and Libya, Saddam and Iraq," Tollifson noted at one point. "They are so intimidated by a bureaucratic process and by a government. The other day I was with a woman doctor from the Philippines who was testing. She was so nervous, she was afraid to say her name. If the fear is going up to that level, they've got to be put in a fair environment—let's give them a church or a community center, where they won't feel afraid."

Tollifson also doesn't think that new citizens should have to know any more than current citizens do, even though they are at a totally different and potentially rich period in their lives, the period of being a student, when so much can be learned that serves as a base for what happens later. "Some study guide questions are beyond what most American citizens are expected to know," he went on, "like 'Why is Congress a bicameral body?' 'Ben Franklin said that the better part of a man's education is what they get for themselves.' I have a lot of problems requiring people to go to school for two hundred hours to learn all that stuff. . . ."

But there are serious questions to be raised about what *kind* of citizen this mass-production line is turning out, over what kind of a "citizenship mill" these new partners are running, and what the entire process, with its pitiful lack of content and context, will mean for the future of American citizenship in general and of these new citizens in particular. (And, dare one ask: Just exactly how many Iraqi and Libyan new citizens *are* there every year?)

☆

Obviously, in such a complicated and spread-out "universe" as this new and devolved naturalization system, it is impossible to assess the panorama in any comprehensive way. Even the INS, it admits fully, cannot do that. So, we must defer to the reports of reasonably fair-minded persons from around the country.

Commissioner McNary's 1992 memo says, for instance, that the petitioner for citizenship "must demonstrate an understanding of ordinary English literacy and a knowledge and understanding of the history and form of government of the United States"—but as a matter of fact, that is not at all what is happening.

In a rare newspaper look at what is happening, *Newsday* special correspondent Thomas Elias writes from Los Angeles (January 8, 1996):

> More applicants than ever before are winning U.S. citizenship without having to learn enough English to answer the rudimentary questions on the multiple-choice test of the Immigration and Naturalization Service. All of the INS-operated . . . test centers and the 828 other organizations authorized to give citizenship tests can now administer them to qualified applicants in languages other than English. . . .
>
> The non-English tests, often given in Spanish, Korean, Vietnamese and Tagalog, have been available at INS offices since 1967 to any citizenship applicant who is over 50 and has lived legally in this country more than 20 years, or over 55 years old and has lived here legally more than 15 years. Not even the INS knows precisely how many applicants for citizenship fall into those two age and residency categories. . . . But the foreign language tests are being offered in hundreds of new and more re-

mote locations, making them available to potential citizens who can't reach the more centrally situated INS offices.

Elias then reports that the ETS told him that about 7 percent of those taking the exam on its most recent test date, December 16, 1995, took it in Spanish, and that that date marked the first time that ETS and its more than four hundred affiliated testing centers had offered the test in a foreign language. In 1996, he goes on, ETS said it would offer the exam in several other languages, including Korean and Vietnamese.

He notes that there is a Herencia de Aztlan Foundation (Heritage of Aztlan Educational & Cultural Foundation) with offices in Santa Ana, Modesto, Pomona, and Bakersfield, California, offering the civics exam in Spanish. It has "helped more than 4,500 immigrants start the citizenship process since 1992." How very interesting! He never mentions, probably because he doesn't realize it, that Aztlan is the name radical Chicanos use for the Hispanic "republic" *of the entire Southwest:* as mentioned previously, they want to reclaim the region for Mexico. If you can't leave them, join them, I guess.

Daphne Magnuson of U.S. English, the 640,000-member group dedicated to making English the only official language in America, is then quoted as protesting that "to participate in the democratic process, people must know English. By allowing these tests in other languages , the government is sending a destructive message."

Elias also mentions that on July 2, 1993, in Tucson, Arizona, U.S. District Judge Alfredo Marquez gave the first naturalization ceremony ever conducted in a foreign language: in Spanish, for seventy-five Spanish-speaking immigrants. What was most telling about this incredible act was the fact that the woman who suggested giving the ceremony in Spanish (not the oath) doesn't even speak Spanish but "just thought it would be a neat thing to do." The judge also said that he thought it was a "nice gesture" and that "we are here to do anything to make these people happy."

But many old-style Americans were not happy for themselves or the citizens so sworn in. Mauro Mujica, then chairman of the board of U.S. English, wrote,

As a Latin American immigrant myself, I find this highly objectionable. I came to this country more than 30 years ago, knowing full well that in order to assimilate into the U.S. society, I had to master the English language. . . . Let's . . . put aside for the moment the "politically correct" notion of so-called cultural "rights." The fact is, these people came of their own free will. They, like most other Third World immigrants and refugees, have come to the United States for its blessings, most notably our democratic institutions and free enterprise systems. They have, in most cases, left their native lands out of desperation—but they chose to come here!

Am I missing something?

Or, as another good observer, Anthony Flint of the *Boston Globe*, wrote in 1994, after researching the test for the paper,

Test-takers say they now know U.S. history well and that the anxious days of preparation were worth it. But the test does not seem to carry quite the impact of the experiences of those who passed through Ellis Island. There is nothing to suggest the test prompts assimilation in any particularly powerful way.

The reason, in part, is the facts-on-parade nature of the test itself: it is a plain-wrapper version of the nuanced contours of the republic, made up largely of straightforward dates and figures. Some questions focus on the finer points of American civics, such as the majority in Congress required to override a presidential veto (two-thirds), how old one must be to run for president or senator (35 and 30, respectively). One immigration specialist said he tested his American-born staff on such questions, and several failed. Just as notable, however, is the lack of big-picture questions. Critical analysis of what led to the Civil War or why women were granted the vote is not required. Race relations in America gets one question about Martin Luther King Jr., who is identified in test worksheets as "a leader in a national civil rights movement to get rid of laws and practices that are unfair to African-American and other minority group members."

No one is suggesting that immigrants be asked to make critical historical analysis any greater than what natural-born citizens

could provide. But the just-the-facts emphasis creates a somewhat narrow—if not arcane—view of U.S. culture and society,
some say, that could turn a meaningful civic exercise into a version of historical Trivial Pursuit.

☆

As for corruption: Channel 5 in Saint Paul, Minnesota, in 1995
provided one of the most cogent looks "inside" one of the major
commercial enterprises, the Florida-based Naturalization and Assistance Services, Inc., or NAS group, mentioned previously, which just
happens to be the group with the extraordinarily high 94 percent
"pass rate" on the citizenship test.

Channel 5's investigative group, run by journalist Robb Leer,
went into one of the sessions and found the NAS office there in
Saint Paul giving "costly crash courses in a corrupt environment."
NAS, they said, contracted with the federal government, and collected $215 (a notably high amount) for a three-hour "course" in
which no fewer than 98 percent (an extraordinary percentage)
were adjudged to have passed. The news section showed employee Nancy Clemens telling the would-be citizens the "key
words" they had to remember—and telling them directly not to
bother about remembering whole sentences. She asked them when
the Civil War was, then told them, laughing, "Don't write that
down—it won't be on the test." At every turn, the "students,"
many of whom unquestionably came there in good faith and with
good intent, were manipulated by the cynically simplistic approach. They were allowed, even encouraged, to share answers
and to check tests beforehand, and they did.

When channel 5 showed their video to INS Supervisor John
Klow, they asked him, "Is she teaching a test on U.S. history or
how to pass a test?"

Klow answered, with some anger, "She's teaching a course on
how to take a test. If notes are being passed, that's a violation. If
people can look at other tests, that's a violation. . . ."

Channel 5 concluded that, in citizenship testing, "'Going private' means big bucks." And when they showed their video to
Republican Congressman Lamar Smith, he said, "That's terrible,
that's dishonest. I can only hope that it's not being condoned by

the INS." And when channel 5 asked questions of several of the petitioners there that day, the results were not edifying.

"When is Independence Day?" they asked one. "I don't know" was the answer. "Can you write English?" they asked another. "Naaahhh," the man virtually grunted. "You passed the test?" they asked another. "Yes," the person replied, "but I don't know how I passed." The NAS unit was duly suspended from INS but only, at least as of this writing, temporarily.

This is not to say that there are not good private or community testers; there are many, and the others should not be unfairly tarred with the brush of the cynical crowd. Indeed, channel 5 went to another group, the International Institute; that was a very different story. Their training was serious and conscionable, and they charged only sixty-five dollars for eighteen hours of education, with a 70 percent pass rate. Still, all too often, as Robb Leer summed up, "big bucks, little teaching, takes the place of naturalization."

But the further interesting aspect of the Saint Paul case was that the INS *did* act. All NAS operations across the country were suspended for two weeks before their tentative reinstatement; and the INS investigators, operating on the human and reasonable supposition that where there's smoke there's fire, went to Honolulu to investigate NAS operations there. This inquiry resulted in four indictments against the Friendly Teaching and Testing Service for "conspiracy to defraud the INS." Its "teaching" was found to be as shoddy in Honolulu as in Saint Paul. (The degree of "friendliness" has not been psychometrically measured, at least not to this writer's satisfaction.)

Meanwhile, the Saint Paul NAS office was closed for good, and U.S. Congressman Lamar Smith readied congressional hearings on the entire situation. At the very least, this case showed that the INS was becoming aware of how dangerous to its public image its controversial policy of farming out its duties could be; surely it will be even more so in the future.

☆

But testing was only part of the Great American Citizenship Dumb-Down. Also being devalued was the vote, always considered the precious core of citizenship. Consider the following two indications of such debasement.

First is the "motor-voter" bill, signed into law by President Bill Clinton on May 20, 1993, and requiring driver's license applications and welfare offices to be used to register voters. It also requires states to conduct mail-in voter registration, discourages states from verifying eligibility or citizenship, and expressly states that mail-in registration forms may not include any requirement for notarization or other formal authentication.

Paul Craig Roberts, of the Cato Institute, wrote at the time, "The Democrats could not have made it any clearer that the purpose of the law is to overturn safeguards against the registration of non-citizens," and noted that no fewer than sixty-five special interest groups—including the League of Women Voters and MALDEF—"lobbied for passage of the bill," while "some lobbied against the verification of citizenship, claiming that it was discriminatory against those with non-Anglo surnames." Then he paused and asked one of those questions considered "unforgivable" in the new world of pro-immigration activists: "Let's think about that for a minute. Isn't it discriminatory against U.S. citizens, including those undergoing the lengthy naturalization process, to make it easy for illegal aliens to register as voters?"

When I spent a most revealing week on the Texas-Mexican border in the spring of 1995, the last thing I was looking for was anything to do with the "motor-voter" law, whose official name is the National Voter Registration Act. But my very first morning in Brownsville, there it was, on the front page of the local paper, the *Brownsville Herald*! I wrote at the time in my column from the area:

"I did not have to wait long to find myself up against the most serious new problem in the seemingly endless mazes of illegal immigration. The potential for non-citizen voting was all over the front pages . . . and so was the incredible way in which the federal government is actually willy-nilly encouraging it. . . . As *Herald* staff writer Anthony Gray declared in his articles about the effects of Motor Voter in 'The Valley,' 'A federal mandate requiring state agencies to offer voter registration to applicants for social services may be dramatically increasing the number of illegal voters in counties along the U.S.–Mexico border.'"

Then Gray fingered one of the typical problems in these "equalizing" measures. "Compounding matters," he went on, "the new voter-registration application does not require an applicant to state where he was born. Furthermore, state agency employees are prohibited from making a determination on a person's citizenship status for voter-registration purposes, even if they see documents that state that a person may not be a U.S. citizen."

In fact, I wrote in my column, "all a person has to do is go to state agencies—such as the Department of Public Safety or the Department of Human Services—and ask for an application for a voter-registration card."

"As long as you have a mailing address," Gray told me, when he stopped over at my hotel, "you get your vote. In theory, you could make up a fictitious person and vote fictitiously."

What was certain was that Gray and many electoral officials in Brownsville and elsewhere along the teeming border were worried. I wrote that elections administrators were saying that the new federal voter registration mandate had increased the number of registered voters in the county from 105,000 to 116,000 in only the few months between January and May of 1995—but that they had neither the mandate nor the enforcement capacity to determine who those people were, much less whether they were citizens. Already there were significant claims of mail-in fraud.

But far more serious than the potential for immediate fraud, I wrote, was "the infinitely larger question of how and why America is so disorganizing and disconnecting itself—and, thus, ultimately disenfranchising itself."

The second instance of vote devaluation was Oregon's first mail-in voting experiment in the winter of 1996. This was twenty-four years after the 1972 Democratic Party "reforms," which gave us the end of the party caucuses and thus the end of the selection of the American presidential candidate by the wise elders of the party. It was twenty-four years after American "representative democracy" in the party was essentially replaced with the deceptively more representative "direct democracy" system of the primary.

The first results in Oregon seemed to be promising, pleasing. Voting went up dramatically that winter. Everyone said how "easy" it was, not to have to engage in all that bothersome old community business of meeting one's fellow citizens at a voting place, to go out in the snow. . . . The mail-in saved the state a million dollars by forgoing the traditional polling places. And the rest of the country began thinking, "Hey, we should do this, too!"

But some of our best and most serious (and most practical) thinkers began having second thoughts."Who could oppose a process that increases voter turnout and costs less money?" Norman Ornstein, the brilliant senior fellow at the American Enterprise Institute, asked in a column in the *Washington Post.* "The answer is, anyone who values a deliberative process in campaigns, elections and government." Most significant, Ornstein argued, "is the fact that the mail ballot turned the Framers' concept of an election and the vote itself upside down. Elections are not single events. They are an integral part of the political and governing processes, linked to the campaigns that precede them and the policy-making that follow them."

He went on:

> The Framers saw all the pieces as tied together by deliberation—a process of give and take, debate, discussion and dialogue, leading to greater public understanding of the choices facing the country, the strengths and weaknesses of the candidates voters can choose from, and then to a choice among them. . . . Just as significant, the mail ballot increases turnout at the cost of erasing the immense benefit, symbolic and otherwise, of the act of going to vote. Gathering in a public place to make a choice in a private polling booth is one of the great expressions of human freedom. When voters make their individual and private choices while surrounded by ther fellow citizens, it underscores both our individuality and our collective responsibility. Going to a school or other neighborhood polling site underscores that the vote is a precious thing, one that requires just a small amount of energy and sacrifice by citizens to protect their basic rights.
>
> The mail ballot turns that sacred experience into the equivalent of filling out a Publishers Clearing House ballot.

At every turn, changes were isolating American citizens ever further from one another, not to speak of isolating the new citizen from the old.

☆

Critics of these changes abound.

Willa Johnson, head of the Capital Research Center, which does respected work on foundations and their programs, says that "groups counsel the new immigrants on welfare benefits and the other side of the problem," instead of counseling them "on adapting to the American way of life." She continues, "Actually, their activities are counterproductive of the interests of the people they claim to help; for they only advance policy agendas or their own agendas to perpetuate their organizations."

I sat for several hours one day over a fascinating lunch with Francesco Isgro, a charming young lawyer who is the son of Italian immigrants and rose to become a major lawyer at the INS as well as a professor of immigration law at Georgetown University. Indeed, we met near the INS offices in downtown Washington at a new Brazilian extravaganza restaurant, Coco Loco, close to Washington's Chinatown. Why, I asked him, did he think citizenship had become so unimportant?

He began: "In the earlier days, the volume of litigation involved in citizenship was huge. It was because so many people were struggling to get citizenship, and they would take it to the courts. In the old days, because becoming a citizen was not an easy matter, people were always challenging denials of citizenship—now, such cases do not exist. The mere fact that someone is here means Congress is giving them all kinds of benefits, benefits that originally related to citizenship. Today court cases are rare, and the only ones we even have are people who are losing citizenship, like Nazis or hate groups. The Supreme Court says we must treat everyone 'equally.'

"We have tried to make the acquisition of citizenship as easy as possible, even to the point where outside consultants administer the test. We have private companies administering the oath, without even judges. Today's INS is even telling them we *want you to be a citizen*"! (In fact, in its new "campaign to promote naturalization," which began in the summer of 1989, INS field offices were suddenly instructed to "get out there" to local events and speak on citizenship, and the INS even launched a contest for the best essay on "what being an American means to me." One of the *winners* wrote in Spanish!)

"When I move on to my own personal experience," Attorney Isgro continued, his voice assuming a tone of real pain, "well, I just can't understand why we are cheapening it so much. It is the most important thing you can get and the most important thing that a country can give."

INS historian Mike Miller agreed, sadly. "It is almost impossible to lose one's citizenship today," he told me. "When I came to the INS in 1956, they taught us that if you naturalize in the United States and go back to your country of origin for two years, you lose your citizenship—it would show that you never intended to stay in the United States. In those days, if you naturalized in another country, if you were in service in the military, or if you held high political office in another country, you would lose it.

"Today," Miller continued "the courts have gotten to a point where, even if a person moves back to his home country after naturalizing here, or even fraudulently withheld from the INS the fact that you did not intend to live permanently in the United States—that, therefore, you fraudulently naturalized—the person simply moves back in and the courts won't touch him. It is almost useless for the courts to bother." Legal thinking on this? "The federal courts are not sympathetic to enforcing the law, which is still ostensibly on the books. The federal courts, really, really, really hate to take someone's citizenship away.

"Most countries don't allow you even to renounce citizenship. You can do it, but you're stateless. The United States takes them back on parole status. Remember the case of the "black Hebrews" who renounced their American citizenship in Israel? That was one of the few cases where the United States wouldn't take them back. That case showed about the only way that you can lose citizenship."

Immigration law was also diminished when the top INS lawyer for many years, Alexander Aleinikoff, who left and then returned under the new administration of Commissioner Doris Meissner in the mid-1990s, argued constantly that it was time to no longer distinguish between citizens and legal aliens. In addition, a large and powerful legal group—most of them in the disputatious AILA, or American Association of Immigrant Lawyers, and often immigration "ambulance chasers" determined to bring in as many newcomers as possible (for both ideological and financial reasons)—has cheapened immigration law. How far we have fallen from the days in which lawyers and the INS respected the idea and process of citizenship! From the early years of the 1950s to 1982, all INS examiners had to be lawyers; then the INS started phasing them out because of their habit of suing for higher-grade civil service jobs and more money—and, being lawyers, they of course got it. Maybe we're lucky they're gone?

☆

Even while some cherished U.S. citizenship traditions were being eroded, some immigrants were insisting upon importing questionable practices from their homelands to America. "FEMALE GENITAL MUTILATION BY IMMIGRANTS IS BECOMING CAUSE FOR CONCERN IN THE U.S.," the *New York Times* headlined in December 1995. Clitoridectomy, or female circumcision, a barbaric practice from the Middle East and Africa, had been transplanted to America.

I had been traveling to Egypt, that magnificent country, since 1969, when I first went as a foreign correspondent for the *Chicago Daily News*. And I early came across this horrible practice, designed ostensibly to "keep women pure." At age nine or ten, a terrified girl is tied to a tree; a family member or "doctor" takes a razor or a knife and cuts out her clitoris. That way, the girl will never be "evil," she will also never have any sexual pleasure; she is maimed for life, and some girls died in the operation.

But now, that practice was being brought in by African and Arab immigrants to America. Please understand, they were not *asking* for the right under law to perform this awful "operation," they were *insisting* upon it. It was *our* duty to be understanding and tolerant and (the key word) "nondiscriminatory," even if they were not. (The idea of "reciprocity" does raise its head, however.)

It doesn't end there. In Connecticut in 1993, Binh Gia Pham covered himself with gasoline and burned himself to death: he was protesting the suppression of Buddhism in Vietnam. His friends recorded his death, then called the police. The district attorney of De Kalb County, Georgia, had to contemplate pressing child molestation charges against a South American woman for stroking her male child's genitals; was it just a "cultural thing?" In 1989 in New York, Dong Lu Chem, a Chinese immigrant, murdered his wife, whom he suspected of infidelity, with a hammer, but got only five years' probation. The judge had listened to an anthropologist's testimony of how serious infidelity was considered in China!

People were beginning to talk soberly about the right to a "cultural defense" or courtroom attempts to get foreign-born defendants off by invoking the cultural mores of their "home countries."

But history clearly shows—and any study of human nature obviously sustains—that there *are* no vacuums, particularly in culture. If the United States was not going to insist upon the *primacy* (not the exclusivity, but the primacy) of its cultural principles, then it was deliberately leaving a big, yawning space that would naturally be filled by other folks with other strokes.

We had become so proudly tolerant that we would feel "guilty" if African or Arab immigrants were told that you do not mutilate your little girls in America! So, why should anyone have been surprised at what was happening?

Dan Stein, an immigration-control advocate and the talented head of the Federation for American Immigration Reform (FAIR), calls this regression *"morphing from immigration into colonization."* To put it less formally, America is now looked upon by a small but significant minority of immigrants not as a place where they come to be Americans, but as one where they can "rightfully" impose their own values.

And, of course, at the very top of these new cultural impositions is language. English is the language of the world, the language of commerce and of diplomacy; to get ahead not only in America but across the globe, one needs to learn English. Yet, many of the very activist groups who are licensed to give the citizenship test are lobbying for lesser English capacitation—or for a country in which many languages are the norm.

Dan Stein is right: This is no longer assimilation, this is a reverse colonization!

☆

Consider the experience of two other important countries, in order to see how the United States fits into the entire world picture. First, the Netherlands, one of the richest, most advanced, and most cultured little countries on earth.

Hans Moll, the fortyish editor of Holland's prestigious newspaper *NRC Handelsblad,* still looked in part a "sixties child" when I had a charming lunch with him one sunny day of June 1994, in an old Amsterdam café. His shirt was open, he wore tight jeans.

But he was balding now, and he had changed dramatically in his thinking about immigration, and particularly about acculturation. He began by reminiscing about how it all started.

"After World War Two," he said, "we young people were opposed to the old ways of thinking. In the nineteen sixties, there was a strong cultural relativist undertow in intellectual thinking—the idea was that 'all cultures were the same.' Then came the new immigrants, with different ways of thinking. From the old Dutch colonies: from Indonesia, from the Caribbean, from South Asia. . . . Probably the largest group was Muslim. When I was growing up, we made a laughingstock of the Roman Catholic Church, but when the Islamists began to come, we stopped making those religious jokes. Nobody said anything against Islam." He paused. "We were all cowards," he added.

He then went on to outline in an unusually cogent manner how "cowardice" in dealing rationally with the reality of cultural difference is, ironically, in large part responsible for the following sentiments currently predominant across Europe: (1) resentment against aliens in general, (2) strong feelings that European countries have been "taken" by Islam, and (3) a conviction that it was high time that those nations demanded far more commitment from refugees than had hitherto been the case.

Most interesting to me was the fact that Dutch men and women in their forties, such as Hans Moll, were no longer deluded—nor too embarrassed by political correctness to say something. "These immigrants, they take an oath to nothing here," he went on. "My girlfriend works with asylum-seekers. She sees them as a microcosm of conflicts to come. She's for a stern approach, making things clear from the moment they come: what can be done and what can't. We had a typical case—a guy from Zaire, stabbed by a Turk. The Zairean had been granted asylum in northern Holland, and he had the idea that all girls were available. Well, he took liberties with a Turkish girl, and her brother stabbed him." He shook his head.

"Socialization of the immigrants into Dutch society? There is none whatsoever," he concluded sadly.

Indeed, that summer, as I roamed across Europe from Amsterdam to Helsinki, from Oslo to Saint Petersburg, from Zagreb to Paris, everywhere I found a new openness. No longer were people of goodwill shamed into remaining still about issues; they did not put up with "racist . . . xenophobe . . . nativist . . ." name-calling. They were finally talking about the real problems, which were at heart not the problem of the immigrants but the weakness of the "receiver countries" to assert, protect, and treasure their own cultural strengths.

When I stopped in Paris to see how the French were handling these issues, I found them trying desperately to deal with "cultural immigration" among Islamic refugees, almost all from northern Africa. Largely because of the nasty civil war in Algeria, terrorism was rife against the French state. Large numbers of immigrants were insisting that Islamic laws and practices be applied to them.

Since the French Revolution, the French had reveled in the idea that France was so strong, its ideas so powerful, its style so unassailable, that anyone in his right mind would choose to be French! But by the 1990s, the point of critical mass grew close in terms of the sheer numbers of Muslim immigrants as they began to impose their own cultural patterns on historic France.

Jacques Chirac, then mayor of Paris, went so far as to warn publicly: "In demographic terms, Europe is disappearing. Twenty or so years from now, our countries will be empty, and no matter what our technological power, we shall be incapable of putting it to use."

Behind those words was the French government's prediction that, by only the year 2000, fully 60 million of the 130 million population in just Algeria, Tunisia, and Morocco would be under twenty years of age and "without a future"—and, therefore, looking for someplace to go to find one.

Activist and fundamentalist Muslims living in France began "testing" the French public school system, insisting that Muslim girls be permitted to wear traditional head coverings in the schools. (The girls, as "at home," were not consulted.) Islamic religious leaders began saying outright that "Allah's law takes precedence over French law." Cases of clitoridectomy were suddenly all over the French courts, while the headlines daily spoke of French police arresting militants supporting Algerian and other radical fundamentalists intent upon overthrowing their home governments from the "tolerant" streets of Paris. Should it really have been any surprise that, in 1994, French police were staging massive crackdowns on Islamic activists who had been infiltrating the three million Muslims in France?

The wholly expectable outcome was that the people of France reacted violently, as all societies finally do when their government has not bothered to represent their real wishes and deal with such provocations to its own culture in a rational manner—they veered strongly to the right. "When we send home several planeloads, even boatloads and trainloads, the world will get the message," announced Charles Pasqua, the hard-line cabinet minister in charge of security and immigration affairs (interestingly paired now in France). "We will close our frontiers." He also announced that France would become a "zero immigration" country, thus marking an astonishing reversal of its two-hundred-year-old policy of generous political asylum.

The French tightened their immigration laws at once. Meanwhile, in England, extremist Muslim groups that had formed a "Muslim Parliament" as an announced prelude to forming "Muslim states" in Europe exemplified another troubling phenomenon, "cultural colonization" by political organization. These states would embrace polygamy, instantaneous divorce, and the abolition of mixed-sex workplaces and public transport. In still another manifestation of this "new age," Commonwealth emigrants from India set up a "British Hindu Untouchability" scheme, or, in effect, "no-go" areas for untouchables—in England, the country that prided itself as being the world's very wellspring of equality before the law!

The result? The *Wall Street Journal* headlined a story about Europe in the spring of 1994, "FLOODED BY REFUGEES, WESTERN EUROPE SLAMS THE DOOR ON REFUGEES." This was so sad because a moderate, balanced, rational policy—in time—could have headed off all of the hatred.

You remember Philip Nolan? America's famous "Man without a Country" who was doomed to sail forever on the seas of the globe, never hearing the word "America?" Well, contemporary France has his counterpart.

Somehow a small man with thinning black hair, Iranian-born Merhan Karimi Nasseri, got stuck in the Charles de Gaulle Airport in Paris in 1988. His papers had been stolen; France would not let him in, and, since no country would accept him, it couldn't expel him either. Supported by friends and family, he spends his days and nights on a plastic bench in the basement lounge, writing his diary, reading discarded newspapers, watching television. He wanders about; the police know him, pause to chat with him.

It is a real story of Europe for our times: a Europe "without borders," yet a modern "man without a country."

☆

The United States has a brand-new immigration policy, and the new commissioner, Doris Meissner, is beginning to control the borders with substantially stepped-up patrols and other active measures. She's also encouraging naturalization with her Citizenship USA program, begun in the summer of 1995.

I went to see her in her office at the INS building on I Street in Washington in February 1996 and found her to be a charming, extremely knowledgeable, fair-minded woman. Behind her, she had years of experience in both the Justice Department and the INS, and at the Carnegie Endowment for International Peace, where she was for six years their resident immigration specialist. I asked her for her philosophy.

"It's very basic stuff," she started off. "I do believe that one source of our strength is our immigrant heritage; I do think that new citizens are a continuous sense of renewal and rebirth of our values. This is a tradition so precious and unique that it's fundamental to our identity and very much something you have to protect." She paused. "But," she went on, "it can only flourish and survive if it takes place in the realm of rules that are fair, that seem to be fair, and that are upheld." She spoke of a "balanced program," which is what she has achieved: on the one hand, moved large resources to "manage the border," which she admits has been out of control, and on the other hand, avidly encouraged naturalization. In fact, she has encouraged naturalization so much that many criticize her for being a "citizen mill," for pushing people through without true civic socialization, even for wanting to help the Democrats in the upcoming elections by increasing the number of people who can vote for them.

Commissioner Meissner thinks it would be a good idea to look at the Oath of Allegiance and get some redrafting. It dates from the last century, and it is kind of odd. It pledges the new citizen to "absolutely and entirely renounce and abjure all allegiance to any potentate, state or sovereignty" and to promise to "bear arms on behalf of the United States," whenever required, "so help me God." "I have raised the question of whether the Oath is relevant today, with its 'princes and potentates,'" she said. "If we're really serious about bringing the immigrants into full membership in the community, let's see what they pledge to, what their core duties are supposed to be. All they really pledge to do is 'bear arms.' The language is anachronistic. . . . *Abjure?* Is 'bearing arms' the only participation they pledge to? I watch them at the ceremonies: they're just mouthing the words."

Yet, despite Commissioner Meissner's talents, the actual testing process is more standardized than ever, less concerned with history than ever, more relegated to pushing people through and creating what are in effect only "economic immigrants" to America. Today's INS, which has all but thrown aside the old textbooks for American history, now says it is going to create a new text like the one that Citizenship and Immigration Canada puts out. But my heart fell when I saw it. It is physically attractive, but akin to a well-designed, forty-four-page comic book on Canadian history, with little block graphs, simple pictures, and text so easy that it must be at a sixth-grade level. Is that really all there is?

Also, Meissner said she was going to "encourage citizenship" not because belonging to the country was something even moderately valuable but because "naturalization helps counteract anti-immigrant attitudes. When people become citizens, they accept our values, and most Americans are reassured." Even her arguments for naturalization ended up being a new kind of self-esteem commission for immigrants!

Many observers seem more concerned than Meissner about the fact that immigrants *don't* accept our U.S. values.

As Willa Johnson of the Capital Research Center worries, "There is concern on the Right and on the Left over the degree to which you control or do not control the entry of people into any society. It has a decisive impact on what that culture is going to be. With unrestricted immigration into the United States, for example, you inevitably change the pattern of American culture, because you tip the balance. Up to a point, you increase diversity, and that is good." She paused, then finished up, "But beyond a certain point, you risk diluting, if not changing, exactly those political institutions that allowed this to flourish."

"There probably *is* a potential for a *Lebanon in America* today," Mike Miller summed up in his conversation with me. "We saw the unrest and explosiveness among the aliens in the Los Angeles riots! If we get large groups from a lot of countries, the fear is that we may end up with those biases they bring with them and that, if they have to get close enough together, we may end up with warring factions."

Others worry about the education, not of the new citizen, but of the children of the old citizens. "The fact is, these Americans are people who created modern freedom," House Speaker Newt Gingrich says, "and when you learn that sixty percent of the high school seniors graduating this year do not know enough history to perform the task of citizenship, it should terrify you. They can't compete in the world market because they're not learning math and they're not learning how to write English. And they can't be good citizens because they don't know enough to be good citizens. . . .

"And if this country does not insist on English as a language, we are going to dissolve. You watch Québec. Go visit Belgium. And ask yourself: Do you really want this country to collapse into a Balkanization of languages? And I would urge every state to look at every way you can to reinforce English as a language and to say to every new migrant—and I am for open legal immigration—that our heroic destiny is to allow people from across the planet to come here and pursue happiness and then to lead the entire planet to happiness.

"But if we do not insist on a common language in this country and we do not enforce a common language, we will dissolve as a civilization. And it will happen within fifty or sixty years. And people will look back on us and say: 'What were they doing?'"

William Bennett, arguably the man who cares most about the downgrading of American culture and education today, comments that "pinning the blame on immigrants for America's social decay is a dodge and a distraction. And it happens to be exactly wrong. One can make a strong argument that many new immigrants have been corrupted by those same degraded aspects of American culture that trouble so many American parents." He quotes the Czech playwright Milan Kundera as saying that "the first step in liquidating a people is to erase its memory. Destroy its books, its culture, its history. Then have somebody write new books, manufacture a new culture, invent a new history. Before long, the nation will begin to forget what it is and what it was."

Our collective cultural task, then, is to remember "what we were and what we still are. If we once again get that right, then immigrants will fit in and flourish, as they always have. If we keep getting it wrong, then it won't really matter where the people come from. For whatever their place of origin, they will be citizens without a culture, and they will bear children without a future."

Even some of the great enthusiasts of the New Way—and of the Era of the Standardized Test and of the Death of History and Civics—seem at times to have second thoughts: sad, sentimental second thoughts.

At the end of my long talk with Skip Tollifson, the exams maven of the INS, after all his enthusiasm about the sheer numbers of immigrants being naturalized, he suddenly grew thoughtful when I pushed him on content, history, patriotism. "Yes, this is more a place of business than a place where you want to promote national pride," he said. "It's like the country's afraid of nationalism. When people meet me, they say, 'Oh, you're Tollifson, you're Norwegian. . . .' Hey, I've never been to Norway. But in Berlin, everybody would know he's a German.

"This is a country that can be patriotic without being nationalistic, but it also kind of stinks. Columbus Day? We celebrate with a sale at Sears. Martin Luther King Day? Even the stock market was open. The problem is that you and I end up having this discussion about things that are very important. Perhaps we should be sending different signals: I'm in this little office, not even any flag. . . . Is this all there is? It's like 'Mr. Jones here, as soon as he puts his coffee cup down, he'll swear you in.'"

The serious young new historian of the INS, a Nebraskan named Marian Smith, sat with me one day in her office at the INS and remembered from her love affair with INS history the way it "used to be," back in the twenties, thirties, and forties. "We'd send out a list of aliens to the schools. We'd send the *Federal Citizenship Textbook*. Immigrants would take classes there. That was 'Americanization.' Those were the days when we had time, money, time from middle-class women who were at home. The 'work of the nation' was being done. . . ."

What happened? I asked her. Why the change?

"Its roots are in the New Left scholarship," she answered thoughtfully, "and those roots were actually in the nineteen thirties. The government has to not offend the middle in America, and something as mundane as a *Federal Citizenship Textbook* is a mirror to what flies. When the history revisionists got power in the sixties, they found they could also influence the federal textbooks. They'd had Vietnam and Watergate, and 'we don't care what someone with a third-grade reading level from Guatemala might need, we're ready for some critical thinking!'"

She looked at me very directly, then said, a note of sadness in her voice: "If you empty something of content, it's not controversial, is it?" Another pause. "But that is only surprising if you think of citizenship as *an attachment of the heart*. If you don't, if it's simply production, then this is not going to work. . . . Things like that make me sick inside . . . to lose something so precious, through neglect." She had started our conversation matter-of-factly, about the history itself; now she looked so melancholy.

Ironically, Commissioner Meissner herself is critical of the lack of civics, the lack of content—and soul and spirit—in the testing. "In fact, we are in the period of highest immigration in our history," she told me thoughtfully. "This is an epochal period. We did it before, but then we had schools, labor unions, community groups, which were the institutions by which we carried out the citizenship training: we don't have those institutions now. . . . Then, we were also perhaps clearer about our position in the world.

"I . . . had to make the decision to do the first thing first—to handle applications effectively. The more qualitative efforts, I won't make yet. . . . But my whole intent will be to vastly upgrade the quality of the knowledge in the testing. We want national standards, a knowlege of English and civics. I'd like us to have a debate in our neighborhoods: What are our values today? What do we want people to know? I see us eventually getting there, but numbers got ahead of us. In terms of the interest groups, I'm cautious about them being heavily engaged in the testing. They should help in getting applications prepared, but they have to be involved in a context of more rigorous oversight.

"We've been very clear: We are not trying to dilute the testing, we're trying to raise standards. If we do that properly, we'll be making a real statement about what we consider important, about what message we're conveying to them. Barbara Jordan's Commission on Immigration Reform talks again about 'Americanization'— it's a non-PC word, but it captures it, doesn't it?"

☆

Despite these plans for the future, from all reports and all the surveys, the major reason immigrants naturalize is economic. It was after California voters threatened to cut benefits to aliens with Proposition 187 in California in 1995 that surges of new immigrants assaulted the INS, leading to Tollifson's aforementioned backbreaking sixty-day naturalization saga in Orange County.

Until Proposition 187, there was no rush to naturalize at all; the great majority even of legal aliens were no longer bothering to naturalize in America. Indeed, whereas 67 percent of legal aliens became citizens in 1946 (when the country was filled with confidence after its unparalleled victories in World War II), only 37 percent of America's approximately ten million legal aliens were applying for naturalization in the mid-1990s (when the nation was burdened still by memories of Vietnam, cultural disintegration, and moral decadence).

But the new "economic citizen" is really not much in the grand scheme of human experience. By far the most brilliant analysis of this type of citizenship is one I found in a French intellectual quarterly, *Elements*. Alain de Benoist wrote of the modern state's dilemma—seeing the citizen only as a consuming, buying, paying being:

> The equation implied between an economic duty (the payment of taxes) and the attribution of a political right (the right to vote in municipal elections) is a perfect illustration of confusion and of the increased primary of the economy. The reciprocity between rights and duties cannot be exercised on the same level.
>
> In other words, there can't be political rights only in exchange of political duties. . . . In the republic, thousands of people are not working and not paying taxes, and this does not diminish their citizenship, which is derived from a different order. . . ."

A watershed study done in 1993 by Johns Hopkins University and sociologist Alejandro Portes, the first in fifty years to study the children of U.S. immigrants, shows that few even want to call themselves "American," preferring, for instance, to call themselves "Cuban-American" or "Haitian-American" (at best).

The *New York Times* coverage of the important study, on June 29, 1993, was headlined "A FERVENT 'NO' TO ASSIMILATION IN NEW AMERICA." According to the article, the direct relationship between immigration and citizenship has changed in America over the decades and over the centuries (as has happened elsewhere) quite simply because the world has changed.

But does that justify the denigration of the Jeffersonian dream, denigration manifested in the "one-stop " Immigrant Service Center of the Caribbean Women's Health Association in Brooklyn, whose director Marco Mason says belligerently, if not grammatically, "This group is entitled to their fair share."

Ironically, at the 1996 meeting of the American Association for the Advancement of Science, investigators found that the more new immigrant families and their children assimilated into America today, the *worse off* they soon would be. "Families that adopt American manners too readily seem to lose the motivation they arrived with and slide gradually into poverty," the *Economist* reports. "It used to be straightforward. Immigrants arrived. They were poor. They worked hard. They became assimilated, both culturally and economically. The adoption of American ways went along with upward economic mobility. But today, for many immigrant families . . . studies suggest that the reverse is true. The families that succeed economically are those that manage to draw on what America has to offer without abandoning their ethnic and cultural distinctiveness."

The magazine sums up the findings of two fine sociologists, Alejandro Portes and Ruben G. Rumbaut, who conducted the study "Children of Immigrants: The Adaptation of the Second Generation" (not to be confused with Portes's aforementioned 1993 study): America "is bad for your motivation."

☆

Papa, My Father: A Celebration of Dads, by Leo Buscaglia, is one of the most poignant depictions of the 1920s–1960s generation of immigrants to America. "Papa," a Jewish immigrant from Poland, came to the States to live in Gallup, New Mexico, where there was work in the mines.

The plan was that Papa would go to America and work hard until he had accumulated enough money to send for his family. His long-term plan was to amass a small fortune, buy a home, educate his children, then return to his small village, to live out his years in security and dignity. That was the scenario for many immigrants, but it did not quite work out that way, either for Papa or for most others.

The majority of immigrants never went back again. The United States became their permanent home. Their dreams eventually faded into nostalgia for their homeland, expressed plaintively on cold winter nights and during long, hot summers. They lived out their days in a love-hate relationship with the Old World and the New.

So it was with Papa.

Finally the time came when Papa wanted to apply for citizenship. He had not done so because he was embarrassed by his lack of fluency in English. So he went to night school to learn better English, picking his clothes for the first night of school with great care and even getting a haircut, and kissing Mama good-bye "as if he were setting off on a six-week cruise" when he walked out the door.

It was with a great sense of relief that we watched Papa leave the house, with his required two witnesses at his side, to take the exam. No sooner had he left than Mama started praying: rosaries to Our Blessed Mother, special vows to Our Blessed Father, flowers and candles to a myriad of saints.

"You don't have to pray, Mama," we assured her. "Papa knows everything. He knows more than the judge." We wouldn't allow ourselves even to imagine what life would be like if Papa failed to pass. Happily, when he returned a few hours later, his face shone with the unmistakable light of success. I can still picture him striding triumphantly up the walkway in what was undoubtedly one of his proudest moments. . . .

... Papa was disappointed that he had not been asked enough questions. After all his studying, anxiety, and worry, only three things were asked of him: What is the highest court in the land? Who was the third president of the United States? What is a democracy? His preface to each of his responses, according to witnesses, was, "That's an easy one . . ."

The swearing-in ceremony was all that was left to make Papa, at last, a real citizen. With hundreds of others, he was required to take the oath of allegiance. We all dressed in our Sunday-go-to-church outfits, squeezed into our dilapidated car, and drove to the courthouse downtown, where the final ceremony was scheduled.

When we entered, the citizens-to-be and their families were separated. Papa was soon lost in a crowd of people whose cultural diversity seemed less apparent in the light of their shared accomplishment.

And, today? I took a dear friend, Cecilia Coder, to lunch one day to hear about her experience, and when this lovely, thoughtful, intelligent young woman related her citizenship experience, certain things became clear about our "utilitarian" process today. I should say first that Cecilia ("Ceci"), who is married to the son of my closest friend, Mary McDermott Coder, is exactly the kind of new citizen we want. Born and raised in Peru, she is an immensely talented, decent, and, well, just nice human being.

"At the very beginning, it was very exciting," she began, "even going to get your green card. Then, all the papers. Sometimes it was scary and exciting: you don't know what they'll say. I found always the people at the desks were very nice, very helpful. The only thing that drives you nuts is at twelve o'clock they close for lunch; even though there are hundreds of people there, they close.

"You turn your papers in in a different room. After checking on you for several months, they call you. You go to a different room: more sophisticated but the same building. Your number comes up. There is a flag at the entrance of the building. Not inside. Once they call you, the officers are in a hurry, but they're nice, they've never been jerks. A lot of younger people: twenty-eight years old.

"I'll never forget the time I first went in and my picture was wrong. The officer told me I had to have it taken again. I said, 'Oh, but my place . . .' He said, 'No, I'll keep it for you.' I remember that. Then I went to take the test. I was asked what were the colors of the flag. How many stripes and stars are there and what do they represent? Where was the national anthem written? And, 'Name the congresswoman of your county.' Then it was, 'Okay, you can go now, you're a citizen.'

"That was it. 'Thank you very much.' I thought everything was too quick, too easy. Anything inspirational? No—and I felt disappointed. Then the swearing-in. Maybe because it was not in a courtroom. . . . It was just a different room. I was in line with a bunch of people. I had to turn in my green card. We waited for the judge. This guy in blue jeans and combat boots came out and said, 'The judge is now coming in, you have to raise your hand.' I felt like an idiot, like a kid. Then the man in jeans told us, 'Now, in case you want to ask for your sisters to come to America . . .'

"The judge came in. He gave a short speech, saying he was proud of us and 'Congratulations, you're all now citizens of this wonderful country. Good-bye!' Then he left—and everybody left."

In place of the charm and civil manners of Papa's citizenship experience, disappointment from the greatest nation in the world, and even suspicion because it asks so little of citizenship petitioners that something seems not quite right! In lieu of the message that Papa got from America, Ceci got the message that, really, you haven't joined very much.

☆
☆ ☆

5

The Ford Foundation
as the New Electorate

Breathes there a man, with soul so dead,
Who never to himself hath said,
This is my own, my native interest-group.
with apologies to Sir Walter Scott's *The Lay of the Last Minstrel*

That transformed, fraudulent, and even often disgraceful "naturalization" process in America today does not stand alone—it is
paralleled by changes in the old ideas of radical individualism and
of individual-merit citizenship that profoundly underline the arrant sloppiness of America's modern approach to its citizenship
bond. For the dumbing-down of the tests, the giving-over of a
once-noble naturalization process to ethnic lobbies, and the total
lack of any penalty for abusing American citizenship are backed
up by a phenomenon still unknown to most Americans; the rise
over the last thirty years of activist forces advocating "group
rights," using the power of the courts to enforce them, and thus
leading, with guileful indirection, to the creation of bartering and
eternally warring new groups that on many levels are in principle
and in practice *taking the place of citizenship.*

To understand this complicated process, let us start with one
spring day in the early 1980s. I was meeting that day by accident
with two representatives of one of the major and supposedly representative "Hispanic" groups, the National Council of La Raza.
One of the group's leaders, a "professional activist" of Japanese
descent, was a young man of considerable charm and intelligence
named Charles Kamasaki. Both were unhappy with the tilt of one
of my columns criticizing illegal immigration, and I have made it

a habit, whenever possible, to talk to my critics and test my convictions against their arguments.

So, after discussing the question of illegal immigration for a while—they remained for it, and I remained against it—I thought to ask them more about their group. It was a thoroughly innocent move. "How many members do you have?" I asked, genuinely interested, as always, in the structure and funding—and thus the real power—of any organization. To my surprise, the two young men just looked at each other, shrugging without embarrassment.

"Well, we don't *have* members," Kamasaki responded simply.

Perhaps I should interrupt here to add that I gained my interest in organization—how structures work, whom they represent—early. Indeed, I learned basic principles from a rare genius in this field, the tough and brilliant Chicago organizer Saul Alinsky. In the early sixties, Saul was a treasured and highly instructive friend and mentor to me, and he instilled in me a passion for analyzing strategy and power, real and mythological, which I then employed working in virtually every culture across the globe. Thus, at moments such as this, whether with the "Razas" of America or with the liberation movements that spanned the map from Lebanon to Angola to Cambodia, I automatically applied Saul's thinking—and questioning. (I also knew all too well, and reflected on with some amusement, the derision that would have characterized Saul's response to an organization so insensitive and arrogant in the era of civil rights as to call itself, translated from the Spanish, "The Race"!)

But to return to that day, I was, frankly, a little taken aback. "You don't have members?" I repeated. "But how do you fund and support yourself?"

The two smiled as though they did not have a care in the world, and, indeed, financially, they did not. To promote and push through their programs and policies, they needed no elections, no campaign strategies, and none of that bothersome business of fund-raising or member-seeking. At the same time, of course, they basically suffered accountability neither to disparate sources of funding nor to the fickle interests of individuals.

"The Ford Foundation!" they answered, almost in unison.

To back up a bit, the National Council of La Raza had been founded as early as 1968 as the Southwest Council of La Raza.

Kamasaki explained to me that Ford, as well as other foundations, agencies, and philanthropies, had been looking for Latino groups to fund because they determined that "the real problem was that they didn't have the kind of mediating community-based organizations and institutions in the Latino community (as in the more traditional American communities)." Although La Raza at that time claimed 150 organizations in thirty-six states, they still did not have real members. "Our membership and principal constituencies are and always will be organizations," he went on. "We have become the Latino equivalent of the Urban League."

Indeed, if you look at one representative year of "The Race," you will find how groups such as La Raza, which is typical, do exist and prosper. Listed on its 1989 Internal Revenue Service Form 990 are the following figures, which reveal the fascinating and disturbing story underlying the new political dynamics in America.

Of a total revenue of $3,553,606, La Raza received $2,562,224 in direct support and $991,382 in government grants. Direct support was listed as $590, 000 from the Ford Foundation, $200,000 from the Rockefeller Foundation, and $75,000 each from the PEW Foundation and the Mott Foundation. The following government agencies also contributed: the Department of Health and Human Services, $321,083; the Department of Labor, $188,150; the Small Business Administration, $176,164; and the Department of Education, $142,649. The Ford Foundation was listed again under "notes payable" for $121,166, to finance debts, loans, and debt relief. (In fact, if we look at other years, we see that Ford Foundation grants to La Raza have gone from $630,000 in 1968 to a low of $150,000 in 1971 to $830,000 in 1988 and to a whopping $1,250,000 in 1991.)

Yes, even the American government was contributing to La Raza and other groups—under laws that came out of the social activism of the sixties requiring organs of government, as well as corporations and banks, to donate to and help such activism. That many of these groups then fought government programs in the courts and elsewhere did not seem to register in the minds of many congressmen or bureaucrats.

Likewise, the fact that much of the thinking of these groups completely denied and even negated the capitalist/citizen, work-ethic, no-zero-sum-game philosophy that American free enterprise was built upon didn't stop corporations from donating money.

They gave because the new laws encouraged them to do so but also because it made them feel good, tolerant, and nondiscriminating. And so, the big conferences of La Raza are filled with corporate visitors fêting and giving both funds and recognition to a group that has virtually no members and no real grassroots but knows well the activist public relations lingo of this era. There you have the "New American Citizenship": the self-interested "get" group selling and bartering ethnic imagery to the self-interested "sell" group.

That day marked my first venture into one of the stranger political worlds of our times: the world of laterally funded ethnic and special-interest lobbies. This world is characterized by its absence of membership and thus its lack of responsibility to anyone outside itself, as well as by its lack of accountability to any power but the activist officers of the big foundations. This world has none of the requisites of or restraints upon political power as we have traditionally known it in democracies because these organizations come laterally into substantial power in the nation—and, in terms of special issues, often definitive power—using largely legal challenges to traditional power. Because they are funded laterally by the big foundations, even though their numbers are very small, their actions can and do constitute a kind of megaphone exaggerating their ideas and influence.

Perhaps Richard Estrada, the superb columnist for the *Dallas Morning News*, put it best when he warned in the summer of 1995 that "we should remember that for all the media attention devoted to organizations such as La Raza, the Mexican-American Legal Defense and Educational Fund and the Puerto Rican Legal Defense Fund, one basic fact is often left out of the coverage: These organizations depend largely on liberal foundations, huge corporations or other organizations for their financial support—but not on the Hispanic rank and file."

Arthur Schlesinger Jr. has written about this new "indirect democracy" syndrome, saying that, in our earlier days as a nation, "civic participation was what indoctrinated (new citizens) into America. Today, ethnic lobbies fulfill exactly the opposite function. They are not supported by the majority of their people and they are paid for by American foundations supported and run by the Left. . . . Are we now to belittle 'unum' and glorify 'pluribus'? Will the center hold? Or will the melting pot yield to the Tower of Babel?"

To black professor and writer Shelby Steele, this process is even more ominous than it at first seems. The California scholar sees it as inevitably leading to a "grievance identity," which allows you, the victim, to "turn your back on the enormous and varied fabric of life. There is no legacy of universal ideas or common human experience. There is only one dimension to your identity: anger against oppression. Grievance identities are thus 'sovereignties' that compete with the sovereignties of the nation itself. Blacks, women, Hispanics and other minorities are not even American citizens anymore. They are citizens of sovereignties with their own right to autonomy."

I want to reiterate here that there is nothing deliberately evil about what these activists and their groups are doing, nothing illegal. Many of their organizers are "good" people who, in line with their beliefs, are doing "good" things. But it is also incumbent upon us to remember that, while they have an absolute right to organize and/or to be funded, so do we others have the conscience-inflicted responsibility and a civic right to at the very least begin a national debate over these new principles. For in reality they serve to distort and endanger American political and, above all, civic life.

The foundations have their own very specific political and ideological agendas, which these devolved civil rights activists and advocates then impose upon the country. The dénouement of this new power-structuring-without-accountability finally is obvious to me: Power in America today in key areas relating to American citizenship often comes, on a variety of levels, not from our old "consent of the governed" but from the passions of young ideologues who ironically capture the "capitalist" monies of the foundations that the old (whatever else they were!) citizenship-conscious robber barons and other more enlightened tycoons such as Henry Ford established to "do good." Thus, self-interested advocacy groups, using civil rights tactics designed for totally different claims and situations in the 1960s, are in still another area shaping American political life.

The effect of this syndrome on the nation is not minor; in fact, it is intense because this "ethnic representation" basically aims, implicitly but also explicitly, at replacing citizenship rights/duties with rights/privileges based upon one's ethnic background (real or imagined, genuine or re-created-for-effect), with group rights and the imperatives of one's supposed victimization at the hands of the old, coherent, common-value central society! These new-style organizations, which carry self-interest to a new level, are on nearly every count the ones leading the fight against stronger tests for citizenship, for unrestricted immigration, and for the weakening of linguistic unity.

Since the victimization syndrome feeds the ambitions of these young ideologues of ethnic groups, that victimization must be eternal, its demands insatiable, its agenda never fulfilled. There can be no resolution—and there will surely never be any absolution. The syndrome does indeed keep the ethnic/special-interest pot of demands boiling like the waters of the first level of purgatory, for the intent of these ideologues is not to join the system as needs and inequalities are dealt with and fade away but to create an alternate system—one not of productivity and equality but of permanent dependency and eternal outrage. (Such carryings-on would have sent a spasmic Saul Alinsky bellowing to high heaven, something he did in classic Homeric style. He would have been the first—and the loudest—to point out that this is abysmally wrong because it does not *empower* people but makes them only *more* subservient. As usual, he would be right.)

☆

But let us look at the Ford Foundation itself, which we will use as an example of what other foundations are doing, and how this one-time bastion of American capitalist influence and money was turned around to establish the broadest funding behind America's influential but largely unrepresentative ethnic and special-interest lobbies.

We choose mainly to look at the Ford Foundation because, with assets in excess of $4 billion, it is the leading funder of such advocacy groups. Ford grants, totaling $175 million per year by the late 1980s, were pouring out of the foundation at the rate of approximately $700,000 per working day, or some $100,000 per working hour. Such enormous resources, matching or exceeding many of the most generous grant programs of the federal government, can indeed make a difference.

But there is another important factor at work here. In contrast to earlier days of the foundation, money often can be allocated now without approval by the foundation board. This makes it possible for impassioned or determined staff ideologues to push the politics of programs in whatever direction they choose. And so we find still another area where devolved power has little or no accountability to any larger authority or principle.

The Ford Foundation was not always this way. When the original Henry Ford and his son Edsel founded the foundation in 1936 with an initial gift of $25,000, it was a highly respected organization involved almost exclusively in traditional Ford family philanthropies. But in time the foundation was championing causes substantially at odds with that very system that spawned it—in tandem with parallel changes in American education, political representation, and civic consciousness.

In fact, the first phase of the radicalization of the Ford Foundation came as early as the 1950s, at exactly the same time that civic education was being destroyed in our schools and universities. It was then that the foundation board was enlarged, effectively taken over by "liberals," and moved to Pasadena, California. The new architects of change in the foundation, under Paul Hoffman, leader of the Marshall Plan, were convinced social engineers of an early variety; they immediately embarked upon highly controversial black and Hispanic "freedom" programs, legal aid for the poor, and even (amazing, for that era!) cultural and social exchanges with Eastern Europe. By then ensconced in "progressive" and booming California instead of stodgy and limiting and disintegrating Detroit, the foundation, as Ford biographer Walter Hayes puts it, "had more freedom to plan the transformation of American society." Meanwhile, Henry Ford II "began to have his first experience of what happens to perfectly normal, even distinguished people when they are provided with the power to give away money they have done nothing to earn."

For a time, after 1953 when Hoffman resigned and the offices moved to New York, the foundation reverted more or less to its original intention, founding such stellar groups as the Institute for Strategic Studies, giving $6.2 million to build a new United Nations library, and introducing family planning to India. But troubles returned with a vengeance in 1965, when McGeorge Bundy became the foundation's president. One of the original Camelot knights of John F. Kennedy's circle, Bundy ironically had considerable responsibility for the very Vietnam War that so energized the activist generation he would later fund from the elegant new headquarters on Manhattan's East Forty-third Street. It was common wisdom that Bundy was morally striving to make up for "Vietnam." No matter, nobody's perfect, and Bundy soon tried to make up for any transgressions by employing the foundation monies to socially transform urban America.

"The foundation was," writes Hayes, "accused of making grants even to street gangs, and critics said that its activism on social and racial issues was actually contributing to violence." It was at this time that the foundation also proudly became the major force in establishing the Mexican-American Legal Defense and Educational Fund (MALDEF), which would soon become one of the most radical pro-immigration and anti-citizenship lobbies.

Simultaneously, Henry Ford II was close to "going crazy" with Bundy's "progressive"—and, to his mind, wastrel—politics. Ford dealers across the country were bitterly complaining to him that Bundy's policies were ruining their businesses: Thousands of Americans were refusing to buy Fords because of what they read and believed about the foundation's "radicalism." Even worse, at least for the foundation, Bundy oversaw an era in which the foundation's portfolio of investments went from $3.7 billion in 1966 to $1.7 billion in 1974. In only eight years, it had overspent its income by an average of more than $100 million a year and succeeded in halving its resources!

Finally, in 1974, the Ford family and motor company broke financially with the foundation, and the foundation disposed of its remaining Ford stock, now to depend upon other more diversified income sources.

Henry Ford II's melancholy letter upon his own resignation as trustee, a post in which he had served since 1943, came on December 11, 1976, a date that in many ways marked the end of a period of Americana. Charging that the foundation no longer understood America as a whole, Ford wrote in what was to become his historic and famous missive that "the diffuse array of enterprises upon which the Foundation has embarked in recent years is almost a guarantee that few people anywhere will share a common perception of what the Foundation is all about, how it sees its mission and how it serves society. . . ."

Then he asked the activists to try to understand the very system that made their enthusiastic philanthropy possible. "The Foundation exists and thrives on the fruits of our economic system," he commented. "The dividends of competitive enterprise make it all possible. . . . In effect, the Foundation is a creature of capitalism—a statement that, I'm sure, would be shocking to many professional staff people in the field of philanthropy. It is hard to discern recognition of this fact in anything the Foundation does. It is even more difficult to find an understanding of this in many of the institutions, particularly the universities, that are the beneficiaries of the Foundation's grant programs."

Ford went on, "I'm not playing the role of the hard-headed tycoon, who thinks all philanthropoids are socialists and all university professors are Communists. I'm just suggesting to the Trustees and the staff that the system that makes the Foundation possible is very probably worth preserving. Perhaps it is time for the Trustees and staff to examine the question of our obligations to our economic system and to consider how the Foundation, as one of the system's most prominent offspring, might act most wisely to strengthen and improve its progenitor."

Actually, as Hayes points out, Ford was not even conservative. He was "a very liberal man himself, generous, concerned for people, often surprisingly and instinctively sensitive to the tenderness of others, and he was, to a large extent, color-blind. . . ." But his was an old-fashioned liberalism—Lyndon Johnson was his kind of president—and he was an engineer of the automobile and the hospital and the traditional university and not of this new kind of social change created by eternal confrontation.

To give only one measurement of the foundation's agenda and intent: By the 1980s and '90s, almost every major political and legal opponent of immigration reform other than business organizations and agricultural workers was receiving major funding from Ford. The foundation went further in advocating funding from other major foundations for immigration policy—thus, its influence was truly more pervasive.

Indeed, Ford played the leading role in founding and building what are now the Hispanic organizations to such an extent that

even the leftist magazine *Ramparts,* writing about Hispanic interest groups in 1970 and comparing them to the U.S. invasion of
Mexico in 1846, comments, "There has been a new invasion of the
Southwest. This time, it is the Ford Foundation, not the U.S. Army,
and it is backed by dollars, not soldiers."

Nothing was being done in the dead of night. Indeed, the foun-
dation activists were proud of what they were doing. "Hispanics:
Challenges and Opportunities," a 1984 working paper from the
Ford Foundation, explains:

> The Ford Foundation's interest in the Hispanic community
> dates back to the Sixties, when efforts on behalf of the civil rights
> of blacks and other minorities first gained prominence in domes-
> tic programming. Since that time, the Foundation has worked to
> insure that Hispanic concerns are well-represented not only in
> the civil rights area but in all domestic programs for the disad-
> vantaged. In civil rights, for example, the Foundation helped
> establish the Mexican-American Legal Defense and Educational
> Fund in 1972. . . . In the area of community and economic devel-
> opment, foundation support in 1968 helped create the National
> Council of La Raza (NCLR) which provides Mexican-American
> communities and organizations with technical assistance and
> which has also become an effective voice for Mexican-Americans
> and other Hispanics. . . .

Then, prophetically, in the conclusion, the report notes the
change in the foundation's work with Hispanic organizations to
a civil rights-oriented approach.

"The old approach is no longer sufficient," the report concludes. "What Hispanics have need of today is what blacks needed
twenty-five years ago: greater knowledge and understanding of
their economic, social, and political situation and of the roots of
their disadvantage, and the development of an infrastructure that
will increase their participation in the mainstream of society."

Still another published Ford study comments on the year
1978–1988: "One Foundation alone, the Ford Foundation, provided
over half (54 percent) of the support for Hispanic needs and concerns. The Ford grants were nine times greater in value than the
foundation providing the next highest amount. . . . MALDEF

obtained almost one-third of all monies given to Hispanic-controlled agencies."

Let's back up. In the late sixties the civil rights fight had basically been won, leaving confused and at loose ends those of my generation who had cared passionately about this struggle—and who risked our lives for it. (I covered Civil Rights in the South, went to the march on Washington, wrote about it in Chicago.) What would come next?

It soon dawned upon many of the activists and organizers involved that, were they to accept the fact that the civil rights war was over, they would be dinosaurs. So, partly out of sincere conviction and partly out of cynical self-interest (depending upon the person and the immediate needs and motivations), the techniques and passions of civil rights were projected onto other groups—in particular, the Hispanic or Hispanic-American community—that had not suffered centuries of discrimination and hatred and segregation as slaves, and then as half-free Americans, which had been the experience of the American blacks. Indeed, including Hispanics, legals or illegals, under the civil rights umbrella seemed to many of us who had cared deeply about black Americans' unprecedented suffering as the greatest possible insult to black Americans' memory of oppression, and to their own well-earned rights.

You see, there were other ways to "do it"—proven and effective ways for people to get ahead, integrate, and assimilate. They could have integrated through jobs, through economics and entrepreneurship, helped along by moral appeals to that American sense of justice and of decency that had been reawakened and already sharpened by the civil rights fight. But by applying these civil rights demands and tactics inappropriately to the Hispanic-American community, and backing them with the legal methods that all America was coming to hate, a bitter focus on "rights"—in place of fairness and economic progress—became the norm. The Hispanic immigrant community (*not* the totally different Hispanic-American community of citizens), which was just getting on its feet, was particularly vulnerable to any influences inculcating a victimization mind-set rather than the citizen virtue of self-reliance.

As Peter Skerry, author of *Mexican-Americans, the Ambivalent Minority*, UCLA professor, and one of the best and fairest analysts of the Hispanic-American community and these new dynamics, has written:

> In today's post–civil rights political culture, many groups have enormous incentives to depict themselves as suffering some version of the racial oppression experienced historically by blacks. They are encouraged to do so by the breadth of the civil rights legislation that Congress passed before the great upsurge of immigration after 1965. It was an historical accident. . . . But, bestowing benefits intended for black citizens upon newly arrived immigrants has led to confusion in area after area of public policy. It distorts common understanding of the problems immigrants face, complicates our efforts to solve them, and encourages immigrants to see themselves as victims of deprivation and discrimination; and results in policies that are frequently inappropriate.

He then bitingly, but accurately, calls the kind of politics that this brings forth "patron-recipient politics which fosters the political equivalent of welfare dependency."

One night, Skerry and I spoke for several hours about these topics, and at the end of our talk, he looked rather sad and added, "The only morality that is left is tolerance and lack of discrimination—that's pretty thin."

No longer was the unique, tragic, and ultimately triumphant history of African-Americans to be specially recognized, their unique suffering specially rewarded. All that history was just "forgotten" in the indiscriminating New Left litany of "everybody's deserving, everybody's got absolute rights." The fact that black Americans were brought in slave ships, against their will, sold as slaves, whipped and punished at will by their "masters," then lynched, or persecuted even after "liberation" was nothing special.

Now, any Mexican or Latin American—or, soon, South Korean, Pole, or Vietnamese—who voluntarily left his homeland, traveled at his own will to the United States (almost always for economic reasons), and did so most often breaking the laws of this new land (that he most probably illegally entered) was considered equally qualified to receive "compensation" or "benefits" from this land (that he had not even pledged allegiance to).

In short, as an assertive governmental role was encouraged on all levels to protect the "special" needs of various "groups" ranging from African-Americans to Hispanics, homosexuals, and women, what is sometimes called a new *"ideological structure"* was being created in America as part of a new *"socially constructed reality."* We had moved from the old system of political bosses, with all that meant in terms of a new people advancing through their own energies in a system that stressed economics and business as the way "up," to professional ethnics, with all that meant in terms of a reliance on victimization beliefs and tactics that could be met only in the activized courts of the post-1960s world.

But what we were seeing concerned far more than immigration; rather, it was an assault on the vaunted historical independence of the American citizen and his way of life. We were also seeing, on more metaphysical and philosophical levels, a *veritable assault on majoritarianism*—the rule of the majority, which had always protected and defined American citizenship.

Allan Bloom perceptively wrote in his classic book, *The Closing of the American Mind,* that

> much of the intellectual machinery of 20th century American political thought and social science was constructed for the purposes of making an assault on that majority. It treated the founding principles as impediments and tried to overcome the other strains of our political heredity, majoritarianism, in favor of a nation of minorities and groups each following its own feelings and incentives. . . . In 20th century social science . . . the common good disappears and along with it the negative view of minorities. This breaks the delicate balance between majority and minority in constitutional thought. When black power . . . supplanted the civil rights movement . . . its demand was for black identity, not universal rights. Not rights but power counted.
>
> Yet the Constitution does not promise respect for blacks, whites, yellow, Catholics, Protestants or Jews. It guarantees the protection of the rights of individual human beings.

Rule by the majority, with protection for minorities, was democratic rule; rule by the minorities, in terms of their interests being legally "protected" by advocate/lawyers with their eternal lawsuits, meant civic chaos. And all of these assaults were underlaid by the new "philosophy" of multiculturalism that was quickly becoming the predominant idea-base of the sixties activists who had taken over the universities and their legal counterparts in the courtrooms of the country.

☆

What really *is* multiculturalism? Does it mean that every campesino who crosses the Rio Grande illegally carries Gabriel García Marquez's classic and wondrous works in his head? Or that he perhaps has Octavio Paz's *Labyrinth of Solitude* hidden away in his pocket, to read to his children at night in the barrios around San Diego? Or does the immigrant maid in Laredo dwell at night on the writings of the brilliant and doomed Mexican nun of three centuries ago, Sor Juana Inés de la Cruz, to find solace for her station?

Does it mean that our colleges and universities are now truly enriched by the magnificent writings of other cultures? The Indian Upanishads, perhaps? Confucius's Analects? The Koran? Rabindranath Tagore's great philosophical writings? Does it have anything to do with the fact that, after all, this country has always historically been the most truly multicultural of any country in the world?

The answer to all of those questions is "No." Multiculturalism, as it is understood in the "politically correct" academic and organizational worlds today, symbolizes no less than a root change in our birthright and is one of the major movements weakening citizenship.

I grew up on the South Side of Chicago, where virtually every neighborhood was of a different culture, a different religion, and a different ethnic or racial memory. As a consequence of that childhood and of the fact that I was an early fighter for civil rights for black Americans, I have few guilt feelings about slighting other groups—in fact, my whole life has been a celebration of the great in other cultures and religions and languages. Our neighborhood at Eighty-third and Ada Streets, in what the maps told us was "Foster Park," was in truth so predominantly Irish Catholic that I, who was from one of the few German Protestant families in the area, was sixteen before I knew that I lived in Chicago and not Saint Sabina's parish!

When in later years my dear Chicago friend, the great humanist/ priest Monsignor John Egan, asked me once why I had not visited Ireland, I answered, "Jack, I was *born* in Ireland!"

Each neighborhood of small one-family bungalows, with tiny rooms that somehow were able to hold the abundance of people and love that existed inside them, had its own Croatian church, Jewish synagogue, Baptist church, Polish Catholic rectory, or black evangelical house of worship. Much of the time, we all got along pretty well (sometimes not so well), but multicultural it surely was! And as I began traveling everywhere in the world for my paper, the *Chicago Daily News,* as the first woman foreign correspondent in the country, I was able to utilize that intimacy with and instinct for other cultures—my intense and driven curiosity about them— that began on the South Side.

As I traveled around the world, too, I noticed something rather pertinent to our subject: Virtually no other countries in the world *were* multicultural—at all—or even made the slightest pretense of being so; and most of them were composed of warring "ethnic groups," rampaging through their historic differences instead of working toward any promise of cooperative unity. Indeed, they were ready to take on their "neighbors" at the slightest real or imagined slight, for they lacked a common uniting belief and had not the slightest idea of how ever to find one.

But in the sixties, everything in America changed. The original civil rights fight—for rights in practice for all races, as guaranteed in theory by the Constitution—had nobly appealed to the conscience of the nation. But when civil rights was distorted by activists and organizers in the post–civil rights period that began at the end of the 1960s and passed into the '70s and '80s, that original appeal was transformed to target the guilt of the nation. Many wished to share in the profitable victimhood. Laws were put on the books by sympathetic and well-meaning legislators and put over America by activist sixties judges, guaranteeing not equality of opportunity now but equality of outcome. Affirmative action personified a new concept of equality—total social equality—that unfortunately was never remotely possible in practice, anywhere. Society was asked to assign positions on the basis of group membership, which was in truth a new racism.

In this new era of divisiveness-at-the-service-of-ambition-and-theory, groups even fell back upon—symbolically, of course—speaking "private languages" of citizenship with, as Duke University proponent of postmodernism Fredric Jameson puts it, "each individual coming to be a kind of linguistic island."

From the 1960s onward, the liberal notion of "cultural pluralism" became the dominant conception of civic identity in American public laws: The civil rights convulsion and acts of the sixties promoted social equality for black Americans, other minorities, and women; the 1965 Voting Rights Act furthered their political equality; the Immigration and Naturalization Act of that same year was supposed to terminate perceived former "ethnic"and "racial" discrimination by opening American immigration to the needy Third World. This new America believed passionately what the Founding Fathers had known to be untrue: that you can force "virtue" down people's throats.

Language was playing a new and important role. The idea of self-sufficient "language minorities" came out of the civil rights bills; they were ultimately defined by Congress to include Asian-Americans as well as "persons of Spanish heritage," effectively giving these groups, who formerly were judged on merit and on America's original radical individualism, ethnically separate and special voting rights. New programs were being created to address the special needs of "ethnocultural minorities."

(A historical parenthesis: We surely know the degree, most often with evil intent, to which "ethnicity" can be created—and re-created—for distinct purposes. Stalin, for instance, decided to re-create ethnic groups in the Soviet Union, even though the czars had always downplayed it, fearing this version of "group rights" would threaten Russian power. Stalin's evil desire was to build ethnic hatreds into the system, so he could manipulate them. The brilliant Soviet scholar Paul Goble tells this fascinating story: When asked "who" they were, most people in the Soviet Union in Stalin's time did not know. Since one did not easily turn down a "request" from Joseph Stalin, they invented "ethnic names"; the upshot was that "seventy percent of the 400 names of ethnic groups in Stalin's last list mean only 'human being' in their languages.")

The most insightful analysis that I have seen of multiculturalism and its political repercussions comes from scholar John Fonte of the American Enterprise Institute. He says that we are going through a transformation from "liberal democracy" to "the alternative world view of cultural democracy, challenging the basic principles of liberal democracy on practically every important issue."

"At the heart of the liberal-democratic world view is the concept of the individual citizen," Fonte writes. "Traditionally, the legal and moral authority of political liberalism is based on the rights and responsibilities of individual citizens, who are equal under the law and together form a self-governing free people. . . ." But in the new "cultural democracy" of the multiculturalists, "the major actors in the civic culture are no longer individual citizens operating through voluntary associations, but distinct peoples, ethnic groups, and cultural blocs with their own world views, values, histories, heritages, and sometimes languages, which often require different legal rights and separate educational programs. Cultural democrats . . . weaken the concept of citizenship itself by blurring the distinctions between citizens and non-citizens.

"Multiculturalists," he sums up, "are extremely uncomfortable even with the very idea of an American people."

The programs that the multiculturalists or "cultural democrats" espoused, conceived, and carried through were, of course, possible only because of the growth of Big Government that began with Lyndon Johnson's Great Society—and its sudden largess. The amount of money going to and from government was growing exponentially, along with the new entitlements by race and by group, so it was not surprising that the special-interest groups forming around these new realities (often inspired by antitraditional American sentiments, as it turned out) should discover rather quickly that all they needed to do, for power and satisfaction, was to petition the government. To repeat, the growth in special-interest groups is directly related to the growth in Big Government.

In short, this led to an entire skewing of the political processes of the country, which had been so meticulously laid down by the Founding Fathers. Beginning with the words and concepts *cov-*

enant, compact, citizenship, the great American discussion has ended up in the rather less noble *rights, entitlements, privilege.* The splendid Shelby Steele, ever prescient and (even more important) ever honest, notes that

> historically, entitlement was based on the rights of citizenship elaborated in the Declaration of Independence and the U.S. Constitution. This was the kind of entitlement that the original civil rights movement leaders claimed for blacks: recognition of their rights as American citizens to equal treatment under the law. They did not claim, "We deserve rights and entitlements because we are black," but, "We deserve them because we are citizens of the United States. . . ." The politics of difference changed all that. Blacks and other minorities began demanding entitlement solely based on their history of oppression, their race, their gender, their ethnicity, or whatever quality that allegedly made them victims. . . .

Steele even goes so far as to trace how sovereignty is increasingly bestowed by government on other institutions, on "little nations within the nation," in effect on groups organized around unassuageable grievances. These fiefdoms, he continues, have become "ends in themselves," providing careers for a "grievance-group executive class" that can thrive and prosper only if the grievances are permanent. The utterly predictable result? An increase in racial, ethnic, and sexual divisiveness.

The term *political correctness* was not new when it sidled into American consciousness in the 1970s through the sixties radical activists in the universities. In fact, it was an old term, a purely totalitarian concept used proudly by the Nazis and Stalinists to assert the right of those in power to suppress all but the party line's official lies. The American leftist philosopher Herbert Marcuse, who influenced sixties radicals' thinking so profoundly, called upon just such a sense of political correctness when he taught a new generation of Americans, among other things, that "tolerance for the expression of intolerant attitudes, like racial discrimination, should be repressed for society's good."

What is essentially a new metaphysical underpinning for American life—alternately called "political correctness" (for the application) and multiculturalism (for the ideology)—has of course come out of the alienation of the young over the Vietnam War, the urban riots of the 1960s, the hatred for presidents such as Richard Nixon, plus the end of the vast educational expansion that took place since World War II. It dawned, as Professor Albert Michaels has put it, in "an unprecedented outburst of anti-anti-Communism, anti-Americanism and anti-Capitalism within many American universities. . . ." There, the new leftist leaders "claimed to want peace and equity but most, especially younger faculty, sought salary increases, easy promotions and administrative power. Collectively called the 'New Left,' they combined a hatred for the American system with limitless personal ambition" and yet at the same time looked to government for their salaries and for power to change society in their image. And, soon, the clash between ethnic particularism and democratic universalism seemed to be defining America in place of the old Left-Right conflicts.

Within multiculturalism and political correctness, there are two major philosophical and metaphysical undercurrents: *postmodernism* and *deconstructionism*. Postmodernism, which replaced modernism in America (and perhaps also the nation-state), as defined by conservative William Phillips, I believe correctly, includes: a belief in a widespread relativism in moral, political, and philosophical matters; a commitment to social changes, vaguely reminiscent of old radical doctrines; a theoretical emphasis on rights over duties; a belief in unrestricted personal freedom, particularly in sexual matters; a general rejection of the existing social system; a radical revision of academic curricula; an atmosphere of leftism and anti-Americanism permeating the whole.

Deconstructionism, postmodernism's brother, basically means the destruction of anything promulgating unity: to deconstruct is to make simpler and to replace a former unity with a new, existential way of seeing things that announces the total absence of unity. Deconstruction also means a fierce emphasis on relativism and on the indeterminacy of the meaning of all texts.

In short, deconstructionism is the father of the intellectual disintegration of American universities and the destruction of intellectual rigor and integrity so that every concept and every idea is equal; and it is also, not accidentally, the mother of the division of the country into ethnic and special-interest groupings, with their special rights and privileges.

The ongoing attack on the traditional historical American model, the brilliant columnist and writer Charles Krauthammer writes, "takes two forms. First, it challenges the idea of a common Western culture, and, secondly, it challenges the idea of a common American citizenship."

Finally, we begin to see multiculturalism for what it is and is not. It is *not* some new respect for other cultures nor some attempt to build into the American academy a true knowledge of the great works of other cultures or religions, or a knowledge of historical experiences.

No, multiculturalism is in truth a carefully designed power play by the sixties "leaders" and activists who see the division into cultural and other units in America, allied with its concomitant victimization, as a way to erect a new America and to rule it. It has nothing to do with being free to practice your own cultural customs—America has always had that—but rather concerns the rewards you can claim according to the power you can call forth in the name of your culture, and thus the imposition of your own ideas and power.

Some of our best thinkers believe we are probably too far advanced along the route of this mind-set to turn back. "The modern era has come to an end, at least within the United States," historian James Kurth has written.

> The United States is no longer a modern society, but a postmodern one. And, as we shall see, it no longer resembles a nation-state, but rather a multicultural regime. . . .
>
> Post-modern society, and especially American society, is not characterized by standardized schools engaged in mass education in a national, often high, culture. Rather, post-modern society is characterized by an organized media engaged in mass entertainment. . . . Post-modern society is not characterized by large conventional armies, based on mass conscription and providing national defense. . . . Post-modern society is not characterized by efficient industries engaged in mass production, principally for a national market. Rather, it is characterized by

financial enterprises and industrial management engaged in
multinational operations within a global market.

And this multicultural society, if it does overtake traditional
America? Well, first, nobody is going to die for diversity, affirmative action, or bilingual education. So the emphasis on the multicultural agenda at the expense of the inspirational qualities of
unity means a dangerous watering-down of the levels of passion
and commitment to nation, with all that means in terms of intellectual, artistic, and moral excellence. Multiculturalism depends
upon a clash of principles, whereas a working society must be
organized upon one or a few central principles.

☆

One does not have to be one of the disdained and dismissed—and
sometimes, indeed, dangerous—Commie-bashers to see the effects
of America's cultural exchange with Marxism from the early 1900s
onward. One finds now within American institutions elements of
class warfare (political correctness), the techniques of mind control and of intolerance for other ideologies (multiculturalism), the
"trials" of dissident thinkers (the persecution of moderates and
conservatives in the universities and the academy), the collective
guilt of groups (white males), and the defining of collaborator
groups (any group that does not accept their ideas).

In this world, there is no redemption, no forgiveness, no transformation—the very soul of the Reformation, the Enlightenment,
and liberal capitalism, which formed American citizenship, was
under attack in these popular new realities.

America's growing "politics of litigation," moreover, fed directly into these totalitarian concepts. For its part, it destroyed
exactly the debate that is always utterly essential to good citizenship and "downgraded all political argument not conducted in
front of a judge," as the prescient columnist John Leo puts it. Or
as the fine University of Chicago theologian and philosopher Jean
Bethke Elshtain has written, "the tendency to remove political dis-
putation from the political arena into the courts" is a tendency
Americans have witnessed over the past four decades "to derail
public debate by judicial fiat." This leads to the prevalence of absolute and unreconcilable and nonnegotiable demands and to "or-

ganizations whose primary goal is to give no quarter in any matter of direct interest to them and to them alone. Juridical politics
is 'winner take all' built on an adversarial model."

And, of course, far from being the transformational ethic of the
original America, political correctness actually *freezes* exactly that
change in America that always allowed and encouraged American citizens to move and mix and try to become more than they
were. Citizenship made America open, fluid, equal; political correctness makes it closed, static, unequal.

Interesting none of the great works of other cultures mentioned
earlier are anywhere to be found on the multicultural reading lists;
almost all books on such lists are quite deliberately volumes of the
complaints of American society's new victims. In fact, multiculturalism is the true racism. Every tenet underlying the actions
of the "multiculturalists" is really saying, and quite openly, that
the differences between people are in the blood—in *la raza*. They
deny differences in the excellence, in even the developmental
efficacy, of different cultures at different periods of history, and
yet they base their whole philosophy upon supposed differences.

The multiculturalists are really talking about becoming immediately citizens of interest groups—and, pretty soon, if their thinking and actions are carried to their logical ultimate dénouement,
citizens of ethnic conflicts. For that is what inevitably comes.

Multiculturalism thus finally becomes nothing less than an
alternative to citizenship, the mythological/metaphorical grounding
for the breakdown of American citizenship.

☆

Multicultural advocates did not have to look very far to find ready-
made many tools to diminish the power of American citizenship.
The Fourteenth Amendment to the Constitution, for example,
states, "All persons born or naturalized in the United States and
subject to the jurisdiction thereof, are citizens of the United States
and of the state wherein they reside. . . ." Illegals from Mexico and
through Mexico learned that they could cross over into the United
States, have their babies in El Paso or Tucson, and—voilà!—they
had a little instant citizen in the family, who could bring everyone
in the family over in later years. (But the Fourteenth Amendment
was put into the Constitution for a very specific reason: Drafted

soon after the Civil War, its intent was to grant citizenship to the freed slaves and to recognize these longtime and long-suffering natural Americans as full Americans. The amendment was never intended to give preference to foreigners, especially those breaking the law in coming here and taking all the benefits, while at the same time bearing none of the rigorous exactions of real citizenship.)

For their part, the activists soon could—and did—organize and activate illegal aliens on all levels to get benefits formerly accruing only to citizens: welfare, hospital service, even education for their children. (This led directly to Proposition 187 in California in 1994.) These aliens, in turn, provided the reason and bodies needed "out there" to keep the foundation grants coming to pay the activists' salaries.

One has to believe and admit that there is among many activists a sincere wish for these newcomers to America to be made better off through their efforts. But removing or trying to remove the immigrants from the traditional political power fight that all other groups had to go through has actually put them at a severe disadvantage. Because of this activism, they are denied access to the modernizing factors of American life that so transformed all other cultural travelers in earlier days. Instead of being counseled by these putative leaders on adapting to the American way of life, they are instead counseled on welfare benefits and other "entitlements" they ostensibly "deserve" and have the "right" to here. Essentially, this only makes them doubly dependent—first, on their "leaders," and second, on government.

As the fine *New York Times* writer Richard Bernstein has commented, correctly, "the educators who push the idea that America has no common culture nor anything redeeming to offer the world—that all cultures are equal and some breed success better than others—are in fact doing a terrible disservice to those oppressed whom the ideologues claim to champion." This is just another example, on the "ethnic" level, as Myron Magnet has written, that the "Have-nots" have been incapacitated for upward mobility by the sixties culture of the "Haves," which tells the "Have-nots" that they are crippled by victimization, in need of therapeutic preferences, and that their self-destructive behavior is a natural expression of a history of oppression.

In short, the activists want to mold "the people" into one group that can be controlled by a central theme—*manipulable victimiza-*

tion. This is, of course, negative, self-pitying, and essentially self-hating. But there is an alternative: to be assimilated into the central theme of Americanization, which is positive, uniting, and respectful of self and of nation.

Social engineering creates dependent individuals, passive clients for social-welfare programs, overseen by the very same activists and their friends who so believe in government programs. Thus they are deliberately cut off from the people who could best give them the values with which to succeed in this new society. Meanwhile, too, those same citizens, instead of reaching out to immigrants and serving as models of citizenship, see the newcomer only as a threat to their own values. And so, the chasm is constantly enlarged and deepened—and that is exactly what most of the activists want.

Hispanic immigrants are also being placed into a rigid and separate group that threatens to usher in the next phase of racial warfare, in particular as Hispanics pass black Americans in numbers. As Peter Skerry writes, "Mexican-Americans are being encouraged to dwell on the undeniable injustices of the past rather than to seize the opportunities of the present." If left unchallenged, he says, the "tempo of race politics" threatens inevitably to set black American against immigrants, and probably Hispanic America, legal and illegal, in particular. This largest bloc of ethnic voters is being fought over by the two major parties, yet, it is not being assimilated as fast as it possibly could and should be because of the Hispanic activist agenda.

This type of activist control-from-above has inevitable consequences that are in truth the antithesis of democracy and of democratic organization. "When you have all these groups which have no members," Peter Skerry says, "it changes the whole dynamics of everything. Members keep you real."

☆

Let us look at the most dramatic example of the power of this new political bonding and its corrosive effect on America: the famous MALDEF, or the Mexican-American Legal Defense and Educational Fund.

MALDEF has had a turbulent history and an energetic and determined leadership, but it was always a creature of the Ford Foundation. In 1990, grants from Ford were $1,575,000, up from

$425,000 in 1977 and $233,600 in 1983; during the eighties and afterwards from one-third to almost half of its total annual revenues were from Ford alone. MALDEF, the strongest institutional expression of the "racial minority view" of Mexican-Americans, has also received help from a handful of other major foundations, corporate sponsors, and even the federal government.

MALDEF was founded by activist Pete Tijerina in 1968, the same year it received start-up funding from Ford. Some of the Ford money was siphoned off to Jose Angel Gutierrez, notorious author of "Kill a Gringo" and other militant statements. Gutierrez's comments were one reason for a famous four-hour grilling of McGeorge Bundy, then president of the Ford Foundation, by the House Ways and Means Committee, who accused Ford of funding "political advocacy." When Tijerina finally resigned, the central offices were moved from San Antonio, Texas, to San Francisco.

It was in MALDEF's "San Francisco self" that its litigational strategy was very deliberately adopted and implemented. Borrowing directly from the litigational tactics of the National Association for the Advancement of Colored People (NAACP), MALDEF soon adopted its test-case precedent, based upon the NAACP's *Brown v. Board of Education*, the historic case in which the U.S. Supreme Court overturned school segregation. Soon MALDEF was arguing the case for free education for Hispanic children in America, regardless of citizenship or even citizenship-intent, which culminated in the 1982 *Plyer v. Doe*, the case in which the Supreme Court did indeed guarantee public education to illegal alien children.

MALDEF, with teams of lawyers, determined to treat every problem of the Hispanic-American or illegal community as a civil rights problem, and so it engaged many "causes," one victory being the bilingual voting amendments of 1975. Also in the area of voting rights, MALDEF was behind redistricting of political districts in order to give minorities—Hispanics, Koreans, et cetera—more electoral power in 1982. It was MALDEF that waged the decade-long battle against immigration reform throughout the 1980s. Peter Skerry notes, "It did so without widespread grassroots support, a fact that was certainly evident to the participants in that battle, at the local as well as national level." But it did so with clear Ford Foundation support; indeed, in August 1983, Ford issued a working paper on refugees and migrants and at the same time initiated massive funding to defeat immigration reform.

MALDEF bitterly fought and modified the Simpson-Mazzoli bill, which was finally to become the Immigration Reform and Control Act of 1986. It argued before the Congress that the legislation's proposed sanctions on employers' hiring undocumented or illegal workers, which was the key to the entire legislation, would lead to widespread discrimination against "all brown-skinned people." It tied up congressional negotiations over the bill for months, always at crucial moments. In the end, MALDEF diluted the effectiveness of employer sanctions and, as Skerry puts it, "succeeded in defining the terms of the debate and thereby persuaded many Americans that racial discrimination was an overriding concern of Mexican-Americans," which further distorted American reality. But during that immigration debate, illegal immigrants were going into MALDEF offices every day, pleading with the group to support the bill because they would become legalized—and have the right to apply to become citizens through its amnesty provisions.

It was typical of MALDEF's work that the organization was also responsible for an out-of-court settlement in 1992 by which the INS agreed to give aliens apprehended while illegally crossing the border a written notice of rights, including the right to consult with an attorney. (Here one again sees clearly the extension of rights formerly accruing only to citizens being extended even to people who were clearly breaking the law.) Typically, too, San Francisco Bay area lawyer, Joaquin Avila, a consultant to MALDEF, came forward with a statewide ballot initiative to end the citizenship requirement for voting. "People who contribute to the economy, culture, who pay taxes, should have the right to vote," he declared. (And here one sees the struggle to make such citizenship privileges as voting available to not only legal aliens but, most probably, even illegal aliens.)

James Q. Wilson calls this political representation hoax "vicarious representation."

Peter Skerry says that MALDEF is typical of public interest organizations in that "in one sense, the organization behaves like any group of ambitious, well-trained lawyers. But without any members or clients to which it is answerable, MALDEF can't take a much broader, longer view than any conventional law firm. This was of course what the Ford Foundation had in mind when it established MALDEF."

Meanwhile, to back up its congeries of commitments and ambitions, MALDEF gave scholarships to promising law students; they were then obliged to work for MALDEF for some years before moving on to greener corporate or other pastures. And at the same time, MALDEF was virtually isolated on the immigration question from more serious, less showy Hispanic interest groups such as the G.I. Forum. These groups had actual *members*. And members feared the effects of uncontrolled illegal immigration because, as normal human beings, they had established lives and positions that were threatened by illegals—they were *citizens* who had not only privileges as such but duties as such, men and women who had something to lose. But none of this stopped the litigators of MALDEF.

Even as one considers MALDEF as the classic case of these new forms of *non*representative government, one must add that other Hispanic organizations do differ in their approaches, even when they often support the same goals. The G.I. Forum, founded just after World War II by Mexican-American veterans who found discrimination upon their return, has long been one of the most effective of Chicano political groups—and one of the most moderate. Unquestionably the most procitizenship organization is NALEO, or the National Association of Elected Latino Officials, which was founded by its national director Harry Pachon, a Colombian immigrant in the 1970s as a network of and for Latino elected and appointed officials. NALEO is funded by foundation and corporate donations and is highly respected in diverse circles, its constituency being the 4,202 Latino elected officials in the country. Another effective pro-immigration group, LULAC, the League of United Latin American Citizens, began in the Southwest in 1929 as a procitizenship group and later changed, but only somewhat. Another great Texas organizer, Ernie Cortez, comes directly out of the Saul Alinsky tradition, and is by all accounts doing superb citizenship work in his areas.

But one social element is similar—and, indeed, strikingly so— in all of the groups. All the leaders and most of what followers exist are upper-middle-class Hispanic-Americans; some call them "Yuphies" (young urban professional Hispanics).

Yet it was MALDEF that captured the public imagination, and the Far Left soon stepped in on its side. Linda Wong, who had been with the Far Left National Lawyers Guild and was by then MALDEF's principal immigration policy advisor, actually said in 1985 that job displacement or wage depression is due to the "real" cause of American imperialism. American involvement in El Salvador raised its controversial head; the question of foreign policy and local citizenship-related policies arose.

The reaction of the spokesmen from some of those extreme groups to the testimony of Colorado Governor Richard D. Lamm before the Joint Economic Committee of Congress on immigration in May 1986 is revealing: Lamm, a man of great talents and reason, began by warning of the risks of massive immigration. "Ethnic, racial and religious differences can become a wedge," he said. "They can grow and eventually splinter a society. Our own society has been the exception to this historical pattern, but it is a mistake to believe that our success has been serendipitous or that it will continue to defy history without our work and care. . . . Can we have today's immigration, virtually out of control, and still remain 'one nation, indivisible'? I believe this is a closer question than most realize."

The next day at a press conference of Hispanic "leaders,"one immigrant rights activist commented, "I think it's typical comments of a lame-duck politician looking for a job someplace else. . . . Book sales must be low if he has to do something like this to try to get publicity." And Ernest Martinez, executive director of a local Hispanic group, Servicios de la Raza, described his agency as one "whose mission is to treat the mental and social problems of Hispanics caused by the oppression, discriminatory stereotyping and cold-blooded disrespect inflicted on Hispanics and Chicanos by people like Governor Lamm."

Civil discourse, utterly essential to any democratic society, is thus being degraded and debased in America.

☆

Come with me to Brownsville, Texas, a charming old city near the delta where the Rio Grande meets the warm, blue-green glimmer of the Caribbean. Unlike the cities of the western and central parts of the river, this city/town of Brownsville has little of the Latin American about it; it is American southern, with mosses and heavy sighs, its memories not of the Mexican-American War but of the Civil War.

One day in the spring of 1995, I was sitting with several excellent and committed teachers and principals in the Brownsville Independent School District, which has the huge educational job of caring for forty thousand children, the largest group of students together anywhere in "The Valley," this very far southern area of Texas abutting Mexico. I soon began to suspect, however, that they must be not educators at all but magicians, for they were surely being asked to perform magic! Here is the amazing conundrum that faces them:

Illegal immigration in America is, well, illegal. Yet certain legal precedents and practices not only force American school districts to educate the children of illegals, but also forbid schools from even daring to ask the children or their parents if they are citizens, legal aliens, or neither. In its wisdom, the federal government will reimburse the school district for the illegal children attending school in Brownsville (probably a year after the fact). Here's where the magic comes in: Only magicians, you see, can figure out how to get federal reimbursements for students from the federal government when they are expressly forbidden from counting them to know how many of them there are!

Dr. Jose Manzano, one area administrator with the district, tried to explain. "Basically, we cannot check who is legal here," he began, already looking defeated. "Texas law says we must educate everyone who comes, legal or illegal." Now, Dr. Mona S. Hopkins got into the fray. "So, for funding purposes, we will say we have thirty-five thousand illegals," she chipped in. "We have an attendance office, which keeps 'records' for three years—in order to get the federal funding. Then after three years, we don't keep up with them anymore; federal laws do not allow us to do that, either."

I told them frankly that that seemed bad enough to me. Such intelligent, committed people, trying to work in these chaotic border areas, already have sufficient problems, I thought, without having such absurd and contradictory tasks imposed upon them. In a city of only 130,000, a school district of 40,000 students is simply enormous and has to be overcrowded; it is expected to rise to 55,000 students by the year 2000. On top of that, many children are coming at ages ten or twelve from Mexico, having had no schooling at all. Bilingual education is the same mess here that it is everywhere; and this system of odd and amorphous "laws" forces everyone essentially to lie. Everybody knows, for example, that many, many children pour across the bridge from Matamoros every day to be schooled—all at American taxpayer's expense, of course. But no one will say it.

As we talked, I finally asked: "And what are these laws that forbid asking students about their status?"

The educators thought for a minute. They looked at one another. Then they thought some more. "Everybody says there is a law," Dr. Hopkins finally volunteered. "We've tried to find it . . . but we never could."

Thus emboldened by my fears about what activists were doing with their interminable social engineering, I then set myself the task of looking for "the law" or "the laws." Everyone was helpful. But no one really knew what or where the law was. (Apparently, I misunderstood the spirit of American law: I had thought it was designed to be clear to citizens and not a mystery. I was wrong.)

I spent hours and hours phoning—to officials who should have had this simple information at their fingertips, journalists, educators . . . I simply could not locate these slippery laws and, frankly, I soon began to wonder whether they actually existed. And finally I discovered that they do—barely. Here are the two best versions of the outcome of my devoted search:

- "There is no written law which prohibits asking students if they are illegal," says William Rentfro, the attorney for the school district. "There is no regulation adopted by an agency and there is no legislation. However, across the entire United States, you are not able to ask these questions." He then explained why: In the activist-sponsored legal cases of 1982, the Supreme Court finally ruled that free eduation is not a "fundamental right" (i.e., for illegals), but that illegals should be educated if they are resident in the United States for "public policy" reasons. Not educating them would, in effect, create a "permanent underclass" that would be a great drain on society.

"This being said," he goes on, "once the courts found it was illegal to discriminate on that basis, there was no reason to ask them [what their status here was]. It was said to have a 'chilling effect' on people."

• The Texas Department of Education could come up with only Chapter 552 of the Education Code. This requires educators to "maintain confidentiality over all personal educational records." So it seems that these confidentiality laws, originally put forward by conservatives in the 1970s, have come to be used by pro-immigration people to push their cause—with great and anarchistic success.

I kept thinking that I must have missed something; this was all too absurd to take seriously. But I had not, and it was not. The federal government had paid this district $450,000 for the two years previous to my visit to educate illegal children, of whose numbers or status we have no real idea because we are forced to educate them without knowing who, what, or where they are. This is taxpayer money, remember, the money we all earned by *doing* things and not just *saying* things!

☆

In that same spring of 1995 I traveled all along the Texas-Mexican border from Brownsville to Laredo, interviewing widely, and at the end I summed up my gratifying findings—that Hispanic-Americans were, if anything, more patriotic, more citizenly, and more American than perhaps even most other Americans—in the following column:

> Brownsville, Texas—If there are two American judges in the entire nation who are more pro-citizenship than Filemon Vela and Ricardo Hinojosa, it would be hard to find them. They approach naturalization with the passion of love.
>
> "One of the great experiences we have in this country is when we make new citizens," the venerable Judge Vela told me, sitting in his elegant office in Brownsville, where he has served as federal judge for 15 years. "They are asked to commit their loyalty to us. The fact is that these people who become naturalized citizens outdo us, teach us."
>
> When I spoke to the equally respected and dedicated Judge Hinojosa just up the Rio Grande in McAllen, he too reminisced

about his court ceremonies. "As a judge, I am exhilarated to take part. I call out each by name. I see how happy they are to receive citizenship.

"I also tell them that I'm a little jealous on this day. That those of us who were born here, we don't remember the day we became citizens. We celebrate our birthdays—but they have birthdays and citizenship."

Despite these words, these two remarkable men are not in the slightest permissive when it comes to the duties that citizenship confers. As Judge Vela says: "I tell them, 'If you are going to live in this country, you must commit yourself to it. You have now renounced your loyalties to the past.'"

And from Judge Hinojosa: "I tell them on this day to think about all the men and women who gave their lives for our rights."

The problem starts when people repeat the fashionable line: "There is no border here." They say that because so many people are mingling and moving back and forth across this fascinating and easygoing border every day as though they did belong to some third "country." In this new, virtual–North American Free Trade Association world, four-lane highways link Texas directly to Mexico City, and Mexican students pay "in-state" tuition at Texas' border universities.

But this is not one world. Laws are different on each side of the border; the police are different, the environment is different, corruption is different. Mores and morals and memories are different. And perhaps most different of all is the Hispanic American from the Mexican.

Professors in the border universities say that their Hispanic American students show no interest in even crossing the Rio Grande to visit Mexico. Every time I tried to speak Spanish to an American of Hispanic descent, he or she politely but firmly answered in English. Poll after poll of Hispanic Americans across the country show that the vast majority want immigration and border patrol—and fully 90 percent of them belong to none of the fashionable radical activist groups. . . .

Indeed, most members of the Border Patrol and the Immigration and Naturalization Service that I met—not to speak of the city managers, the police and the businessmen—were Hispanic

Americans, proud of their citizenship and quite clear about it. And, of course, there are the judges, who are entrusted with one of the highest honors the nation can bestow.

I then went on to say that, yes, there are radical demonstrations, regularly recorded by the press, usually against cutbacks in the "right" of welfare payments for illegals; and there are the professional "Chicanos" who vow that their hearts and souls will always remain in Mexico. "But that is surely not the way it is in these other parts of the country," I wrote. "Here, on the other hand, the Hispanic Americans I met make you proud to be an American."

In short, according to every survey and poll and surely according to my own investigations and interviewing, most Americans of Latin American or Spanish descent are hardworking middle- or working-class people, mostly white, with some Indian or black admixture that is not at all dissimilar to the mixture of America as a whole. They want to live their lives, raise their children, and be good citizens, and above all they represent far from cohesive societies regarding their ethnicity. Alejandro Portes, the Cuban-born sociologist who teaches at Johns Hopkins University in Baltimore, is only one of many who now argue that "Hispanic" ethnic solidarity is ultimately a political creation rather than one based on the real experiences of the groups so labeled. He is quite right.

Indeed, the very word *Hispanic* (which I use very reluctantly, it is so imprecise) not only barely covers this rich and varied cultural group but is an "invented" word, created by government bureaucrats. It emerged as a descriptive group label only in 1980, when the U.S. census used it for the first time in its forms—a direct result, one might note, of the perfervid lobbying by groups such as MALDEF to "group-right" the American population of Spanish and Latin American descent.

The truth is that there is no "Hispanic" race—*Latin, Spanish,* or (since we must use it) *Hispanic* are the words used for many peoples and races from a rich culture that originated on the Iberian peninsula in Spain and/or Portugal, with a great admixing of Arab culture from the Arabian peninsula and North Africa.

And the final truth is that there *is* no "Hispanic" community in America, either. There are Mexican-Americans, Cuban-Americans, Puerto Ricans (who are, of course, American citizens), Spanish,

Portuguese, and the aristocratic descendants of the first settlers in the Southwest who were awarded land grants across that region by the Spanish crown. In their own terms, there are *Mexicanos*, Latin Americans, *Hispanos*, Latinos, Chicanos, *la raza*, *batos*, *batos locos*, Mexican-Americans, Mexicans, Spanish-Americans, wetbacks, *tio tacos*, *braceros*, green-carders, Uncle Tamales, *cholos*, greasers, beaners, and *pochos*. The 1980 census showed that fully 18 percent of the country's population was some sort of "Hispanic," compared with 14.8 percent only ten years before, and that they came from all the rich and variegated cultures of Latin American countries plus Spain and Portugal.

Richard Rodriguez, the great Mexican-American writer and pro-assimilationist, tells the story of meeting a woman at Middlebury College in Vermont and having her insist she wanted him to speak only Spanish with her. He said, no, he would speak English. She responded that she was proud of being Indian, and said, "Soy Azteca" (I am an Aztec). "And I said," Rodriguez concludes, "well, at least notice the paradox of what you are saying. You are using the language of the Conquistadores to say that you are Aztec."

☆

Every consequential poll of the American-Hispanic community has shown clearly that on issues related to American citizenship—*all* the issues, whether illegal immigration control, bilingual education, citizenship duties, belief in the unifying force of the English language—the Hispanic-American community is totally and unreservedly American. To name only one, the Roper poll of 1985 found that 91 percent of Hispanic-Americans were in favor of stopping all illegal entries and that 77 percent wanted to reduce the quotas for immigration.

Still another indicator of Hispanic or Hispanic-American attitudes toward citizenship is to be found in the National Latino Immigrant Survey of NALEO, the National Association of Latino Elected and Appointed Officials, the major procitizenship group among the Hispanic organizations. Only 35 percent said there was discrimination against Latinos in the United States; only 18 percent were afraid of losing the culture of their home country; only 17 percent even planned to return to their home country; and a mere 15 percent felt they would be mistreated by the U.S. Immigration Service.

But the stunner of them all was the 1993 Latino National Political Survey, conducted by Rodolfo O. de la Garza, the respected professor of government at the University of Texas at Austin, ironically with funding from the Ford Foundation. (It surely did not expect the outcome, and there were indications that it tried to downplay the embarrassing results!) This comprehensive poll of Hispanic-American attitudes, goals, and hopes illustrated once again how ethnic political leaders were not advocating the causes that their communities supported. It found that 80 percent of Puerto Rican–Americans, 75 percent of Mexican-Americans, and 66 percent of Cuban-Americans wanted to reduce immigration to the United States. It also showed that most "Hispanics" think of themselves as neither Hispanic nor Latino. Most consider themselves moderate to conservative ideologically and support a common national agenda that includes traditionally liberal positions on domestic issues; and most do not have a particular interest in Latin America.

But an even greater shocker was the fact that fully 90 percent of those interviewed said that none of the ethnic organizations spoke for them or for their ideas. (Peter Skerry had already found that only 8 percent of Hispanic-Americans even used the word "Hispanic" to describe themselves.) They spoke English better than Spanish and thought newcomers should use English. As to motivation, they were surely reacting on a self-interest level as well as on a patriotic level, and trying to keep foreign competitive labor from destroying their lives and lifestyles. Then, really challenging the suppositions on which the activists' policies were based, a majority denied ever having been discriminated against.

As the brilliant black economist Thomas Sowell wrote in his column when the poll was released, "All this is miles away from the picture broadcast through the media and taught in 'ethnic studies' programs in academia. It is likewise miles away from the shrill cries of ethnic 'spokesmen' who are forever demanding more programs that teach in foreign languages under the misleading label of 'bilingualism.'" He further remarked, and this is an important footnote to the Hispanic-American "experience," that polls of thousands of black students on dozens of college campuses found also that most believed that everyone should be admitted to the schools under the same standards. "Yet minority preferences and quotas polarize many of these same campuses, because the vocal 'leaders' and strident organizations demand that admissions be based on demographics rather than academic qualifications.")

Time magazine's columnist Richard Brookhiser perhaps analyzed the power dynamics of these new groups best in writing that

> the assimilation of Hispanics is news because two allied groups of political operators are trying to pretend that it isn't happening. Leaders of ethnic communities fear the success of members of their communities because it makes special favors unnecessary and deprives leaders of their status as favor brokers. Meanwhile, liberal believers in the problem-solving omnicompetent state mourn any group's graduation from maladjustment because it gives them one less thing to do at the office. Both sets of people would protest that they are motivated by idealism and a desire to right wrongs. Always distrust a saint when his charity generates his paychecks.

☆

It was not surprising—indeed, it was inevitable—that all of these developments would lead to the formation of still more ethnic lobbies and political organizations, and even to the threat of separatist groups *within* the United States.

Already, the U.S. government was even sponsoring and subsidizing—via special tax funding—special-interest caucuses of "ethnic" congressmen and women in Congress. By the 1990s, there were caucuses of Albanians, Asian Pacific nationals, Indians, Eastern Europeans. . . . As always, "short-term" and "special" benefits tended to become permanently expected "rights." When the new Republican majority tried to cut these subsidies (which, remember, were often dedicated to break up the nation into specially privileged groups), the Hispanic groups in the Congress cried to high heaven: the elimination of the tax funding was "racist," "mean-spirited," even "an attempt to impose censorship." (By this reasoning, refusing to pay for another's antagonistic accusations and even his lobbying against your interests is considered "censorship.")

The new Republican majority decided that the caucuses could, of course, continue; they would just have to pay for themselves and not expect the five million dollars in subsidies that, by the way, paid for the jobs of ninety-six people working for them.

By the spring of 1996, what was surely the most important new development in America's citizenship debate had received remarkably little attention: Immigrants' groups, and even aliens' groups, were suddenly organizing, forming lobbies, and even incipient political parties to represent their own exclusive interests. A new stage had been reached as, for example, technologically sophisticated Chinese students, many of whom remained in America after the massacre at Tiananmen Square, were organizing, using E-mail, to stay here longer; Congress even pushed through the Chinese Student Protection Act, which granted permanent residency to more than sixty thousand Chinese students and their family members living here temporarily (thus setting a dangerous precedent, many thought). And the Armenian Assembly of America had been successfully lobbying Congress to slow development of the rich Caspian Sea oil fields, whose cultivation would considerably lower world oil prices (but would also bring wealth to their enemies, the Azerbaijanis).

Representative Lee Hamilton summed up the new syndrome one day when he said with some astonishment that "there has been an explosion in ethnic group participation in politics in this city." He thought for a moment then added, "What is often missing is analysis of the national interest."

In addition, we were seeing one of our first real secessionist movements since the Civil War in Beautiful Hawaii, where a movement demanding independence from the mainland had thousands marching in torchlight parades. The *Washington Post* duly reported that by 1993 there were "at least a dozen organizations struggling to define Hawaiian identity." One, Ka Lahui, headed by an educator, was trying to create a self-governing "nation within a nation" of Hawaiians under the federal policy that allows "all Native Americans to be self-sustaining." Both Presidents Reagan and Bush had refused to treat Hawaiians as Native Americans eligible for nationhood and for title to lands taken from them in an American coup in 1893; but the independence people were hopeful about Bill Clinton. The editor of the *Honolulu*

Advertiser, Gerry Keir, was quoted: "Ten years ago sovereignty was talked about only on the fringes. It is now an issue squarely in the mainstream of public debate." And the islands' first Hawaiian-ancestry governor, John D. Waihee III, supported the secessionists by flying only the Hawaiian flag over the capitol and government buildings.

If this sounds more than a little like the Québec separatist movement or the beginnings of the Serbian ethnic war, it was. And if it sounds a little like the beginnings of separatism on the mainland, well . . .

In fact, in the Southwest there was already, even though small, a disturbing and potentially dangerous secessionist movement. Chicano art exhibits are traveling around the country focusing on the utopian Hispanic idea of Aztlan, which includes a swath of America from Texas to California, ceded by Mexico to the United States in 1848; now radicals in the Hispanic movement demand that we return it in order for them to set up an "independent nation."

And in San Diego and other cities in the Southwest, there is a movement called MEChA (the initials for the Spanish-language name for the Chicano Student Movement of Aztlan). Far from being democrats, MEChA activists such as Miguel Perez state with equanimity that once Aztlan is established, non-Chicanos "would have to be expelled" and anti-government demonstrations would have to be quashed.

There are some problems with their analysis. For one, since the Aztecs originally came from Asia and never lived in the Southwest, syndicated columnist Raoul Contreras of San Diego suggests with more than a touch of irony that "their mystical homeland is some-where in Siberia." In addition, students at the University of California insisted upon creating a separate Chicano studies department, despite the fact that no other ethnic group has such a department—and, after a window-breaking protest, the UCLA chancellor backed down. "Ethnic studies" are already mandated at the University of Wisconsin and at Texas A & M.

Chicano students at the California universities and elsewhere are not at all the new immigrants they are assumed to be. They are not even the sons and daughters of the new immigrants; indeed, they are the alienated and fashionably deracinated grandchildren of the original immigrants. They did not *start out* with their modish Chicano ideas of Aztlan. These came to them *at* the American universities!

We see the odd turns of this entire syndrome: It is not that the "Hispanics" don't assimilate, it is that they assimilate too quickly so that, cut off from their past, the following generations find their "roots" in the alienated American university setting.

But still another leader of MEChA did say something deeply troubling: that members of his organization do not feel affinity with the United States because *"this country does not give you very much to feel part of."* He is right, and *that* should be the real guilt of the made-to-feel-eternally-guilty old Americans! With the watering-down of citizenship that we see around us, and with the lack of pride of Americans in America and their lack of reasonable authority in enforcing the coherence of their country, America ironically is playing directly into these irredentist claims, however strange and wildly unrealistic they are. Worse, America is giving little reason to such disaffected young men and women to want to belong to America.

Arthur Schlesinger Jr., one of the nation's greatest historians, fingers still another related problem, which is adding to the diminution of citizenship power. He says first that "spokesmen with a vested interest in ethnic identification turned against the idea of assimilation." Then he adds, with his exquisite instinct, that another factor leading to the "ethnicity" of America today is the face of "waning American optimism about the nation's prospects." How true! Not only American prosperity and power depend upon those "prospects"—so, as a matter of fact, does American confidence.

Again, it is surely not at all the immigrants' fault that Americans have so wantonly thrown away their birthright. When the center does not hold, particles dispel, to find new identities and new faiths, always; usually this development occurs when empires are approaching their end.

☆

Let's revisit the Ford Foundation. It funded another study, begun in 1987 and completed in 1993, using dozens of researchers and professors who examined (1) how high immigration transforms communities and (2) the effectiveness of various attempts to mold "inter-ethnic relations." At a press conference in June of 1993, Robert Bach, a radical multiculturist and principal author of the seventy-two-page "Changing Relations: Newcomers and Established Residents in U.S. Communities," concluded that there were only infrequent "dramatic episodes of violent conflict" but that relations between natives and newcomers were damaged by competition, tensions, and opposition, with the use of different languages being the worst "single source of contact." (Bach, by the way, would also become the top adviser to the INS in 1995; he had also done in-depth work in Cuba and Vietnam.)

But what did the foundation people conclude? After noting a "diminution of living standards for many . . . class polarization and . . . widening differences between high- and low-income groups," they determined with extraordinary logic that the cause was not immigration, but Americans' and their institutions' weaknesses in being able to adapt to it!

"Immigration itself is not the difficulty," the report states. "The problem that many observers claim faces America—the potential for fragmentation—is not produced by immigrants or by their diversity." Author Bach, a professor of sociology at the State University of New York at Binghamton, stated unequivocally that "the problem in America may not be diversity but homogeneity."

There you had the "new mentality," shorn of any shame, in total and quite amazing candor! What now–INS idealogue Bach was saying is that *America as we have known it—and Americans as we have known ourselves—must be changed,* not really to facilitate immigrants' progress but to facilitate the vision of America dreamed up by the activists and the Ford Foundations of the world.

The problem is ours, don't you see? We have been too successful, too rich, too prosperous, too great a force in the world, *too homogeneous!* Let me be ironic for a moment: We Americans should understand that we are the ones who have no "right" to keep ourselves the way we are.

6

"Roaming in a Land of Strangers"

*The dogmas of the quiet past are inadequate to the stormy present. . . .
As our case is new, so must we think anew and act anew. We must
disenthrall ourselves and then we shall save our country.*
Abraham Lincoln

*There are historical forces too powerful to be contained. . . . Citizenship
is one of them. There is, in other words, a suicidal strain in the citizen,
a death drive which is very evident today.*
historian Ralf Dahrendorf

Whenever Americans talk about immigration and how it affects
our daily lives and our citizenship, the first "truth" someone inevitably puts forward is "After all, we are a nation of immigrants!"
It is invariably stated as a kind of biblical verity. Conversation
stops, as if a Roman Catholic pope has spoken among the faithful
on questions usually undiscussible and answers always infallible.

And it is there, right away, that one finds encapsulated the first
misunderstanding about immigration in America today.

First, all countries in the history of mankind are nations of immigrants at one time or another. Even the American Indians (Native Americans) originally emigrated, beginning their trek from
Central Asia about 30,000 B.C., following the bison to Alaska across
the Bering Strait, and then southward into North and South America.
(Mankind's wanderings are often oddly inspired!) Throughout
history, cultures have crossed and recrossed, with stronger cultural
traits adapted from people to people, as cultures rose and fell,
justly or unjustly. Before World War II, it was generally the great
empires that spread ideas, carried products, and imposed law and
religion from continent to continent—across the Silk Road, down

the dangerous waterways, around the Cape of Good Hope, and so forth.

Second, while America is a nation of immigrants, what is primarily true is that *America is a nation of citizens.*

Immigration was the first and most crucial step in forming America, but it was also the unfinished, tentative step. Citizenship was the final polished and noble step. One was marked by the uncertainty and disconnectedness of youth; the other, by the maturity and seasoned certainty of adulthood. One was characterized by the sadness, loneliness, and even tragedy of uprootedness; the other, by the joy of renewal with reconnection in a voluntary bond to one's fellow man.

One is marked by loss; the other, by gain.

Inevitably, the uprooted person's mentality changes during this process as he is literally faced with the dramatic chance of being—in civic and political terms—born again. Poets experience that type of rebirth often and of course more breathtakingly than do we ordinary mortals, as do theologians and men and women with a sense of mission; but the only rebirth that all naturalized Americans can take part in is the sobering and (at least once upon a time) "sacred" ceremony of citizenship.

Actually, the whole idea of America-as-a-nation-of-immigrants is inaccurate, even absurd. At no time, except in the unquantifiable Colonial era, has the American population ever been composed of less than 85 percent native-born citizens. In 1850, only 9.7 percent of the population was foreign-born; in 1900, it was 13.4 percent; by 1950, it was only 6.7 percent; and even as late as 1990, it rose again to a mere 7.9 percent. But percentages are not, by far, the most important part of the immigration question.

To constantly freeze the American experience at the immigrant stage, a clearly unfinished stage in the long human struggle for ever higher forms of human organization and being, is to profoundly misunderstand the ideas underlying the American experience and the common experience of virtually all civilized nations in modern history.

Yet, that is what we have done and are doing.

Consider Emma Lazarus's famous words on the Statue of Liberty: "GIVE ME YOUR TIRED, YOUR POOR, / YOUR HUDDLED MASSES YEARNING TO BREATHE FREE, / THE WRETCHED REFUSE OF YOUR TEEMING SHORE, / SEND

THESE, THE HOMELESS TEMPEST-TOST TO ME./I LIFT MY LAMP BESIDE THE GOLDEN DOOR!" Even that quotation distorts the American experience. First, the words are not inscribed *on* the statue, as is generally assumed; they are on a small plaque inside the base on which the statue stands. Second, her words were not written in response to any American experience but rather to the Jewish experience in the Russian pogroms following the assassination of Czar Alexander II in 1881. Emma Lazarus's loyalties were not primarily to America at all; while she was surely an ardent and valiant young woman, she was not an American but a Zionist. Her words were added years after the dedication of the statue, which came to America in 1886, although it was a gift from France to commemorate the American centennial of 1876. And the statue, far from being intended as a beacon to immigrants, was actually designed to stand for "Liberty Enlightening the World": France was thanking America for inspiring her revolution, for inspiring her to duplicate U.S. successes in that country, and not for encouraging Europeans to emigrate from their homelands.

The statue is not the only immigration story that's been distorted, however.

First, the situation on the ground:

By the 1990s, America had more than 1 million legal immigrants entering the country every year. From 1983 through 1992, 8.7 million men and women arrived to become, first, legal aliens and, then, American citizens; that was the highest number of immigrants in any ten-year-period since 1910, the high-water year of American immigration. Because of the 1965 immigration bill and its "family reunification" portions, some 3.5 million family members are in line to come; once here and once citizens, they can then bring in *their* direct relatives.

But at this same time, another estimated 300,000 a year were pouring across America's borders illegally. The Immigration Service and other immigration specialists estimate that between 3.2 and 5.5 million have come illegally over the past ten years. Almost all were from the impoverished Third World of Latin America, Asia, and the Middle East, those parts of the world that often were furthest from the standards of American prosperity and most remote in education and experience from the political, religious, and social principles that built America.

To get some idea of the scope of the problem:

In 1975, America had about 200 political asylum–seekers, people who wanted to make the case to America that they were deserving of asylum because of persecution or because of the real fear of persecution in their countries of origin. By 1992, U.S. applications were up to an astounding 103,000, and the American courts faced the problem of having to deal with a backlog of some 300,000 cases.

By the time the census was reported in the summer of 1995, it was revealed that the percentage of the country's population that was by then foreign-born was at its highest level since World War II—and was increasing exponentially at a record pace. The proportion of Americans who had been born elsewhere rose to 8.7 percent in the previous year, or to 22.6 million people, with about 4 million of them estimated to be in the United States illegally. This proportion of immigrants was the highest since 1940, when it was 8.8 percent, according to a Census Bureau report, "The Foreign Born Population: 1994," although less than the modern historic high of 14.7 percent in the flood year of 1910.

The writers point out that most of the increase stemmed from the watershed 1965 Immigration Act, while many analysts warn that past waves of immigration have helped to fuel the ranks of xenophobic and sometimes violent groups, such as the Know-Nothings in the nineteenth century and the Ku Klux Klan in the 1920s.

Now let us look at world parallels:

By 1993, the annual "State of World Population" report issued by the United Nations Population Fund stated that people were moving across international borders—and, it is important to note, from the countryside to the city, everywhere—in larger numbers than ever before in history. And this migration, behemothian and transforming even by accident, "could become the human crisis of our age." It painted the chaotic picture of tens of millions of people on the move, often leaving behind horrendously desperate circumstances but often also carrying horrendous problems with them.

The population of the world has gone from 800 million in 1776—to 1.9 billion in 1924, to 5.8 billion in 1996. At the same time, the population of the United States has gone from 2.7 million in 1776 to 114 million in 1924, to 265 million in 1996.

By the 1990s, 100 million international migrants were already living outside the countries in which they were born, an astonishing 2 percent of the world's population!

Meanwhile, the world has seen a concomitant "relentless movement of people from the countryside to the city." Across the globe, the world's poorest human beings have moved in massive numbers from rural to urban zones, especially to the Third World's increasingly dangerous "megacities." Whether it is a Mexico City with 33 million people, a Karachi that by the mid-1990s has sunk into internal civil war, or even a New York that has in many respects come to resemble the Hobbesian "war of all against all," three major outcomes are assured: These huge and unwieldly new cities of the world are becoming *criminalized, decivilized,* and *deculturized,* as are of course the suffering people trapped in them.

In the Middle Ages, when the feudal estates began to break down and the former serfs fled to the cities of Europe, poets breathlessly put forth the historic cry that "the city makes man free." In the twentieth century, it has been precisely from those urban morasses that the soulless anomie of modern life has morbidly issued.

In short, what happened in the middle of the twentieth century was something that the world had never seen: Human beings were moving en masse across borders and over nation-states. In many cases, they were challenging status quos and even inadvertently neutralizing treasured historic patterns of behavior.

When I interviewed the United Nations high commissioner for refugees, Norwegian diplomat Thorwald Stoltenberg, in his office in Geneva in 1990, he went so far as to say thoughtfully and sadly that "in many ways, I feel there are similarities between 1945 and 1990. Then, the war had ended and, despite the many hopes for the future, those hopes fell into the cold war and that enveloped us for forty years. Now that war has ended and again there are hopes for the future. But now, the mass movement of peoples represents a new form of North-South problem that has become the next East-West issue."

And this is only the start. According to the International Labor Organization, the total labor force of the Third World countries will be 600 million to 700 million people larger in the year 2000 than it was in 1980. To employ all those additional workers, the developing countries would have to create more jobs than now exist in Western Europe, Japan, the United States, Russia, and all the other industrialized nations combined. Rather obviously, that is not going to happen, and for a serious nation to ignore the implications is little less than a criminal dereliction of its duties to its own citizens.

Nowhere are these ominous new developments—and their dangers—as immediately discernible as in China, a country that we should watch carefully with regard to immigration, alienation, and the great displacement of peoples in today's world.

In the summer of 1995, I went to China for the third time and was stunned at what I saw. China was always a universe of peoples, 85 percent of them peasants living out on that great but agriculturally impoverished land mass. But something new was happening: Even by official admission, there were between 80 and 100 million Chinese roaming homelessly, and often hopelessly, around China. That means that, of a country of 1.2 billion, roughly 1 in 12 to 15 was now "floating." The government itself says that only about 44 million of those are registered with public security departments for temporary urban resident permits, although it was desperately trying to get them all to register. And, despite its "1 child per family" policy, you go to bed every night there thinking, "People, people, people, . . ."

I went one day to see Zhao Gwangzhou, the charming and cultivated man who is president of the Academy of Sciences, and, even as crowds teemed on the old street outside, he told me, as we discussed population problems, "We hope that population will decrease by twenty twenty or twenty thirty and level off. But at that time, the population of China might reach one point six billion."

What population could China, with its poor land, reasonably support? I asked.

"Eight hundred million," he responded.

I wrote at the time about the "floating migrants," trying to capture in words the poignancy of their fate: "You see them everywhere: homeless men roaming the streets of China's cities; farmers from the hills of Sichuan sleeping at night on the construction sites they work by day; country boys with suitcases held together by ropes; and brutal criminals kidnaping Hong Kong businessmen who dare to do 'business' in this 'new China.'"

It's an explosive situation. The countryside is pulling away from faraway Beijing, as always throughout Chinese history. New warlords are arising in region after region. Crime and criminality-as-a-way-of-life are burgeoning everywhere, as is uncertainty and fear.

Here I see the final contradiction of Communism, which was supposed to show people where they belonged—and how—and to offer them and force them into "the faith." But now, China and Russia are illustrating that that faith failed and that they do not know where to go next with the question *Who belongs where?*

But these problems of internal immigration are also leading directly to political developments in China, as in Russia and elsewhere, that no serious person could want to see. I predicted the summer of 1995 that "the only other faith besides making money in China or Russia then becomes nationalism, which may well be invoked in the next 10 years, essentially in order to retie the people to the society. Until then, China is riding a bike that it needs to pedal faster and faster, if only to keep those masses of people from falling off into the road."

By the winter of 1996, it was indeed a new and virulent nationalism—gazing outside in order to call attention away from or to try to assuage these problems inside—that was informing Chinese foreign policy, as she began to threaten to attack Taiwan and even Los Angeles, and as 1997 and 1999 takeovers of Hong Kong and Macao loomed.

☆

As immigration began to transform *this* country, America was no longer a "melting pot," but rather a tapestry, a kaleidoscope, a quilt, an orchestra, a weaving machine, a tossed salad, a mulligan stew, a stir-fry. . . . By the 1990s, *Time* magazine said that America was "too complicated and diffuse to be described as a melting pot, or even a goulash or a mosaic, that society today is really a collection of intertwining subcultures. . . ."

Should it really have surprised anyone that in the early 1990s a great paper such as the *Los Angeles Times* would decree in its politically correct new handbook for reporters that illegal aliens should be referred to as "illegal immigrants" or "undocumented immigrants"? Or that, in 1980, New Left groups would meet in

Mexico and decree a "Bill for Undocumented Workers" that demanded for them all the rights formerly reserved for citizens? Should we be astonished that one of the major organizers was the National Lawyers' Guild, an early recipient of Ford Foundation funding? Or that one article called for the right of illegals to "a proper public education in their native language, using English as a second language," and that another called for the "right to vote in local and state elections . . . without having to become citizens"?

Should it have shocked Americans to find that others foresaw horrendous things to come for the United States, if we continue in the same direction? That observers such as Professor John Gray of Oxford University had come to view America as an inevitable "proto-Lebanon," soon to be riven by ethnic strife?

In his aforementioned remarkable study on how America has moved from the old traditional individual-merit-based "liberal democracy" to the New Left's "cultural democracy," John Fonte says that "the majoritarian principles of liberal democracy are increasingly under attack in the name of supranational and subnational ideas of multiculturalism, diversity, multilingualism, Balkanization, political correctness, racism, feminism, ethnicity, immigration, assimilation, the melting pot, the mosaic, the salad bowl, *Laïcité*, . . . sovereignty, globalism, national identity, religious fundamentalism, cultural nationalism. . . ." What is really being contested in all of these conflicts, he concludes, is "whether liberal democracy will survive or whether it will be reconstructed into a new form of governance."

☆

Elliptically offering us the possibility of an answer to that question, the respected Vernon M. Briggs Jr. of the Center for Immigration Studies has managed to underline in one short list of his own questions every inanity of America's immigration problem. He asks:

- How can it be that the annual number of legal immigrants admitted each year is totally unrelated to changing domestic economic conditions from year to year?
- How can it be that 520,000 of those persons who are admitted each year are granted admission solely on the nepotistic basis

that they are related to adult U.S. citizens or permanent residents—as opposed to being admitted for any skills, or education, or locational preferences they might have that the nation
may need?

- How can it be that additional immigrants (55,000 per year,
  beginning in February 1995) are admitted simply on the basis
  of a lottery—the ultimate antithesis of responsible policy-
  making?
- How can it be that 10,000 immigrant visas are available each
  year for millionaires who can buy their admission in return for
  a faint promise to invest in some sort of job-creating activity?
- How can it be that, despite mounting evidence that illegal
  immigration is continuing to soar, Congress refuses to address
  the flourishing business of fraudulent document abuse and
  grossly underfunded border enforcement agencies?
- How can it be that, of the tens of thousands of persons already
  in the United States who seek political asylum each year, only
  20 percent actually show up for subsequent hearings on their
  status?
- How can it be that over 50,000 persons will be admitted in 1993
  as political refugees from the former republics of the Soviet
  Union, when the cold war is over and the United Nations high
  commissioner for refugees has conceded that almost no one
  currently emigrating from this region is a refugee?

Briggs does offer one primary explanation for such present
lunacies: "U.S. immigration policy is essentially a 'hodge-podge'
of politically-motivated initiatives that pays no attention to its
collective economic implications." He could have added that
what we see in immigration "policy" is simply a reflection of
what we see on so many other levels of American life: an unwillingness to make even relatively painless reasonable choices to
assure our very health and security as a nation and an unwillingness (in immigration policy) to look the fraudulent charges of
"racist" and "nativist" and "exclusionary" in the eye and reveal
them for what they are.

But, there is a key new element in immigration that escaped
even this perceptive observer:

This new immigration is not the old emigration from one country to another because of famine, war, or national collapse. It is not

the phenomenon of peoples making a practical and moral decision to stay in America. As *Providence Journal* columnist Philip Terzian has written, "This is not immigration in any historic sense; it is the economic transfer of bodies across borders—and, it must be said, a certain prescription for just the sort of ethnic discord that sent European refugees flocking to Ellis Island."

In short, many people are coming to America today not to become part of the polity, but essentially to get a job.

☆

Any realistic questions about citizenship and belonging revolve about the question of time and space.

In 1776, when the American polity and experiment was born into a world that knew immeasurably more misery than joy, it was a world of only 800 million people—only roughly three times the American population today. Almost without exception, it was a world of monarchies and other autocratic systems, a world of subjects but not citizens.

Within America itself, one could not even correctly speak of a "frontier"—all of America was a frontier and, moreover, it was a land of majestic natural riches and soaring possibilities. And those possibilities were realizable because the Founding Fathers—almost all English (and, after them, other Protestants, Roman Catholics, and Jews of Europe)—carried with them the implicit agreements on politics that would forever save America from the political chaos of the Old World, with its ancient hatreds and eternal conflicts.

The Founding Fathers favored open immigration, but they were also specific about the context in which it must be pursued. They were not at all ashamed of welcoming immigrants only if they intended to become "Americans." Not only were they deeply proud of the unprecedented system that they had created in the New World, but they knew well that it depended upon a common consciousness and upon a shared conscience; they also feared that concentrating foreign populations on American soil would exacerbate the risk of factional and sectional conflict of the terrible sort that they had themselves so deliberately fled in Europe.

As for illiterates, they were not welcome at all. Those wise men had not a second's hesitation in recognizing the need to build upon the base of an educated citizenry, and they also had a sure sense of the social and moral limits even of their great continent and their seemingly horizonless world.

"I do not wish," James Madison said, without apologies, "that any man should acquire the privilege of citizenship but such as would be a real addition to the wealth or strength of the United States."

Even as they believed that citizenship was a transformational experience that they passionately wanted to share with the world, the Founding Fathers never entertained any idea of an America as a refuge nation for all the poor of the globe, no matter how deserving. They knew the limits of their capacity; they understood that "space"—social, educational, cultural, environmental, psychological, economic—would allow for only so much expansion before they lost their edge. America could be looked upon as the philosophical "home" of all mankind, but it could never be its physical home.

Rather, their idea was of an America that would stand as an *exemplar nation*, which the rest of mankind could learn from, if it so wished. America to them represented a kind of new colonialism—but an odd colonialism, being one of ideas! (This idea of exemplar nations will be picked up again later, in terms of foreign policy influence.)

Even General Washington was worried about the many foreigners in his officer corps. This did not in the slightest reflect any disrespect for his valiant foreign companions-in-arms such as the Marquis de Lafayette, whom he admired inordinately. Rather, he feared that too great a foreign presence might weaken the morale and cohesiveness of his citizen-troops.

Finally, all of the Founding Fathers came together in the belief (it did not, frankly, seem such an outrageous idea at the time!) that immigrants must be profoundly socialized into an understanding of American ideals.They knew a lot of big truths and little truths: In terms of the social compact, they knew that becoming citizens helped to make men responsible for one another and for the polity they shared—and that being citizens together made men capable of being and behaving as friends.

All of the questions America faces today about immigration—and, thus, citizenship—were present in some form from the very beginning days of the audacious young republic; but they were dealt with very differently then and generally more realistically. In part, this was a result of the fact that the early leaders in America were balanced men and women who knew that human beings had to be formed in morality and in the operating of the institutions of this new and different society. In great part, too, this approach resulted from the Founding Fathers' knowledge, as historian Arnold Toynbee hammers home in his works, that "the same elements that build up an institution eventually lead to its downfall—because something that was good in the past does not necessarily mean that it will continue to be good in the future."

☆

At least two of today's major citizenship/immigration problems stem from earlier days of American history.

First, from the very beginning of the republic, the most important right and duty of citizenship was the vote. During Colonial times and post-Revolution, voting rights were clearly tied to property rather than citizenship, the reasoning based upon early English rights to own property, which argued that such ownership gave a person the economic freedom that singularly allowed him political freedom. It was a workable and correct assumption—for its time.

But when the property and tax-payment tests began to fade in importance in the early nineteenth century, the states turned to more broadly based eligibility standards such as gender and citizenship. The war of 1812 spurred a number of states to prohibit voting by aliens. But just when the exclusion of aliens from the suffrage had become predominant in America, a contrary trend began to emerge because of the wide-open states and territories of the South and the West seeking to attract new settlers.

In 1848, for instance, Wisconsin even amended its constitution to grant suffrage to aliens, but only to "declarant aliens" or those who had already announced their intention of becoming citizens. Actually, at that time the issue of noncitizen voting became the center of a political and social tug-of-war between the North and the South that continued right up to the eve of the Civil War. With a more conservative outlook, southern senators were trying hard to stop noncitizen voting in the expansion of the western states, while the northern states were in general upholding the new practice, basically because they wanted to encourage immigration in order to develop the country as rapidly as possible.

In those early years of American history, noncitizen voting ebbed and flowed in tandem with the need for immigrants. So it was to be expected that, after the great tide of immigration between 1890 and 1924, those states that had extended the vote to aliens intending to naturalize began to abolish that practice. Indeed, the last such state, Arkansas, did so in 1926; and since that year, aliens have been *legally and officially* unable to vote in federal or state elections in the United States.

Yet, by 1986, the *Los Angeles Herald Examiner* was reporting that no fewer than twenty-five congressmen or women owed their jobs to the "illegal vote." The reason was not even very complicated: Because of America's pitiful refusal to keep track of illegals (the fashionable word was "residents," which could just as well have been phrased "strangers abroad in the land"), they were being counted as citizens in the census used to apportion congressional districts.

Second, the "birthright citizenship" of the Fourteenth Amendment (discussed in the previous chapter) has become a problem. As the *Reader's Digest* has duly reported, so many illegal alien women just walk across the border to give birth that (1) two-thirds of births in the Los Angeles County public hospitals are to illegal aliens; (2) New York City hospitals spend an estimated five hundred million dollars a year on care for illegals; and (3) in Dade County, Florida, there are 16,395 undocumented children in public schools, placing an estimated sixty-eight-million-dollar burden on taxpayers.

Both the vote problem and the birthright problem are classic examples of what happens when a law or practice that is right for one age is not corrected in another, quite different age.

☆

We can probably say fairly that when most Americans look at immigration today, they know intellectually, they judge morally, and they feel viscerally that something is very, very wrong. But the whole immigration problem is so complicated and contradictory—and the din of voices focused obsessively on them are so busy crying "racist . . . nativist . . . immigrant-basher"—that they begin to grow terrified at the prospect of even approaching the subject, much less addressing it. The entire panorama tends to blur before their eyes and finally they just abandon even any realistic or just search for rationality, justice, or truth at all.

American immigration, while never easy to understand, can be simplified immensely by looking at the patterns and flow of immigration here; in fact, America has been characterized by clear "waves" of immigration, which were almost always followed by substantial or even lengthy periods of low to no immigration. The "high" or peak years were from 1851 to 1854, from 1866 to 1873, from 1881 to 1883, and—by far, the peak years—from 1905 to 1924. That last period offers the most revealing lessons for Americans today: The country was finally shocked by its numbers, not to speak of its early example of "cultural colonialism," then on the part of the German immigrants who actually wanted German taught in the American schools.

Those waves did not come out of the sea of humanity accidentally, of course; most were not flotsam and jetsam thrown up on the beaches of America, they were men and women who deliberately moved to America, for specific and most often serious reasons—no food in Europe, no space in Asia, no justice in Latin America. They didn't want to serve in the German military; they were Jewish scholars forced to flee the Nazis; they were Polish peasants for whom the land no longer cared, . . . Italian workers, Greek sailors, Russian refugees, even Albanian poets.

Between 1905 and 1924, the population of the world had grown from 1,683 million to 1,942 million. That period witnessed the terrible First World War, and on top of that the chaos of the Bolshevik Revolution, the collapse of the czarist Russian state, the rise of Japanese imperialism, the disintegration of Germany, and the slow death of European colonialism. It could hardly be considered a wonder that people were fleeing from nation to nation in figures never before seen in any epoch. Meanwhile, in America, people were beginning to fear not only the Europe of so many wars, but the new and aggressive Soviet Union with its universalist ideology that so definitively challenged democracy and capitalism. Should it really have been any wonder that America soon began watching for "Communists" within, eventually putting through laws, such as the McCarran Act (1952), to flush them out?

Not surprisingly, a stunning 9 million immigrants poured into the United States between 1905 and 1924, the heaviest period of immigration until today's. The American frontier may have officially been closed, but the vision of "America, the frontier of the whole world" was more prominent than ever.

Also not surprisingly, Americans began to feel overwhelmed then, as now.

National immigration policy until the twentieth century was more implicit than explicit, but after the turn of the century the federal government acted to try to bring some order into that chaos.

Americans then were not modest—and certainly did not feel guilty—about protecting what they had with so much pain and blood created. National standards for immigrants were made in 1906. In 1911 came the famous immigration report put into motion by President Theodore "Teddy" Roosevelt, in which the U.S. Commission on Immigration stated in the strongest terms that the continuation of unlimited immigration was "not in the national interest" and put a lid on the number of immigrants, setting the strictest limits in America's history.

This "Dillingham Commission," in its forty-two-volume report, put forward the following two significant principles to guide America on immigration, principles that the United States would do well to review today. On the commitment part of citizenship: "While the American people, as in the past, welcome the oppressed of other lands, care should be taken that immigration be such both in quality and quantity as not to make too difficult the process of assimilation." On the often-neglected commercial and economic aspects of uncontrolled immigration: "The development of business may be brought about by means which lower the standard of living of the wage earners. A slow expansion of industry which would permit the adaptation and assimilation of the incoming labor supply is preferable to a very rapid industrial expansion which results in the immigration of laborers of low standards and efficiency, who imperil the American standard of wages and conditions of employment."

Those recommendations were followed first by the Quota Law of 1921, "the first law to put a quantitative number on immigrants to be permitted to immigrate to America," and then by the crucial and pivotal Immigration Act of May 16, 1924. The 1924 act placed the first permanent limit on immigration, ruling that national groups already in the United States (according to the censuses) could be enlarged annually by only 2 percent of their numbers.

The upshot was that almost all immigration from Asia was banned and immigration from the eligible countries of the Eastern Hemisphere (almost all European) was limited to 150,000 a year. Most of that was reserved for the British Isles and Germany; Southern and Eastern European countries, the source of most immigration at the time, were limited to tiny quotas. In fact, 1924 spelled the beginning of the forty-year moratorium that allowed the United States to assimilate and absorb the large numbers of immigrants it had been accepting.

America was thus given crucial "breathing space" in which those immigrants already in the country could be assimilated, socialized, and integrated into American life at a reasonable, just, and moral pace.

Harvard sociologist Nathan Glazer wrote that "we can phrase the intentions of the 1924 act in quite another way: it said that what America was in 1920, in terms of ethnic and racial makeup, was in some way normative and to be preferred to what it would become in the absence of immigration restriction; and it said that the United States was no longer to be a country of mass immigration. The 1924 law called for a remarkable scholarly exercise to determine the national origins of the white population: each country would have a share in the quota of 150,000 proportional to its contribution to the makeup of the white population."

At that stage, alarm bells were going off over new fears: Illegal immigration from Mexico across America's southern borders was just beginning. The U.S. Border Patrol and the Immigration and Naturalization Service were created in those years of sober reassessment and concomitant retrenchment. Yet, Mexico's population was still small and the distances to hitch up with the gringo economy were still enormous, so the problem of emigration was still manageable.

☆

I have spent a good deal of my life in southern Wisconsin. My family had a small summer cottage on one of those beatific Wisconsin lakes, and I was at least half raised there. I am convinced that, if there is paradise in America, it is in that good state. Its hilly, pastoral loveliness, abundant farmhouses and barns, progressive politics—all make Wisconsin, more than a physical part of America, a state of mind. The goodness and decency that at best characterize America are to be found "up there" in that state, sitting proudly and independently between Lake Michigan, Minnesota, and Illinois.

But, Wisconsin is also a long way from any of the "troubled" borders—by that I, of course, mean generally Mexico, New York, and Los Angeles. No, I must correct myself: Wisconsin *used to be* a long way from trouble. Today, as is true of nearly every corner of the Middle West, that good state is vulnerable to the undermining problem not of immigration (which they need and welcome), but of uncontrolled immigration (which is transforming many communities in unhealthy ways they certainly would not choose).

The pleasant, leafy, middle-class city of Wausau, Wisconsin, not very far from Milwaukee, would become one of America's first case studies of immigration problems in the early 1990s. As Methodist layman and writer Roy Beck states in a classic article published in the *Atlantic Monthly* (this study later to appear with others in his book *The Case against Immigration: The Moral, Economic, Social, and Environmental Reasons for Reducing U.S. Immigration Back to Traditional Levels*): "After the turn of the century, immigration caused a social upheaval in Wausau. Back then, the Germans and Yankees were distinct ethnic groups, neither of which found particular strength in diversity. From 1880 to the start of the First World War, Germans streamed into Wausau, eventually overwhelming its New England Yankee founders." Indeed, Germans became the predominant ethnic group around 1910, and soon the immigrants transformed the town from conservative Yankee Republican bulwark to German socialist powerhouse. The Germans took over the county seats and county offices and, soon and not surprisingly, "amid the political turmoil, natives felt like foreigners in their own home town."

Not to be casually ignored is the fact that that was the age of the sweatshop, inner-city conflict, and ethnic hatred, when the Ku Klux Klan set itself up against the decent forces of the nation; this, indeed, is what always happens when a nation or a group allows imbalances in population and thus in power to occur and permits an original population to realize its threatened state.

But any further undesired changes in Wausau—and the nation—were squelched by the 1924 immigration moratorium, which lasted for nearly forty years. The law provided the nation the time needed to absorb and assimilate the new immigrants, the Ku Klux Klan's dark powers faded, and the country was again reclaimed for restrained and balanced citizenship.

But—and one cannot stress this factor enough—here we also see, writ small and writ real, the importance of *uncontrolled* immigration with regard to economic and technological development.

Beck relates that "improvements in technology and productivity which supported the middle-class-wage economy that Americans took for granted" continued for several decades; then, in the 1970s, a renewal of mass immigration, combined with the natural and welcome entry of baby boomers and married women into the workplace, began to divide the nation between "haves" and "have-nots" and to lower the technological capacity of the country. That economic decline was quite simply inevitable.

During those forty years after that watershed year of 1924, America pulled back, with great effort and sacrifice absorbed newcomers, and reconstituted itself. But above all, America socialized its new citizens—the process was called "Americanization" at the time—in one of the greatest efforts at transforming disparate peoples into one civic culture that the world has ever seen. Even Henry Ford, attempting to remake his immigrant workers into ideal employees with all sorts of disciplines and incentives, believed that "these men of many nations must be taught American ways, the English language and the right way to live." And even as early as 1919, at least fifteen states realized that there could be a linguistic immigration (the conflict with the pro-Berlin American German community during the war was a first great warning of immigrants determined to hold on to—and even impose—their own language) and decreed that English would be the sole language of school instruction. Gradually, with the opposition to German in the schools and with the acts of Germany in two world wars, this early language threat faded away, only to emerge in other forms with Spanish half a century later.

As Professor Morris Janowitz of the University of Chicago, one of the finest scholars of "Americanization," has written, "There was a great deal of rhetoric about 'Americanization,' especially during World War I and the strained period thereafter. But . . . ethnic identifications, except for some limited radical groups, did not serve as a basis for political separatism in America. To the contrary, ethnic attachments were compatible with and contributed to the dominant trend toward political acculturation. . . ."

It is wrong to see that vast movement as in any way trying to erase the immigrants' original culture. It was not that. What America aims at, as the prescient former governor of Colorado, Richard Lamm, has put it, is "not homogenization but harmony." "Americanization" called for (and one hopes, would call forth) two essential responsibilities on the part of new immigrants as they entered American society: *"to obey the laws of America and to harmonize with American society, not to be homogenized by it."*

One cannot sufficiently emphasize the degree to which this respect for the original cultures of the immigrants, on personal and community levels, was so totally different from the vaunted "multiculturalism" of the later years. Far from giving up their original cultures, the newcomers were asked only to learn English, promise to obey American laws, have a sort of vague "attachment to the Constitution," and swear allegiance to a political creed that in fact exemplified a universal cultural inclusiveness and which had built into it a unique respect for their cultural (if not political or military) origins.

Those were amazingly minimal and modest requests for any polity to make of new citizens, particularly one as desirable to enter as the United States, the most prosperous and advanced nation in human history. Yet, even those consummately reasonable requests are today no longer made.

☆

Prior to World War II, the political system organized communities, and particularly service in the armed forces carried newcomers into the great agreement of America. "Before, there was ward politics, party conventions, schools of Americanization and assimilation," Professor Phil Martin of the University of California at Davis has written. But since the war, America has seen a "new politics" that actually lives off ideas of racial aggrievement, exaggerates any social or economic disparity, and debases and destroys the old public debate on behalf of the new power of the courts, the foundations, and other essentially nonrepresentative groups. As citizenship historian T. H. Marshall puts it, civic education has devolved into "a subtle form of political indoctrination and agitation."

Indeed, in the deceptively complacent fifties that gave way to the cultural and political upheaval of the sixties, and just before the consolidation of new citizenship and immigration ideas in the seventies, America saw its traditional concept of freedom greatly overhauled, not always by neutral or knowledgeable parties.

"In our lifetime," Lawrence Auster, one of the most sensitive commentators on immigration, has written,

> American democracy has been radicalized, the idea of equality has been extended from the carefully defined political sphere where the American founders located it to the idea that everything is equal, that all types of men and all types of behavior are equal. . . . In order to avoid being inhumane to illegal immigrants, we give illegals virtually all the privileges of citizenship, and so on. But freedom used to have a more complex meaning. It meant ordered freedom, freedom within the constitutional and moral order that made that freedom possible. Freedom also meant national freedom, the sovereignty and distinctiveness and the will to defend it.

In the sixties and particularly because of the disastrous war in Vietnam—seen as "immoral" by large sections of the American populace (and as incalculably stupid by others, including me)—everything changed. Many of the old American elites were responsible for the policies of the war and the dumb determination in pursuing it; Vietnam came close to destroying those elites and their values at the same time. After Vietnam, there was no more draft to equalize Americans and immigrants alike. After Vietnam, the great United States of America was a different country: *disillusioned, disheveled, dispirited.*

Other nations, even great nations, have fought wars and gone on. But for America, with its intense, unbending moralism, *losing* a war was different. It meant not only that that generation of thinkers had failed, and that America too was capable of doing something really awful, dumb, and cruel, but that the entire venture of America was flawed, fruitless, finished. America was not used to considering itself with qualifying adjectives. And so, many sectors of America, particularly and not surprisingly its academic youth, came to deny everything American.

In the words of history professor Albert Michaels of the State University of New York at Buffalo, the old ideas gave way under the onslaught of a "loose, fluctuating, university-based alliance with a fundamental world view," namely, *"multi-culturalists, feminists, radical homosexuals, new historicists, Marxists and extreme environmentalists."* (Italics mine.) They were the new "alienated intellectuals," and they sought to discredit the American system and destroy the business elite "which they both envied and hated."

It was these young Americans in this new era with their new ideas that led to the "deconstruction of the American nation." Harvard sociologist Nathan Glazer lists their characteristics: "official bilingualism and multi-culturalism, multilingual ballots, defining citizenship so as to include all children born here, the abandonment of English as a prerequisite for citizenship, the erosion of citizenship as the solid qualification for voting, the extension of welfare and education benefits as a right to illegals and their children, and congressional and state legislative apportionment based on legal and illegal population."

And then, on top of all that—and in many respects *because* of all that—came the 1965 immigration law. Although few people understood it at the time, the law introduced to an unsuspecting America the idea of a utopian world, without borders, where it is not an exaggeration to say that the decisions on who should be Americans would no longer be made in America but rather in Mexico City, Seoul, or even Warsaw.

☆

What the 1965 law foreordained in terms of the very makeup of America was little discussed—and, when it was discussed, consequences were denied. Peter Brimelow, one of our most provocative writers on immigration in America, remarks perceptively that "U.S. immigration policy was not transformed without debate.

There was a debate. It just bore no relationship to what subsequently happened. . . ."

Senator Edward Kennedy, one of the perfervid supporters of the bill of the "new egalitarianism," and his utopian-minded group of supporters assured America during the debate, "First, our cities will not be flooded with a million immigrants annually. Second, the ethnic mix will not be upset."

Every single assurance of Kennedy's turned out to be shockingly false. The American people should relinquish any idea that the flooding of America with a million immigrants annually and the resulting perversion of the ethnic and cultural mix were somehow accidental. "The current wave of immigration, and America's shifting ethnic balance, is simply the result of public policy," Brimelow states correctly. It was that *deliberate* change in policy that "opened the Third World floodgates after 1965."

It was what the 1965 law meant in other terms—most important in terms of the centrality of citizenship—that has shaken the nation ever since. For it effectively took the responsibility for citizenship away from the American government and gave it squarely to the newest immigrants, and then to their children, and then to their aunts and uncles, and then to their cousins, and then . . . and then . . .

Before 1965, the major principle of immigration policy was to take skilled people proportionally from the countries of origin of present American citizens; after 1965, American immigration was deliberately opened to the Third World—indeed, to the point of nearly being reserved for it. Not only were the poorest and least developed peoples of the world, whose cultural habits were furthest from America's, given preference, but they could now bring their entire extended families to America. This, of course, had to swell the ranks of unskilled workers and take much-needed jobs from the American poor, particularly the American black community, which deserves far better.

Before, immigrants were expected to embrace American values; after 1965, Americans were forced or felt they were being forced to adapt to foreign cultural values. Ironically, these were often the same cultural values that for centuries had caused hardship, misery, and conflict in the immigrants' home countries, had made it impossible for those poor lands to develop, and finally had forced people to flee to America. In place of America's taking in new immigrants according to what the country needed, massive numbers of new immigrants were taken in on the principle of "family reunification." Before America tried to take skilled individuals who would raise the economic and industrial levels of America for everyone; now the focus on "family reunification" was so intense that, by 1986, only 4 percent of newcomers were being admitted on the basis of skills!

Some other figures: In 1910, nearly 90 percent of American immigrants came from Europe; in the 1980s, more than 80 percent came from Asia and Latin America. From 1930 to 1960, about 80 percent of America's immigrants came from European countries or Canada; from 1977 to 1979, only 16 percent did, while Asia and Latin America accounted for roughly 40 percent each. By 1979, as a direct result of the 1965 immigration bill, the nine leading "source" countries for legal immigration were Mexico, the Philippines, Korea, China and Taiwan, Vietnam, India, Jamaica, the Dominican Republic, and Cuba.

By then, a mere 3 percent of the immigration allowance was allotted to the United Kingdom: the country whose people were the original citizens of America and whose historic principles were the basis for the American Constitution, American law, and the American language waited in a humiliating tenth place! No preference was any longer given to the countrymen of those who had formed America, sacrificed for it, loved and hated it but always been committed to it.

History is replete with the sagas of great defeats, of peoples wiped off the face of the earth, and of cultures transformed through clashes with others. Across and throughout history, nations fell, disintegrated, lost their nerve, made disastrous decisions, fought wars of self-destruction, and were not wise enough to sustain themselves. But I, at least, have never been able to discover another nation in human history, much less a great and powerful one, that literally *willed* itself out of existence through lethargy and, worst of all, guilt over things it did not even do.

The 1965 immigration bill did not, of course, come out of nowhere. It grew from a complicated body of legal and judicial decisions and administrative rulings; from crass and cynical political decisions in the U.S. Congress by which senators and congressmen tried to satisfy constituents such as the rich growers and farmers of the Southwest and Northwest at the cost of the American polity; and from a series of lawsuits, state by state and court by court, filed by the activists and young lawyers of the sixties New Left and the new ethnic and special-interest lobbies. Eventually, the New Left–oriented courts made so many decisions breaking down the original merit-oriented America into specially privileged ethnic and other interest groups that paradoxically it no longer benefited anyone very much to identify as an American citizen.

"The consensus of 1924 was finally swept away in 1965," Harvard's brilliant Professor Glazer concludes, swept away by "a coalition that consisted of Jews, Catholics and Liberals, who had for years fought against the preferences for Northwestern Europe and the restrictions on Asia. The new immigration act abandoned all efforts to make distinctions among nations on grounds of race, size or historical connection."

On October 3, 1965, in a ceremony at the foot of the Statue of Liberty, President Lyndon Johnson solemnly signed into law the Immigration Reform Act of 1965. Americans would eventually understand that that watershed moment marked the beginning of the end of their sovereignty. Although few people grasped it at the time, the law imposed upon America the idea of a utopian world without borders—and without borders, if the history of the world is any guide, nations soon come to know only chaos, anarchy, and disintegration.

At the same time, on the larger world stage and particularly across that same Third World—Vietnam, Lebanon, India, Central America, Angola, Mozambique, Equatorial Guinea, Iran, China, Bosnia, Somalia, Rwanda, Haiti, and beyond—from which more and more of the new immigrants were coming—the forces of disintegration were moving ever more rapidly, outpacing the forces of cohesion and inclusion.

Only a very few voices of distress and despair were raised then. The American writer Theodore White predicted "a stampede . . . almost an invasion. . . ." The French writer Jean Raspail foresaw the future in his prophetic book *The Camp of the Saints*, in which he pictured a boatload of Indians landing on the southern frontiers of France from India and walking inland, thus "invading" Europe "peacefully." Father Theodore Hesburgh, the brilliant president of the University of Notre Dame, where so many foreign students and leaders have come to be educated and prized, echoed those forebodings. He told me in the early eighties, as we sat on his lovely campus in Indiana, "Immigration is one of the great sleepers in the world. Twenty years from now—it sounds like science fiction, but it isn't—India may have bad harvests. . . . Suppose one hundred million Indians put sacks of rice on their shoulders and start walking toward Europe. . . ." That wise and cultivated man looked me squarely in the eye as he said this; then he asked me: "What do you do?"

Actually, Europe was already going through a slow-motion version of the Raspail/Hesburgh scenario. Germany in particular offers a valuable case in point, for it shows us what happens when (1) a country brings massive numbers of foreign workers in, usually to do the "dirty jobs," without much thinking about the consequences, (2) a country pushes its own citizenship into moralistic positions that cannot be sustained by reality, and (3) the workers thus brought in with a hope for change become disillusioned and—naturally and inevitably—form their own power groups, totally changing the society they once so humbly entered.

Germany's idea of citizenship, unlike America's, was always one of blood. You had to be born a German, and so an ethnic German from Kazakhstan or the Crimea, who wandered there under the reign of Catherine the Great, would find it easy to become a citizen (again), while the children of immigrants who came there forty years ago will never be accepted. But after the horrors of World War II, under the shadow of the Allied victory, the postwar leaders of a guilt-ridden and defeated Germany *did* put through the country's first constitution. In atonement for the crimes of the war, this astonishing document offers anyone who can demonstrate virtually any likelihood of political persecution in his homeland the guarantee of safety and asylum in Germany.

All a person had to do for years after that war was utter the magic word "asylum" at the German border and voilà! he was a ward of the German state. He could stay in the country as long as it took to process his case, often two to three years, and while he was there, he would receive an average of $350 in a monthly allowance, plus free housing and medical care. The not-surprising upshot was the fact that, by the 1990s, Germany sheltered no fewer than 1.4 million refugees from every place around the globe. It was taking in 60 percent of the asylum seekers coming to Western Europe each year, five times the number taken by Britain and France combined. Its courts were swamped: With only 1,200 adjudicators, the backlog of cases quickly rose to more than 418,000!

When the Berlin Wall came down in the late fall of 1989 and East Germany disintegrated, and then Yugoslavia, Germany was simply overwhelmed. By the end of 1992, she had 500,000 asylum cases!

In June of 1993, I sat in the neat, busy offices of Barbara John, the commissioner of foreigners' affairs for the Senate in Berlin, as she tried to explain to me her job. "We have one hundred ninety thousand applications already this year," this handsome, serious woman began, "but people don't support this policy anymore, and those who are full of aggression in our society feel this."

Changes soon came. That July, Germany eviscerated Article 16, which had brought in so many immigrants. Overnight, Germany's immigration policy became one of the most restrictive in Europe, largely because of the vicious rising "skinhead" violence against foreigners. In 1992 alone, there were some 2,000 attacks on foreigners, with 17 people killed. This violence, in turn, provoked other fears. "Our secret fear," one Berlin official told me, "is that certain groups of young Turks, already organized in street gangs of both Left and Right, will bring this whole thing to an explosion. In short, for the first time, there are two sides to the internal conflict."

Now, Germany was faced with new questions, in particular about the large Turkish worker community it had brought in after the war: Is a Turk born in Germany a citizen? Should he be able to become a citizen? What kind? Should Germany retain its old "blood citizenship"?

Or, as correspondent Marc Fisher, a specialist on Germany, wrote in the *Washington Post* in 1995: "Many citizens—especially in academia and politics—proudly view their country as the world's first post-modern state: selfless, rational, eager to be blended into a united, non-national Europe. Unfortunately, that intellectual ideal stands apart from the natural, emotional desire for belonging, for identity. After the essential question *'Who am I?'* comes the obvious follow-up: *'To what do I belong?'* Germany is not yet ready to answer that question."

But, ahh, I thought, at least she is asking it!

As it turned out, Germany's policy of taking just about every-one in the world was neither humane nor truly compassionate. In its lack of concern for the cultural nexus of German citizens them-selves as they turned away from the old extreme German nation-alism, this policy sparked extreme and radical solutions that effectively set the country back instead of moving it forward.

Finally, the "German Turks," rightfully and naturally enraged by the violent actions and attitudes against them, began pushing their "cultural rights." Girls must wear veils to school; they wanted to slaughter animals according to Muslim ritual; they were de-manding Muslim burial grounds. Finally, of course, they formed a special Turkish political party, the Democratic Party of Germany, to represent the interests of all immigrants.

It was all so totally inevitable.

☆

The American response to problems parallel to Germany's in the 1970s and 1980s was, well, hardly anything at all. Rather, there was a strange and eerie mood of (let us call it by an accurate, if pain-ful, word) *submission* on the part of the largely well-meaning citi-zens of the most successful and emulated country in the history of the world.

Americans had lost their confidence, particularly in any area that might even minutely be thought of as involving any kind of "discrimination" (even discrimination by moral or principled de-cision) or any lack of total, radical egalitarianism. They had fought one of the greatest moral and political battles of all time with civil rights, but then they had allowed the original civil rights principles to be transferred lock, stock, and barrel to immigrants who had suffered none of the biblical tribulations of black America. They had been subtly and not so subtly brainwashed by the liberal and radical utopianism that came out of the sixties—and, by the way, out of the effects of grappling with Marxist influence since 1917— into being utterly terrified by any accusation, however accurate or misapplied, of "intolerance" and "racism." (No one seemed to notice that America's basic moral good sense on these topics, of course, was the most important element behind her conscientious concern.)

The "New Left" elites certainly were not alone in changing the public agenda regarding immigration! Indeed, these changes in the very spirit of a great country could not have been brought about so forcibly and in such a brief time without the joining-in of mainstream forces.

If we try to separate out some of the yarns from the weave of the changes that have occurred over the years, let us start with *the experts*. Yes, one of the most important partners in the changes surrounding American citizenship, working hand in glove with both the ideological elite of the Left and the commercial elite of the Right, is the expert, born of the "professionalized" society and endowed with "wisdom" that ordinary people—citizens—do not possess to deal even with their own lives, much less with today's larger problems.

Harry C. Boyte, the enlightened Minnesota thinker and activist on citizenship subjects, traces the trend in the prestigious *Kettering Review:* "After World War II . . . a view of the professional, manager and expert as the significant problem solver spread through European and American politics alike." An "ideology of care" developed toward the "unfortunate" and (the term more often used now) the "victim," especially the illegal immigrant. "The growth of professional services in every field," Boyte sums up, "from education to traditional unions to voluntary organizations like the Red Cross and the YMCA—more and more rendered citizens as clients, not problem solvers, and detached professional knowledge from any larger civic meaning or context. . . ."

The not really surprising outcome was a distinct "decline in civic involvement in politics," so much so that mere citizens became *"outsiders and tourists of the age. . . . From a nation of citizens, we have become a nation of clients. . . ."* (Italics mine.)

David Mathews, the thoughtful president of the Kettering Foundation, picked up the "expert" discussion here. "In the twentieth century, the world became too complex," he mused one day in the foundation's Washington office, as we discussed all of the factors underlying the death of citizenship in America. "Americans began to think that only the experts could understand it. Among engineers, for instance, there is an utter disdain for citizenship. Ironically, the Soviet Union was our mirror image. The modern technocratic world has come in the end to have a common parent: technocracy, the belief in technology, perfection-through-technocratic perfectionism. People who see the world through the lens of certain knowledge."

"And then, when you link 'salvation' to it," I suggested, "you can sacrifice anything to it?"

He nodded. "Remember how Václav Havel said after Czechoslovakia was freed from Communism, 'The people who ran the state told us that they *knew how*. They said not to believe your eyes. Until we all got together later and found that we were all thinking the same thing.' They gave us the dominant metaphor. The twentieth century disavowed and disallowed our ability to know in common."

Finally, what the "experts" do to us in citizenship is to kill any real chance for political debate: everything is their knowledge married to personal taste. They destroy exactly the self-regulation so necessary for an autonomous life and for responsible citizenship. They actually encourage ethnic conflict by making technological answers so frighteningly predominant. On the contrary, normal human beings cannot live by technology alone; with the present dearth of broader beliefs in the citizenly state, they fall back on old, narrow, and dangerous ethnic ties.

☆

The second new partner in these changes in American citizenship is the transformation of "rights" in America.

Harvard Law School Professor Mary Ann Glendon defines Americans today in haunting words: "Buried deep in our rights dialect is an unexpressed premise that *we roam at large in a land of strangers*." (Italics mine.) It is Glendon who, in her watershed writings, has most persuasively alerted us to the danger of today's extraordinary predominance, in the national parlance and thinking, of "rights" over "responsibilities." She too locates the beginning of these changes in the civil rights fight that ensued after World War II, as "older constitutional law professors who had given pride of place to federal-state relations and the commerce clause were succeeded by men and a few women who focussed on advancing equality and personal liberty by means of rights."

But it finally came to the point in America where, Glendon goes on, "the language of rights is the language of no compromise.

The winner takes all and the loser has to get out of town. The conversation is over."

This has resulted, she rightly says, in a "neglect of the social dimension of personhood, and a consequent carelessness regarding the environments that human beings and societies require in order to flourish." In a terrifying way, the shift in importance from responsibilities to rights would lead us back to that until now blessedly lost time in history when the fount of public virtues had run dry and there were "subjects still, but no citizens."

Scholar Robert A. Goldwin further notes how the old political-rights doctrines, those on which America was founded, "held that individual rights are natural and inherent in every human being." But, he says, "theoretical formulations concerning natural rights have been out of favor for a long time. We now avoid calling rights natural and speak instead of 'human rights, civil rights and political rights.'" His comments are particularly important to remember in terms of the international scene—and changes there in the formulations of power, in the duties or nonduties of nations.

And the great Russian writer Alexander Solzhenitsyn thus defines this whole syndrome:

> In Western civilizations—which used to be called Western-Christian but now might better be called Western-Pagan—along with the development of intellectual life and science, there has been a loss of the serious moral basis of society. During these 300 years of Western civilization, there has been a sweeping away of duties and an expansion of rights. But we have two lungs. You can't breathe with just one lung and not with the other. We must avail ourselves of rights and duties in equal measure. . . . The only thing we have been developing is rights, rights, rights, at the expense of duty.

In the end, a Faustian alliance of both Far Left and Far Right is behind the fight against immigration control.

Interests weigh in just behind ideology, and often become indistinguishable from it. The American Left in these issues, as we have seen, wants, in its final gambit, "open borders" with the entire world. That is one emanation of its basic hatred for America, hatred for the "stodgy, hypocritical Vietnam-killers" that are the old generation. One pro-immigration zealot, economist Julian Simon, has written about how on the New York subway (of all places!) he "delights in looking at the variety of faces I see. . . . When I visit New York . . . I get tears in my eyes. . . ." (Columnist George F. Will has characterized the impulses of pro-immigration groups aptly: "The anti-assimilationist impulse may emanate primarily from those native-born intellectuals who believe America is a sick, racist, sexist, exploitative, oppressive, patriarchal, etc., society into which no self-respecting person would wish to assimilate.")

Parts of the leftish and/or more ambitious hierarchy of the Roman Catholic Church equally want uncontrolled free immigration. Indeed, the head of the Catholic Conference's work with migrants and refugees, Jesuit Father Richard Ryscavage, has said no less than that immigration is "the key to our future and the key to why the church is going to be very healthy in the 21st century." When the Catholic Church unites with the Left, you find a lineup of free-immigration groups and organizations such as the following getting together against "employee sanctions" (to control illegal immigrants through control of hiring): the American Civil Liberties Union, the League of Latin American Citizens, MALDEF, and the National Council of La Raza.

But, while the Far Left, perhaps somewhat unfairly, gets the most attention for their sympathy for illegal immigration, they are far from alone.

The prestigious *Wall Street Journal* constantly editorializes for *totally open borders*! Its reasons seem to be a combination of the utopianism of the American Right and simple, all-out greed. (Yes, the Right in America also taps into utopianism—witness even Ronald Reagan, when president, wanting to share "Star Wars" with the Russians in the interests of "peace.") *Journal* editorialists have argued that, with open borders, immigrants would spontaneously become citizens. Other ideological conservatives argue from a pure "our-interest" position, insisting that "no one else will do this work." (Read: "We like our cheap maids.")

Still other conservatives see immigration only through a "free enterprise" prism: to them, the movements of peoples are no different from the movement of products. That this is cynical, as well as abysmally ignorant, never seems to occur to them. Then there are the "virtue Republicans" who see, in Hispanics in particular, people who prize "family virtues." And some conservatives, such as writer Ben Wattenberg, equate a country of masses of people with power in the world.

But by far the largest and most important forces in the American Right who want open migration are the farmers and growers, most of them in the Southwest and Northwest, who want cheap and exploitable labor, and almost always for reprehensible reasons. Cheap and malleable labor with, for the more passive and fearful illegals, none of those pesky old American "rights" to bother the bosses, is what they desire. But exploiting illegal labor is counterproductive, not only to the cohesion of the country but to the real interests of the American economy. For the fact is that cheap labor from abroad, used originally after World War II with the organized bracero program, keeps growers and industrialists from mechanizing and moving into the modern age. It also "protects" the owners of businesses, at least for a while, from the unspeakable "horror" of unionization.

The wise Otis L. Graham Jr., in his *Rethinking the Purposes of Immigration Policy*, sums up the real problem for the United States in the selfishness of this part of the Right with regard to immigration. "The U.S. can either evolve toward a high technology economy, with a labor force of constantly advancing productivity, wage levels and skills, or it can drift towards a low technology, low skill and low wage economy, marked by widespread job instability and growing income disparity. Immigration policy will be important to the outcome." He warns of "the demographic transformation of the U.S. in ways the voters have not authorized and the alteration of the very structure of our economy through the distortion of the functioning of the domestic labor market and the supplying of chiefly low-skilled labor."

With both extremes of the political spectrum thinking exclusively of their own interests, you can add to the Right's end of that coalition fighting against immigration reform or employee sanctions the following groups: the Associated General Contractors of America, the U.S. Chamber of Commerce, the American Retail Federation, the Kmart Corporation, and the National Restaurant Association.

The actions of all such groups have had economic, social, and political effects on America that are impossible to overestimate, while other countries have taken the common-sense road:

- Modernization and postmodernization of any economy puts a premium on linguistic unity; because of the pro-immigration sentiments, America has become a nation of linguistic confusion.

Professor Nathan Glazer suggests that one major reason the East Asian economies are doing so much better than America's is that "they do not have to worry about educating to their language and customs, as we do, 600,000 immigrants a year and an unmeasured number of undocumented immigrants. Those countries that have invested in their own human resources . . . have been the economic successes of the 1980s. There is no reason to think matters will be different in the 1990s." You pay for linguistic pretensions.

- Advanced economies obviously require—and the smart ones, such as Singapore, insist upon—highly skilled and educated workers.

Yet, America keeps taking immigrants whose skills have declined sharply over the past few decades relative to the skills of natives. George J. Borjas points out, "Newly arrived immigrants admitted in the late 1950s had about half a year more schooling than natives did and earned about eight percent less per hour. Immigrants admitted in the late 1970s had 0.7 fewer years of schooling and earned about 17 percent less than natives." America pays for that wanton disregard for reality.

- More homogeneous countries and countries where individual merit reigns instead of group rights are more peaceful economically.

Harvard University economist Robert Barro points out a reasonable rule of social economy: "If diversity is great . . . then there is a strong incentive for people to spend their energies in efforts to redistribute income rather than to produce goods. In particular, a greater dispersion of constituent characteristics leads to the creation of interest groups that spend their time lobbying government to redistribute resources in their favor."

Governments can redistribute ad infinitum; wiser countries, with an integrity of production, flourish.

- Racial balance and reasonable racial harmony is maintained by a tough-minded and wise setting-aside of jobs for, first, one's own citizens.

"Since 1965 . . . the black working poor have suffered again from competition," Michael Lind, the fashionable young scholar who wrote "The Next American Nation: The New Nationalism and the Fourth American Revolution," has stated in the *New York Times;* the competition this time pits Latin Americans and Asians against black Americans. "There can be little doubt that many employers discriminate against African-American workers and in favor of immigrants, who are more likely to accept low wages and poor conditions without complaint." Black Americans deserve better at the end of the "American Century" than being frozen out of the existing jobs.

Neither the utopian Left nor the greedy Right ever really thinks about the ultimate, long-range economic costs to America of their beliefs and actions; they think only of the immediate benefits to themselves, whether of power through immigration or of money through exploitation.

If they did think of long-range costs to the country, they might listen to Houston political scientist Donald Huddle, who, with immigration specialist David Simcox, did the most comprehensive study of immigration costs in a massive study undertaken in 1993. It was carefully based upon projections of the rate of immigration and the rate of public service expenditures on immigrants, subtracting the taxes paid by immigrants and adding the costs of native workers displaced by immigrants. They concluded that over the decade between 1993 and 2002, immigration would cost the United States $668.5 billion, or two-thirds of a trillion dollars!

And the House Republican Research Committee reported in 1993 that "in 1992, an illegal alien population estimated at 4.8 million . . . tapped into public benefits and ran up a $7.6 billion tab that was paid for by the American taxpayer. In the next ten years, these costs are likely to exceed $105 billion." Moreover, by the 1990s, few serious analysts really disagreed with the general thesis that not only was illegal immigration destabilizing, it was costing the United States economically on every possible level. In effect, writes George Borjas, "the United States has become an importer of relatively unskilled labor."

Finally, Otis Graham hits upon a crucial truth when he notes that U.S. immigration policy has no real thought-out goals; rather, it has what he calls "revealed goals" that simply "came about" because of immigration laws that the American people were simply not "let in" on.

Consider the reality we face:

Illegals are putting ever more massive demands on American welfare systems. Borjas has found that, even though immigrant households in California make up about 8 percent of the population, they account for 13 percent of the expenditures in cash-benefit programs. Elderly foreign parents of children already earning in America are inflicting insufferable abuses in American welfare programs, in particular the Supplemental Security Insurance (SSI) program. They have effectively found what can only be called an attractive new "retirement plan in the United States," or, as the Heritage Foundation calls it, a "deluxe retirement home for the elderly of other countries." In 1994, there were nearly 738,000 lawful noncitizen residents receiving SSI aid, up from 127,900 in 1982—a 580 percent increase in only 12 years!—and the trend is accelerating.

But perhaps worst of all, the United States government is not defending the security of its own citizens. Twenty-six percent of the 76,000 inmates in federal prisons are now aliens. By 1996, the World Health Organization is reporting that new and reemerging diseases—HIV, the Ebola virus, tuberculosis, bubonic plague, and yellow fever are reaching epidemic proportions across the world; obviously, America's porous and laughable borders leave Americans dangerously open to these ravages, which are carried by unchecked human beings. (This health-care laxness has a long history: In the early eighties, for example, 70 percent of the sudden rise in tuberculosis in American cities was directly ascribed by medical groups to the immigrant community.) Internationally, "alien-smuggling" is now a major crime syndrome that threatens America in particular, since this is where most aliens want to go. (Finally, on February 7, 1996, President Bill Clinton released a "presidential initiative to deter alien smuggling," which for the first time saw this crime as a huge problem, which earns smugglers billions of dollars and causes untold human agony.)

Everything that America's weak haplessness in formulating an immigration policy touched was being corrupted: every human being, culture, American citizen, immigrant, other government, potential criminal in the world, and principle that we have exemplified and lived by in our national life.

In 1981, a presidential Select Committee on Immigration and Refugee Policy, led by such distinguished and moderate public servants as Notre Dame's Father Hesburgh, had come out strongly in saying that immigration was "out of control" in America and advising with unmistakable urgency that illegal immigration should not be sanctioned at all. But Congress paid no attention to this "early warning."

By 1995, still another immigration commission, the bipartisan Federal Commission on Immigration Reform, headed by the courageous and effective Barbara Jordan, put forth the same recommendations as the 1981 commission and, earlier, the Dillingham Commission: limited family-reunification immigration, elimination of the annual allotment of ten thousand visas for unskilled foreign workers, a national identity card.

Before her untimely death in 1996, Chairman Jordan wrote prophetically,

> Americanization means becoming a part of the polity—becoming one of us. But that does not mean conformity. We are more than a melting pot; *we are a kaleidoscope, where every turn of history refracts new light on the old promise.* Immigration imposes mutual obligations. Those who choose to come here must embrace the common core of American civic culture. We must assist them in learning our common language. . . . We must renew civic education in the teaching of American history for all Americans. We must vigorously enforce the laws against hate crimes and discrimination. We must remind ourselves, as we illustrate for newcomers, what makes us America. [Italics mine.]

That courageous woman had not only mentioned but actually endorsed *the* forbidden word of the last four decades: "Americanization"!

In the end, every responsible person who has looked into our immigration quandary sees problems. And yet, almost nothing has been done.

☆

Aside from those quantifiable issues of the economic and practical, there's a more profound question to be asked about our immigration/citizenship situation: *Why?* To even begin to answer that question, we have to enter the world of morals and ethics. To that end, I attended a fascinating meeting in Los Angeles, sponsored by the environmentalist Carrying Capacity Network on precisely this subject, "The Ethics of Immigration," and I came out with these conclusions, which were part of a longer column I published for the Fourth of July, 1994:

> Even as we celebrate the principles behind the sacred independence of America this Fourth of July, few ever ask: What is the basis on which our crucial immigration decisions should be made? Indeed, as America flails around in an unrooted and ill-defined immigration discussion that sinks either into maudlin sentimentality or into the coldly cruel, is it not time to inquire, "What *are* the ethical principles that should underlie those decisions?"
>
> First, the sentimental—and talk about strange bedfellows! On this side one does indeed find the Left—but right there alongside it are the libertarians ("free will" individualists), far-right businessmen such as the growers in the Southwest, and many Christians who incongruously believe in utopian open borders because we must love all mankind.
>
> Perhaps libertarian philosophy professor James Hudson of Northern Illinois University best personifies this viewpoint, when he writes peremptorily that there is no "moral propriety in restricting immigration in any way." He counts, then, in political terms, "everyone," not "every citizen of my country."
>
> In short, this position—extreme to be sure, given that the civilized world is just that *because* it has organized the world into nation states—recognizes no right of the citizens of a nation to preference over illegal aliens.
>
> The cruel group on the other extreme wants to close down the United States totally, but frankly this group is hardly ever heard from, largely because of the epithets of "racist" and "nativist" bandied about these days. Then we come to the ratio-

nal and fair-minded centrists, who want to see the United States itself decide what it wants and needs in terms of immigrants.

Philosophy Professor John Lachs of Vanderbilt University supported this position at a recent conference. . . . Implicitly attacking "philosophers who love to disregard the actual," Lachs affirmed that our ethical "obligations are specific, focused on . . . people who occupy some special position with respect to us." Our first duty morally is always to our own parents, children and fellow citizens. Everything else is nonsense that confuses the philosophers' "purified air of the ideal" with the necessary political imperatives and responsibilities of the nation state.

When Professor Garrett Hardin, the renowned scholar on population and global capacity, looks at the ethical question of how and when to be "my brother's keeper," he is even more adamant about first principles—and first responsibilities. "Traditional ethics has an answer to this problem," he says. "Charity begins at home. Why the restriction? Because the greater the distance betwen donor and recipient, the more likely it is that well-meant charity will cause more harm than good."

Moreover, the ethical imperative grows ever more intense when we study the real outcome of pushing for uncontrolled immigration—and the concomitant lack of assimilation that invariably attends it. Because, as Hardin says, "when immigration is at a slow rate, cultural and linguistic distances can be overcome. But when immigration is very rapid . . . the result is conflict."

As for the general altruism of loving everyone in the world and neglecting the reasonable welfare of one's own, perhaps Austrian economist Friedrich von Hayek demolished that pretense most effectively. Loving all the world is a "meaningless conception," he said, emphasizing that man can care only for specific individuals in concrete circumstances.

Moreover, the great diplomat George Kennan has written that, by absorbing the poverty of the Third World, the more prosperous society "is sometimes quite overcome in the long run, by what it has tried to absorb." Any more prosperous society then diminishes itself so that it is no longer an example to the world, and necessarily diminishes the only hope that the poorer countries have to emulate and learn from.

Isn't it odd that a country stumbling over these watershed questions—all of them revolving directly or indirectly about what and who this "American" will become in our confused and contradictory times—should not be discussing what rocks we still stand on?

Who belongs? To whom is our primary responsibility? Where does it begin? Where does it end? What responsibility do I have to my family, to my immediate fellows, to my fellow citizens, to the stranger? These questions are dealt with by most of the world's great philosophers, not to speak of many more of the not so great, and in every sacred book from the Bible to the Koran. I soon found that, on a strictly religious level, many Catholics and Protestants were taking the position that we are responsible for all mankind.

The Catholic Church's "consistent ethic of life" enjoins the real Christian to stand in solidarity with society's weakest members, the elderly, the infirm, the unborn—and now the immigrant, too. "In this view," David Simcox, a Catholic layman and former director of the Center for Immigration Studies, writes,

> setting appropriate immigration levels becomes a critical ethical decision that cannot legitimately be based on national interest, but on an overarching "common good" of all humanity.
>
> The U.S. hierarchy's creeping radicalization of church teaching on immigration blurs the distinction between the state's first obligation to the welfare of its own members and the obligations it may have to all humankind. Rejected is the primary of the contractual obligations among members that has been at the heart of the democratic nation state. National interest as a basis for immigration and population policies is deeply suspect in the hierarchy's view.
>
> In its place, the Church offers a high-minded but amorphous sentiment of a global "common good," but without a global social contract or a global entity to define or implement it.

In the post–Second Vatican Council years since the sixties, the Church initially proclaimed a "right" of immigration but then balanced that supposed right with acknowledgment of the right of governments to regulate immigration. That stance has changed back, and immigration has become yet again almost an absolute right in the eyes of the hierarchy, although there is substantial disagreement on these matters within the general Catholic population.

Many Protestant churches reflect pro-immigration thinking, but what is important in Protestantism is the degree to which almost all of the churches' official professional staffs, usually situated in New York City, far away from their actual denominations, have been taken over by the young leftish activists. Their situation is almost a replica of what happened with the Ford Foundation and its Hispanic groups: They make public policy but hardly represent their "flock."

None of the religious spokespeople, it seems, reflect on the practical considerations inherent in ethical issues, for instance, environmental ethics. So I sought out the opinion of one of the wise men from that California meeting, Garrett Hardin.

When we had lunch in Washington two years later, my first impression of Hardin—a professor emeritus of the University of California at Santa Barbara accused of being "nativist, bigoted, and xenophobic"—was that he was such a gentleman. A courtly man then in his eighties who moves carefully with a walker, a brilliant scientist still filled with a youthful, effervescent joy in life, he is far from the "hate-monger" portrayed by pro-immigration types.

That day, he told me a story—about India, harvests, and the environmental impact of immigration and population—that surely underlines the ethical questions of carrying capacity and environment and illuminates those neglected areas of foreign policy and missionary work involved in the entire immigration/citizenship question.

"Think of things this way," he began. "In nineteen sixty-six to 'sixty-seven, India had a shortfall in agricultural production. America sent ten million tons of grain to India. (One ton of grain keeps five people alive per year.) Then, in nineteen sixty-eight, we did not send grain. I went to India for an interview with the planning commission and they told me, 'When word came down that there would be no grain in nineteen sixty-eight, at first we were very angry; we even thought we had been double-crossed. But, having been told that, we exerted ourselves to provide grain for our people, and now we are out of the woods. It was one of the best things that ever happened to us.'"

The Socratic Mr. Hardin then leaned across the table and asked me, "Let us grant ourselves the most malevolent of motives: Let us ask, 'How can we harm India—*really* harm her?' Quite simply, by sending India a bounty of food, year after year."

To me, he stood for a different worldview, different particularly from welfare-state professionals, both national and international. This was the man who early on described the earth as a "lifeboat"; who coined the more discriminating word "commonism" to replace "one-worldism"; and who managed to make "global" America's own nagging welfare-state worries.

But to understand Professor Hardin, one has to go back to his first really public "shocker." It was 1968; innocently (or at least, so he would have us believe) he wrote a little treatise, "The Tragedy of the Commons," which stunned the scientific community and is now published in one hundred different anthologies and quoted in hushed voices in arcane academic circles. Unlike private property, he begins in his now-classic paper, a commons is a "resource to which a population has free and unmanaged access." It is fine so long as the commons is managed by someone, and so long as the people do not overgraze it or generally overstress it. But if, say, each herdsman increases his own herd at the expanse of the commons, very soon there is disaster ahead for everyone.

By the time we met, Hardin, no stranger to controversy, had extended his thesis to the even more emotion-laden field of immigration and citizenship. He was professing that our unassessed immigration policy, which had as yet seen no rational debate, was one of the major causes of America's ten-million-unemployed problem and of a general diluting on all levels of America's seminal responsibility to its own citizens.

Hardin dismissed (his term) "indiscriminating altruism" and (my term) the "compassion professionals" that have given us everything from essentially counterproductive food programs in India to welfare programs in America that destroy the recipients' spirit and incentive. As he again made his point that true compassion can be given only to those close to you, he reminded me of the French socialist thinker Pierre-Joseph Proudhon, who captured the meaning of real compassion in the last century, saying, "If everyone is my brother, I have no brothers."

Before we left each other that day, I reminded him that "people say you're hard-hearted. Are you?"

He smiled his warm and intelligent smile. "My thinking appears to be hard-hearted—in the near term," he answered. "But that is because I am trying to protect future generations. So, really, I am softhearted in the long run."

☆

One country that has had to learn the hard way how to be softhearted in the long run is the aforementioned Australia, a country with so many similarities to us in its experience with the entire immigration issue that we would do well to consider it again.

Perhaps Dr. Katharine Betts, lecturer in sociology at Swinburne Institute of Technology, has best analyzed the situation there, which as we will see closely paralleled the American experience with political correctness in the universities and the transformation of the old Anglo-Saxon missionary service abroad to such work with immigrants at home. "During the 1970s," she has written,

> a particular ideological climate grew up around the topic of immigration, and attitudes to it came to acquire a special significance in intellectual circles. And, for a series of historical reasons, the question moved from being a legitimate topic of discussion and disagreement to become not a topic but a symbol, a marker of intellectual status and identity. If a person's work brought him or her close to the subject, it could be more important to be ideologically correct than to ask difficult questions. . . . The costs of pursuing them might be too high to pay.

Australia's immigration problem started with space, as was and is the case for so many countries. But while those others suffered from not enough space, Australia suffered from too much. After the emigration from Britain of so many convicts and other poor people to the southern Pacific, Australia had never been a country of immigration, remaining a small continent of English-speakers in a veritable sea of Oriental masses.

But then, in the late seventies and early eighties, the Australian government quite deliberately chose to increase immigration, particularly from its formerly spurned Asian neighbors, as part of an "economic growth" policy pushed by manufacturers and industrialists who wanted cheap labor. As immigration suddenly surged, Australia's very excess of land and resources made many of the utopian thinkers in the universities and the media believe that, morally and ideologically, they must share it with the poor of the world. No longer missionaries to the world out there, they would bring the targets of missionary zeal right into the bosom of Australia, instead! (Who could possibly think there was anything wrong with that?)

Many of the pro-immigration people were themselves tired of their working-class pasts. They wanted to distinguish themselves from it, and from the British/European background of Australia as well. They liked the foreign restaurants that the immigrants brought with them. They were "cultural tourists" who always found, in Betts's terms, "the foreigner they imagine, and the idea of the 'marvellous ethnic' agreed with the liberal values of internationalism and tolerance." The new ethic: Those who support open borders are generous and humane, and those who question large-scale immigration are xenophobic and racist." In their minds, what they were doing was an act of altruism toward the world, with high immigration a form of foreign aid. The Australian Catholic Social Justice Council on Immigration, which called for still more massive increases in immigration, actually argued that "for .03 percent of the world's population (i.e., Australia) to claim a whole continent for itself is a kind of selfishness and injustice which can't be argued for ethnically." Immigration was a way of doing good.

Finally, these new intellectuals utterly despised any idea that Australia might actually need a defense against others: that, too, was an invention of their Australian "fathers" whom they were rebelling against.

When Katharine Betts traced how the self-proclaimed altruistic intellectuals and ethnic lobbies of the Left promoted more immigration, thus coming together in a Faustian bargain with the "growth" industrialists of the Right—and when she tried to make a scholarly case that the great mass of Australians were left out of the "discussion" completely—she was ostracized.

Then, suddenly, in 1992, opinions began to change. New thinking had it that high immigration was causing unemployment and increasing the foreign debt. The 1993 immigration quota would be reduced to 80,000, less than half of the 1989–1990 figure of 170,000. On top of that, the government introduced an English language test to ensure that skilled immigrants could exercise their skills fully in Australia, and immigrants with skills were directly targeted. All three opposition parties called for even further reductions in numbers.

Like Canada, Australia had done a complete turnabout, under seemingly impossible odds, when Australians finally figured out what was happening to citizenship on their continent. Only the United States among the English-speaking countries had not yet really tackled its citizenship crisis. But voices were beginning to be heard.

The able Professor George Borjas looked at the Canadian and Australian examples and noted that because of their changes in law and attitudes, they—not the United States—were now drawing the most talented immigrants. Borjas comments, "In both Canada and Australia, visas are now allocated through a point system, which grades visa applicants in terms of educational attainment, age and occupational background. The presence of relatives in the country is only one factor among many."

If American law were different, he sums up, if these skilled and educated aliens had not been crowded out of the United States by such preferences as family reunification, "they might have come here instead."

But American law was not different—at least, not yet.

☆

There was hope, however. The bright Daniel Yankelovich, for instance, did a Democratic Leadership Council report in 1992 and concluded that there was emerging "a different kind of politics—an approach to governing grounded on the notion of reciprocity." He found "significant public support for the idea that recipients of government benefits should give something back to their community or country and that, above all, they should not expect something for nothing as a matter of right." And the prominent black professor of sociology at Harvard, Orlando Patterson, actually advised incoming President Bill Clinton in the *New York Times* in 1992 to be sure that single welfare mothers accept entailed duty of parenting in return for government help, because, "without such a moral and social contract, the President-elect's domestic plan is headed for disaster."

Polls continued to show more support for immigration control. In the winter of 1996, Negative Population Growth, Inc., released a poll of nearly two thousand Americans showing that most Americans, of every race and income level, wanted less than the three hundred thousand legal immigrants coming in every year. That view was supported by 52 percent of Hispanics, 73 percent of African-Americans, 72 percent of conservatives, 71 percent of moderates, 66 percent of liberals, 72 percent of Democrats, and 70 percent of Republicans. The great majority wanted population stabilization by the year 2050.

Meanwhile, immigration control groups were beginning to arise across the country. The original group, and far and away the most effective, was the Federation for American Immigration Reform (FAIR), which was started by one determined and impressive individual, Michigan resident John Tanton, in the 1970s. After FAIR, different people and groups got together to form the American Immigration Control Foundation, the Carrying Capacity Network, Population Environment Balance, Negative Population Growth, Inc., the American Alliance for Rights and Responsibilities, Californians for Population Stabilization, and the Center for Immigration Studies.

Many of the leaders and adepts of these groups, such as FAIR's extraordinary Dan Stein, were impassioned civil rights activists; they love American history; far from being just restrictionists, they are fair-minded and progressive people. Despite the polls, however, they have until now been fighting very lonely battles; one could mistake them for some of America's original frontiersmen and women, charting new roads and thinking new thoughts.

Is it possible, I asked myself, that times are indeed changing, and that America is beginning to readdress, reassess, and perhaps even prize its "contract" with itself?

☆

My favorite state illustrates the ethical and scientific disasters that happen when immigration is judged strictly in utopian terms.

Wisconsin's little city of Wausau had been able to absorb the early German immigration, although it changed the nature of the town, too, as the original Yankees left and were replaced. But then, Wausau had the forty years' grace period to absorb and integrate the newcomers when America wisely halted immigration from 1924 onward.

Today, Wausau has no such "second chance." Today the new immigration—that of far less assimilable emigrants from the quintessentially different Hmong culture of Vietnam and Laos—is making changes that have staggered the Wausau community.

"It all began simply enough," Roy Beck writes in his study, "when a few churches and individuals in Wausau . . . decided to resettle some Southeast Asian refugees during the late 1970s. To most residents, it seemed like a nice thing to do. Nobody meant to plant the seeds for a social transformation. But this small and private charitable gesture inadvertently set into motion events that many residents today feel are spinning out of control. . . ."

At first, the experiment—which, like so many of the pro-immigration impulses, was fueled by real or self-imposed American guilt, this time from the Vietnam War—seemed to work well. The Hmong were welcomed, and the usual utopian suspects were saying such things as "I have a dream that Wausau will become uniquely cosmopolitan and take advantage of its diversity." When Wausau citizens today look back on their "best times," they think not of the Wausau of 1978 before the refugee influx, but of the Wausau of 1984, when the Hmong—about 5 percent of the city's population—constituted "a delightful spice and community relations were harmonious."

No one knows exactly when things began to go wrong, but soon the churches tired of their charges and generally pulled out of assimilation work; soon the Hmongs' percentage of the population overrode the original settlers as "the volume of immigration crossed some kind of social and economic threshhold."

And today? Seventy percent of the immigrants and their children are receiving public assistance because the economy simply could not assimilate them. Property tax rates rose 10 percent in 1992 alone; Wausau residents were paying three times as much in taxes as an adjoining school district with few immigrants. English was becoming the minority spoken language in several schools; Asian gangs centered in Saint Paul and Milwaukee have extended their operations to once-innocent Wausau; and, because of Hmong "cultural migration"—-the carrying with them of their cultural habits—35 percent of the Hmong girls were pregnant in high school, and the community could not prosecute the boys because of these same "Hmong cultural standards."

We should note that the "experiment" was going well with the first group that came because they were given a lot of attention and socialization into American life. It was the more recent group, not so socialized, not so assimilated, who began imposing their own culture on little, unsuspecting Wausau. Therein lies a fact of enormous importance: Yes, Virginia, *there is a critical mass.* There is a moment, in social or political change, when power shifts irrevocably to the side that has been gaining. Then it is too late to stop or go back: the "decision" has been made without anyone really consciously making it.

Beck sums up: "Many communities find it difficult to impose American standards of behavior on people who claim membership in another culture." But the Hmong are here now, they cannot "claim membership in another culture." And yet they do! And now officials in Wausau simply wring their hands and say there is nothing that can be done about it as more and more Hmong, now relatives, come to Wausau, such a very "unlikely place" for this strange drama, in the farmlands of southern Wisconsin.

The people of Wausau are not racists, nativists, restrictionists, exclusionists, or America-Firsters—indeed, they are just the opposite! But they had assumed that the newcomers were coming to be *part of them*, and not to transform them. Indeed, under what possible principle of personal morality or national interest must long-time Wausau residents acquiesce in the destruction of the life and the community that they have built up—and by people to whom they have no special responsibility, people who have made no commitment to this land?

"The overwhelming emotion seemed to be sadness about a social revolution that the community as a whole had never requested or even discussed," Beck notes.

In short, Wausau, Wisconsin, is a sad metaphor for America today, a tragic example of how the uncontrolled immigration of people from a dramatically different culture, with little socialization into American life, is threatening the very viability of American citizenship.

☆
☆ ☆

7

California—the Way America Will Be

The vineyard, the orchards, the great flat valley, green and beautiful . . . Ruthie whispered, "It's California!"
John Steinbeck, *The Grapes of Wrath* (1939)

We have to face the possibility that we're no longer a state, meaning one people willing or able to be governed for the common good . . . and if what happens here spreads to the rest of the nation, as it often does, then the rest of the nation had better be pretty nervous.
Sherry Bebitch Jeffe, longtime California political analyst and professor at the Claremont Graduate School (1993)

In California, that beautiful place, one can find the realization of every mistake that we Americans have made in the last half of the twentieth century regarding citizenship in a modern nation-state.

California was historically the "dream" in the American Dream. The Northeast was the country's nervous system, with its choking factories, ravenous machines, and hungry workers grappling with the Puritan ethic. The Middle West was the down-to-earth, can-do core of America, with its vast plains, fertile soils, and practical people. California was where the children of those Americans went to be transformed into consummately unpractical Americans. In California, they became actors, singers, movie directors, hangers-on, groupies, scriptwriters, and—if California spun its legendary magic—"stars!"

The world came to America looking for hope and for opportunity. America in turn went to California, looking for redemption from tedium and everyday life, for relief from the necessity of always making mature choices and for a childhood that would last forever. For a couple of centuries, Californians didn't think much about their surroundings; they did not understand that there could ever be any bothersome limits placed upon their own whims, movements, or ambitions. There was always space, always another frontier to escape to, always another new "faith" to try on for the salvation that must surely be somewhere right around the corner.

Only once in a great while did one of the creative denizens of that place/idea/phenomenon/dream/reality that was "California" pause to think about how space defined life, as when two decades ago writer Joan Didion stopped, looked around, and suddenly reflected that "things had better work here, because here, beneath that immense bleached sky, is where we run out of continent."

The moment blessedly passed, and everyone returned to the beach.

Meanwhile, the California that was really almost a "nation" of its own went on blithely reveling in the party that (everyone was sure) would never end.

Meanwhile, too, with California's luxuriant playfulness, Californians reveled in repeating the superlatives that never seemed to soar high enough. Everything was bigger and better and getting still bigger and better; the sky was more brilliant; the sea, more vast. There was more growth, more hope, and more magic per square mile in California than anyplace on earth. Had not California given us Hollywood, the television industry, the aerospace world, whole computer valleys with men and women of new minds that would surely save the world, a place where all peoples could come (no questions asked), Sunset Boulevardiers, guided missiles and Stealth bombs, the Progressive movement, beach bums and bodybuilders, the feminist movement, acid-house music and New Age power, gay liberation, your very own "right to publicity," and redemption for the sins of Vietnam by embracing Vietnamese immigrants? Had not California celebrated EST and therapy sessions that stretched into the glorious sunsets? Had not California spoken to that "child within," making us believe we would stay children forever?

It was in California that the self-esteem movement started; in fact, Santa Clara County had a Self-Esteem Task Force. For balance, the victimization movement started in California, too; court cases became roller coasters on which everyone could have fifteen minutes as a victim. That way, no one was responsible, and of course no one was ever guilty, either! When a *New York Times* writer noted that "Americans had moved from the self-absorbed Me-Generation to the self-absolved Not-Me Generation," he was really referring to California.

Time magazine called the state "America's bright, strange, cultural outrider, a sort of floating state of mind, a golden land unanchored in tradition or guilt, a fresh start, no corpse of the past, no tragedy." Inhibitions were "abandoned on the borders of the state."

There were more Mexicans in Los Angeles than in any other city but Mexico City; more Koreans than in any city outside of Seoul; more Druze than anyplace but Lebanon! California would in the 1970s and '80s take in more immigrants than any state in the nation; if they happened to come illegally, well, for a long time that was all right, too!

By the 1990s, however, in place of multicultural idealism, Los Angeles had become not only one of the least governable cities in the world but one of the most segregated. Crime had risen so quickly in the eighties, largely because there were so many unemployed and/or unemployable young men entering the state, that California embarked upon a ten-year, $3.5 billion prison construction spree, while in the absence of money for court buildings, the judges who were supposed to represent the dignity of the law pushed their piles of briefs in shopping carts from dingy courtroom to dingy courtroom.

"A dejection born of overblown dreams" was the way that Neil Morgan, editor of the *San Diego Tribune,* sadly put it. "CALIFORNIANS GET SICK OF EACH OTHER," the *Wall Street Journal* headlined. "Immigrants are building an ethnic mosaic, but the pieces don't quite fit," *Time* magazine opined. In step with the therapeutic mind-set that Californians had made into an art form, newspapers talked about an "entire state" having an "identity crisis." The sign displayed prominently in a Sacramento government office read: "WARNING: THE LIGHT AT THE END OF THE TUNNEL HAS BEEN DELAYED."

If we were to pause for a moment and consider the core reasons for California's precipitous demise, we would find that most of the state's "sins"—wantonness, disregard for the past and its vexing verities, the arrogant presumption that "we will do what no one has ever done before, with no price to pay"—directly related to the destruction of the citizenship bond. And since the state has always seemed to be (and, indeed, bragged of being) what all America would be next, it is not unreasonable to assume that we can preview America's future by examining California's past and present.

☆

California had started out like the rest of America, of course, with a traditional political organization: two major parties, regular election campaigns with candidates for office chosen by the party fathers, and the Founding Fathers' form of American indirect republican democracy, by which elected representatives made the laws that ruled the nation. But the state, with its propensity to experiment, had been particularly fertile ground for the nationwide Progressive movement, which aimed at controlling the big corporations (in California, the railroads) and devolving power to the people, while weakening the controls of the state political institutions. By the 1990s, experiment after experiment with the political base of California had changed it beyond all recognition, so much so that London's prestigious *Economist* at one point suggested with its usual wryness that the state looked "as if it had been designed by a child on LSD." (The analogy of drug use was, ironically, perfect for California.)

Like most of California's changes, these had *seemed* so right, so liberal, so good. In this brave new world, power had been dispersed . . . decentralized . . . deconstructed. . . . (California was always good at embracing new ideas that were wonderful in theory, abysmal in practice.) Among fifty-eight counties of all sizes, there were more than five thousand special districts, neatly dividing up everything from sewage to air quality. In Los Angeles, any one police car could belong to a dozen specialized forces. By 1993, in the state capital of Sacramento, roughly 85 percent of the state's proposed $451 billion budget for that fiscal year was outside the governor's control, having been preassigned either by ballot initiatives or by federal law; this was surely a "division of powers" that America's Founding Fathers could scarcely have anticipated.

One source of the problem was the impassioned tendency of California, influenced by the thinking of the sixties, to break down—" deconstruct," in New Left lingo—institutions, all in the name of greater individual participation. It *sounded* good.

California was the womb of the ballot-initiative movement, and thus the mother to the Western world's chief experiment with the "direct democracy" that the Clinton administration would later come to applaud. Los Angeles was the first decentralized modern city, thanks to the domination of the automobile in this post-twentieth-century "nation." But the state was also the home of Proposition 13 tax-cutter Howard Jarvis, who in 1978 got Californians to vote to halve local property taxes by the sheer exercise of "popular will." And at the same time, on the communications and "information age" level, his brother-in-ideology Ronald Reagan invented (in California!) the modern politics of the sound bite and the quick fix, while still others, on the Left, were fashioning the "illegal citizen." California seemed to have devised the way to get around government and bureaucracy through opening these direct channels between citizen and power.

California had also gone about as far as any state could go in trying to cleanse politics of its old and cynical flavor; the state nearly tried to abolish politics, and in fact did virtually abolish the political campaign.

William Schneider, arguably the country's most perceptive political commentator, writes of its experiment with "direct democracy" that

> California is well on its way to achieving a new level of perfection in the art of politics—the totally paid political campaign. No speeches, no rallies, no walking tours, no interaction with the voters. Just fund-raising events, television commercials, and direct mail. . . . Most of the primary campaign bypassed the press. There were no events to cover, there were only ads and mailings. . . . First, political parties became irrelevant. Now the press has become irrelevant. Soon the voters will become irrelevant. If an ordinary, unskilled voter tried to volunteer for a campaign in California, there wouldn't be anything for the voter to do. The pros do it all. You want to participate in politics? Give money.

Politics California-style was being shorn of the sacred aura of individual responsibility that the Founding Fathers had attached to it; indeed, in that new fangled nation-state that was Hollywood, politics was simply becoming another form of entertainment, a form that demanded none of the active intensity of the original political life of America. In direct democracy, people thought they were voting, *thought* that their will was expressed and their feelings mattered, but they weren't and they didn't. What happened was that their will and feelings were frittered away in self-expression; there was no longer any system of representation that could give them form and real, as opposed to virtual, power. There was no political vehicle. And so when economic and social problems presented themselves to the state for solution, no one could garner the power to deal with them anymore.

Little wonder that in 1991 Governor Pete Wilson would sum up: "California is ungovernable!"

All of these changes in California had their beginnings in the American ideal of individual human beings free and autonomous. But, in truth, few Americans realized what this new direct democracy was—or what it could be. It sounded good but confused, as though one could not tell the difference between Fidel Castro's "spontaneous approval" by "the masses" in the plaza and American viewers watching television in their homes and employing some electronic method to register their level of emotion about a subject at hand.

It seemed avant, for instance when futurists Alvin and Heidi Toffler advocated "a whole new structure of government," averring that "today's spectacular advances in communications technology open for the first time a mind-boggling array of possibilities for direct citizen participation in political decision-making." And few paused to remember that such direct democracy was actually announced in modern times as the system of Benito Mussolini in his demagogic dictatorship, or that the Founding Fathers had studied similar dictatorial forms and warned against them, saying that such régimes were particularly vulnerable to demagogues and that throughout history they were characterized by cataclysmic shifts from anarchy to tyranny because the only real power allowed was the power of the dictator's fist. (And, where on earth had we left the Enlightenment?)

The modern California-born "proposition movement" was to become in many ways brother to that amorphous and undisciplined "direct democracy," in that both were designed to bypass the old political parties as mediator between the leader and the led. The proposition movement, which led to the "ballot initiative" laws, actually was designed early, in 1911, by the great Progressive governor Hiram Johnson, largely as a way to restrict the power of the Southern Pacific Railroad. Indeed, the state's disastrous workers' compensation program, which by the 1990s was impoverishing the state, also came out of that movement. And who could possibly say it was wrong to help the working class, to have a beneficent state aid the sick or the disabled?

By the winter of 1993, many people *were* saying that. I sat in the lovely and mellow Sacramento for several hours with Russell Gould, the head of the state's health, education, and welfare programs, and he was saying, while shaking his head with sadness (and at times in disbelief), "Workers' compensation is out of control. It is one of our great hidden taxes. Businesses ask, 'Is California the place to expand?' We have the highest premiums in the nation and the lowest benefits. Who's gaining?"

As a matter of fact, a lot of people are gaining, but not those intended. While California's employers payed the highest amounts of money in the nation into workers' comp (17 percent of a company's income is not an exaggerated figure), and thus many simply get up and leave the state for good, fully 70 percent of the funds were going to extravagantly politicized lawyers and forensic specialists, while a bare thirty cents of every dollar went to workers.

"We end up with a system of 'dueling doctors'" was the way Lee Grissom, Governor Wilson's able economics counselor, explained the system to me. "If a worker claims a stress problem, or if you show that ten percent of the stress is work related (it may even be due to a divorce!), you're eligible for workers' comp. There are situations where people were laid off and one hundred forty people filed claims, some of them claiming that 'the termination created terrible stress.' In 1989, there was an attempt to reform the system, but the best of the bills then introduced would still have added eight hundred million dollars to employers' costs!"

Pause.

It is instructive to note here that the continuation of this impossible system of workers' comp is supported by such high-monied lobby groups as the California Teachers Association and the California Trial Lawyers Association, whose activist/directors really make the laws; the comparison to the similar power of the Ford Foundation with regard to immigration law is quite arresting.

By 1992, in great part due to all of these changes and political and metaphysical dislocations, the Golden State was quite simply going bankrupt. In his watershed "State of the State" speech on January 6, 1993, Governor Wilson tried desperately to point up the problem. "California is in crisis," he proclaimed urgently and unashamedly. "We have lost eight hundred thousand jobs. At least one in ten Californians is out of work. As a result, state government lacks the revenues and cannot pay . . . can *not* pay . . . for all the increased services we are asked to provide. It takes three jobs just to pay the cost of sending one undergraduate to the University of California. It takes twenty-two jobs to support one elementary school classroom. It takes five jobs to keep one additional dangerous criminal in prison, and it takes almost a quarter of a million jobs just to meet this year's growth—just the *growth*, mind you—in Medi-Cal recipients.

"And all public programs," he tried to remind the people, "begin not in this chamber but in the sweat and toil of working men and women. . . ."

But by far not all of the state was "working," and the figures on welfare for Californians, figures similar to those on worker compensation, had become staggering. When Governor Wilson came into office in 1991, the state had a $440 billion base income—and a $414 billion deficit. To put it another way, in 1990 California needed twelve taxpayers for every ten welfare recipients; but, the way things were going, by the year 2000 it would have only eight taxpayers for every ten recipients. In short, the center was simply not holding, and people began to wonder when the moment of critical mass came in the Golden State, when a return to the original state became impossible.

The state was rich in welfare programs, but through incessant business regulation and destruction of its tax and revenue base, it had willfully impoverished itself. This development was startlingly similar to the manner in which America was destroying the very bases of its traditional citizenship.

"I was born nine months after Pearl Harbor," Lee Grissom told me. "My whole life, we have been a nation at or recovering from war. And all my lifetime, this state was the bastion of America's military might. California made the weapons to be used against the Soviets. Now, the smugness that Californians experienced is clearly gone. But there is not a sense of hopelessness, just the quiet moment that comes to people when they realize that the status quo must change."

The status quo, in California more than anywhere in the nation, was one in which the *citizen* had returned to the old *subject* of earlier epochs. He had become the subject of special-interests agendas, the devouring welfare system, the self-isolation and selfishness of the new elites, the utopianism of the education establishment, the suburbanization of inner-city civic leaders, direct democracy, television and technology, and uncontrolled waves of illegal immigration.

And, so, many citizens responded in a way that was unexpected: They *moved*! In the twelve months ending in June 1993, roughly 580,000 people left California, 150,000 more than moved in from the other forty-nine states. It was the largest net out-migration number since record keeping began in 1970. California's best middle-class citizens devised ways to abandon the sinking ship and become citizens in some more propitious business and social clime, if not more felicitous in terms of temperature / precipitation climate.

Before, refugees from other states, less blessed than California, had poured into the Golden State; now they were pouring out: to Idaho, New Mexico, Oregon, and Colorado. "They are the harbingers of the future," Richard Lamm, Colorado's talented former governor, tartly summed up. "They have compromised their quality of life, and they are looking for other places to go. If you want to see Denver tomorrow, go to Los Angeles today. When people have screwed up their own areas, then they come here." The frontier was being reversed—and, of little-noted importance, it was not only *white* Americans who were leaving California, it was also large numbers of disgruntled *black* Americans.

"We have hardly a flag in the public schools, no Pledge of Allegiance," Eyala Foster, a serious, middle-class Angeleno who was head of Los Angeles Black Americans for Family Values, told me in 1994. "Some black schools pledge allegiance to Africa. Advocacy groups backed by your tax funds have dealt a devastating blow to the black community. We are in a very serious time in our history. The illegals are not only coming across the border for a better life, but they are bringing their problems with them."

By the winter of 1995, the *New York Times* reported in a front-page story:

> For perhaps half a century, Los Angeles has lured blacks, along with hundreds of thousands of other immigrants from the South and Midwest, with its promise of jobs and the luxury of space. But in the last decade, fed up with high housing costs, drugs and crime, blacks have been fleeing Los Angeles, not only to outlying areas, but also to other states, particularly in the south. In fact, demographers and geographers say, middle-class and working-class blacks, born in California, are on the verge of disappearing altogether from some neighborhoods. . . .

James H. Johnson, a specialist in black migration at the University of North Carolina at Chapel Hill commented at the time, "In a community where you have other ethnic groups growing rapidly, these changes have enormous political and electoral significance."

And hardly anyone noticed the coincidence that it had been *one hundred years since the frontier had closed in 1893!* The centennial seemed to be celebrated in an odd way: Now, the frontier was being reversed.

There was a phrase, "internal exile," that came from the Polish intellectuals struggling to remain moral and responsible human beings while forced to live under Communism. It meant burying oneself in one's own personal life and evading public life; nothing could be more antithetical to America's original spirit. Yet now, many Californians, in their own style, also went into internal exile. Some flocked to self-sufficient, self-governing, gated and guarded communities—the "modern equivalent of medieval city states," the *Economist* calls them. And these new societies had their moats of the mind and spirit around them, as well as physical moats. Columnist George Will notes that "a city [L.A.] where 40 percent of all households have unlisted telephone numbers is experiencing a great withdrawal—from public life, including public schools, into gated neighborhoods, or just indoors, or to suburbs."

California led the nation in the four million Americans living in thirty thousand gated communities, as charted in the aforementioned major study of them, *Fortress Communities*. Interestingly, the Golden State was followed in gatedness by Florida, Arizona, Texas, and New York. This was not surprising: these states had the highest level of illegal immigration, and thus of challenges to the coherence of responsible citizenship. But California gated communities served up nostalgia with a twist: The first walled cities in the Caribbean were the Spanish walled cities, which of course inspired the first Spanish who came as priests and officers to settle the Southwest.

These new distant Americans who sought out the relative safety of gated communities did so for many reasons: Some were the Reichian "symbolic analysts," stopping by "at home" in Anaheim or Whittier en route from Seoul, Singapore, or Samarkand, and soon to be off to Moscow, Magadan, or Myanmar; some were people just terribly afraid of crime and disorder; some were concerned about keeping up the value of their homes. They are called "common-interest" communities, for they have "shared-interest" group loyalty that is considered far more important than that old common good. The study, *Fortress Communities*, calls them "invisible citizens," and in a part of the analysis calls each one of them elliptically "Citizen Who?"

Meanwhile, poorer citizens also "seceded" by not taking part in politics, which is of course the very medium of expression of citizenship. When Los Angeles Mayor Tom Bradley was elected in 1973, 674,555 people voted; the city has grown since then by almost that many, but by 1993, only 598,436 voted.

And still others had more "creative" (some might say more "desperate") agendas, as is made clear in the following discussion of a divvied-up California.

After visiting the state's capitol and its leading lawmakers in Sacramento in January 1993, when Governor Wilson was giving his extraordinary "State of the State" address, I wrote in my column:

> Czechoslovakia has split into two. Yugoslavia is horrifically devolving into God-only-knows how many new countries. The Soviet Union two years ago split into republics, which are now

busily splintering into bits and pieces. Thank God we live in America! Thank God we are part of a nation-state whose universalist idea and federal system keeps us solidly and snugly together.

Oh yeah? Well, if you think that, you haven't talked to Stan Statham, the California assemblyman from Redding. When "unmarryin' Stan" looks at the map of the Golden State, his eyes see not one California but three—and he is gaining more and more support for his consuming idea of breaking up the state.

It was a cool winter's morning when I strolled into Statham's office in the state capitol, and the assemblyman was amazed at how many were agreeing with him that breaking up is not so hard to do.

"I am stunned by what has been happening to the movement," the tall, gray-haired, outdoors-type Mr. Statham began. "Friday of last week, the TV show *Jeopardy* started a new category called the 'fifty-first state.' They're also talking about Washington, D.C., and Puerto Rico and perhaps others—but mainly it's California. Then, over the last eight months, my favorite magazine has been researching the division of California; *National Geographic* is putting out a special section on it in the spring. . . .

"You see, the world is aware that California is broke; my opinion is that it's also broken. By any economist's view, California is dysfunctional. We have multimillion-dollar deficits as a matter of practice. We need major restructuring in everything. . . ."

When Stan Statham got his "outrageous idea," most Californians saw it as some kind of joke. Divide up the state? Into two states? Into three? But then Statham and his staff began going county to county across the state, petitioning the counties to put on the ballot a "nonbinding advisory" on the breakup of California. Thirty-one of fifty-two counties did so; and of those, only three counties voted against approving division. The rest approved by an average percentage of 66 percent, and in the rich and alienated northern counties, they approved by an average of 82 percent.

Not surprisingly, the board of supervisors of Los Angeles County refused to let Statham even make a presentation to them; but, then, that is hardly surprising since they were sitting—with increasing discomfort and desperation—on the very core of the problem!

Basically, what the "three states" advocates were finding was that (1) rich and trendy San Francisco and increasingly impoverished and violent Los Angeles really did not want to be in the *same* state together anymore, (2) rural California didn't want to be in a state with *either* of them, and that (3) *nobody* wanted to be in a state with Los Angeles. Thus, the idea to form three new states: prosperous North California (population, 2,350,725; estimated budget, $3.6 billion), roughly above San Francisco with citizens of the old style; Central California (population, 10,146,200; estimated budget, $15 billion), stretching roughly from Santa Barbara to San Francisco and also largely with citizens of the old style, intermingled with trendy San Franciscans; and the once-Dionysian but now-miserable South California (population, 17,853,900; estimated budget, $27 billion).

As not only Stan Statham but more and more Californians spoke seriously about the prosperous parts of the state simply "opting out" of the tarnished goldenness of California, one had to stop and say, "Hey, no, this is not supposed to happen here! That is Yugoslavia, Lebanon, Armenia. . . ." Only it was happening here —and it will indeed happen more often if the nation does not rationally affirm its unity.

I wrote at the end of my column on Stan Statham and his scissors poised restlessly over the map of California:

> I think the prosperous regions, whether of California or the former Yugoslavia, would take on even more responsibility for others if they believed it could do any good. The tragedy of the onerous burden of Los Angeles is that there is no end to it. Even now, with the state broke and everybody knowing the problems, nobody is willing to address the city's massive illegal immigration, the corrupt welfare programs and the pitting of modern "tribe" against "tribe" (blacks, Hispanics, Koreans).
>
> It is simply a fact of human nature—as inevitable as the sun rising—that, if well-meaning people are too long kept from solving problems on terms acceptable to the principles, moral and otherwise, of that culture, they will simply opt out. And is the responsibility really, then, theirs?

It is wrong to claim that the massive immigration to California is the core of the state's problems. There are many reasons, including selfish American elites, utopian political thinkers, and "progressive" educational thinkers who do not believe in any socialization

at all. Even illegal immigration cannot be said to constitute anywhere near the whole problem. But by the hundredth anniversary
of the closing of the American frontier in 1893, there was no question that immigration—and, in particular, massive and growing
illegal immigration—had become one of the two or three decisive
elements in pushing the state just over the brink of collapse.

Without uncontrolled immigration, the state might still make
it, even with its other problems of political disintegration through
political decentralization, the excesses of direct democracy, and
sheer economic foolishness. But with immigration such as no nation or state has seen throughout history, California simply does
not have a chance.

As the *New York Times* wrote of Los Angeles on October 30,
1994:

> The economy is down and resentment of the immigrant in-
> flux is up.
>
> The city has become a giant jigsaw puzzle that no one knows
> how to put together anymore. Once a laid-back expanse of pas-
> tel neighborhoods, its spirit exemplified by skate-boarders and
> Christmas at the beach, Los Angeles is splitting into separate and
> often clashing pieces. Of the estimated five million immigrants
> who moved to California since 1970, two-thirds moved to the vast
> sprawl of the Los Angeles basin.
>
> In less than a generation, they remade what had been a bas-
> tion of predominantly white Protestant migrants from the Mid-
> west. Today one out of every four people in Los Angeles County
> and the four counties that surround it is foreign-born. One-fifth
> of America's immigrants call the area home.
>
> This human influx left a legacy of social dislocations. In Pico
> Union, Mexican-Americans compete for low-wage jobs with
> thousands of largely unskilled refugees displaced by war in Cen-
> tral America. In Monterey Park, affluent Taiwanese and Hong
> Kong Chinese began a building boom, rankling defenders of the
> status quo, whose anxieties emerged in rancorous debates over
> foreign-language signs. In South Central Los Angeles, the dense
> presence of Korean-owned liquor stores in a predominantly black
> and Hispanic community set off an acrimonious dispute about
> economic exploitation. . . .

But to understand what California is facing one has to travel again to the border, to that 1,951-mile-long "world" that marks the only place on earth where a rich industrialized country directly meets the Third World of dulling poverty, political and economic underdevelopment, and collective ambition to share the wealth of rich nations. California's immigration problems—and, thus, the critical mass of her social and human problems—began in the dramatic ways the border has changed over the last half century.

In 1981, when I visited the border on one of eight visits between 1968 and 1993, I found myself talking with Robert Mitton, a veteran immigration official on the San Isidro "crossing" with Tijuana. "I remember twenty-five years ago," he reminisced at one point in our long talk. "I would find a group of Mexicans marching through the desert toward the border. They would be carrying smoked carp in one pocket and a tequila bottle filled with water in the other. Violence was so repugnant to these ranchero agricultural people that, if somebody got into a fight, they would crouch down and lower their eyes. They couldn't even swing fists, but they would always keep their word. We could only admire these people."

And today? "Now it is all reversed," he summed up. "Now more than fifty percent of the illegal aliens here come from a new hard-core unemployed in the barrios of Mexico City. They call them 'pachucos.' And, whether in the United States or in Mexico, the hard-core unemployed are people who move toward violence. . . ."

The physical border itself was, of course, the same: Five-sixths of it constitutes a swatch of scrub desert whose eastern end is a delta region of thickets and swamps, while the Pacific end is thoroughly unremarkable dry, barren hills. Historically, the boundary stayed more or less the same after being drawn following the American invasion of Mexico in 1848—when, Mexicans still remember, Mexico was forced to cede the northern two-fifths of its territory to the "Colossus of the North" in the Treaty of Guadalupe Hidalgo—and the subsequent Gadsden Purchase (1854).

But socially the border has been transformed in the last half of the twentieth century by the new restiveness fueling masses of mankind on the move, by the technology that made such moves possible, and by the sheer pressures and power of overpopulation. What is sure is the fact that the "borderlands" represent such a new

entity—such an original geopolitical, economic, and human "construction" or "occurrence"—that names and phrases proliferate
wildly as people try to define its unique reality: *unified border region, third nation, MexAmerica, poverty cesspool, world of its own, col-
lision of cultures . . .*"

At the time of World War II, Tijuana was a pretty, sleepy, small
town. (It is still a remarkably pretty and civilized city of 1.2 million, clean, prosperous, and modern, with broad streets, five universities, and job opportunities available at every turn. Immigrants
regularly pass those jobs by for better-paid ones in the States.) It
was known best to the gringos from the North for its block-long
outside bar, where San Diego servicemen liked to go for Mexican
"flings." By the 1990s, Tijuana was the unofficial but real capital
of the "borderlands," a world as new as California had been in its
joyful youth, a "zone of influence" through which passed astonishing numbers of the world's population. It was also largely
through this crossing that tens of thousands of Central Americans
passed in the 1980s, as liberal or leftish city councils from Los
Angeles to San Francisco passed resolutions and ordinances declaring their cities to be "sanctuaries" for illegal immigrants from
Central American civil wars and repression.

By the 1990s, 54 million people passed through the Tijuana–San
Isidro crossing every year legally, but the serious problem was not
the legal visitors or aliens with green cards allowing them to work
legally in the United States. The serious problem was the 2 million
or perhaps even 3 million illegal aliens who cross every year. Estimates are that by the early 1990s, more than 2 million illegal immigrants were living in California with at least 550,000 U.S.-born
children—twice as many as a decade earlier. California was receiving 1,519 immigrants a day, while it had lost 400,000 jobs in 1991
alone, more than half in construction and manufacturing. By then,
fewer than half the children in the Los Angeles schools spoke English; in Santa Ana, 70 percent did not speak English.

Crucial was the fact that fully 90 percent of Mexican immigrants
in Los Angeles were not citizens; only around 30 percent were flu-
ent in English; and only 20 to 25 percent completed high school.

Not only have the *numbers* of illegal aliens changed dramatically, the types have changed as well. Instead of Robert Mitton's
poor but noble rancheros, the newer immigrants are everything

from the criminal pachucos to the restive, hardworking but most often uncultured poor from Mexico's crowded cities and (more and more) displaced middle-class urban workers.

When I visited the border again in 1988 and spoke with Dr. Jorge Bustamente, head of the Mexican government-funded Colegio de la Frontera y el Norte, or the College of the Frontier and of the North, this respected "first scholar" of the border explained to me that, actually, bad economic times such as Mexico witnessed in the early eighties did not act as an instigator to emigration. "When the economic crisis began in Mexico," he told me, sitting in his neat office in Tijuana, "we thought that it would operate as a pushing factor. That was not the case. We found it made many think of leaving, but they couldn't afford to do so." So, he went on, most of the hundreds of thousands of illegal aliens who try to cross to the United States each year—in addition to the fifty-four million legal crossings back and forth—were by then middle-class urban workers, a dramatic change that was confirmed to me by the *colegio* when I again visited in 1993. This was in some ways good, but it meant that besides bringing skills to America, illegal immigrants were now taking the upwardly mobile jobs that citizens should have. It was also—still—illegal.

This sociocultural phenomenon may not seem important to many Americans, but as a matter of fact, it is crucial because it means that contrary to what the pro-immigration people constantly and simplistically insist, even very real and extraordinarily fast economic development inside Mexico (which will not happen) would not stem the tide of illegal immigrants. In our lifetimes American wages will always be higher than in Mexico, and so even the better-paid will continue to come. The answer, then, is not to be found in blithe assertions claiming that "development inside Mexico" will or would solve the problem.

But let us pause here for a moment and concentrate on the questions that begin to nag at me. One surely has the right to say that, yes, the border is always historically interesting—and, yes, the border is economically important—and, yes, it is politically and even geopolitically of consequence to the United States. But does it really have anything to do with citizenship? Is it possible to claim that those masses of (more or less) poor people, deserving and undeserving, could actually threaten the hoary concept of American citizenship? What could those people possibly have done to threaten the great sovereign state of California?

The answer is that, yes again, illegal immigration is indeed a swing element in the breakdown of California as a workable and prosperous state. A healthy citizenship—indeed, any citizenship— depends upon the commitment of the great majority of persons living in a nation-state *to* that nation-state; this is true both in a spiritual/patriotic sense and in a purely economic sense. When large numbers of people live outside the commitment to the principles of a state, inevitably and invariably other loyalties become dominant and fill the vacuum—or a passive anomie and alienation soon lead to a loyalty to those other "citizenships": gangs, militias, even gated communities.

This is as utterly expectable as any law of physics, and if one needs social proof, one needs only to look at Beirut . . . Bosnia . . . Rwanda . . .

One might further note that illegal immigration debases citizenship in myriad ways: by using services meant as a reward for citizenship and its duties, by debasing the concept of citizenship and disheartening true citizens, who then retreat into exile. It also destroys the crucial aspect of "reciprocity" both between individuals and their fellows, and between the individual and the state. Even between states, without reciprocal obligations there is no comity and no real equality. It is simply common sense to see that one does not have the moral or ethical right to ask things of others based upon principles that one does not oneself accept and observe.

☆

The inevitable results of California's uncontrolled immigration can now be seen everywhere. Los Angeles County alone offers *the* nightmare scenario for the entire country. After a meeting on immigration problems in the offices of the U.S. senator from Kansas, Robert Dole, in the summer of 1993, Michael D. Antonovich, of the Board of Supervisors of the county, sent me information showing that "illegal immigrants and children impose a $1.43 billion per year burden on Los Angeles County in health and welfare, justice system and educational costs. On the other side of the ledger, illegal aliens generate revenue to the county of only $36.2 million. The net impact on the county budget is catastrophic and the net impact on American taxpayers more generally is one-half billion dollars per year. Again, this is just for Los Angeles County."

Basing his figures on well-accepted county studies and statistics, Antonovich goes on to still other areas where illegal immigration is rapidly destroying human services that centuries of American citizens set up primarily for the benefit of citizens. "Sixty-three percent of all children born in our county hospitals at taxpayer expense are born to illegal alien mothers," he continues. "Such children now represent 30 percent of all Aid for Dependent Children cases in Los Angeles County and their annualized AFDC costs total over $400 million." Then there is "the onslaught of illegal alien criminals."

Although, he says, "our nation's immigration laws bar criminals from entering the country, criminals circumvent the law rather easily because of our porous borders. In Los Angeles County, illegal aliens account for more than 11 percent of all inmates in the county's jail system. A joint County–Immigration and Naturalization Service study found that almost 80 percent of deportable aliens in the county's jail system in May, 1990, who were returned by the INS to their countries of origin, illegally reentered the country and were arrested again within one year of their release. . . ."

More on the serious abuses of health care by illegal aliens: Medi-Cal (Medicaid in other states) was established in California to provide health care for needy California residents, but in the 1980s and '90s it had become a veritable magnet for illegal aliens and unscrupulous foreign visitors, whose demands together caused costs to skyrocket from $187 million in 1989 to a projected $1 billion in 1993, tenfold increase in only five years!

Indeed, a 1993 series in the *San Diego Union-Tribune* on "Medi-Cal, the New Gold Rush," outlined how "health care pilgrims" have made their way from countries as disparate as Armenia (for liver transplants), Syria (for cancer care), and Hong Kong and Mexico (for heart operations and bone-marrow transplants). The fraud is now so rampant, the paper said, that the statewide cost of the special program for illegal aliens topped $700 million in 1992, up from $190 million in 1989, its first year.

The respected Center for Immigration Studies estimated that illegals in general cost the U.S. government $5.4 billion in health care, housing and energy assistance, education, welfare, and prison expenses in 1990. (In one case of fraud typical in such assistance programs, an extremely wealthy woman, of the Tijuana family that owns the twenty-three-story Fiesta Americana hotel-office complex, came to California, misrepresented herself, and got free care— although her bills totaled $635,000!)

When this series came out, I wrote in one of my columns about what seems to me the core mystery of this entire illegal alien situation:

> While we bankrupt our own country, we make con-men of the world's people, who know they can lie to come here to get what they don't deserve. For our part, we are vacillating and unclear about what commitments newcomers should make to America and we offer few incentives to reward loyalty to this country. And at the same time, we overload our own citizens and destroy the unity of America in the name of people who have not even chosen to make any commitment to this country. It is staggering.

But the crisis of health care and illegal aliens did not end there. For the new "Health Security" card that was being proposed by the Clinton administration in 1994 and '95 to "assure health care for all Americans" was in fact a Trojan horse that could intensify the immigration problem. For the Clinton administration's neat wallet-sized card could easily have become the first official American identity card, as ripe for counterfeiting as many other documents today.

Not only the border cities but even the downtown sidewalks of cities such as San Diego have become virtual document-producing factories, another example of how the immigrant's first and generally most formative experiences with America are those of fraud, dishonesty, and illegality. (Are these really the qualities one wants to encourage in new citizens?) You can buy anything you want— Social Security cards, driver's licenses, voting cards—and, voilà, you are "legal" and you can get a job! Employers are supposed to check documents or be fined. Some do, some don't, and some can't.

So, under the Clinton health-care-reform scenario, the card that virtually would have become the first American ID card would have gone to countless numbers of illegal aliens—good or bad, saint or criminal, devoted mother or drug junkie—who would be effectively "legalized" overnight. Wouldn't this have been one of the greatest threats to responsible citizenship?

☆

In the summer of 1990, I spent a day driving around with Los Angeles "gang cops" in the most bleak, ugly, and dangerous areas, where Hispanic and black gangs kill one another on whim. Their language is as strange and different as that of a Lebanese militiaman or a Serb "Chetnik": *Rifa* means to rule; *Puto* marks on the walls were the symbols of homosexuals; *Rasco* is the gun; *Hoopdee* is a car ride; and *homeboy* is your gang comrade.

What was happening in American inner cities was only a reflection of what was happening around the world. One could see in East Los Angeles the same phenomena one saw among the militias in West Beirut or the young thugs in Liberia or Sierra Leone: Violent young men who didn't belong to anything formed groups they *could* belong to; they created their own symbols, even their own language. In Bosnia, the early Serb militias were so disorganized, they pinned their "unit's" colors on their sleeves; in the West African social collapse, militias dressed in women's wigs and clothing, in part to show how grotesque they knew they were. (Nature abhors a vacuum—again!) Why be surprised, indeed, in East L.A. or, for that matter, Omaha or even Minneapolis, when these California gangs spread there next? America had given them no symbols to recognize and embrace anymore.

In 1977, just before this special "gang unit" was formed, L.A. had 180 gangs; by 1990, it had 900. In 1977, it had 20,000 gang members; in 1990, it had between 90,000 and 100,000. They were getting younger (some were only eight years old) and they were getting meaner, with 3,539 lives lost to gang warfare in the United States between 1979 and 1989. "The *Los Angeles Times* Monday edition runs a scorecard of the dead over the weekend," Captain Raymond E. Gott of the sheriff's office told me, looking somber indeed. "Gangs are breeding more gangs early on. The underclass is breeding more of an underclass." He paused.

"I don't see much hope," he went on. "It's not just the minority communities. We've developed a society that is very materialistic, that has no impulse control, and that is not willing to 'work for it.' What worries me is that when you talk to one of these kids who has just done a drive-by shooting, and you ask him how he feels to have killed somebody, he just says, 'That guy shouldn't have been there.' There is no remorse, no caring, nothing."

We are living in a time when more and more world-defining movements are not toward consolidation or definition of society, but toward breakdown, disintegration, and cultural nihilism. The increasing "powers" of the post–cold war period are not mass armies but (Central American and other) guerrillas, (Lebanese and Serbian) militias, and (American) street gangs. These gangs even have many of the strange pieces of clothing and emblems of the militias in Beirut and Rwanda and Liberia. ("I man a checkpoint; therefore, I am," Fouad Ajami's generic Beirut militiaman had said.) As communications and technology diminish the historic importance of the oceans as America's protection, we are every day less immune to the troubles of other areas of the modern world.

Moreover, Americans in general should not believe that such gang warfare is exclusive to cities with high rates of illegal immigration such as Los Angeles. Although the gangs started largely in the illegal-immigration barrios of cities close to the border, they are now traveling across the country. In the Pew Partnership for Civic Change's 1994 report, "Youth Violence—Gangs on Main Street, USA," selected cities with populations of 50,000 to 150,000 were asked to identify the top three issues facing their communities, and nearly a third of them cited youth violence and escalating gang activity as major problems.

Meanwhile, in America's quintessential "gang capital," Los Angeles, whose name in Spanish ironically means "City of the Angels," gangs have grown to outnumber the police by five to one. The *Los Angeles Times* has commented that "Latino gangs have been rejuvenated by a new generation of Mexico and Central American immigrants. On the streets and behind bars, they have come to the realization that—if only through sheer numbers—they have the potential to dominate the underworld. . . ."

Finally, as they spread across the country, the gang leaders were even going into politics; occurring in many places was a "criminalization of politics" that was about as far from the old citizen-politician as anything could be.

There was little question that illegal immigration was a major factor in the awful riots of May 1992 in Los Angeles, for instance. Indeed, Los Angeles County Assistant Public Defender Michael Judge found at the time that approximately 40 percent of the defendants facing criminal charges for looting during the riots were Hispanic, and the *San Francisco Chronicle* quoted "Latino activists" describing many looters as "desperate . . . immigrants who were not finding the American dream they came to find." Indeed, many analysts called the riot the "first immigration riot."

The fact was that America's refusal to control its borders and the "multiculturalism" breaking America down into warring interest groups were actually fueling violence and racism. "Conservatives have warned that the multiculturalist prescription of diversity at the expense of common culture would lead to tribalism and eventually to separatism and violence," Lance T. Izumi, former speechwriter for California Governor George Deukmejian, has aptly noted. "The ultimate effect of uncontrolled immigration has been to turn California's urban areas not into the multicultural fantasy land of brown, black and yellow brotherhood, but into our own budding version of Bosnia."

☆

We need to pause here again and reiterate an important verity: The blame for all of these immigration-linked problems, which are growing more and more dangerous to the reality of a united and coherent America, does not lie with the immigrants. True, they are deliberately breaking the law when they come here illegally; true, they have an abnormal level of violence and social disintegration in their neighborhoods; true, until very recently they were not becoming citizens even when American society was making it absurdly simple for them.

But the real blame lies with America. It is the United States that refuses to control the border; the United States that somewhere along the way lost its nerve and, with it, its confidence; the United States that has dumbed down and ideologized its universities with so much "ethnic sensitivity" and so many "ethnic studies" that American principles are either not heard or completely cut out of the curriculum.

When, say, a young Mexican- or Hispanic-American man comes to most American universities today, what does he study? The American civics curriculum that once taught the American principles that are now *the* model for development across the entire world? No, today he will be studying "Chicano studies" at Berkeley or "multiculturalism" at Stanford. At Stanford he will get a reading list including almost none of the great—and now hated—"Western civilization" writers but a lot of "victims" discussing their "terrible victimization" in America. He is far more likely to become acquainted with the "internal colony model" of Mexican-American New Left academics who see Chicanos as "a conquered people, whose alienation from their lands, language, and culture gives them much in common with American Indians and blacks." He is much more likely to read the Mexico City newspaper *Excelsior*, which editorialized in 1982 (to cite only one example) that the "Colossus of the North" (the United States) would "in the long run have to pay the price for their rich natural resources" because "there will not be in any part of the world privileged minorities, nor territories reserved for selected races or dominant groups" and that, further, "the biblical teaching, people of the earth, does not recognize frontiers nor admit of privileges. . . ."

If he enters the once-exemplary California university system, he will find that it now teaches American history as only one of many histories and under the sobriquet of "European-American" history— although where these educators find "European-Americans" is a mystery, since nobody I know has ever met one! As an "American" student, he will study the ancient African civilizations of Cush and Mali as well as the "suffering of native people at the hands of missionaries in the California missions." And he also will learn something else: Across the board, the American system today works, sometimes accidentally but often deliberately, against assimilation. Moreover, a newcomer to America not unexpectedly will soon learn that, if he can illustrate enough "oppression," he will be rewarded by the inappropriate overhang of the original civil rights laws.

How could he possibly come to feel—or be—American?

In his extensive definitive research on the Hispanic-American community in the United States, Peter Skerry came to the conclusion that ideological Hispanic-Americans, particularly in California, those seeking their "Chicano" or other roots, were not at all the first-generation immigrants, who might have some real reason for complaint, but were actually their children or grandchildren—who went to Berkeley and took "Chicano studies" taught by feverishly ideologized New Left ethnic activists.

Two persuasive critics of the multiculturalism practiced at its spiritual alma mater, California's Stanford University, wrote *The Diversity Myth*, taking the whole multicultural mythology apart. "It's completely anti-intellectual," according to Stanford graduates Peter A. Thiel and David O. Sacks. "Multiculturalism is about studying less, not more. It has nothing to do with other cultures and no stress on foreign languages. It's anti-Western, not non-Western. Multiculturalism and political correctness are different sides of the same coin. Multiculturalism is the side where you look for the victims. Political correctness is the side where you go after the victimizers."

☆

The reason always given by both Leftist and Rightist pro-immigration people for their stance was that "the border cannot be controlled anyway." But by the 1990s, the United States had lost that excuse. For in both San Isidro/Tijuana and El Paso/Juárez, the borders *were* being largely controlled—and this was being accomplished, interestingly enough, by the first two Hispanic-American border chiefs.

In San Isidro, Chief Gustavo de la Vina had quietly gotten truckloads of old military parts for nothing and built a fourteen-mile fence along the most-used crossing point between there and Tijuana; it had not by any means totally stopped the illegals from passing over, but it had slowed the traffic immensely—and, perhaps most important, it gave the signal to people on both sides of the border that "business as usual" was no longer the accepted mode!

But it was in El Paso that by far the most successful "control" of the border was instituted, this time by Chief Silvestre "Silver" Reyes, like de la Vina a solid and upright man who kept saying, "I only wanted to do my job; if they didn't want me to do my job, they shouldn't have sent me here!" As a matter of fact, Chief Reyes was the very first Hispanic-American to become a Border Patrol chief, his grandfather having come from Mexico.

"We had a situation here with almost institutionalized undocumented entry through the Rio Grande that people had gotten used to for decades," this serious, dedicated, pleasant man remarked, sitting in the picturesque "Old Texas" offices of the patrol near the El Paso airport. "It was largely due to the fact that our strategy was unworkable. We were trying to arrest people after they came in, and that was chaos for everybody. It made our agents vulnerable to [charges of] human rights abuses and raised the stress levels for everybody.

"I perceived a community-wide frustration with a situation that was simply out of control. I'd never seen anything like it: You couldn't go anywhere in the city without meeting panhandlers."

With accidental symbolism, Chief Reyes had taken over on July 4, 1993; by September 19, he was ready to put into practice his new "strategy that would work."

Before, the agents were not placed directly on the border itself, which in spots brings El Paso right up against its Mexican urban counterpart of Ciudad Juárez and in other parts is relatively open brush country. They were back in the city, which meant spending futile hours chasing illegal aliens or undocumented workers through the maze of city streets and alleys. So he began by moving his agents right up to the border. Having cleverly scrounged $250,000 out of Washington to cover massive hours of overtime, he took four hundred agents and covered a twenty-mile border stretch, stationing them within visual distance of one another from Anapra, New Mexico, to Yaleta, Texas. There they were—and are—twenty-four hours a day, seven days a week. By Tuesday, September 21, the reality had settled in, with shock on the Mexican side of the border and generally pleased relief on the American side.

By the time I visited in November of 1993, apprehensions of illegal immigrants in El Paso had plunged by 81 percent since the crackdown; the streets of El Paso were virtually free of panhandlers; and crime in the city had been reduced by 46 percent. There had been no confrontations whatsoever with agents and not a single allegation of human rights abuse. Perhaps most revealing, most polls showed that roughly 95 percent of El Pasoans approved of the actions.

No one mentioned it, but something else had occurred as well: A rare strike for *strengthening* American citizenship had actually taken place by this simple act of doing what every nation-state is supposedly obliged to do—defend the country's borders and assure its security. By 1993, an overwhelming majority of Americans—86 percent, according to reputable polls—considered illegal immigration a major problem, with nearly three-quarters in favor of using the National Guard to patrol the border.

It should be noted that the immigration onslaught was dangerous not only to California and the other southwestern border state of Texas; uncontrolled illegal immigration was endangering *all* of the states at America's peripheries. By 1994, New York was reeling, with reports showing that legal and illegal immigration was costing New York a minimum of $5.6 billion annually. And in Florida, nine hundred persons were arriving every day, the entire prison and police system of the state was collapsing, and the governor was suing the federal government to try to force it to pay the huge bills for social benefits for illegal aliens. It was not surprising that old Americans were fleeing those states that had traditionally served as centers of upward mobility or that that new exodus was prompted by the movement of migrants from abroad into those states.

Indeed, by the 1990s, the pattern in Florida, America's fourth largest state in population, looked disturbingly similar to the pattern in California. Its governor, Lawton Chiles, called the state *"more a crowd than a community."* In Dade County—Miami—more than 25 percent of the public school students had been born outside the country, and the largest hospital had spent $300 million in the last year treating illegal immigrants. Florida began deporting criminal aliens. Noting that the state had a "feeble public sector that extends from universities to environmental protection to criminal justice," *U.S. News & World Report* editorialized in 1993 that "Florida's predicament looks like America's, writ in a shaky hand: *affluence but attenuation; separateness of the old and the young, the well-off and the scrambling; a beautiful environment but a weak sense of guardianship; old traditions trying to set roots in sandy and swampy soil."* (Italics mine.)

By the year 2020, the Center for Immigration Studies reports, little Florida's population will pass 22 million at present rates of growth, which is a population 50 percent higher than would be the case without immigration. These analysts report further that about 40 percent of immigrants there have arrived since 1980; that half of Miamians aged five and over speak English poorly or not at all; that 750,000 school children will have been added to the state's schools between the 1990s and 2020, requiring a new school to be built every five days for the next twenty-five years just to keep up; that the state's population increased 32 percent during the 1980s but that road capacity increased at less than half that rate; that Florida's valuable and necessary wetlands have been reduced from 51 percent of the state's area in 1900 to less than 30 percent today.

It is a state—and a world—where too few have taken E. M. Forster's advice: "Only connect!" Or the serious environmentalists' warning call: "Only save!"

The present is scary, but predicted population growth is scarier still. California's population, for instance, has gone from 20 million in 1970 to 23.7 million in 1980 to 29.8 million in 1990 (a million more than all of Canada!): demographers say that, at current rates of increase, the population will rise to 40 to 50 million in the next quarter century and to 80 to 120 million in the lifetimes of children today. Fully 85 percent of the newcomers of the 1980s were Hispanic or Asian; it is estimated that by the year 2000 there will be no ethnic majority in California but only minorities (including "European-Americans"). Meanwhile, not too far into the twenty-first century, America's population could well be upwards of 500 million!

In sum, California is growing faster and the fertility rate of California is higher than any other industrialized nation in the world thanks to illegal immigration. That fertility rate is higher than in Mexico itself, and indeed Mexican immigrants have more children in California—an average of six children per family— than they do in Mexico because they are healthier and get better care in California. This new California is growing faster than India! There is no truth to that bit of "common wisdom" that says immigrant women will have fewer children as they become more prosperous. Indeed, the truth points the other way as America's frontiers, long the very symbol of her independence and spirit, move in upon her.

When will critical mass be reached? When will the moment of no-turning-back come? When do the illegal aliens, with no commitment to the country and no respect for its common principles, form their own political power groups to challenge the old citizens' America? In fact, that is already happening.

☆

The great historian Arnold Toynbee warned, "When a frontier between a more highly and less highly civilized society ceases to advance at the more backward society's expense, the balance does not settle down into a stable equilibrium but inclines with the passage of time in the more backward society's favor."

In the winter of 1996, as I was finishing this book, I found myself writing:

> Blessed as it was by its beautiful and bountiful continent, America never had to make these kinds of difficult decisions before, never had to choose one good over another, never had to do all those tedious things that crowded Europe and teeming Asia had had to do. It was always "Just move on!"
>
> But by the end of the 20th century, America itself had changed —it was in danger of drifting toward becoming a Third World nation, and crucially important parts of it, like once-glorious California, were actually moving backwards in time and backwards in development. If there was one predominant reason for this, it was America's unwillingness to make hard decisions over who belongs to America, what it means in a redefining world to BE an American and what commitments America feels it has the right to expect and (yes, even) demand of its residents.

The great American diplomat George F. Kennan lived good parts of his young life in California, and early on he saw the state as a gloriously beautiful but essentially childlike place—and, thus, a place that could not make hard decisions (and, then, did not usually need to). From his memoirs:

> California reminds me of the popular American Protestant concept of heaven. There is always a reasonable flow of new arrivals . . . people spend a good deal of their time congratulating one another about the fact that they are there; discontent would be unthinkable; and the newcomer is slightly disconcerted to

realize that now, the devil having been banished and virtue being triumphant, nothing terribly interesting can ever happen again.

. . . Southern California, together with all that tendency of American life which it typifies, is childhood without the promise of maturity—with the promise only of a continual widening and growing impressiveness of the childhood world, and when the day of reckoning and hardship comes, and I think it must, it will be—as everywhere among children—the cruelest and most ruthless natures who will seek to protect their interests by enslaving the others; and the others, being only children, will be easily enslaved. In this way, values will suddenly prove to have been lost that were forged slowly and laboriously in the more rugged experience of Western political development elsewhere.

And just as I quote Kennan's poetic but melancholic words, the unbelievable is happening: California's economy is beginning to improve, but, more important, Californians are beginning to rally—albeit through a questionable vehicle—against their disintegration. And the rebellion started in Northern California's Marin County, with its glorious vineyards, exquisite villas, and tie-dyed politics. It started in the North and not in the South because, in 1992, the northern town of San Rafael, outside of San Francisco, voted to use municipal funds to build a hiring hall for itinerant day laborers, and local businessman and political consultant Rick Oltman decided "This is enough!"

"On some days we had six hundred day laborers hanging around the street corners waiting to be picked up for jobs," he recalls. "People were getting tired of pulling their cars into a local business and having it surrounded by people looking for work. So the city comes up with the idea of building a hiring hall. And we said, 'Wait a minute!' According to the Immigration and Naturalization Service, eighty percent of these guys are illegal. Well, the City Council told us where to get off."

It was the worst parts of the surrealistic San Diego experience all over again!

Oltman organized a small band of rebel-citizens and they began videotaping the people hiring the illegals. The group was going to turn over automobile license-plate numbers to the INS. Soon and not unexpectedly, confrontations occurred; Oltman commented,

"The wackos from San Francisco and Berkeley would come and picket. At one point I was assaulted. But when we finally started talking about having the mayor recalled, the City Council backed down."

From that moment on, Oltman's group linked up with like-minded California groups and tried to get legislation passed to make illegal what actually already *was* illegal: the hiring of illegal aliens. But the politicians refused to take the citizens seriously until the rebels formed the Citizens' Committee on Immigration Policy, which linked with the "Save Our State" campaign to put forward the now-famous Proposition 187, which would bar illegal immigrants from most government services and which passed the state by a substantial margin in the fall 1994 elections!

Proposition 187 was far from perfect and was criticized as being mean-spirited and niggardly because it could, if implemented, cut the innocent children of illegal aliens off from school, medical care, and every avenue of belonging in this society. But columnist George Will called Proposition 187 "the result of one subvention of representative government after another. There probably would be no Proposition 187 if elected officials, in Washington and Sacramento, had not been corrupted by the culture of judicial activism and been delighted, as the 'political class' often is, to allow a court to take custody of an inconvenient problem. . . . Californians are trying to reclaim a right of self-determination."

Dan Stein, director of the Federation for American Immigration Reform, called it a "new era in populist politics" and said he found it "difficult to see an era of more grassroots democracy." And Sherry Bebitch Jeffe, arguably the best political analyst mind in the state, noted: "Voters have more faith in issues than they have in candidates. They have lost interest in candidates and campaigns. They're so cynical about politicians' ability to produce and they're focusing on initiatives. It's a means to take control." A concurring view: "The political dimension of citizenship is going toward a desire to be more active and citizens taking a more direct role in shaping policy," Don E. Eberly, president of the Commonwealth Foundation in Harrisburg, Pennsylvania, commented at the time. "The direct-democracy movement is very much reflective of that."

When Proposition 187 passed that fall of 1994 with a 67 percent majority, other changes followed. Santa Clara's Self-Esteem Task

Force closed its doors. Bilingual education was criticized as it became clear that children learned in English in an English-speaking country better than they learned in Spanish, Korean, or Urdu! And Pete Wilson had the ultimate temerity to call for a national identity card, common throughout Europe.

And when I went to the border at San Isidro that fall, I found a totally changed atmosphere and situation. Gus de la Vina had been transferred: He was now one of the more powerful regional directors of the INS. The agents were immensely more optimistic than in those troubled earlier years. The federal government's new Operation Gatekeeper had provided for three hundred additional officers immediately and for an increase in the border force of 60 percent, to sixteen hundred agents, by 1995; new lights and vehicles were now found regularly along the border, and a new technology called biometrics was being used to fingerprint and photograph every alien arrested (possible because of advances that allowed machines to take a person's fingerprints in twenty-five seconds). As they built up a database, the agents could now tell, from the machine, how many times an illegal had been arrested—before they sent him back. The intent was multipurpose: One objective was to arrest, deport, or imprison illegals wanted for crimes; another was to keep a record of illegals in the United States.

In fiscal year 1994, arrests of illegals decreased 15 percent from 1993; in 1993, they had decreased five percent from 1992. Before that, they were steadily going up. In the first fifty days of the fiscal year beginning October 1, 1994, they had decreased 26 percent. This meant that far fewer were coming—deterrence *does* work!

And then, swiftly, came the astonishing response.

☆

More than seventy thousand people marched in downtown Los Angeles in October 1994, to protest Proposition 187. The rally was topped off by a sea of the flags of Mexico, El Salvador, and other Latin American countries and placards characterizing Governor Pete Wilson as a pig, comparing 187 to Hitler's racial laws, and calling just about everybody they did not agree with "unreconstructed racists." In this and other demonstrations, always bordering on the obscene and violent, signs and slogans read: "GO BACK TO EUROPE . . . PILGRIMS GO HOME . . . YOU HAVE RAPED OUR CULTURE AND

LANGUAGE . . . REVOLUTION IS THE SOLUTION . . . WE WILL OVERWHELM YOU . . . WE WERE HERE FIRST . . . YANKEE GRINGO RACISTS . . . ATZLAN—THIS IS MEXICO!" They also flew the thirteen-star early Mexican flag that implicitly denies that California and indeed the entire Southwest are part of the United States, while a man in "whiteface" wearing a blond wig ran through the crowd to be pelted and spat upon before they beat up and "killed" an ugly and contorted effigy of Governor Wilson and put it in a "coffin."

"We want everyone to know that Mexicans have the same rights as anyone else here and that they'll never be able to throw us out," Erica Zaragoza, fourteen, one of the marchers from Montebello High School, shouted at the rally. But Mexicans do not have the same rights here; they are not citizens of the United States.

I wrote at the time a carefully but strongly worded column, which I would construct even more adamantly now, warning these "protesters" about their wrongheadedness. I saw them grossly perverting the American right to free speech and demonstration in the same way that Latin America through the centuries had doomed itself—via vulgar insults and political machinations—to bitter upheaval and subsequent brutal repression. I warned them that they had gone too far; indeed, that they ought to have the common sense to realize that they had handed the "Save Our State" citizens a veritable wealth of invaluable arguments and proof for their cause. I told them that now they would be watched very carefully—and with good reason—for it was American citizens who had, through their carelessness but also through their innate historical kindness, allowed them to come to this country. Theirs was a mistake on a grand scale, for it was the first time that Americans could really see what their own sloppiness and unwillingness to make hard decisions about immigration and citizenship had really wrought—and how lacking was any sense of Americanness or respect for America among these visitors.

To add insult to injury, other countries entered the fray. Even miserable little Nicaragua in Central America "totally rejected the contents of Proposition 187 because it violates the human rights of fellow citizens and those of Latinamericans [*sic*] in California," according to a government statement released from Managua.

Nicaragua? *Nicaragua?*

I had been going to Nicaragua as a foreign correspondent since 1968, when I first visited for the *Chicago Daily News*. I had hated the old Somoza dictatorship, just as I hated all the Old Right dictatorships in Central America and the Caribbean. But, as much as I hated to admit it, Nicaragua under Anastasio Somoza was a poor and repressed but workable country. By 1994, Nicaragua was what the avatars of development in the 1980s and '90s liked to call a "failed nation." The Marxist Sandinistas who had taken over in 1979 had spent most of their time marching around in little uniforms and singing the "Internationale" as they bankrupted the country. (They never claimed economics was their talent.) By the time of the L.A. rally, more than 60 percent of the population was unemployed and Nicaragua's income was lower than Haiti's.

One could be forgiven for asking: What right did such a country have telling the sovereign American state of California what to do on a perfectly legitimate subject of interest to it?

But it soon got worse, as Mexico, the country that had historically carried the principle of nonintervention to the sacred level of a Roman high mass, got into the picture, for the first time claiming Mexico's right to intervene in American states on behalf of Mexicans there legally or illegally. Mexico's deputy foreign minister, Andres Rozenthal, declared that the government of Mexico would "work actively to prevent the passage of the anti-immigration initiative 187." All ten Mexican consulates in California worked openly for 187's defeat. More than two thousand demonstrators marched in Mexico City in front of the U.S. embassy, denouncing "damned gringos!" while an American flag was burned. (Only three months later, Mexico was begging American help as its currency collapsed.)

Rozenthal had already in effect established a new "doctrine" on August 13, 1994, just as the turmoil of 187 was starting, regarding Mexico's relations with its over-the-border citizens. "Mexico's recognition of her sister community on this side of the border has been belated," the ambassador stressed several times. "For many decades in our history, those of us born or living in Mexico ignored our compatriots in the United States and failed to recognize their true value. . . ."

And Manuel Tello, Mexico's minister of foreign affairs, wrote to Oltman with some rather stunning suggestions about the quid pro quo for the future. He recalled how, that August during the Mexican elections,

> hundreds of private U.S. citizens, political party representatives and American embassy employees were in Mexico to watch our presidential elections, supervise the balloting and freely give their opinions as to the process and its results. Although until recently such open involvement by foreigners—especially by Americans —in as sensitive an internal matter as our presidential elections would have been strongly opposed, we now understand that things have changed, that Mexico is more open to international scrutiny and that our new NAFTA partnership with the U.S. and Canada obligates us to accept debate and criticism regarding issues that until recently were considered as belonging to national sovereignty.

Then came Tello's démarche, his challenge to 187. "On the U.S. side of the border," he concluded, "you must accept a similar involvement, especially when the immediate interests of your neighbor are so evidently at stake."

What we were seeing was something curious indeed: one country placing demands upon a more powerful neighboring one—as an exchange for the first country's observing international norms that it claimed it was going to observe anyway. It was an absorbing example of how illegal and uncontrolled immigration inexorably moved on to influence foreign policy. But Mexican demands of 1994 should not have been surprising; in his annual *informe*, or "State of the Nation" address, in Mexico City on November 1, 1993, President Carlos Salinas de Gortari had already claimed, as he attacked American "human rights abuses" toward Mexican immigrants that "the treatment accorded our migrants should be according to Mexican law." He then added that "the defense of sovereignty is not an outdated concept; it is the ethos of our being."

My respected friend Richard Estrada, the brilliant columnist for the *Dallas Morning News*, called this the "politics of aggrievement." He believed, as do I, that Mexican policy had evolved to the point where it was now designed not to discourage illegal emigration from Mexico but to encourage it, and then to "manage" and to "regularize" the phenomenon. This policy was to be carried through by the fifty-one Mexican consul generals in America, and nobody spent a lot of time recalling that Mexico had a law explicitly forbidding surreptitious entry into neighboring nations and that, as Salinas admitted freely and without any perceivable guilt, he had recently expelled 125,000 Central American illegal aliens from his own vulnerable southern border.

By the spring of 1995, I was reporting on still another ploy of Mexico's to control and use its large illegal population in the United States. This time, the Mexican government had determined to establish Mexicans' right to "dual nationality" in America.

To hear Ambassador Alejandro Carrillo Castro, secretary of international relations for the ruling Revolutionary Institutional Party, tell it, the idea just bubbled up spontaneously from Mexicans in Chicago some years ago. "It was then that I first heard the demands of Mexican residents, who said they were not becoming American citizens because they were afraid to lose their rights as Mexicans," he said. Still other Mexican diplomats explained the measure in terms of Mexico's historical supernationalistic chauvinism. A Mexican who left Mexico to become a citizen of another country was always considered a kind of Judas. So, the dual-nationality idea would "modernize" Mexican thinking on these sensitive issues. Under the new law, Mexicans could become actual citizens of the United States while still being able to own land and do business in Mexico. But they would not actually be dual citizens, and they could not vote in Mexico.

There was my old friend, a man I respect, Jorge Bustamente, quoted in the Mexico City newspaper *Excelsior* as encouraging the idea so that Mexican-Americans could vote in the next U.S. presidential election to defeat a presidential campaign by California Governor Pete Wilson, a prime backer of Proposition 187. It was clear to me that this maneuver on the part of the Mexican government was designed to create a kind of political lobby of newly enfranchised citizens of Mexican descent whose cultural allegiance would remain where *they* belonged, in Mexico! Don Jorge went so far as to say publicly that the dual-nationality ploy was designed to allow his countrymen "to defend the interests of Mexico in whichever country they reside."

While Mexico was arguing that its voluntary adherence to the North American Free Trade Agreement treaty now made it incumbent upon the United State to take on responsibility for Mexico's excess population (even those in the United States illegally and thus deliberately breaking the law), NAFTA, pushed through by the Clinton administration in 1993 and '94, was *not* solving the human and social problems that "internationalism" and "globalization" were supposed to solve, particularly for a state such as California, which in most ways exemplified this new international climate. As Harvard University political theorist Michael Sandel so cogently noted: "There is one thing NAFTA cannot provide, and that is a sense of belonging. NAFTA has no flag you can salute, no national anthem you can sing, no real sense of community to which people can relate." Sandel was one of those truly *new* thinkers who were beginning to realize that these supposedly novel international-organization "answers," far from replacing the old conception of community, demand more of it. "If we do not build local communities with which people can identify," he has said, "we will find ourselves without any form of political community that expresses our shared identity, and knits us together in the families, schools and neighborhoods that democracy requires."

Nor did sleepy and inattentive America realize that Mexico's "neighborly intrusions" were already taking place in this country. In that same Los Angeles of the Proposition 187 rally, for instance, none other than the famous and tough L.A. Police Department was by then into Phase 1 of a special course, "Mexican Culture Training," taught by Mexican consular officials and professors from the University of Guadalajara. This was done at Mexican initiation so the police can "most importantly listen" to the Mexican population in California, legal and illegal, and understand "the plight of the Mexican immigrant to the United States," according to the promotional material on it.

Richard Weinstein, urban affairs specialist at the University of California, Los Angeles, summarizes the threat involved in such concessions made by government agencies, especially in cities: "The multiethnic factor in governance and politics in big urban centers is going to be the central issue for the future, and one that we are unprepared to deal with. The difficulty of talking across cultures and across languages and across traditions—the kinds of things that have divided nation-states for centuries—are to some degree being miniaturized within our cities."

Now, one of the important ethical and moral principles that should attend international "conversations" such as the one between Mexico and the United States over illegal immigration is that of reciprocity. It has long been recognized in jurisprudence and in moral philosophy that one party to a conflict cannot demand from another what it does not itself observe. Yet, few countries of large outward emigration are willing even to consider such ethical or even international-law issues when they are not in their own best interests, despite the fact that they often make claims against them. (A friend of mine once asked an Indian authority in New Delhi what it would take for him to become an Indian citizen. The man just stared at him, disbelieving, obviously thinking about all the poverty and misery in India, and asked in stupefaction: "Why would you want to be an Indian?")

Does Mexico practice any of the high principles it demands of the United States? No! Mexico's immigration "policy" can only be called xenophobic and disgraceful. On its southern border, where poor immigrants from Central America cross, Mexican troops with guns and dogs drive them back, often into the arms of medieval military forces such as Guatemala's. By and large, foreigners cannot own property. Mexico summarily deports illegals and requires legal residents to prove a minimum monthly income and pay yearly residency fees. Foreigners get no welfare or unemployment benefits in Mexico at all. And on the northern border, Mexican emigrants are routinely beaten, robbed of all their belongings, and sometimes murdered before they cross over to America; their attackers can be criminals but more often are the Mexican police, renowned for their brutality.

But I have personally never heard a complaint from a Mexican immigrant on the border about American Border Patrol or INS brutality. (The unforgivable beating of runaway illegals by California police in the spring of 1996 is a different issue.)

So much for reciprocity and the ethics of truly international law.

☆

America's other neighbor, Canada, provides lessons in many of the same issues faced by the United States in its relationship with Mexico.

Canada, with twenty-eight million people, for the first eighty years of the twentieth century shared idealism with the United

States; indeed, since it was not a world power, Canada could exercise her idealistic propensities toward the outer world more aggres-
sively and unapologetically. Canada moved toward becoming the
country with the highest per capita immigration rate in the entire
world: given her population base, her immigration rate was twice
as high as that of both the United States and Australia, the only
other major immigrant-receiving nations.

The reasons put forward by the pro-immigration lobbies in
Canada were at first essentially altruistic. Canada had vast natural resources, immense open spaces; Canada should help relieve
the pressures on the teeming world out there. Soon Canada became
a virtual magnet for immigrants from all over the world, many of
them from Indian or Asian cultures totally different from, or even
antithetical to, Canada's essentially British culture. Immigration
numbers increased threefold between 1985 and 1995.

In 1991, Canada's population of 27.3 million included 4.3 million immigrants, with large numbers in the big cities. Of cosmopolitan Toronto's population of 3.9 million, fully 1.4 million were
immigrants. Canada was creating many of the same cultural bottle-
necks as had been created in the United States. Although Canada
did not have a Ford Foundation, it had in its very bosom the
"Québec reality," and it had the charming and bright and public-
spirited Pierre Trudeau, the separatist Québeckers' first prime
minister. The Canadian "experiment" in mixing all sorts of people
began with Trudeau and his administration in the early 1970s, and
with his vision of creating in largely homogeneous Canada (except,
interestingly enough, in his native Québec) a "cultural mosaic" of
interracial tolerance and harmony.

Canada's attractive prime minister would not only provide
Canada with a non-English population, but he would offer the
world an alternative to his arrogant American neighbors' beloved
"melting pot." The experiment even had a mantric slogan: "LET'S
CELEBRATE OUR DIFFERENCES." But by the mid-1990s, the celebration
was over.

It was a Trinidadian writer, Neil Bissoondath, a Canadian citizen since the seventies, who more than anyone defined what went
wrong in Trudeau's cultural disaster. "Multiculturalism was supposed to coalesce into a new sense of Canadian identity," the famous writer told the *Christian Science Monitor* in 1995. "Instead, it
has helped tear Canada's identity apart. It has told those of us who

have come here from elsewhere that what matters more is the past
. . . what defines us is our ethnic or racial identity. It has caused
many of us to disregard the larger possibilities around us, of belonging to a larger country like Canada."

Before the party ended, however, ethnic groups demanded the
right to wear religious headgear—in all public circumstances, and
at all times. They fought to have Canadian schools recognize their
holy days alongside Christian holidays. In 1994, Canadian Sikh
army veterans, originally from India's Punjab, were not permitted
to join in Remembrance Day ceremonies with a branch of the Royal
Canadian legion in Surrey, British Colombia, because the legion's
bylaws prohibited the wearing of headgear—and the Sikhs refused
to remove their turbans. The Royal Canadian Mounted Police, famous for their legendary red and black uniforms, *did* dilute their
own heritage when they permitted their Sikh officers to wear their
turbans instead of regular RCMP hats. And at a 1992 festival cele-
brating Macedonian heritage, an estimated three thousand Macedonian and Greek youths fought in the streets of North York, north
of Toronto.

Like its big and powerful neighbor, hospitable Canada had
invited all of the world's problems right into its living room.

At the same time, undigested immigrants were costing Canada
money. Canadian officials announced that their taxpayers were
paying the equivalent of $518 million in U.S. currency a year to
cover welfare costs for those same immigrants.

It was not surprising that Canadians would eventually rise up
against the idea imposed upon them by Trudeauian multiculturalism: that the "New Canada" was nothing in and of itself but simply the sum of its parts. In fall 1994, for instance, an Environics
Research Group poll showed that public support for Canada's
multicultural policy had fallen from two-thirds to about half since
1989. And a Decima poll showed that 72 percent of Canadians
thought ethnic groups should adopt a Canadian value system. In
that same survey, fully 41 percent agreed with the sentence: "I am
tired of ethnic minorities being given special treatment."

The "Land of Oz" paradox that Canada had become was best
expressed in the Canadian press by Grant McCracken, a cultural
anthropologist with the Royal Ontario Museum in Toronto, when
he said, "A national identity in its classic form is a claim to same-

ness of some kind. It's just strange to think of a claim to sameness built out of many forms of claims to difference."

In November of 1994, Canada announced that it was reducing, for the first time in a decade, the number of immigrants it would accept. Preference would now be given not to "family reunification" but to skilled workers and businessmen. Canada tightened its control of immigrants coming for welfare, and even put visa officers and immigration-control agents in foreign airports and transit lounges, where Third World passengers changed planes to enter Canada, often for improper "refugee" status and often without correct papers. Now, the state got tough. Immigration agents actually carried one Zairean woman to the plane to deport her, but not before she was injected with sedatives three times because she refused to go voluntarily. That, of course, is unfortunately what happens when standards are not observed all along.

☆

California was always the "first"—the way California went was the way America soon would go. In only a few decades, California had traveled a long way down the new sociological superhighway: from a land of citizens to a land of immigrants to, increasingly, a land of conflict and, worse, incoherence. The hopeful element was that Californians were finally aware of what was happening, they were angry, and they were seeking new ways to pull themselves together in some form of unity again.

But the big question still remained: Could California go back? And, since the rest of the country always followed the Golden State: Could America still go back?

Or could she perhaps go forward—to a new mix of qualities, incorporating the best of the old with the promise of the new? Was some healthy *new* form of citizenship possible? In the words of Abraham Lincoln, "as our case is new, we must think anew and act anew . . . disenthrall ourselves . . . and save our country. . . ."

8

The Struggle for America

*Americans of all ages, all stations in life, and all types of
dispositions are forever forming associations. There are . . .
a thousand different types—religious, moral, serious, futile,
very general and very limited, immensely large and very minute.
Thus the most democratic country in the world now is that in
which men have in our time carried to the highest perfection the
art of pursuing in common the objects of common desires. . . .*
Alexis de Tocqueville, *Democracy in America* (1845)

*The most whimsical yet discomfiting bit of evidence of social
disengagement in contemporary America that I have discovered is this:
more Americans are bowling today than ever before, but bowling in
organized leagues has plummeted in the last decade or so. . . . We are
bowling by ourselves. . . .*
Robert D. Putnam, "Bowling Alone" (1995)

What I am convinced America needs to renew and reinvigorate
its civic conscience is *another voice*—the voice of the rational, compassionate, tough-minded middle that we have so tragically lost
in the last three decades. It needs a voice that understands the
realities of relationships in America and in the world and one that
is unapologetic and wise about defending the interests of America
and humankind. A voice that knows how and when to make
choices.

It needs a voice that understands that utopianism leads only
and inevitably to the realization of its own worst fears, but that
sensible human evolution, nurtured by civic and classical education, still offers mankind that "last best hope." But one that also
knows that our present overemphasis on the commercial—the

thoroughly inappropriate marketization of our civic and spiritual life—is as dangerous as defining-down. It needs a voice that is equally impatient with the Far Left and the Far Right, that on every level eschews racial or religious prejudice but is unregenerate about judging individuals and nations on manners and morals.

It needs a voice not laden with guilt unless appropriate and genuinely compassionate; a voice that does not treat other adult human beings as though they were children but as the fellow citizens that they can be. It needs a voice that realizes that, without the United States and its leadership, this world could easily sink back into the predominant anarchy and chaos that has so often characterized the past.

And, yes, it needs a voice endowed with the conviction that citizenship is not a static creature, but rather one that can indeed be renewed, reinvigorated, even reinvented in some ways, if only the human spirit and intelligence—and, perhaps above all, will—are applied.

We don't really know if a nation-state can call itself back to *original principles*—or, better, move forward to new expressions of those principles—to preserve the original intent of the nation without some extraordinary jolt, such as war or revolution or famine. But what we do know is that, in the last two years, there has been an incredible spontaneous movement in America for reviving the spirit of citizenship.

The adherents are to be found among all classes. It is especially satisfying that the intellectual elites are playing such an important part. What we have experienced since the sixties is the predominance of an intellectual elite that is multiculturalist, pseudo-Marxist, and clearly anti–traditional American, so the present trend is a refreshing change.

These are not, in general, typical "Be a good citizen!" community organizations, although, thank God, there are many of those. Rather, those I see sprouting like the grass in April after a long winter are organizations seeking to rediscover and reestablish citizenship.

Some talk about "American pluralism and identity"; some, about "re-creating a real balance between our rights as individuals and our social responsibilities; some, about "remoralizing" or a "new social covenant" or re-creating "homeland imagery."

Luckily, that *new voice* is beginning to be heard: across the country, our cities, the linked trajectories of our civic consciences.

☆

On February 8, 1993, I went to the National Press Club for "Citizens' Inaugural Day," the kickoff of "The New Citizenship." A broad coalition of national, state, and local groups as well as prominent individuals had come together in a serious deliberative debate over how to revitalize citizenship. They proposed a partnership between citizens and government, one that would "shift from the current model of government as the provider of services to client-citizens to a model that fully engages the citizenry in solving our nation's problems."

Harry C. Boyte, one of the citizenship movement's leaders and codirector of the Center for Democracy and Citizenship at the University of Minnesota, got up and said, "We've got to stop being complainers about government. If something is wrong, we as citizens should make it right. Conventional wisdom sees citizenship as a kind of cuckoo clock—it makes noise and goes away. . . . Nor should citizenship be sentimentalized, because citizenship means contributing—it is tough, serious work. We want a serious national discussion on citizenship, we want to work with President Clinton on problem-solving and we want to build around this body to reinvent citizenship. . . .

"America is developing a culture of outsiderness, of complaint and innocence. Citizens view politics as a spectator sport, dominated by experts who are expected to fix all our problems. That's why the project's theme is that we can't reinvent government without reinventing citizenship."

Then, the immensely talented political scientist Benjamin R. Barber, of Rutgers University, took on some of our simplistic present-day notions of citizenship. "A lot of Americans believe that citizenship has to do with adversarial protest," he said. "The 'We won't take it anymore' syndrome. But it is not enough to protest and assume someone else will fix it. Protest is a starting point, a way to engage people—it can't be the final step." Then he went on to say, "Citizens are not born, they are made. We acquire civic skills. Men may be born free, but *they are not born citizens.*"

Then there are noble men such as the George Washington University sociologist Amitai Etzioni, whose passion for many years has been his work on the "communitarian movement," which he dreams will bring Americans back to a sense of community through a real balance "between our rights as individuals and our social responsibilities." As he expressed at this "Citizens Inaugural Day," he believes that "we have gone from the old establishment to moral anarchy because it is much easier to destroy. When you attack institutions, you form an easy negative coalition. It is easy to attack the old family, for instance, where the father had all the power—but, what then are you for?"

If I were to list all the individuals, groups, foundations that right now are working toward *new citizenship*, we wouldn't finish this discussion in weeks. Start with the Kettering Foundation, the communitarian movement, the Bradley Foundation, the Commonwealth Foundation, the American Enterprise Institute, the Heritage Foundation, the Federation for American Immigration Reform, the Institute on Religion and Public Life, the National Center for Neighborhood Enterprise, the Hudson Institute, the National Endowment for the Humanities, the Firethorn Institution of Dallas, the "Respond to a Crisis in Character" coalition, the "Renewing American Civilization Project," the Congressional House Wednesday Group's "New Social Covenant," the National Civic League, the Council for the Advancement of Citizenship, and many more.

Indeed, one morning in February 1996, I picked up my *New York Times* and, at the very top of the front page was the headline, "IN ERA OF SHRINKING BUDGETS, COMMUNITY GROUPS BLOSSOM." The story told how voluntary organizations, civic associations, and neighborhood groups were "growing in number and in strength, taking on responsibilities that were once the province of government agencies and getting more attention from government officials." Their numbers had gone from thirty-five hundred in New York in 1977 to eight thousand in 1995!

Fueled by shrinking local, state and Federal budgets and armed with fax machines, newsletters, a mastery of legal nuance, and enthusiastic members willing to give their money and time,

they are moving beyond their traditional role of pestering officials to get potholes filled and streetlights fixed. Communities that
never organized before are forming neighborhood associations,
groups that had fallen apart or fallen silent have once again
started making noise, and immigrants have found a voice in
neighborhood life through such organizations. These groups are
often banding together, forming, for example, a coalition of communities and businesses in Flushing, Queens, or an umbrella
organization of neighborhoods in Manhattan. . . .

Ha! Think about *this* case: The Pew Charitable Trust suddenly
shifted its funding priorities in the 1990s to support new projects
aimed at the restoration of civic society, especially in neighborhoods struggling with economic upheaval. The great irony: Pew
had been working in Eastern Europe and focusing its energies and
funding there before they took on the American civic problem. Paul
Light, their public-policy director was quoted: "We had a growing sense that the democratic flame was burning less brightly back
home."

But what is *really* exciting is the *new conceptual thinking about
citizenship.* It's almost as if you could re-create love or loyalty or
faith through your own will and intelligence and spirit, then say
to the world, "Here, this is what it is!"

In fact, the *new voice* was already speaking.

You remember that Carrying Capacity conference in Los Angeles on the "ethics of immigration?" Well, everywhere I look
today there is another related conference, seminar, "conversation" on "Empowering People," "The Real Citizenship," "Citizenship U.S.A." It's very exciting indeed, particularly coming during
probably the most vulgar and divisive political campaign in
American history.

In fact, citizenship issues have permeated the 1996 campaign
since the very beginning—from the question of immigrants to the
reality or unreality of "globalization" to the practice of reaching
and capturing voters on the basis of television and private wealth.
Civility? Did you see those Republicans screaming and shouting
at each other, insulting, degrading? Did you see the negative cam-
paigning getting worse?

Yet, even in those very same days, beneath that appalling political surface of American life, I was finding everywhere what I
call the real citizens' "trying to bring morality back into American
civic life" movement.

To find that new citizenship, come with me for a moment to a
"Real Citizenship" meeting, held in February of 1996 at the American Enterprise Institute. Father Richard John Neuhaus, that brilliant Catholic priest, started out by arguing, eloquently, that what
America must now do to extricate itself from the morbid clutches
of Big Welfare is to consider any charitable or civic work "public"
if it serves the public good; in effect, "it is public by virtue of the end
it serves and not its auspices." Instead, what we have done is given
the state—with that supposed "superior" allied knowledge of the
experts—such total power over the "welfare" of its citizens that it
is nearly destroying them.

"The state is there to serve civil society," he went on, "but the
state is only one agency within society, and it is not identical with
that society. We have to liberate ourselves from the misconstrual
that, when we say 'we,' we mean the state. That . . . is what the poor
have been burdened with, in the most horrifying manner."

Such meetings were not just "talk." Republican Senator Dan
Coats of Indiana was working with the irrepressible William
Bennett to put "tough-minded compassion" into the debate; in
order to *do* that, he was sponsoring in Congress nineteen well-
thought-out bills that, in different ways, would allow citizens
to earmark tax money for private / public charitable organizations
and thus strengthen those groups who really know how to *solve*
problems.

The splendid thinking congressman, David Boren, went home
from one of these citizenship brainstorming sessions to Oklahoma
to be president of the state university, convinced that we had to
start rebuilding from the bottom up. Social thinker Daniel Yankelovich, emphasized that "mutuality works," even in economics—
whereas adversariness only destroys. The brilliant Robert Woodson
Sr. of the National Center for Neighborhood Enterprises, stressed
that the bureaucrats of the welfare state always built upon the
weaknesses of the poor, but it was preferable to "build upon
people's competences, not on their failures." To his clients, he said,

"the one-legged carpenter is of value because of his skills; but to the rehab hospital, he is of value because of his debility."

Listening to these refreshing citizens, I saw acted out right there before my eyes the old "deliberative democracy" in action, totally different from the politically correct and essentially passive "plebiscitary democracy." I had begun comparing observation of the 1996 campaign to having one's appendix out, living on Slim-Fast for a year, or taking a long trip through the sand dunes of Arabia's legendary Empty Quarter without water or even an aspirin to relieve the pain. But with these citizens, I had a glimmer of hope that the trip to a new civility might even proceed with some felicity.

The "secret" of these thinkers of the modern "catacombs," many of them actually Christians, was beginning to be analyzed on many fronts.

It was David Mathews, president of the Kettering Foundation, which has done some of the most impressive analytical work on citizenship, who told me one February day in 1995 in the foundation's Washington offices, "There is an *extraordinary secret political life* in the country today. It defies all conventional ideas of politics. People think I'm talking about traditional politics, but, no, it is different in method. In objective and organization, it is not old-fashioned citizenship politics. People are doing it because they are desperate."

He struggled to define it, adding, "the process is invariably deliberative; it is not your old citizen activism and not Ross Perot—it's something in between. It's not quantitative but qualitative. But it is the hardest story I've ever tried to tell."

I told him it was confusing me, too. What kind of citizenship was it?

"A lot of it is driven by people who have been through the mill," he went on, searchingly, carefully. "What comes out of it? The product is in different ways working together. This sets loose a variety of actions, sometimes almost evangelical, sometimes almost old-fashioned barn-raising activities. It's basically about banding together and sharing. But that passed from us in the twentieth century—we passed into this real romance with the orderly, scientific way of doing things; the use of the experts was very captivating. We thought that, in the twentieth century, the world had become too complex, that only the experts could understand it.

"Citizenship lost its vocabulary. People lost the vocabulary on how to join together. The twentieth century wiped out the vocabulary that served us so well from the Greeks onward. And it's not only us: at least ten countries that I know of have forums for reviving citizenship. . . ." At that point, Mathews even waxed a little Jeffersonian. "People don't have to be *given* these political interests," he added, "they are not acquired from 'outside,' they already have them. . . ." And at that moment I thought of my respected friend Askar Akaev, the president of faraway Kirgizstan, who essentially had told me the same thing.

At that moment, my mind switched back to that beautiful Fourth of July at Monticello and what the historian David McCullough told us about Thomas Jefferson and his group believing that citizenship issues were *natural* to human beings, and they *came out of the human soul.*

☆

But the *new voice* was not only talking, debating, deliberating; in fact, the *new voice* was also painting, sculpting, designing. . . .

In the spring of 1995, I was in Sarasota, Florida, where I go in April to spend some wonderful days with friends; we went to visit the Ringling School of Art and Design, sponsored by the Ringling circus family. For sixty-five years, this cluster of pink Spanish buildings, surrounded by the languid Gulf Coast mosses, was one of the creative centers of the country. Now that school had become a dynamic center *bringing together art and citizenship.*

Arland Christ-Janer, an elegant and cultured man who has been president of the school for more than a dozen years, has always been a Renaissance man, with a divinity degree from Yale and a law degree from the University of Chicago; he has been president of Cornell University, Boston University, and Stephens College. And he does not believe that art, as beautiful as it is, is only "art for art's sake." At its best, it also *inspires other endeavors*—akin to citizenship's "multiplier" effect.

"Students who come here have decided on their commitment to the visual arts," he began. "It's unusual that everybody does one thing here: create! They have to work very hard; this is a professional art school. Now, I majored in Greek at Carleton College," he went on, "and I realized that the word *school* from the Greek means 'leisure.' This meant that you were relieved temporarily from your duties as a citizen, but so that you could refine the powers of your intellect and become a better citizen later. At the end of it all was *not a job but being a citizen. . . .*"

The Ringling School has all the high-tech gear and knowledge that one could wish for; but Christ-Janer scorns the idea that life begins and ends with technology. To the contrary, "as worldwide communications draw more and more on visual images, artists and designers have a growing role in creating meaning and influencing perceptions," he said. The artist-as-citizen? Actually, the idea is very old; all the great artists of earlier eras were considered to be citizens, with concomitant duties. But in the current era of "economic man," where the overemphasis on the free market has most often snuffed artistry and the spirit out of public life, this was fresh air that I was breathing.

And so, in an era when it has been fashionable for artists in America to pose as unrelievedly alienated from society and spurn any archaic notion of a "common good," the Ringling School established a tough and accredited liberal arts curriculum that links the artist to society through an awareness of his or her citizenship. In "American Creativity" classes, students become aware "of the ethical questions embedded in twentieth century American culture and ways in which the arts have addressed them—and of the moral and ethical questions involved in making art and their role as responsible visual communicators." Then comes the practical application. Through "Student Life" programs, they practice these principles, giving their Saturdays for months to paint murals in hospitals, assist in building houses with Habitat for Humanity, work with injured dolphins. All involve artistry *and* citizenship.

This unusual school, way down there on the beautiful Gulf Coast of Florida, where one might reasonably expect to find people taking a more languid view of life, is offering an astonishing living example of a noble return to "the whole" at precisely the moment when so many Americans are realizing what they have lost and are having the tremulous feeling of a possible civic turnaround. Perhaps surprisingly, there are a great number of Christ-Janers "out there" in the country, their talents already enlisted in the struggle for renewal.

☆

What will happen to America if we do not pause at this point in our national history to take stock, to correct mistakes, to regain our national principles?

I do not think that America will "collapse," as so many other nation-states have collapsed in our era, although that would be easier than what will surely come if we do nothing.

What is already happening to America is that we are being neutralized in terms of our effectiveness as a nation. Perhaps better said, we are neutralizing ourselves. We are at the beginning of a slow-motion breakdown, not unlike, actually, the odd slow-motion disintegration of the Soviet Union. America's is a disintegration that is political, social, and economic, but above all moral and philosophical. It finds its most ready example in *citizenship,* since that is *the only bond we have that involves every American in a commitment to every other one;* and, as it occurs on every possible level of the national debate, it takes many public forms.

To sum up:

Americans have allowed themselves to be afraid and often even ashamed to expound their national principles. At the time when the American experience and experiment constitutes the living civics class for mankind, Americans are embarrassed to take pride in their own work. Americans will not make the simplest moral or even security decision if it involves employing authority against someone, as in the crucial decision of how many new immigrants they want to let in. At every turn they have divorced morality and ethics from civic life—"made naked the public square," as the eloquent Father Neuhaus sadly describes the melancholy emptiness where the American soul once was. All but gone is the very civility that is so essential to citizenship, what social thinker Charles Murray has described as "deference or allegiance to the social order befitting a citizen."

Above all, there is the shocking dumbing-down of just about everybody. A recent *Washington Post* poll shows that today's high school graduates appear to know less about government and politics than their educational equal of five decades ago.

As our education system becomes more and more dumbed down, those human beings who persist in calling themselves

"Americans" will have come to the point that editor and writer Lewis Lapham so eloquently and frighteningly describes:

> People unfamiliar with the world in time find themselves marooned in the ceaselessly dissolving and therefore terrifying present, divorced from the future and the past, surrounded by the siege of images in the mirror of the news. The media promote the impression that the urgent questions of the moment—war and peace in Bosnia, the budget, global warming—arrive uninvited and unannounced, like monstrous apparitions from the depths of the sea. The spectators forget how and why events come to pass, not knowing where to find their place in the human story, condemned to a state of constant dread. . . .

I got some valuable insights into the cause of that state of constant dread when last in lovely Finland, from the famous and multitalented young artist Bjorn Weckstrom. I had stopped by his beautiful studios in downtown Helsinki, and soon noticed, in addition to the gorgeous silver jewelry, exquisite sculptures, and fine drawings, a sketch of a lonely and unhinged man sitting before an empty television screen. The man seemed to gaze into nothingness as he crooked his arm vacantly under his chin. I looked quizzically at Bjorn for help.

"That's Icarus, the son of the Greek inventor Daedalus, in front of a television," he immediately said. "What I'm trying to express is the problem of identity of man today, the need to be someone even for a short moment . . . to get the attention of the mass media." Then he grew very serious. "This is a very obvious problem in the supertribe in which we have been living. A hundred years ago, people were living in small communities. Everyone had an identity known by the whole village. . . . Those times gave people stability and a kind of harmony. . . . But now . . . the borders of the tribe have been moving out. It was enough before to do something just in front of the village. You knew you had been doing something great. But now to be somebody, you have to be on television, you have to catch the attention of the media."

Weckstrom's point is simply another way of describing how technology is transforming leisure, "privatizing" and "individualizing" our leisure time and keeping us from truly social behavior, a point that is excellently expressed by Robert Putnam in

"Bowling Alone": "Time-budget studies in the 1960s show that the growth in time spent watching television dwarfed all other changes in the way Americans passed their days and nights. Television has made our communities (or rather, what we experience as our communities) wider and shallower." The great New York University communications genius, Neil Postman, traces this phenomenon in his books, claiming that we create technology that does not remain neutral but busily proceeds to re-create us. The reason for this is that, as he writes in *Technopoly*, technological progress works most efficiently "when people are conceived of not as children of God, or even as citizens, but as consumers."

This brings us to the crucial question of whether changes in the relationship between man and technology make citizenship more important or less important. Given the essentially alienating nature of these relationships with their unquestionable tendency to unlink people from previous communities and commitments, it is hard to argue—in fact, I would say it is impossible to argue—that citizenship could become anything other than much, much more important.

In addition to the dumbing-down of education and the intrusion of alienating technology in our lives, the dying-out of trust is another big problem. Unlike all those other societies that have been cursed to live without rules or law, with the constant rampages of conquest ever destroying their cultures and hopes, Americans have always invested one another with a high level of trust. They could do that *because* their citizenship provided them with a very public complicity in the fate of their nation; fighting one another would be self-destructive. Now, as the *Washington Post* reports in a major series, "The Politics of Mistrust," in 1996, "*America is becoming a nation of suspicious strangers. . . .*" (Italics mine.)

But let me repeat that what I see is not an actual collapse, at least not one felling us with one dramatic sweep. Rather, what has been a largely unified, coherent, law-abiding "America" will be a crowded, bickering, highly criminalized, *incoherent* nation. Citizenship will have been so overtaken by group rights, on both explicit and implicit levels, that any sense of community responsibility or civic potency will largely have died.

The country—if we will be able even to call it a country by then—will be mired in its differences instead of being forever more enriched by the political and conceptual unity of its culturally, racially, and religiously diverse elements. The promise of the "last, best hope of mankind" will be frozen because everything freezes up for good and forever in zero-sum games. Those who will suffer most are the poor because there will be no elite culture anymore to inspire them or help them up the ladder. There will be no way to control or maintain the environment because that cannot be done without a decent, reasonable, and voluntarily accepted central authority.

The borders, while not "open," will be effectively porous because Americans will have lost even any spirit to make choices or protect what they have built and fought for. Everyone will vote, even noncitizens or visitors from abroad, and so the vote will mean nothing; every "civic duty" will get more and more dumbed down, and corruption will of course flourish in such a mood of ultimate permissiveness. Americans will serve in foreign governments and even police forces without question from "home"; enormous possibilities for corruption will flourish, most important for bringing the international mafias more deeply into American society.

But perhaps saddest of all is the fact that most people will not even realize what is happening for a long time, for in truth the country is cursed by its inherent prosperity. By the time Americans know what's going on, it will be too late. . . .

And, of course, the gradual decay of "America the Beautiful" into "America the Expendable" will have enormous consequences for the entire world. As we saw with the terrible war in Bosnia, the "new internationalism" was no match for the deliberately reawakened "ethnic wars," which started as a contrivance of the Serbian president. China and Russia both threaten to "lead the world," but without any of the principles of America. The Pacific rim Asian countries are economically thriving but show no political or civil leadership capacity. Africa is dying, terrorist movements proliferate across the globe, and internal disintegration is more and more like a sickness that passes from country to country, ignoring borders.

Just in case you are thinking that I am too pessimistic or that I exaggerate the urgency necessary to even begin addressing these serious matters, I suggest you consider my early trips to Belgrade, Kosovo, Croatia, and doomed Bosnia; in 1989, 1990, . . . even as late as 1994, the world could have acted with relative ease and total effectiveness against the Serbian aggression. Only a few thousand troops, if any, would have been needed if the analyses of the situation were correct and other military methods were masterfully applied. Those of us who *chose to know*, knew; but those who *chose not to know* were making public policy.

By the time the world acted, 250,000 were dead; every principle of Western civilization had been ravaged by the new Balkabarians; and the West, the "new neutralists" in the United Nations, and other international agencies had over and over "excused" their cowardly inaction, which turned out to be passive observation of a massacre.

☆

When will we pass the point of no return, of critical mass?

Henry Kissinger, for one, has predicted to me, that America will be "irrelevant" by the turn of the century if our present national proclivities continue. I would say about 2020, perhaps before.

In the 1930s, the preeminent professor of anthropology at Columbia University, Dr. Ralph Linton, wrote that a culture changes for all time when there is no longer enough that most citizens agree upon to hold them together, warning even then that "in modern civilizations . . . the core of culture is being progressively reduced. Our own civilization, as it presents itself to the individual, is mainly an assortment of 'alternatives' between which he may or frequently must choose. We are rapidly approaching the point where there will no longer be enough items on which all members of the society agree to provide the culture with form and pattern. The disruptive trends in our own culture have not yet had time to work themselves out completely."

Writing particularly about the disintegrative effects of life in American cities, Linton found that

> such a condition is fatal to the effective operation of democratic institutions, since these depend upon a high degree of cultural participation, with the united will and consciousness of social as apart from individual interests which this confers. A low degree of cultural participation makes the rule of organized minorities not only possible but almost a necessity if society is to be maintained as a functioning entity. . . .

The situation which confronts us today is not altogether unique. Something very much like it existed during the later phases of the Roman Empire. . . .

In fact, the study of empires in general shows us a lot. John Bagot Glubb, the famous British historian and the general who organized the Jordanian Legion as the legendary "Glubb Pasha," is one who has carefully analyzed and compared empires: They go through their phases of great military might and expansion, followed by their commercial periods, until finally they dissolve in a morass of moral decay. Young people become minstrels and pop singers, and the once-great cities stagger under the proliferation of masses of noncitizens who flock to them. They usually disintegrate within fifty years of their "highest pinnacle of glory."

He states in his book *The Course of Empire* that in the Baghdad of the tenth and eleventh centuries, when the Seljuq empire is first rising then fading, Arab historians "lament the deterioration in sexual morals, the use of obscene language in conversation and the influence exercised over young people by 'pop' singers." An "evil playfulness" among the young overtakes and juvenilizes the entire society. A decline in morals and in stamina takes place, men "become once more selfish and materialistic." The end of empire almost everywhere is followed by a dreadful period characterized by a "revival of tribalism." The empire suffers "the loss of the bravest and most enterprising citizens, who either go abroad to the outposts of empire or are killed in war, leaving the timid and selfish to breed the next generation at home." Meanwhile, "the great influx of foreigners to the capital of a great empire may also exercise a considerable, if imperceptible influence. Ancient Rome, imperial Baghdad and modern London and New York have all absorbed very large numbers of persons of other races. The inhabitants of such cities exercise a disproportionate influence on policy. . . ."

The collapse of empires, the book goes on, "is usually attributed to the demoralizing influence of luxury and wealth. This is certainly true, though rather in the field of moral than of physical degeneration." This, in turn, leads to vulgar materialism and to the decline of religion, heroism, and idealism, resulting in "a cynicism, which justifies the decline of heroism by 'debunking.' Religion is alleged to be false, heroes have never existed and there is nothing real except material objects." Worse for us today, we live in—rather than the old elitist societies of imperial England or imperial Baghdad—a generally classless society, "all members of which read the same newspapers and listen to the same broadcasts" and who "will all become decadent together."

Glubb Pasha dreams for a moment that good empires might pause, study where they are in this seemingly inevitable "course of empires," and avoid the faults that clearly led to the ruin of so many. But then he thinks anew, and, smitten with realism, sums up: "In our present stage of human development, such hopes may well be illusory, for levity and triviality often seem to be typical characteristics of decadence. Nation after nation has sung, danced and trifled itself into chaos and slavery."

☆

But what about all those romantic new forms that are supposed to be re-structuring the world? What about the replacement of the nation-state? The economic globalization phenomenon? The great "information revolution," the "global village" that is supposed to unite us all in new links between human communities?

Sorry.

Early in 1996, always prescient and ever provocative, the *Economist* ran a lead piece that happens to be right. "THE NATION IS DEAD," it headlined. "LONG LIVE THE NATION STATE."

The article begins by repeating the usual litany:

> The nation-state is not what it used to be. Ignored by the global money markets, condescended to by great multinational corporations, at the mercy of intercontinental missiles, the poor thing can only look back with nostalgia to its days of glory, a century ago, when everybody knew what John Bull and Germania and Uncle Sam stood for. It seems inconceivable that so diminished a creature can much longer continue to be the basic unit of international relations, the entity that signs treaties, joins alliances, defies enemies, goes to war. Surely the nation state is in the process of being dissolved into something larger, more powerful, more capable of coping with the consequences of modern technology. . . .

Surely? That opening is only tongue-in-cheek; the conclusion of the article is that the nation-state remains totally necessary for a civilized world. Through its coherent form alone, the people "possess the necessary sense of identity"—a shared language, a shared religion, a proud ownership of some special political idea—and hold that identity in common with the government, both being "part of the 'we.'" The new cross-border ties are no match for the old nation-state and will take its place no more than the United Nations took the place of the United States in Bosnia.

Economic globalization as an alternative to national citizenship?

One splendid young writer, Michael Ignatieff, captures my thinking on this subject when he writes in *From Blood and Belonging: Journeys into the New Nationalism* that the self-styled "cosmopolitan" is *actually more dependent* upon the nation-state than anyone else in today's supposedly floating internationalist world. "With blithe lightness of mind," he notes, "we had assumed that the world was moving irrevocably beyond nationalism, beyond tribalism, beyond the provincial confines of the identities inscribed in our passports, toward a global market culture that was to be our new home.

"In retrospect, we were whistling in the dark. The key narrative of the New World Order is the disintegration of nation states into ethnic civil war; the key architects of that order are warlords. The repressed has returned, and its name is nationalism." Ignatieff comes to a fascinating conclusion: "I've lived all my life in sated nation states, in places that have no outstanding border disputes, are no longer ruled by foreigners or oppressors, where citizens are masters in their own house. But among the Crimean Tatars, the Kurds, and the Cree, I met the hungry ones, peoples whose very survival will remain at risk until they achieve self-determination, whether in their own nation state or in someone else's."

Indeed, true universalism is really protected only by mutual obligations, codified in law and citizenship, which in turn are only possible under the nation-state system, at least until we all become perfect human beings.

Probably no one has better described "the hungry ones" in our time and in our new language of development and desperation than author Robert Kaplan, who has wandered on foot through the worst of the failed corners of the world. In *The Ends of the Earth: a Journey at the Dawn of the Twenty-first Century*, this keen and evocative observer finds everywhere, in place of the old constituted traditional societies even of Africa: "young men with restless, scanning eyes, surrounding my taxi, putting their hands all over the windows . . . young men everywhere, hordes of them . . . like loose molecules in a very unstable social fluid, a fluid that was clearly on the verge of igniting." Independently corroborating my most troubling early findings, Kaplan describes how, from West Africa to the Balkans to places like Azerbaijan, "you go into a bar and you find young men with nothing to do. . . . They sit around all day and drink and talk. Communism created an Orwellian underclass of violence-prone, semi-criminal, urbanized peasant males who, as long as there was order, were kept at bay. Then suddenly they all got uniforms and became members of militias. Here you have urbanized peasants who don't know who they are but only know who they are by knowing what they hate." Kaplan believes that the real questions in these unnerved and unnerving parts of the world are not those of self-determination and independence but those of identity. Therefore, the problem for the still-intact world is not to create formal democracies but to create workable civil societies. "The border between violence and pure crime is collapsing," he says, and "violence is becoming more criminalized. . . . We must also think of identity in terms of emerging concepts, in terms of drug cartels, mafias, shadowy Islamic terrorist forces. These are the outgrowths of identity that don't fit our modern two-dimensional map of seventeen countries. War has become more and more criminalized, and you need to factor it in with environmental stress, over-population . . . and a general breakdown of society."

This condition, he repeats over and over, is spreading toward the rest of the world, including America. Kaplan warns against what happens when one adopts abstract, utopian, or postmodern ideas about how the nation-state is no longer necessary or desirable. He decides "the political and categoraphic implications of postmodernism—an epoch of themeless juxtapositions in which the classificatory grid of nation-states is going to be replaced by a jagged glass pattern of city-states, shanty-states, nebulous and anarchic regionalism. . . ." He identifies the same new warriors of whom I became ominously aware in the 1960s, '70s, and '80s, and who are taking the place of the old national armies ("dinosaurs about to go extinct") in their dark and threatening new forms: "Chetniks in Serbia, 'technicals' in Somalia, Tontons Macoutes in

Haiti, militiamen in Liberia grotesquely garbed in women's wigs and clothing as they go about coldly massacring their own people." And he asks the somnolent West to remember that "in places where the Western Enlightenment has not penetrated and where there has always been mass poverty, people find liberation in violence—worrying about mines and ambushes frees you from worrying about mundane details of daily existence."

As I wrote in chapter 1, remarkably similar factors recur in every example of national fragmentation: the death of an all-encompassing ideology whose "truths," until now, held the answers to the major questions of life; the deconstructing of nations in the name of ambitious individual egos; the breakdown of one language as *the* unifying element in society; the growth of one definable population group at the expense of the others; the sudden sundering of legal or legitimized population/power imbalances; affirmative action policies or other policies of preference or equity that come to be perceived as unfair and unbalanced; the sudden insistence by minority groups on having a separate law; and—always—the fact of the dominant society's waiting too long to confront divisive elements.

Even as I write this, I pick up the newspaper and read headlines such as "REGIONAL CONFLICTS THREATEN 42 MILLION AROUND THE WORLD." I read surveys indicating that 30 percent of the American people believe there will be no United States of America a century from now. I read that the jailed Palestinian terrorist in the brutal *Achille Lauro* hijacking escaped jail in Italy by using the self-styled, homemade passport of a group called the World Service Authority (WSA)—an organization that, incredibly, issues fifteen thousand passports and other documents a year for what it considers a "boundaryless world." And a handful of countries actually accept them.

All of these developments should alert us urgently to the breakdown of nation-states—and thus to the breakdown of citizenship around the world. But there is one more crucial element that comes into play here. Just as Americans are losing that old "language of citizenship," so are the people who should be the leader of the world losing the old language of moral leadership that essentially springs forth from citizenship. Eschewing American or Western "triumphalism," Western leaders in Bosnia, the prototypical state of the post–cold war world, have greeted the massacre of tens of thousands with neutralist and nonjudgmental cries of "Nobody's guilty . . . nobody's innocent . . . just make peace. . . ." What we are seeing on the world stage is analogous to what we are seeing in America: moral judgment and principled commitment slipping away. Ironically, globalization of the economies of the world— which, theoretically, was expected to modernize everybody over-night—is a major factor in creating ethnic or disintegrative warfare. The reason is that it creates new classes at the top at the same time that it leaves behind, alienated and deracinated, too many at the bottom, who must seek emotional solace somewhere.

Globalization, of course, is real, and it can do some great things for mankind. The problem occurs when we persist in thinking that globalization is somehow irresistible—and somehow uncontrol-lable by governments—and that modern men and women with-out countries, of the truly transnational corporations, can actually owe allegiance to no nation and still be safe and thrive. That is what is untrue.

In a seminal article in the *Financial Times*, economics writer Martin Wolf points out that the openness of economies today is no greater than before 1914. Nor is global economic integration irresistible, he argues. In fact, governments (the still-extant power structures of those old nation-states) "have chosen to lower trade barriers and eliminate foreign exchange controls. They could, if they wished, halt both processes." He sums up: "The opening of national economies to international trade and capital flows oc-curred not because it was irresistible, but because it was benefi-cial. Globalization is, if not a myth, a huge exaggeration."

The late Christopher Lasch had the last word. "The 'citizen of the world' . . . is not much in evidence," he wrote in his last book before his death. "We have a universal market, but it does not carry with it the civilizing effects that were so confidently expected. . . . Instead of generating a new appreciation of common interests and inclinations—of the essential sameness of human beings every-where—the global market seems to intensify the awareness of eth-nic and national differences. The unification of the market goes hand in hand with the fragmentation of culture. . . ."

But, then, what about the "global village," which was supposed to take the place of the nation-state and make us all spontaneous "citizens" of one another's lives?

It was the late Marshall McLuhan's perception that the world was inexorably moving toward a kind of one-stop information system. Everyone would know everything. The world would be, in short, one village. With everyone able to know everything, human beings would instantly bond. Differences in culture, in race, in religions? All would disappear. A most brave new world.

In fact, that mood of universalist exaltation was captured in the early 1990s when Ted Turner, founder of the Cable News Network (CNN), the first worldwide television news network, was given an award from Georgetown University's School of Foreign Service. He suggested that the school might want to change its name to something like the "School of World Affairs" or of "Global Togetherness." Why? "Because," he said, "nothing is foreign anymore!" (He also once had a rather good-sized zoo at his home; but he wanted to mix the animals up and have them all live together in Turner's version of the "peaceable kingdom." Not surprisingly, many of them ate one another and the "utopian community" was soon abandoned.)

But instead of a global village, we see increasingly a world of the most ancient and retrogressive types of villages; instead of the creativity that comes from unity, we witness worlds of ever more murderous apartness; far from bringing people together, all that wondrous and supposedly transformational "information" is actually driving them apart.

That does not mean that these modern waves of change should or will ever be obliterated. But a healthy, thriving, and rational citizenship is surely going to be *more* important in a world of high technology.

☆

There is no alternative to the individual citizen of a liberalized but still-coherent nation-state, from which he or she can engage the world. There is no alternative to civic loyalty. Is the current picture of reengaged American citizens, forming groups to "disenthrall" the nation from the recurrent extremes of utopian and cynical philosophies, the gasp of a slowly fading order—or the herald of a Renaissance?

Time is growing short. The revival of citizenship has to be done soon, it has to be done seriously, it has to be done, period.

I remain convinced that the nation will rally at this important moment in a Renaissance to preserve the best of the past and to mate it with the best of the present and the future—so that we can and will be *Americans once again*.

Selected Bibliography

Abshire, David, and Brock Brower. *Putting America's House in Order: The Nation as Family*. Westport, Conn.: Praeger, 1996.

Auster, Lawrence. *The Path to National Suicide: An Essay on Immigration and Multiculturalism*. Monterey, Va.: American Immigration Control Foundation, 1990.

Barber, Benjamin R. *Jihad vs. McWorld: How the Planet Is Both Falling Apart and Coming Together and What This Means for Democracy*. New York: Times Books, 1995.

Barry, Brian, and Robert E. Goodin, eds. *Free Movement: Ethical Issues in the Transnational Migration of People and of Money*. University Park, Pa.: Pennsylvania State University Press, 1992.

Barlett, Donald L., and James B. Steele. *America: What Went Wrong?* Kansas City, Mo.: Andrews and McMeel, 1992.

Beck, Roy. *The Case against Immigration: The Moral, Economic, Social, and Environmental Reasons for Reducing U.S. Immigration Back to Traditional Levels*. New York: W. W. Norton & Company, 1996.

Bennett, William J. *The De-Valuing of America: The Fight for Our Culture and Our Children*. New York: Summit Books, 1992.

———. *The Index of Leading Cultural Indicators: Facts and Figures on the State of American Society*. New York: Simon & Schuster, 1994.

Berger, Peter L., and Richard John Neuhaus. *To Empower People: From State to Civil Society*. Washington, D.C.: AEI Press, 1996.

Betts, Katharine. *Ideology and Immigration: Australia, 1976–1987*. Melbourne, Australia: Melbourne University Press, 1988.

Bloom, Allan. *The Closing of the American Mind: How Higher Education Has Failed Democracy and Impoverished the Souls of Today's Students*. New York: Simon & Schuster, 1987.

Bock, Alan W. *Ambush at Ruby Ridge: How Government Agents Set Randy Weaver Up and Took His Family Down.* Irvine, Calif.: Dickens Press, 1995.

Boorstin, Daniel J. *The Image: A Guide to Pseudo-Events in America.* New York: Atheneum, 1961.

Borjas, George J. *Friends or Strangers: The Impact of Immigrants on the U.S. Economy.* New York: Basic Books, 1990.

Boss, Carl. *The Two Revolutions: Gramsci and the Dilemmas of Western Marxism.* Boston: South End Press, 1984.

Bowen, Catherine Drinker. *Miracle at Philadelphia: The Story of the Constitutional Convention, May–September 1787,* with a foreword by Warren E. Burger. Boston: Little, Brown and Company, Atlantic Monthly Press, 1966.

Boyte, Harry C. *CommonWealth: A Return to Citizen Politics.* New York: Free Press, 1989.

Brimelow, Peter. *Alien Nation: Common Sense about America's Immigration Disaster.* New York: Random House, 1995.

Brubaker, William Rogers, ed. *Immigration and the Politics of Citizenship in Europe and North America.* Lanham, Md.: University Press of America, for the German Marshall Fund of the United States, 1989.

Cushman, Thomas, and Stjepan Mestrovic, eds. *This Time We Knew: Western Responses to Genocide in Bosnia.* New York: New York University Press, 1996.

Diggins, John Patrick. *The Rise and Fall of the American Left.* New York: W. W. Norton and Company, 1973.

Dionne, E. J., Jr. *Why Americans Hate Politics.* New York: Simon & Schuster, 1991.

Eakman, Beverly K. *Educating for the New World Order.* Portland, Ore.: National Book Company, 1991.

Eberly, Don E., ed. *America's Character: Recovering Civic Virtue.* New York: Madison Books, for the Commonwealth Foundation, 1995.

———. *Building a Community of Citizens: Civil Society in the Twenty-first Century.* Lanham, Md.: University Press of America, for the Commonwealth Foundation, 1994.

Etzioni, Amitai. *The Spirit of Community: Rights, Responsibilities, and the Communitarian Agenda.* New York: Crown Publishers, 1993.

Flexner, James Thomas. *Washington: The Indispensable Man*. New York: New American Library, Signet, 1984.

Fonte, John, and Andre Ryerson, eds. *Education for America's Role in World Affairs*. Lanham, Md.: University Press of America, 1994.

Fukuyama, Francis. *Trust: The Social Virtues and the Creation of Prosperity*. New York: Free Press, 1995.

Garling, Scipion. *The Immigration Handbook: A Basic Introduction to Immigration Policy, Practice, and History*. Washington, D.C.: The Federation for American Immigration Reform, 1995.

Gibson, James William. *Warrior Dreams: Violence and Manhood in Post-Vietnam America*. New York: Hill and Wang, 1994.

Glazer, Nathan, ed. *Clamor at the Gates: The New American Immigration*. San Francisco: Institute for Contemporary Studies, 1985.

Glazer, Nathan, and Daniel Patrick Moynihan. *Beyond the Melting Pot: The Negroes, Puerto Ricans, Jews, Italians, and Irish of New York City*. Cambridge, Mass.: MIT Press and Harvard University Press, 1963.

Glendon, Mary Ann. *Rights Talk: The Impoverishment of Political Discourse*. New York: Free Press, 1991.

Glubb, John Bagot (Glubb Pasha). *The Course of Empire: The Arabs and Their Successors*. Englewood Cliffs, N.J.: Prentice-Hall, 1965.

Hale, Edward Everett. *The Man without a Country*. Sandwich, Maine: Chapman Billies, 1994.

Hardin, Garrett. *The Immigration Dilemma: Avoiding the Tragedy of the Commons*. Washington, D.C.: Federation for American Immigration Reform, 1995.

Harris, Sam. *Reclaiming Our Democracy: Healing the Break Between People and Government*. Philadelphia: Camino Books, 1994.

Henry, William A., III. *In Defense of Elitism*. New York: Doubleday, 1994.

Hoffer, Eric. *The True Believer: Thoughts on the Nature of Mass Movements*. New York: Harper and Row, 1951.

Hollander, Paul. *The Survival of the Adversary Culture*. New Brunswick, N.J.: Transaction Books, 1988.

Hughes, Robert. *Culture of Complaint: The Fraying of America*. New York: New York Public Library and Oxford University Press, 1993.

Ignatieff, Michael. *Blood and Belonging: Journeys into the New Nationalism.* New York: Farrar, Straus, and Giroux, 1993.

James, Daniel. *Illegal Immigration: An Unfolding Crisis.* Lanham, Md.: University Press of America; and Washington, D.C.: Mexico-United States Institute, 1991.

Janowitz, Morris. *The Reconstruction of Patriotism: Education for Civic Consciousness.* Chicago: University of Chicago Press, 1983.

Jenks, Rosemary E. *Immigration and Nationality Policies of Leading Migration Nations.* Washington, D.C.: Center for Immigration Studies, 1992.

John D. and Catherine T. MacArthur Foundation. *A National Conversation: On American Pluralism and Identity; Commentaries on American Pluralism and Identity; Scholars' Essays.* Chicago: MacArthur Foundation, 1994.

Johnson, Haynes, *Divided We Fall: Gambling with History in the Nineties.* New York: W. W. Norton and Company, 1994.

Kaplan, Robert D. *The Ends of the Earth: A Journey at the Dawn of the Twenty-first Century.* New York: Random House, 1996.

Kemble, Penn, ed. *After the Cold War and the Gulf War: A New Moment in America?* New York: Freedom House, 1991.

Kettner, James H. *The Development of American Citizenship, 1608–1870.* Chapel Hill, NC: University of North Carolina Press, for the Institute of Early American History and Culture of Williamsburg, Va., 1978.

Kimball, Roger. *Tenured Radicals: How Politics Has Corrupted Our Higher Education.* New York: HarperPerennial, 1990.

Kittrie, Nicholas N. *The War against Authority: From the Crisis of Legitimacy to a New Social Contract.* Baltimore: Johns Hopkins University Press, 1995.

Lasch, Christopher. *The Revolt of the Elites and the Betrayal of Democracy.* New York: W. W. Norton and Company, 1995.

Lean, Mary. *Bread, Bricks, Belief: Communities in Charge of Their Future.* West Hartford, Conn.: Kumarian Press, 1995.

Lind, Michael. *The Next American Nation: The New Nationalism and the Fourth American Revolution.* New York: Free Press, 1995.

Lutton, Wayne, and John Tanton. *The Immigration Invasion.* Petoskey, Mich.: Social Contract Press, 1994.

Mathews, David. *Politics for People: Finding a Responsible Public Voice.* Urbana and Chicago: University of Illinois Press, 1994.

McCarthy, Eugene. *A Colony of the World: The United States Today.* New York: Hippocrene Books, 1992.

McGiffert, Michael, ed. *The Character of Americans: A Book of Readings.* Homewood, Ill.: Dorsey Press, 1964.

McGowan, William. *Only Man Is Vile: The Tragedy of Sri Lanka.* New York: Farrar, Straus, and Giroux, 1992.

Mills, Nicolaus, ed. *Arguing Immigration: Are New Immigrants a Wealth of Diversity . . . or a Crushing Burden?* New York: Simon & Schuster, 1994.

Moynihan, Daniel Patrick. *Pandaemonium: Ethnicity in International Politics.* New York: Oxford University Press, 1993.

Murray, Charles. *Losing Ground: American Social Policy, 1950–1980.* New York: Basic Books, 1984.

Murray, Charles, and Richard J. Herrnstein. *The Bell Curve: Intelligence and Class Structure in American Life.* New York: Free Press, 1994.

National Center for History in the Schools. *National Standards for United States History: Exploring the American Experience, Grades Five–Twelve. Expanded Edition.* Los Angeles: University of California, 1995.

Nisbet, Robert A. *The Quest for Community.* New York: Oxford University Press, 1981.

———. *Twilight of Authority.* New York: Oxford University Press, 1975.

Peirce, Neal R. *Citistates: How Urban America Can Prosper in a Competitive World.* Washington, D.C.: Seven Locks Press, 1993.

Pfaff, William. *The Wrath of Nations: Civilization and the Furies of Nationalism.* New York: Simon & Schuster, 1993.

Porter, Rosalie Pedalino. *Forked Tongue: The Politics of Bilingual Education.* New York: Basic Books, 1990.

Portes, Alejandro, and Ruben G. Rumbaut. *Immigrant America: A Portrait.* Berkeley and Los Angeles: University of California Press, 1990.

Postman, Neil. *Amusing Ourselves to Death: Public Discourse in the Age of Show Business.* New York: Penguin Books, 1985.

———. *Technopoly: The Surrender of Culture to Technology.* New York: Vintage Books, 1993.

Rauch, Jonathan. *Demosclerosis: The Silent Killer of American Government.* New York: Times Books, 1994.

Reich, Robert B. *The Work of Nations.* New York: Vintage Books, 1992.

Richard, Carl J. *The Founders and the Classics: Greece, Rome, and the American Enlightenment.* Cambridge: Harvard University Press, 1994.

Rifkin, Jeremy. *The End of Work: The Decline of the Global Labor Force and the Dawn of the Post-Market Era,* with a foreword by Robert L. Heilbroner. New York: G. P. Putnam's Sons, 1995.

Rischin, Moses. *Immigration and the American Tradition.* Indianapolis: Bobbs-Merrill Company, 1976.

Russell, Cheryl. *The Master Trend: How the Baby Boom Generation Is Remaking America.* New York: Plenum Press, 1993.

Samuelson, Robert J. *The Good Life and Its Discontents.* New York: Times Books, 1995.

Schama, Simon. *Citizens: A Chronicle of the French Revolution.* New York: Alfred A. Knopf, 1989.

Schmuhl, Robert. *Demanding Democracy.* Indiana: University of Notre Dame Press, 1994.

Schuck, Peter H., and Rogers M. Smith. *Citizenship without Consent: Illegal Aliens in the American Polity.* New Haven, Conn.: Yale University Press, 1985.

Selznick, Philip. *The Moral Commonwealth: Social Theory and the Promise of Community.* Berkeley and Los Angeles, Calif.: University of California Press, 1992.

Shklar, Judith N. *American Citizenship: The Quest for Inclusion.* Cambridge, Mass.: Harvard University Press, 1991.

Schlesinger, Arthur M., Jr. *The Disuniting of America: Reflections on a Multicultural Society.* Whittle Direct Books, 1991.

Sinopoli, Richard D. *The Foundations of American Citizenship: Liberalism, the Constitution, and Civic Virtue.* New York: Oxford University Press, 1992.

Skerry, Peter. *Mexican Americans: The Ambivalent Minority.* New York: Free Press, 1993.

Smith, Clint E. *The Disappearing Border: Mexico–United States Relations to the 1990s.* Stanford, Calif.: Stanford Alumni Association, 1992.

Sowell, Thomas. *Race and Culture: A World View.* New York: Basic Books, 1994.

Teitelbaum, Michael S., and Myron Weiner, eds. *Threatened Peoples, Threatened Borders: World Migration and U.S. Policy.* New York: W. W. Norton and Company for the American Assembly, Columbia University, 1995.

Thomas, Andrew Peyton. *Crime and the Sacking of America: The Roots of Chaos.* McLean, Va.: Brassey's, 1994.

Tifft, Wilton S. *Ellis Island.* Chicago: Contemporary Books, 1990.

Toffler, Alvin and Heidi. *Creating a New Civilization: The Politics of the Third Wave.* Atlanta: Turner Publishing, 1994.

Toynbee, Arnold J. *A Study of History: Abridgement of Volumes 1–6 and of Volumes 7–10.* New York: Oxford University Press, 1987.

U.S. Department of Justice, Immigration and Naturalization Service. *Federal Textbook on Citizenship: Our United States, Becoming a Citizen Series. Book 2.* 1963. (This and the following publications under the U. S. Department of Justice entry are all distributed through the U.S. Government Printing Office in Washington, D.C.)

———. *By the People . . . U.S. Government Structure: An English as a Second Language Text,* 1987 and 1988.

———. *For the People . . . Citizenship Education and Naturalization Information: An English as a Second Language Text,* 1987 and 1988.

———. *A Reference Manual for Citizenship Instructors,* 1987.

———. *United States History, 1600–1987.* 1987.

Wilson, James Q. *On Character: Essays by James Q. Wilson.* Washington, D.C.: AEI Press, 1991.

Wright, Robin, and Doyle McManus. *Flashpoints: Promise and Peril in a New World.* New York: Alfred A. Knopf, 1991.

☆
☆ ☆

—————

Index